Harvard Studies in Business History XXXI

Edited by Alfred D. Chandler, Jr.
Isidor Straus Professor of Business History
Graduate School of Business Administration
George F. Baker Foundation
Harvard University

Contents

MAPS

CHARTS

Moving the Masses

Introduction:
The Challenge to Urban Transit

In 1880 public transportation in large American cities was provided by numerous, competing horsecar companies. The firms were autonomous and their operations uncoordinated. Public policy, which dealt primarily with the grant of franchises and charters, provided little or no control of operation, technology, or extension of service. By 1912 a monopoly in each city operated a system, or a coordinated network of electric-powered streetcars. In the largest cities subways offered rapid transit through the center city toward the suburbs. City and state agencies now regulated the operation of a crucial utility, and in some cases the commissions even built and administered high speed rights of way.

The demands on local transportation and the responses, both private and public, to that challenge are an integral part of the business and urban history of the late nineteenth century United States. Transit development reflected the changing nature of American enterprise: the rapid application of new technology, the expansion of output, and the coming of new men, the so-called robber barons or industrial statesmen, who directed the creation of large enterprises which replaced many small units with a few, dominant firms. And though European cities offered examples of technique and technology, the evolution of urban transit systems most clearly revealed the character of the large American city: the pervasiveness of business leadership in urban decision making and the interplay of interests within that group; the fragmentation of city government, often led by venal or mediocre politicians; the different timing and patterns of growth among evolving metropolises; the advent of private monopolies of public utilities; and the coming of progressive urban reformers with their mistrust of large business units. Most important, transit development reflects two dominant themes: the constant pressure of rapid growth in city population and area and the requirements of the technology developed to service that growth.

The City and Public Transit in 1880

The changes in the late nineteenth century city that promoted the demand for urban transit systems are a familiar tale. Movement was certainly a predominant characteristic of the exploding industrial metropolis. Huge numbers of people—both foreign born and native—swelled its population, and industrialization quickened the pace of life. The population influx concentrated more people in the central district. Increased activity downtown forced the construction of taller buildings to give business the required operating space. Simultaneously, these and other changes in urban life encouraged many occupants to relocate within the city.[1]

By 1900 such experiences were common to the thirty-eight big cities in the United States with populations exceeding 100,000.[2] Four of them had become industrial metropolises whose populations surpassed the million mark. New York (including its New Jersey suburbs) had 4,607,864; Chicago had 1,837,987; Philadelphia 1,623,149; and Boston 1,249,504. A gap of almost one half million separated Boston from Pittsburgh, the next closest with 792,968.[3] Each transcended old political boundaries as the compact pedestrian city of 1850 became a sprawling giant with a diameter of twenty to twenty-five miles. With greater size came specialization of area and separation of home and work. For an increasing portion of the population, the old center city remained the locus of business while residences were moved outward. Within the business district, too, came separation by function as retailing, financial, manufacturing, and wholesaling enterprises clustered in identifiable areas.

In big cities as well as in large metropolises, the growth of population, area, and specialization heavily burdened public transit, that is, facilities for transportation by common carrier in the municipality and its suburbs. A larger population meant more passengers. Of more importance, the city's expansion caused more frequent use of public transit. The number of rides per capita rose faster than the population. Specialization of activities in different areas demanded new routes along the increasingly congested streets of the business district. The rise of suburbs compelled local transportation to cover ever lengthening distances. Additional traffic and greater distance required faster speed, larger capacity, and more extensive range from public transit lines.

The steam-powered commuter railroads, horse-drawn omnibuses, and horse railways developed for the mid-nineteenth century commercial city failed to meet these needs. Steam railroads serviced a small and decreasing fraction of local movement. Their massive engines were ill suited to frequent stops and starts. Antagonized by their noise and dirt and fearful of the dangers of explosion and collision, citizens fought to keep them off the streets and out of the downtown area. Steam railroads carried passengers from the outermost suburbs but could not offer transportation in and around the city.[4] Commuter roads generally moved less than 10 percent of local traffic. Even in the exceptional case of Boston, whose lines transported more than the New York and Philadelphia roads combined, steam commuter traffic was scarcely more than one fifth the number carried by streetcars.[5]

Local transit had originally depended upon the omnibus, a horse-drawn stagecoach operating on city streets. First appearing in the 1820s and 1830s, omnibus companies were small enterprises, operating only a few vehicles and requiring little capital investment. By the 1850s numerous firms existed in New York, Boston, Philadelphia, Chicago, and other large cities. Although companies had definite routes and schedules by the 1830s, they operated independently without coordinated schedules or transfers. Because their owners used the public streets as rights of way, they paid license fees or taxes and were subject to city regulation of fares and stopping places in exchange for a franchise, or the right to operate, from the city council.[6] But the initiative to organize and function, the choice and purchase of equipment, and the selection of routes belonged to operators; the council only approved or rejected.

In the 1850s entrepreneurs began to build horse railways to compete with omnibuses. By the outbreak of the Civil War, horsecar lines rolled over rails in the streets of most major cities, including New York, Boston, Philadelphia, Pittsburgh, Baltimore, Chicago, Cincinnati, and St. Louis. They quickly replaced the omnibus lines with service which was cheaper, quieter, smoother, and faster. By 1860 horsecars annually carried forty-five million passengers in New York and almost fourteen million in Boston. They provided the primary means of transportation within the business district and captured commuter train traffic in the closer suburbs.[7]

Like the omnibuses and the steam-powered railroads, horse railways were privately owned and operated. Profit-seeking entrepreneurs initiated the switch from omnibus to horse railway, selected routes, and arranged for finance, construction, and organization.[8] And like the omnibus lines, horse railways were constructed and operated on the public streets by many separate companies.

The use of city streets inevitably embroiled transit operators in municipal politics. Franchises were crucial, and negotiating their terms before a frequently inept and sometimes venal local government required careful lobbying and a none too strict conscience. In exchange for rights of way and franchises, horsecar owners accepted limited regulation by the city council. Controls varied from case to case, but included license fees, fare regulation, and such duties as snow removal, paving, and street repair, which gave cities indirect remuneration.[9] For the most part, however, regulation was left to a market characterized by limited competition among firms in the central city.

Horsecar lines did differ from the omnibus pattern in one important way. Because they were also railroads, they had to obtain state charters as required by general railroad law. Thus they fell under the control of the state legislature and sometimes the state railroad commission as well as under local authorities. Since nineteenth century municipal corporations were creatures of the legislature, the state assumed ultimate authority over this urban service and delegated to the city the regulatory powers it deemed necessary.[10]

As a result, regulation of horse railways was often confused, contradictory, and unenforced.[11] Politicians in New York, Boston, and Philadelphia neither planned nor coordinated street railway development. What direct control there was had little to do with the actual operation of a facility for the public's convenience, for before 1890 in large American cities, transit policy centered on the grant of charters and franchises and the compensation to be given in return. The tradition of private enterprise in local transit, the lack of expertise in city and state governments, and a general acceptance of existing service, all combined to leave authorities with no guide to select technology, to devise and coordinate routes, to order extensions, or to increase the number of cars.

The contrast with European cities was clear. The Paris Prefect of Police directed consolidation of omnibus lines in 1854, and the General Council of the Seine created horse railway networks in the 1860s. Between 1878 and 1882 the government of Berlin completed a viaduct railway, and in London the authorities gave careful scrutiny to omnibus and horse railway routing.[12] As John McKay has noted, "National and local authorities had extensive police powers . . . [which] allowed them to regulate the speed and capacity of cars, or require or reject modifications of equipment, as a matter of course."[13]

In the United States horse railways were in widespread use for little more than two decades before the increasing need for improved urban transit outmoded them. Animal power limited the horsecar's speed to about five miles per hour. Assuming a one hour commuting limit for most travelers, horsecars could service only an area within three or four miles' radius of the city center.[14] As growing criticism made clear, the horse-powered public transit of the commercial city lacked the speed, range, and capacity needed for the evolving metropolis.

Local transit operators were as unhappy as the public with horsecar transportation. Horses and their care were a big expense item in railway budgets, accounting for 40 percent of capital investment, while operating costs consumed over 73 percent of gross revenue. Time and money were lost each day for several changes of teams per car. The majority of the stock was always idle. On crowded downtown routes with frequent stops and starts, on longer runs to the suburbs, and on lines with steep grades, horses wearied more quickly and extra teams had to be hitched on. Finally, there was always the danger of a recurrence of the great "epizootic" disease of 1872, a contagion which decimated horse motive power in cities across the nation.[15]

The Range of Technological Solutions

By 1880 perceptive promoters and transit men recognized the need for technological innovation, including changes in both motive power and right of way. The most common response was to substitute mechanical power for the horse to meet the public's requirements and to lower costs and raise profits. As early as the 1860s horse railway firms had experimented with steam-powered cars. But as John McKay has demonstrated in his careful study of European transit, steam proved too costly, too dangerous, and too annoying in congested streets.[16] Compressed air, hot water, ammonia gas, and springs also failed as sources of power. Then in 1873 Andrew Hallidie developed the first successful mechanical substitute for the horse in hilly San Francisco. He used steam engines to power cables as a motive force. Stationary engines revolved drums from which miles of cable moved through slotted conduits between the tracks in the streets. Hallidie equipped his cars with a grip by which the operator or "gripman" could grab and release the cable for starting and stopping.[17]

The superiority of the cable over the horse made the 1880s the heyday of cable cars. In Chicago, Philadelphia, Kansas City, Baltimore, and St. Louis they replaced horses on major lines. At the same time construction began on extensive cable systems in New York and Washington. Cable cars attained speeds of seven to nine miles an hour in business districts and twelve to thirteen miles an hour elsewhere. They operated at constant speeds with no time lost to substitute for weary animals, and the use of mechanical power allowed longer cars to replace the typical twenty-four foot horsecar.[18]

With faster speeds, larger capacity, and greater efficiency, cable cars were considerably cheaper to operate than horsecars. An 1890 U.S. Census survey concluded that operating costs per cable car mile were about one fourth less than horsecar costs. A later comparison of the two when operated by the same company disclosed a saving of almost a penny per car mile over a four-year period.[19] In addition the use of cables reduced operating costs relative to gross receipts—the ratio commonly used by railroad men to measure success. According to the 1890 Census, cable operation left an additional 8 percent of total revenue for fixed costs and dividends.[20]

But there were drawbacks as well. Unlike horsecar lines, cable railways were extremely expensive to install. The cost of railbed alone was, according to one expert, $111,000 per mile of double track cable line, while a similar length of horsecar road cost about $12,600. Cable lines required expensive powerhouses, powerful steam engines, drums, cables, and costly street conduits with pulleys and yokes. According to the Census report, total cable investment per mile quadrupled the horse railway figure.[21] Maximum use of facilities was vital to pay for these high fixed charges, and only the major arteries of big cities could supply the traffic needed for profitable operation.

What was more, cable operation was awkward. Cable cars had to move at a constant speed, which made adjustment in heavy traffic conditions difficult. A broken cable stopped the entire operation. The addition or removal of cars on short notice to match traffic demands was bothersome. And cables worked best in straight lines. Sharp curves significantly reduced their life span. Curves and intersections required expensive construction, complicated operation, and at times proved hazardous to passengers and passersby alike.[22]

The search for an alternative power source continued, in part because of the cable system's awkwardness and inflexibility. Even more important, the high cost of installation made the cable unprofitable for suburban routes whose traffic was neither as constant nor as dense as that of major downtown lines. In 1890, the heyday of the cable car, less than 6 percent of total street railway mileage was cable powered.[23]

The electric streetcar provided the answer. Though experiments dated back to the 1840s, the first practical implementation of electric cars came with Frank Sprague's work in Richmond, Virginia, in 1887 and 1888.[24] Electric traction (so-called because motion depended on the adherence of the car wheels to the rails) revolutionized the industry. By 1890 electric car trackage was 15 percent of total trackage, more than double the cable figure. By 1902 it was 94 percent of total street railway mileage, and cable and horse lines accounted for only 1 percent each.[25]

The new technology offered faster speed, more efficient operation, and greater capacity than did either horse or cable cars. Steam-powered dynamos in plants located at strategic points along the line supplied electric current through a system of overhead wires. The current moved from the wires via flexible connecting poles to each car, where it powered an electric motor geared to the axles. The number and location of cars in service was easily adjusted to demand. Intersections and curves were no longer troublesome. The variable speeds of the motor allowed easy ac-

commodation to traffic conditions. Because animal stamina no longer
limited car size, electric cars eventually doubled the seating capacity of
the old horsecars.[26]

Electric power offered other advantages over horse and cable power.
Although electric lines were more expensive to build than horse railways,
their construction cost and investment per mile of track were only about
half the figures for cable roads.[27] And the new technology was cheaper to
operate than either horse or cable lines. A 1902 Census survey reported
that operating expenses had dropped from 68 to 57 percent of revenue
since 1890.[28] Operating costs for the electric lines on New York's Metropolitan Street Railway Company from 1898 to 1901 averaged about two
thirds of its per-car-mile cable and horse railway expenses.[29]

Electrification wrought tremendous changes in urban transit. Between
1890 and 1902 track mileage almost tripled and fare passengers more
than doubled. The book value of construction and equipment jumped
fivefold to $2,000,000,000. Combination and consolidation of indepen-
dent lines began in the 1880s with the advent of cable power and vastly
accelerated after the development of the electric car. By 1900 unified systems controlling "all or nearly all" local transit had emerged in most big
American cities.[30]

New construction and mergers stimulated considerable financial activity. Entrepreneurs like Charles Yerkes, Thomas Ryan, and Peter Widener
created millions of dollars of new securities—paper issues far in excess of
actual assets. The lure of increasing revenues and the decreasing ratio of
operating expenses to total revenue attracted credulous investors. Frederick Lewis Allen observed that in 1900 "electric trolley lines were booming; the financial journals were full of advertisements of the securities of
new trolley enterprises; to put one's money into street-railroad development was to bet on the great American future."[31]

But like its predecessors, the electric car also had its limitations. Few
noted, as did the 1902 Census, that mileage expanded more rapidly than
did traffic. Promoters, investors, and operators paid too little attention
to the important change in the financial structure of streetcar companies
which resulted from mechanization. The investment for road and equipment on electric railways more than doubled the amount for horse railways. Capital charges to service fixed investment and to replace depre-
ciating equipment created new pressure on revenues. Fixed charges as a
percentage of total expense doubled from 1890 to 1902 when they consumed almost one third of gross revenue. High fixed costs resulting from
mechanization, as well as from overexpansion and stock watering which
accompanied combination, more than offset efficiencies of operation.
Despite electrification, average net earnings as a percentage of street railway revenue actually decreased between 1890 and 1902, while longer

lines and more transfers gave riders greater service for their fixed fares.[32]
Finally, the newest transportation technology—the internal combustion
engine—would eventually make inroads in trolley traffic. Track mileage,
which had almost tripled in the 1890s, neared its peak by 1902.

Even more serious than the nascent competition of the automobile was
the demand for still another form of public transit in the nation's four
largest industrial metropolises. The increasing congestion of city streets
and the development of electric technology in the 1880s and 1890s led to
rapid transit: the construction of high speed lines with rights of way
above or below city streets. Elevated railways and subways provided
urban transportation with still greater speed, capacity, and range.

Though looked upon as risky innovations in the 1890s, neither was
new. The world's first subway began operation in London in 1863. Built
in response to street congestion and the demand for more public transport, London's steam-powered subways served as extensions of the railroads that entered the city. After some early success, the burden of fixed
costs (exceeding one million dollars per mile), overconstruction, and the
unsuitability of steam power for tunnels discouraged imitation before the
development of electric-powered trains in the early 1890s.[33]

Before that time New York's size, population, and congestion had also
led to rapid transit construction. Because of the problems of steam power
and the costs of construction, American entrepreneurs opted for a new
technology for motive power and type of transit. Along Ninth Avenue in
1868 ran the nation's first elevated railway, powered by a cable system.[34]

But the elevated lines also had their limitations. Cable power, which
encouraged the construction of an elevated line rather than a subway,
soon failed and was replaced by steam locomotives. Once again, costs
(about $700,000 per mile) and the unfitness of steam technology for local
transit in crowded cities discouraged further imitation.[35] The ponderous
trains were ill suited to a pattern of frequent stops and quick starts. They
failed to generate adequate average speeds. Their capacity was insufficient, and further expansion was strongly opposed. Citizens objected to
the noise and dirt they generated, to their damage to abutting property,
and to the street-darkening effect of the massive elevated structures. But
despite their drawbacks, elevated railroads were the only form of rapid
transit operating in the United States in 1880.

In the last quarter of the century, then, transit entrepreneurs seeking
profits and inhabitants of such cities as New York, Boston, and Philadelphia, who required better local transportation, could choose among
three types of motive power—steam, cable, and electricity—and three
forms of transit—street railways, subways, and elevated railways. The
pressures of urban growth made transit improvement an urgent necessity, but the high costs and risks of innovation and the technological

limitations of steam and cable for motive power slowed construction. Gradually, however, in response to two powerful forces—urban growth and technological innovation—a solution began to appear.

The Response

The preceding sections outline the challenges to urban transit and the range of technological responses but fail to suggest either a framework for working out solutions or the roles of market, technology, and other forces in shaping the process. A brief review of other public utilities illustrates their pattern of evolution and a scheme of analysis for urban transit. Like street railways, national (telegraph and telephone) and local (gas and electric) utilities were subject to the pressures of a rapidly expanding market and changing technology.

In the case of the telegraph the demand was clear enough. In the westward expanding nation, the ability to communicate faster than a man could travel had obvious benefits. In addition, the advent of the railroad with its special need for information and coordination served as a springboard for the telegraph's adoption. Within a decade of the instrument's invention by Samuel Morse in 1844, a number of businessmen and railroads had established operations.[36]

Competition among autonomous local firms was incompatible with a technology whose advantages lay in the high volume, high velocity flow of messages across a nation. Amos Kendall, Norvin Green, Ezra Cornell, and others organized regional operations and arranged for pools in overlapping territories. When these arrangements proved inadequate to handle through traffic, a series of mergers by Kendall, Cornell, and their associates led to the formation of Western Union in 1866. Large investments by the Vanderbilts then helped finance a national network.

Monopoly control, however, was neither total nor inevitable. Within the next fifteen years, financier Jay Gould, using the Baltimore and Ohio and other railroad lines, twice successfully challenged Western Union. On both occasions he forced the older firm to purchase his organizations at favorable terms and finally attained control of Western Union in 1881. The company's national network, its negotiated settlements with such potential rivals as Postal Telegraph, and its apparently satisfactory service at reasonable rates discouraged further raids by new firms after the 1880s.

While Cornell, the Vanderbilts, Gould, and other promoters directed the creation of the enterprise and the wars for its survival, they were not responsible for its administration. Structure and operation fell to a number of salaried managers who organized the sprawling network into four regional divisions (Eastern, Southern, Central, and Pacific), each headed by a general superintendent. Beneath the superintendents were thirty-three district supervisors, who managed the stations and operators in their territories. This line of authority from station to supervisor to superintendent culminated with the executive committee of the board of directors, composed at various times by Cornell, the Vanderbilts, Gould, and other entrepreneurs. The executive committee determined strategy and finance, and staffs providing auxiliary services helped the managers perform the firm's major function—communication. The men in the line and staff, then, coordinated the flow of information on which the company's existence depended.

The line and staff structure had been borrowed from the innovations of managers on the closely allied railroads and was quickly adopted by the telegraph's next major rival, the telephone.[37] Following its patent and demonstration by Alexander Bell in 1876, a major struggle ensued with Western Union, which was armed with valuable patent claims developed by Thomas Edison.[38] Faced with complex litigation, Bell and his associates surrendered control to William Forbes and other Boston financiers who established the American Bell Company. Forbes and his fellow investors financed battles to compel Western Union to sell its rights and supplied funds for future growth after 1880.

But expansion and the nature of the technology and the product rather than patent control shaped the firm's evolution. In the 1880s a top operating man, Theodore N. Vail, concentrated on the development of long distance technology and traffic. Rapid expansion with investment in proliferating local telephone companies would assure a national network for high volume, through traffic. Following a fifteen-year break with Forbes, which proved the soundness of Vail's strategy, the manager returned to establish a series of regional subsidiaries, rationalizing Bell-owned and -associated local companies. Equipment was supplied by the Bell-owned Western Electric Company, and the American Telephone and Telegraph Company, at first a holding company, soon provided central administration and operated the crucial long distance lines. As in the telegraph case, Forbes and his fellow promoters, aided by J. P. Morgan and Company and other bankers, financed overall strategy, while the professional managers operated the regional divisions, headed staff operations, and evaluated performance. And by 1910 Vail and other top administrators began increasingly to plan strategy as well.

The early history of competition and cooperation, the advent of consolidation to provide crucial high volume flows, the initial dominance of entrepreneurial and financial people, and their later replacement by professional managers who established and administered an operating structure—these patterns are obvious in the evolution of both national utilities. And clearly in both cases strategy and structure owed much to the high volume, high speed flow of information made possible by the new electric technology.

New and changing technology was also important in the evolution of local gas and electric utilities for illumination.[39] In the 1870s came new techniques for generating illuminating gas: first the use of naphtha to enrich coal gas and then the development of the Lowe process to generate cheaper, more efficient water gas. These techniques, along with the invention of the Welsbach burner and other improvements of gas fixtures, meant that gas would continue to be an important illuminant until World War I. But competition came much earlier in the 1880s when the development of dynamos for arc and incandescent lighting sparked the growth of the electric light industry.

Generalization is difficult in the case of gas and electric utility companies, which, like urban street railways, were organized on a local basis. Nevertheless the histories of illuminating gas and electric firms in several large cities in the nineteenth century illustrate familiar patterns.[40] Competition and bitter rate wars alternated with short-lived efforts at cooperation in the last three decades of the nineteenth century. In New York four established regional companies fought bitterly when two newcomers, the New York Mutual Gas Light Company and the Municipal Gas Light Company, introduced the new naphtha and water gas methods. In Baltimore after an 1880 merger had ended the competition begun by the new Consumers Mutual Gas Light Company with its water gas process, officers discharged by the merger joined another new firm, the Equitable Gas Light Company, and renewed the battle. Subsequent price wars sent gas prices tumbling to one fifth of their earlier figure.

Nor was the electrical industry any different. In Baltimore promoters hoping to profit from the new electric lighting technology organized at least four firms in the 1880s. An 1890 consolidation only temporarily stemmed competition, for within five years two new companies entered the field. At first technology did not restrict but stimulated battles as new, unstandardized systems appeared in rapid order, including the Brush arc, Edison direct current, and Westinghouse alternating current methods. In Detroit the story was similar. In the 1880s and 1890s firms representing Brush, Edison, and three other systems struggled for city lighting contracts or for store, home, and office business. Competing firms in gas illumination and electric lighting appeared in many other cities during the same period, including Chicago, Philadelphia, Brooklyn, and San Francisco.

As in the telegraph and telephone cases consolidation came quickly. Combinations generating large profits attracted entrepreneurs, speculators, and bankers during the nation's first great merger wave at the nineteenth century's close. In New York, public utilities promoter Anthony

N. Brady began merging electrical firms in the five boroughs. Meanwhile Harrison Gawtry, who had entered the gas industry with the water gas process in the 1880s and begun merging gas firms into his Consolidated Gas Company, acquired three of Consolidated's four major competitors in greater New York in 1900. At the same time Gawtry saw the advantage of "an anchor to windward" with his competition in the electric industry, and by 1901 he and Brady had joined forces to control the major gas and electric firms of Manhattan, the Bronx, and Brooklyn.[41] In Baltimore, Brady, speculator Thomas F. Ryan, and banker S. Davies Warfield merged gas and electric firms to form the Consolidated Gas, Electric Light and Power Company in 1906. In Philadelphia public utilities promoters Thomas Dolan, Martin Maloney, and others chartered a New Jersey holding company in 1899 to control that city's electric utilities, while Dolan already headed the illuminating gas monopoly.

But mergers were not simply a response to promotional profits and the merger mania. In New York, Chicago, Baltimore, and other cities, combinations began well before the national merger wave. Competition and rate wars drove revenues below costs and wasted capital in duplicated facilities and costly excess capacity at generating plants. In Baltimore the public protested the constant tearing up of streets to lay new pipe during rate wars. Suburban electric operators near San Francisco, who had financed a shoe-string operation and who depended on erratic water-powered plants, found a natural match with the well funded San Francisco Gas and Electric Company, which used dependable but expensive steam power to supply electricity to its growing urban market. And in Detroit, operating man and expert Alex Dow, who clearly foresaw the advantages of unified operation, led the consolidation of that city's electric companies into the Edison Illuminating (later Detroit Edison) Company.

Once again the needs of new or changing technology had encouraged combination. If entrepreneurs like Brady, Ryan, and Dolan and bankers like Warfield repeated the efforts of Gould, Vanderbilt, Cornell, and Forbes, the presence of Dow suggests the importance of operating men in local utilities. Dow thought of the consolidated enterprise as more than an amalgamation of four predecessor plants. Instead the operation was a system with high fixed costs in a large, growing urban market. He oversaw the standardization of meters and pricing, directed the rationalization of old plants, and planned the construction of a gigantic central station with a waterfront location for coaling and cooling.

Dow's planning was long term. In his eyes promoters' profits and investors' dividends represented capital to be hired as cheaply as labor. As vice president and manager Dow quickly dominated Detroit Edison's operations and within five years he was de facto head at the parent North American Company. Within ten years of Detroit Edison's formation and affiliation with North American, he was president of North American and "the head of the table was where Dow sat."[42]

Dow's early and extensive power was probably exceptional. Certainly, company histories emphasize the roles of promoters and investment bankers in the formation and early years of utilities combinations. Nevertheless by the 1890s salaried men had already come to staff and head the administration of gas and electric firms. In New York William H. Bradley became chief engineer of the Municipal Gas Company in 1877 and held a similar position in its successor, the Consolidated Gas (later Consolidated Edison) Company, until his death in 1922. In Baltimore Alten Miller, a former engineer of construction in New York's gas monopoly, became general manager of the Consolidated Gas Company in 1902 with a salary double the president's pay. He reorganized personnel and procedure and supervised all manufacturing, administration, and engineering. Miller was the top operating man in a line and staff structure with functional departments for sales, purchasing, legal affairs, and auditing. When the Gas Company merged to form the Consolidated Gas, Electric Light and Power Company in 1906, Miller became vice president and general manager of the new firm, and within ten years the president of the firm was a career operating man as well.

The histories of national and local utilities offer several parallels. The city-based electric and gas firms repeated the patterns of competition and combination, entrepreneurial promotion, and professional management. New or changing technologies with high fixed costs generated or transmitted high volume products. At both levels combination was closely associated with a need to integrate operation and coordinate the product flow of electricity, gas, or information.

But the evolution of local utilities involved more than economic considerations. They were "quasi public" corporations which by definition became part of politics and public policy. Of course, telephone and telegraph firms were also public utilities. The agitation of Populist reformers for their nationalization or control is well known, and local telephone companies depended on public franchises to operate on urban rights of way. Nevertheless neither telephone nor telegraph companies were nationally regulated during their formation and early years. Not until the progressive era and the second decade of the twentieth century, at a time when monopolies were well established in both industries, was either subject to control by the federal government.

In contrast the local utilities were part of politics and policy from their inception. Some urban public services were already municipally operated, especially those directly related to health and safety. By the mid-nineteenth century such large cities as New York, Boston, and Philadelphia had begun to assume systematic responsibility for sewage disposal and police and fire protection. Water, which such private firms as New York's Manhattan Company had supplied early in the century, was by the 1850s and 1860s increasingly a city operation.[43]

But there were few public operations of gas and utilities, which were less directly related to sanitation and protection and which could be readily sold as tangible commodities. Philadelphia did supply its own illuminating gas until 1897, but the operation was conspicuous as an exception and as a boondoggle creating jobs and revenue for the city's political machine. As late as 1891 only eight municipalities in all the United States had emulated Philadelphia's gas operation, and in 1902 public power lighted less than 8 percent of the nation's incandescent light bulbs.[44]

Nevertheless state and local governments definitely influenced the evolution of gas and electric enterprises. Operation was impossible without a franchise. Franchises not only granted the right to do business on, over, or under the public rights of way but also prescribed the area in which the company might operate. Thus, when the Municipal Company of New York obtained a franchise in 1877 for unrestricted operation, it had a signal advantage over established rivals confined to particular parts of the city. And franchises might or might not be exclusive, an obviously important criterion in stifling competition. Shrewd operators competed vigorously and often unscrupulously before sometimes venal city and state legislatures for coveted franchises and charters. In Philadelphia such prominent politicians as David Martin and James McManus served as directors or officers of electric companies. The unsavory ties between companies and city officials, both real and imagined, were the stuff of many a reformer's and muckraker's cries.[45]

Franchises were only one of many reasons for the intimate connections of utilities and public officials. Legislative action was a city's most effective control over privately owned, public service firms. Thus, when citizens complained about gas rates in Baltimore, the state legislature assumed the power to set rates. When the poles and wires of electric companies cluttered New York's streets, the municipality compelled the firms to bury their wires in conduits called subways. And when agitation in Maryland threatened to establish a public service commission, the Consolidated Gas, Electric Light and Power Company tried to stall the movement with a proposal of partnership between company and city, including city representation on the board of directors and a sharing of all profits above 4 percent.

Public action could also promote or stall company growth. In Baltimore the renewal of the lucrative city gas lighting contract encouraged at least one new entry into the industry, while in Detroit the city agreement for arc lights was half the income of the Brush Electric Light Company in the early 1890s. In contrast the severe terms of New York's gaslight contract became an onerous duty visited on less favored firms.

In general, faith in competition was the norm until the 1890s, and franchises were issued with little coordination or planning in Detroit, Philadelphia, and other cities. To preserve competition Chicagoans fought in the courts for ten years to destroy a trust agreement among city gas firms. Cities' efforts to encourage competition, however, failed to prevent combination and rationalization. Neither Chicago's battle against the gas trust nor Baltimore's threat to investigate an 1880 gas consolidation prevented the evolution of monopoly.

Only gradually did experts and legislators begin to recognize the costs of competition and resort instead to public regulation of evolving gas and electric monopolies. According to the historian of Baltimore's gas and electric companies, though the state assumed power to set gas rates in 1888, competition was still the ideal.[46] Nevertheless, regulatory commissions and agencies appeared with increasing frequency as part of progressive reform at the century's turn. Massachusetts established gas and electric commissions in 1885 and 1887. New York consolidated regulation of its gas, electric, and transit utilities into a landmark Public Service Commission in 1907, the same year that Wisconsin created a railroad commission to regulate all public utilities. And at the federal level the Mann-Elkins Act expanded the Interstate Commerce Commission's jurisdiction to include telegraph companies in 1910.

The experiences of national and local utilities offer two focal points to analyze the evolution of urban public transit systems: private enterprise and public policy. As utilities operators responded to the growing market and the invention of new technology, they followed a pattern of competition, cooperation, and consolidation. The initiators and directors of the new strategy were entrepreneurs seeking promotional and operating profits. But the systems they created and the complex technology they adopted demanded a new operating structure, which quickly came to be administered by salaried professional managers.

Such changes, however, affected more than the operation of private enterprise. Because of the public nature of local utilities, changes and their impact were a crucial part of the lives of urban inhabitants. Thus the evolution of the utility system and the new technology gradually pointed to the inadequacy of the existing public policy of competition and led the way to a policy of regulated monopoly.

Yet the parallel of public transit and other utilities is not perfect. Though public transit shared the experience of fast growing markets and rapidly changing technology, that technology differed from others in its cost. The major cost of gas, electricity, and telephone companies was the construction of their producing or transmitting plants. As Forrest

McDonald has shown, the economics of the electrical industry were central station economics.[47] The object was to maximize off-peak load in order to get fullest use of the high fixed costs of the generating plant. As markets grew, expanding service was a matter of stringing new wire until the capacity of the central plant was reached, and then additional plants were built. In the electric power industry as in telephone, telegraph, and gas operations, the extension of service by stringing wires or laying pipe was relatively inexpensive.

But as we have seen, expanding public transit was not so simple. Not only must costly generators be built, but expensive rights of way as well. The cost of one mile of electrified street railway track in a big city was fifty times that of stringing one mile of telegraph wire and more than quadruple the cost of one mile of gas line.[48] Thus it was much easier for gas, telephone, and electric firms to move with the population to the expanding, less populous suburbs. Nor was the congestion of city streets an obstacle to wire stringing or pipe laying as it was to transit firms traveling on public rights of way.

These differences had important consequences for the evolution of urban transit. Transit firms' inability to expand profitably as rapidly as demand grew and their visible participation in the growing congestion of downtown city streets generated popular criticism and influenced policy. Furthermore, their failure to avoid congestion and the limits of trolley speed and capacity left them unable to meet the needs of the nation's largest industrial metropolises. The resulting resort to rapid transit with its complex technology and much higher costs further altered the transit system and public transit policy.

In sum public utilities, both national and local, changed in response to growing markets and changing technology in the last half of the nineteenth century. But the nature of the urban market differentiated the experience of local utilities by involving them more closely in politics and policy. And the nature of the technological response in public transit complicated its development and separated it from other local utilities. Thus the impact of technological innovation on transit enterprise and policy became the prime factor for change and is the major theme of this study.

The Case Studies

To trace the evolution of urban transit systems and their impact on public policy, the analysis builds on three city case studies. The major determinants shared by cities in late nineteenth century America—urban growth and technological innovation—provide the common ground for comparison. But it is worth treating cities individually in order to appreciate the process of change and the peculiarities of each case. In each market the impact of such factors as city size, the timing and rate of growth, urban topography, and local politics help illuminate the complex relationship between technology and policy.

Only four American cities implemented rapid transit during the period under study: Chicago, New York, Boston, and Philadelphia. Chicago has been the subject of a recent study and will not be examined here.[49] After World War I when the automobile and the bus began to reduce the demand for mass rail transit, other cities showed lessening interest in rapid transit although local governments did plan and build the highways necessary to accommodate the enormous growth of vehicular traffic. More recently, renewed interest in public transit and the construction of high speed lines in San Francisco, Washington, and Atlanta marks a continuation of the policy and technology established in the 1890s, albeit on a regional rather than a city basis.

Since technological innovation plays such a central role in the process, the case studies are divided into two chapters, the first focusing on the mechanization of surface lines and the second centering on the implementation of rapid transit. The exception is New York, which required an additional introductory chapter on steam-powered, elevated railroads. In this, the first American city to have mechanized local transportation, early population growth required rapid transit before the invention of electric technology. The differences between the implementation of steam-powered elevated railroads and the later electric-powered subway illustrate the importance of technological change for shaping alterations in transit policy.

Though the remaining cases follow the conventional, two-part format, each has its own peculiarities. Boston, the second study, was the first big city to have a completed, mechanized surface system and was the site of the first American subway. In this instance a strong tradition of public control, a peculiar political alliance, and the location of a hallowed landmark, the Boston Common, were important determinants of technology and public policy.

Philadelphia, the final case, was more resistant to rapid transit and policy change. Public apathy and a strong affinity for private enterprise left the building of its first subway to its transit monopoly, the Philadelphia Rapid Transit Company. But because the company was unable to sustain construction and service, that city began to assume active development of transit by 1912. In Philadelphia as in New York and Boston, the innovation of new strategy, policy, and organization was an important response to technological change in public transportation.

PART I

East Side, West Side, All around the Town: Transit in New York

IN EACH CASE the area of study is the territory served by the city's transit system in 1900. Normally this definition includes the municipality and at least some of its metropolitan area. Yet New York is more complex. Expansion and change created several New Yorks between 1860 and 1910: pre-1898 New York whose political boundaries included Manhattan and the Bronx; Greater New York, the post-1898 city of five boroughs; and metropolitan New York, which in the early twentieth century encompassed Greater New York, Westchester County, and suburban areas in northern New Jersey.

The distinctions illustrate important differences from the Boston and Philadelphia experiences. In those two cases city expansion absorbed formally or informally much smaller adjacent communities, but in the New York case the merger included Brooklyn, whose population made it the fourth largest city in the United States in 1890. As a result, the early twentieth century city had two large, autonomous transit systems: the BRT, which serviced Brooklyn and parts of Queens, and the Interborough-Metropolitan system, which traversed Manhattan and much of the Bronx.

The latter system is the subject of this case, and thus pre-1898 New York (hereafter called New York) is the physical setting. The evolution of a transit system began in New York before Brooklyn, and the former led the latter in a series of innovations. In 1860 New York's population was almost half again the size of the next largest American city, and by 1880 the Census Bureau recognized New York as a part of something new—a metropolis. As a result New York was the first city whose population size and need for expansion led to rapid transit construction in the United States. Subsequently, New Yorkers witnessed the gradual consolidation and mechanization of their streetcar lines. Finally, New York along with Boston pioneered in the building of subways at the end of the nineteenth century.

These three technological innovations in transit and their impact on public policy serve to focus the New York case and to define its parts. The three-step process also contrasts with the experience of other cities where creation of the surface car system came first and rapid transit, if it came at all, appeared after streetcar mechanization. New York's early and unique growth, then, forces us to begin before the period defined in the study's title and raises several obvious questions. In what ways did its early start affect the evolution of New York's transit system? How were the necessary innovations accomplished? And finally, why did New York's early experience *not* become a pattern for other cities?

1.

Getting Up
in the World

NEW YORK became America's first industrial metropolis. By 1865 the
city's rapid growth had outstripped efforts to supply essential urban services at a comparable pace. Expansion especially taxed transportation
facilities and solving the transit problem raised several difficult questions: the selection of motive power and form of transit; the removal of
legal and traditional barriers to change; and the location of power and
expertise to plan, finance, erect, and operate adequate transportation
lines. The solutions and their limited impact provide a clear test for the
role of technology in the evolution of public transit and public policy.

The Emerging Metropolis

In the decade after the Civil War New York City was Manhattan Island,
twelve miles long and one half to two miles wide, to which the Bronx or
"Annexed District" was added in 1874. Map 1, which illustrates the pattern of construction in Manhattan, reflects somewhat New York's population distribution after the Civil War. By 1880 the retail district was
moving from below 14th Street toward 23rd Street, and many upper and
middle income New Yorkers were relocating residences in midtown. The
island's solidly built-up area extended only to Central Park's southern
edge. To the park's west settlement remained sparse while a number of
New Yorkers had moved into the upper East Side.[1]

Yet the location of buildings understates the concentration of population. In the 1870s cattle still grazed at 42nd Street opposite the new
Grand Central Station and cattle drovers were a major source of traffic
on Fifth Avenue north of 59th Street. One half of the city's million inhabitants crowded into the area below 14th Street.[2] As early as 1850 the
city's population density had surpassed London's, and in the lower East

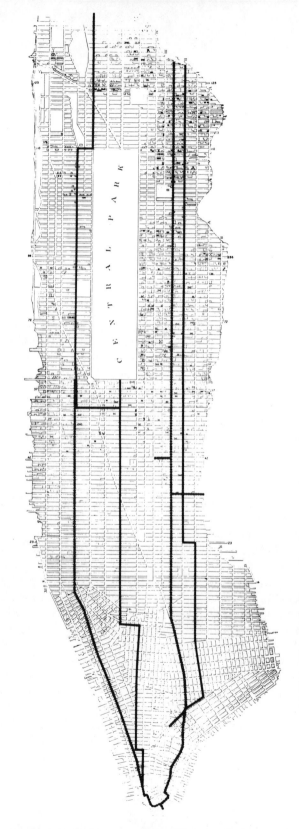

MAP 1. New York City and its elevated railroad lines, 1880. The gray reflects built-up areas. The heavy dark line is the Metropolitan Elevated Company, and the dotted line is the New York Elevated Company. *Source:* U.S. Bureau of the Census, *Tenth Census of the United States: 1880. Report on the Social Statistics of Cities* (Washington, 1886). I, 563; V. D. Leven, *Die New Yorker Hochbahnen* (Berlin, 1884).

Side's Tenth Ward, concentration exceeded three hundred per acre and was climbing to a level "quite possibly" unequaled in the world by 1900.[3]

Already the city had assumed a fast-paced, polyglot character. Alexander Callow has portrayed New York as a "city of contrasts": a "bustling metropolis of strangers" with a "collection of sharply divergent neighborhoods" and a place of magnificent hotels that "clashed sharply with the wretched poverty of Rag Pickers' Row or the violence of Hell's Kitchen." The vibrant city "was an emerging urban giant which, unlike Philadelphia or Boston, was living for the future, not the past."[4] New York was the nation's leading port as well as its primary industrial city, with shipyards, sugar refineries, flour and grist mills, textile mills, slaughterhouses, and other establishments.[5]

By the 1870s the city's economic and population growth had begun the transformation to the industrial metropolis illustrated in Map 2. Across the Hudson River to the west lay Jersey City, already part of metropolitan New York by 1880. The East River separated the city from Brooklyn, which was fast gaining a reputation as New York's bedroom community. Manhattan continued to be the most populous of Greater New York's five boroughs, but its share of the total population declined steadily from 60 percent in 1860 to 54 percent in 1900.[6] As manufacturing, commercial, and retailing districts took shape and expanded the city's business district toward midtown, an increasing number of those who worked in the city began to reside outside lower Manhattan.

The evolving metropolis soon found itself straining against its limited transportation facilities. Ferries were vital links to transport thousands daily across the rivers to New Jersey and Brooklyn. So great was the flow that by the 1880s the Brooklyn Bridge would become the first of many spans and tunnels linking New York to metropolitan New York. Much more flimsy were the links between downtown and uptown. The advent of omnibuses and later of horse railways had allowed some to commute to work, but they were too expensive and too slow for further uptown dispersal.

Omnibus lines on Broadway, the city's major thoroughfare, and on fashionable Fifth Avenue were simply inadequate to their purpose. As one newspaper editor put it:

> Modern martyrdom may be succinctly defined as riding in a New York omnibus. The discomforts, inconveniences and annoyances of a trip in one of these vehicles are almost intolerable. From the beginning to the end of the journey a constant quarrel is progressing. The driver quarrels with the passengers and the passengers quarrel with the driver. There are quarrels about getting out and quarrels about getting in. There are quarrels about change and quarrels about the ticket swindle. The

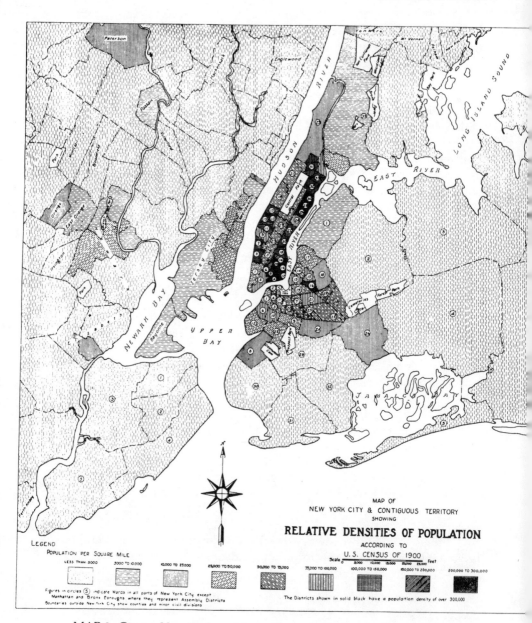

MAP 2. Greater New York and its environs, 1900. *Source: Regional Survey of New York and its Environs.* II: *Population, Land Values and Government* (New York, 1929), 73.

driver swears at the passengers and the passengers harangue the
driver through the straphole—a position in which even Demos-
thenes could not be eloquent. Respectable clergymen in white
chokers are obliged to listen to loud oaths. Ladies are disgusted,
frightened and insulted. Children are alarmed, and lift up their
voices and weep. Indignant gentlemen rise to remonstrate with
the irate Jehu, and are suddenly bumped back into their seats,
. . . [and] involved in supplementary quarrels with those other
passengers upon whose corns they have accidently trodden.
Thus the omnibus rolls along, a perfect Bedlam on wheels.[7]

The omnibus coaches remained on these two streets because influential
property owners and merchants opposed horsecars, which might attract
the masses and spoil quaintness and real estate values. Smoother riding,
cheaper, and more capacious horsecars on rails had quickly replaced
stages elsewhere in the 1850s.[8] Nevertheless, although horsecar fares fell
to a nickel, George Rogers Taylor has calculated that the charge was too
high for workers' daily use. Passengers on horse railways were most
probably skilled workers and people with middling incomes. Ridership
averaged one hundred fares per capita in 1870, high for the era but
hardly suggestive of daily travel by urban workers.[9]

Transit development had its costs as well as benefits. Before a fragmented and sometimes corrupt city government, numerous enterprisers
battled for the profitable privilege of operating omnibuses and horse railways. By 1860 the city council had granted at least eight 99- or 999-year
horse railway franchises with no coordination of routes and little provision for payment to the city. So notoriously venal was the process that a
state legislature increasingly dominated by Republicans with Protestant,
rural constituencies was quick to punish a municipal government run by
Democrats with heavy Irish Catholic support. The legislature rescinded
the city's chartering power and issued its own grants, which established
the routes and duties of the recipients.[10]

In addition to policy problems, technological limitations also marred
the evolution of New York's public transportation. Though they were
a definite improvement, horse railways soon exemplified an axiom
that continued to plague urban transit: betterment of facilities generated greater traffic, which in turn swamped the improvement. Speedily
the populace abandoned stages for horsecars and exceeded even their
capacity. Horse railway traffic almost tripled in the 1860s, reaching
115,000,000 by 1870.[11] The New York *Herald* editorialized that

it is in vain that those who are obliged to ride seek for relief in
a city railway car. The cars are quieter than the omnibuses, but
much more crowded. People are packed into them like sardines
in a box, with perspiration for oil. The seats being more than

filled, the passengers are placed in rows down the middle, where they hang on by the straps, like smoked hams in a corner grocery. To enter or exit is exceedingly difficult. Silks and broadcloth are ruined in the attempt. As in the omnibuses, pick-pockets take advantage of the confusion to ply their vocation. Handkerchiefs, pocketbooks, watches and breastpins disappear most mysteriously. A healthy person cannot ride a dozen blocks without a headache. For these reasons most ladies and gentlemen prefer to ride in the stages, which cannot be crowded so outrageously, and which are pretty decently ventilated by the cracks in the window frames. The omnibus fare is nearly double the car fare, however, and so the majority of the people are compelled to ride in the cars, although they lose in health what they save in money.[12]

Congested streets and an expanding city created additional problems. In lower New York heavy traffic already blocked the streets, and as the retail center gradually moved northward, it carried along the congestion. The glut made speeds of more than 5 miles an hour virtually impossible. On trips to uptown residences, the frequent stopping and starting, the lengthening distances, and the packed vehicles taxed the endurance of the two-horse motive power. Though some lines reached as far as 129th Street, few cars went beyond 42nd Street. There were delays to change teams or to hitch on extra horses to drag cars up the steeper inclines. With the delays and speed limitations, travel between the business district and the area above 42nd Street consumed as much as an hour.[13]

Alternatives were few and inadequate in 1865. Private cabs and carriages carried the well-to-do. Steam railroads were forbidden to travel below 42nd Street because of their danger to pedestrians and the risk of explosions and frightened horses.[14] The only alternative was shanks' mare. By the mid-1860s many recognized the need for a new kind of urban transportation. Mechanization was necessary to facilitate travel in the congested and ever-growing city and to permit northward expansion.

The Coming of the Elevated Lines

Demand for mechanization was well established by the 1860s, but it remained to be determined what form of transit would solve the city's need and just who would supply that solution. How was the city to move from generalized need to concrete answers and implementation?

Urban growth affected many segments of the population, who in turn supplied the dynamic push for rapid transit and encouraged inventors and capitalists to innovate new technology and venture for profit. After the Civil War land speculation above 59th Street anticipated the city's northward spread.[15] To increase the attractiveness of their lots, investors clamored for better transportation. As the New York *Daily Tribune* explained: "Several hundred thousand persons—rich and poor, male and female, wise and simple—earn their living by personal effort in that narrow corner of this island which lies south of Grand-st. We cannot live here; for most of this area is needed for stores, banks, offices, factories, workshops, etc.; and it is inconvenient to live across the arms of the sea on either hand. We want to live up town, or in the adjacent County of Westchester; and we want facilities for getting quickly, cheaply, comfortably, from our homes to our work and back again."[16]

Pressure organizations such as the West Side Association strove vigorously to be "efficient in protecting the interests of property owners, [and] in uniting them in favor of the rapid completion of . . . improvements." Realtors and investors quickly recognized that rapid transit was "of paramount importance" and gave it their "especial attention," and the agitation increased when the depression of the mid-1870s slowed the turnover of uptown land.[17]

Investors' concerns allied them with other businessmen and with civic boosters campaigning for urban development to increase commerce and hold down taxes. Like citizens in many nineteenth century cities, New Yorkers imagined themselves in a race for additional population and business activity. Since 1815 they had wrested leadership from Philadelphia and had fended off Boston and Baltimore for preeminence among east coast cities. But by the 1870s New York's rate of population growth slowed as suburban settlement grew in neighboring Brooklyn and New Jersey.[18]

Though the United States Census had recognized the region as a metropolitan area, that designation was in a sense premature, for, as Seymour Mandelbaum observes, the "region was composed of competitive settlements vying for advantage. They lacked the instrumental arrangements and the channels of communication which would have allowed them to act together to forward the well being of the entire area."[19] Failing to recognize their place in the evolving metropolis, Manhattan's citizens viewed with dismay a possible exodus which threatened their leadership and the erosion of their tax base.

Simultaneously the growth of the city amplified the cost of public services. Increasing population concentration, especially on the tenement-lined East Side, escalated demands for control of fire, crime, and disease and multiplied city expenses. This development allied the tax-conscious with urban reformers who advocated deconcentration as the remedy for urban ills. One critic argued that concentrated population "resulted in increasing the poverty and distress of one-half of our inhabitants; has added largely to the number of our drunkards, thieves and other abandoned and dangerous characters; has debauched the morals of our citizens, and, finally has resulted in an increase of disease and death almost unparalleled among civilized people."[20]

The link between transit, health, and order was a popular one, and the refrain was repeated many times in New York and other cities here and abroad.[21] Transit promoters quickly took up the cry and it is often difficult to distinguish them from reformers advocating transit improvements. The preceding quote is from a pamphlet published by an advocate for a subway firm, and New York's leading advocate of health improvement through transit betterment was Simeon Church, later an agent for the elevated railroad company, who was popularly accepted as a genuine reformer.[22]

Led by Church, reformers publicized the findings of the city's Health Board and Health Commissioners, which revealed overcrowding and squalor reminiscent of the old cities of Europe.[23] Fear of epidemic diseases added bite to their argument that, if Central Park were excluded, New York's population density exceeded the safe limits established by both English and French sanitary authorities. One health official asserted that "to the health and comfort of the poor of New York *cheap and rapid transit* is of the utmost importance, *as the most practicable method of relief from the surplus population.*"[24] In fact, relief would be available only for the upper and middle classes who could afford to buy, build, and travel. If for some reformers cheap rapid transit was a way of bettering the conditions of the laboring classes, for others it offered escape from the bustle of the city to the serenity of the suburb.

Improvement of public transit, then, became a rallying cry for several groups. What they wanted was rapid transit—the innovation of mechanized, high speed lines which avoided the city's congested streets and offered greater capacity. As the New York *World* aptly summed up the facile reinforcement of civic need, reform, and profit, "the growth of the city, the comfort of the people, and the value of property all depend on it."[25]

Responses by investors and entrepreneurs in the postwar economic boom were varied and enthusiastic, and all depended on the creation of new rights of way running above or below the streets. In the next decade proponents organized more than ten elevated and subway companies using stream, cable, and compressed air systems of power. Although proposals for elevated railways dated from the 1830s, the first serious effort at rapid transit in New York was a subway line advocated by the Metropolitan Railway Company in 1864 and inspired by the recent opening of the London subway. The company sought incorporation for $5,000,000, but although its supporters included such prominent New Yorkers as Henry Varnum Poor, Abel Low, and John Jacob Astor, its charter application died in the legislature, apparently a victim of the opposition of street railway and property owners.[26]

Only two projects—both elevated roads—became operational. Despite the appeal of rapid transit, there was considerable opposition—not to the innovation *per se*, but to particular locations or technologies. The local street railways fought every proposal. Much more significant protest came from influential merchants and property owners like Alexander Stewart and the Astor family. Abutters feared damages and decreased property values and merchants objected that construction would block streets and curtail business. Finally, vigorous fighting in the legislature and the courts among groups vying for a particular technology and an exclusive route also accounted for many failures. Subway and elevated partisans were avowed enemies, each quick to trumpet any weaknesses of the other before bewildered representatives from upstate.[27]

Technological constraints and costs virtually eliminated the subway as an alternative. In the 1860s steam was the only practical power, and steam subways with their smoky tunnels were unpopular with investors and riders. James Walker, an early historian of New York rapid transit, has suggested that the success of the London subway removed technological barriers for subways in the 1860s, but he minimized the smokiness of the tunnels and ignored an important difference between the London system and the New York situation. London's early undergrounds were actually a combination of subway and open cut with no long tunnels. New York subway proposals called for a continuous tunnel for most of the route. The ventilation problem and the high cost of construction made subways less attractive than cheaper railways built above the street.[28] And the expense of a path through New York real estate discouraged an open cut or mixture of open cut and subway as alternatives. Even in the estimates of supporters, subway construction would require more than $1,500,000 per mile, almost twenty times the per mile cost of New York's most expensive horsecar line. Indeed with one exception, the subway's per mile cost equaled or exceeded the total cost of road and equipment of any New York horse railway in 1870.[29] None of the subway companies that obtained charters raised the funds necessary to build.

Capital shortages plagued elevated railway proposals as well, because of the costs and risks of innovation. Steam engines, forbidden in downtown New York streets, were not welcome overhead and raised the possibility of large damage payments. The search for a new motive power—either cable or compressed air—meant additional risk. The purchase of a right of way through the most expensive real estate in the nation was not feasible. The obvious solution, the use of the public way, raised opposition from influential abutters. As Sam Bass Warner has shown, the regard for the rights of private property over public welfare was a serious hindrance to improvement.[30]

In New York the issue was more complex. Nineteenth century municipal corporation law and the notorious scandals in local government con-

siderably reduced the city's power. As in most large nineteenth century
cities, a political machine dominated municipal government in New
York. Headed by a boss, the machine was a hierarchy built of precincts,
districts, and wards and fueled with cooperation, patronage, and graft.
At its zenith the boss's power was reflected in his control of the branches
of government—city council, the mayor's office, and the local judiciary.
In New York, as Seymour Mandlebaum has shown, the boss unified a
complex structure of competing branches, departments, and commissions and thus centralized authority.[31] But the boss's power was never
absolute, and in New York it was not continuous. Instead a recurring
cycle of machine and reform politics characterized the city's government.
The regimes of Fernando Wood, William Marcy Tweed, John Kelly, and
Richard Croker were broken with the election of reform coalitions and
the reallocation of authority.

The cycle of alternating reform and machine governments weakened
the possibility of coherent policy and local control. After Albany assumed exclusive chartering powers from a corrupt city council in the late
1850s, abuses and the callous attitude of a rural-dominated legislature
toward the state's largest city fueled demands for greater home rule. But
until 1875 the only local controls over the 999-year horse railway grants
were the rights of individual abutters.[32] Injunctions by property owners
against horse railway and rapid transit lines thus were blows not only for
property rights but for home rule as well.

An additional obstacle to rapid transit was the lack of an adequate
public mechanism for resolving the complicated and interrelated problems of technology, law, and urban needs. The city council and the state
legislature, both battlegrounds for politicians, were without the necessary expertise. The courts were slow and their role was generally negative and regulatory, not developmental. The executive branch both in the
state and the city lacked the clear-cut authority and, like the legislature,
was embroiled in party struggles.[33]

Before 1875 city and state governments had made only one attempt to
deal comprehensively with the transportation problem. An 1866 commission composed of three state senators, the mayor of New York, the
state engineer, and the engineer of the Crotan Aqueduct studied the situation for a year but settled little. The choice of transit routes and technology was left to private companies where it had been and would remain for more than a quarter century.

The commission undertook no active investigation of its own, opting
instead to wait for the submission of plans from interested groups. It
spent six months deciding that rapid transit was indeed necessary and
that routes were required for both sides of the city. In a confusing report,
it found that "the underground plan alone meets the conditions already

set forth as demanded, of speed, safety, economy, and rapidity of construction." But it rejected steam-powered subways and recommended instead the construction of an experimental segment of Charles Harvey's proposed elevated road.[34]

A later judgment by the New York Public Service Commission that the report "was without practical result" emphasized how much the state's place in transportation development had diminished since it built the Erie Canal early in the century.[35] Finance, choice of route and technology, construction, and engineering—functions performed by state commissions building major public arteries in the canal era—were now left to private enterprise. A new technology demanded a coordinated administration of carrier and right of way, which was far more complex than the operations of canal boards. The advent of the railroad had shifted the power of the state commission to private companies by the 1860s.[36] And as noted earlier, local transit already had an established tradition of private enterprise. Not surprisingly, then, the evolution of local transit systems in New York as in Boston, Philadelphia, and other American cities, was initiated by privately owned, profit-based enterprises. Only when they proved unable or unwilling to provide adequate service in the future would city government assume a more active role.

Meanwhile, private interests supplied the solution—elevated railroads —to satisfy the city's need for rapid transit. Beginning in 1867, Charles Harvey and his associates built a single-track line, which rested on a set of posts on one side of Ninth Avenue from the Battery to 30th Street. A cable powered by stationary steam engines propelled the cars.

After the failure of the cable system and early bankruptcy, the company was reorganized in 1871 as the New York Elevated Railroad Company, and its owners successfully petitioned to convert to steam locomotives.[37] Heavy engines and growing traffic soon required double tracks and the more substantial double-post system still in use today. The gradual process of implementation—first elevated roads, then dirty steam locomotives with their smoke and cinders, and finally the massive, street-darkening roadbed—obscured the public costs of the new technology and aided the initial acceptance of the elevated.

By the mid-1870s the New York Elevated Company had demonstrated its ability to build a transit system that could halve travel time.[38] But it was unable to continue. A national depression which dried up capital, opposition from abutters, and a hodge-podge of acts exempting particular avenues as rights of way prevented further construction along the authorized route on Ninth Avenue and blocked any attempt to charter a route on the East Side.

Technological and legal problems stalled a second firm, the Metropolitan Elevated Railroad Company, incorporated in 1872 to run from the

Battery northward along Sixth Avenue to Central Park. Charter provisions limiting the line to inadequate "atmospheric power, compressed air or other power" and injunctions by abutters halted any action.[39] In the absence of city authority, only the state could provide the public aid needed to overcome the many restrictions facing both companies.

The Appeal to Public Aid

While private enterprise supplied the technology and the organization for actual implementation, it did not act in a vacuum. There remained the problem of accommodating transit innovation and public policy. Since the avid interest of many groups complicated the question, public action offered the best means of unsnarling the impasse.

By 1875 a city population in excess of one million and the New York Elevated Company's limited success magnified the demand for rapid transit. Thwarted by the repeated failure of the company to expand after 1870, a few businessmen and reformers turned to government action. Addressing a mass meeting at the Cooper Institute in February 1873, ironmaster Abram Hewitt called for the city to build lines if necessary. A proposal to that effect soon appeared before the city council. Meanwhile reformer Simeon Church persuaded the New York Rapid Transit Association to encourage public construction in March 1873.[40]

But in 1873 and 1874, bills for city finance failed in Albany because of the traditional opposition from abutters and street railway interests and because New Yorkers could not agree to support public development. Church had persuaded the West Side Association to approve municipal construction with a hasty vote at a meeting's end in 1871, but the group quickly reversed itself at the next meeting after realtors and property owners had had time to ponder the issue. As much as these investors wished to develop their property, government finance was too much to accept.[41] Some aid was needed to cut through the mass of entangling injunctions and restrictions, but the searing memory of Tweedism was enough to make even the strongest supporter of rapid transit blanch. What was more, the eagerness of private interests to act weakened the argument for the necessity of public funding and construction. Debate over the issue of government finance deprived rapid transit bills of the unified support vital to their success.

Intrigued by the problem, a blue ribbon panel of the American Society of Civil Engineers studied the issue thoroughly in the winter of 1874-75 and offered a proposal that united rapid transit support. Abandoning city construction, they concentrated on the obstacles to private enterprise. Their report again reflected the difficulties attending the innovation of costly rapid transit technology. As they saw it, "the law-makers have been unwilling to grant charters until they knew on what plans the roads were to be built, and capital has refused to make in advance the necessary surveys and investigations, upon which alone adequate plans could be based."[42] To resolve the dilemma, the committee recommended that a commission of prudent citizens aided by leading officials and engineers establish a route and select a plan and technology. Franchises would be offered to those "who now control the existing lines of transportation in the territory" or to other capitalists if they hesitated.[43]

Because the city was again in the reform portion of its machine-reform cycle, the proposal was a reasonable one. Boss Tweed and his Tammany mayor, A. Oakey Hall, were gone. An anti-Tweed businessman, Mayor William Wickham, quickly sent a bill embodying the ASCE proposals to the legislature. Since it avoided the divisive issue of public finance, the measure had the virtually unanimous support of the city's leaders. Prominent engineers, influential businessmen, the mayor, and major investors in the New York and Metropolitan Companies endorsed the proposal, and it quickly passed the legislature.[44]

The act empowered the mayor, upon petition of fifty householders, to appoint a five-man Rapid Transit Commission (RTC) to establish routes in the city, to design links with ferries and steam railroads, and to plan construction. The commission could implement its plan in one of two ways. It might lay out the route along the rights of way of the existing companies and grant them the power to build the necessary extensions. Or, as an alternative it could create a new corporation to construct the road and supervise its organization by private interests.[45]

As the ASCE panel had envisioned, the RTC acted under business control and with businesslike dispatch. The mayor appointed five businessmen to the commission: banker Joseph Seligman; financier and real estate investor Lewis B. Brown; Jordan L. Mott, owner of an iron foundry and close friend of Mayor Wickham; Cornelius Delamater, head of an iron works; and Charles J. Canda, investor in various iron and railroad enterprises.[46] After hearing plans for various types of roads, the commissioners selected steam-powered elevated railways as the proper solution and awarded franchises to the New York and Metropolitan Elevated Companies. They laid out lines on Sixth and Ninth Avenues to coincide with the elevated companies' routes and mapped out two additional rights of way on the East Side as extensions of the first lines. Finally, they authorized the creation of a third organization, the Manhattan Elevated Railroad Company, to serve as an alternative if either existing company failed to exercise its franchise.[47]

The 1875 act appeared to be a greater step toward innovation of an active government role in public transit than it actually was. The RTC did in theory establish the route, motive power, and type of transit. It also created an instrument, the Manhattan Company, to implement its plans. But in reality the basic decisions were those of private enterprise.

Not surprisingly, the New York and Metropolitan roads were enthusiastic about the possibility of completing their lines on the West Side and expanding up the populous East Side. Prior to the introduction of the RTC bill, major investors in the companies wrote Mayor Wickham to express their support for the plan. In addition, the petition asking the mayor to appoint the RTC was signed by David Dows, a director of the New York Elevated Company.[48]

Because of the private enterprise tradition and the enthusiasm of the companies, much of the vital decision making was a *fait accompli*. The commission did not engage in an open-ended examination of city transit needs, but contented itself with promoting the completion and extension of the New York and Metropolitan lines. Because the best available routes on the West Side belonged to these companies, the RTC had little choice in its award. Although it received more than forty proposals, the RTC negotiated with the two companies almost immediately after its organization, and within six weeks the commission made a formal offer, before even issuing a report. The New York Elevated Company accepted in six days and the Metropolitan Company in one day. The elevated owners quietly bought all the stock of the RTC-created Manhattan Company and divided it equally between the two existing firms.[49]

The 1875 RTC, then, did not build rapid transit but confirmed and fostered private efforts. Nor did it establish itself as a powerful agency of city government. The law limited the commission to a 120-day term, and general acceptance of its decisions came only after careful judicial review in 1877.[50]

Nevertheless, the RTC played a more active role than the commission of 1866. Its performance met most of economist Henry Broude's standards for positive government action: "Giving specific and direct support to industry in the private sector; taking initial risks, leading the way, and removing bottlenecks; and creating a favorable climate which had salutory effects on expectations in the private sector."[51] The commission offered city streets as rights of way, obtained acceptance of routes and construction plans from the Board of Alderman and the mayor, and provided for valuable extensions. Its grants set maximum fares at five cents for workers' rush hours and ten cents for the rest of the day and established time limits and standards for construction to be enforced by city government.[52]

Such restricted action directed by businessmen admirably suited the public's desire for better communication and transportation.[53] The RTC solution of public aid for private enterprise won virtually unanimous approval in New York's newspapers.[54] As suggested by the ASCE report, the provisions of the 1875 act, the RTC's deliberations, the enthusiasm of the elevated owners, and the general approval of the plan, the eventual solution was widely regarded as the simplest, quickest, and most efficient way to obtain badly needed rapid transit. With technology handy, the outlook promising, and capital reassured, private enterprise was prepared to maintain its dominance.

Thus New York's early evolution as an industrial metropolis provoked limited change in transit and public policy. The use of familiar steam technology, the choice of elevated railways, and the city's readiness to promote the enterprise permitted the New York and Metropolitan firms to satisfy temporarily New York's rapid transit needs and obviated any radical alteration in public policy. Not until the 1890s, when urban growth outstripped the elevated system's capacity and compelled the innovation of an expensive and complex subway system, did the policy of public aid for private development fail, forcing the city to assume a direct role in the improvement of local transit.

Not So Rapid Transit

The RTC's grants and a series of court actions upholding their validity in 1877 fulfilled their purpose. Government aid broke the logjam of restrictions and injunction. Promoters with experience and connections quickly appeared to complete the work of the New York and Metropolitan Companies. Cyrus Field of the New York Company and Commodore Cornelius Garrison, Jose DeNavarro, and others from the Metropolitan were seasoned businessmen with useful financial and political ties. Field was well known for directing the laying of the Atlantic cable and was closely allied with Samuel Tilden, Democratic governor of New York and recent candidate for the presidency. Garrison had battled for franchises and favors in the gas utilities business in New York and Chicago, and De Navarro had made lucrative deals with the Tweed machine.[55]

Perhaps more important both groups were able to tap sufficient resources to supply the approximately $18,000,000 needed to construct the roads.[56] To sell his bonds, Field apparently drew upon European contacts dating from his Atlantic cable venture. He also followed the railroads' example and relied on investment bankers for some finance. He dealt with Drexel, Morgan and Company while his rivals at the Metropolitan Company sold bonds through Kuhn, Loeb and Company.[57]

In addition, the Metropolitan builders employed the old railroad technique of using construction company profits to attract investors. The New York Loan and Improvement Company, headed by General Horace Porter and other Metropolitan directors, accepted the contract to build the $9,700,000 road for some $21,500,000 in stocks and bonds.[58] The

watered securities increased in value after the line's completion and offered large profits to early investors. Midway through construction both
firms injected still more water by leasing their lines to the RTC-created
Manhattan Elevated Railway Company, which they already controlled
jointly. Besides producing more insider profits and possibly attracting
more funds, the merger replaced a cumbersome arrangement of dual control and joint use of track with a central administration for a single system.[59]

After 1881, then, the Manhattan Elevated monopolized New York's
rapid transit and reinforced the city's northward expansion. The company operated 81 miles of track on four lines that stretched from the Battery up to or beyond Central Park, as illustrated in Map 1. By 1890 the
city's population above 42nd Street had increased 50 percent in a decade,
while the jump in land values in the three mid- and uptown wards serviced by the system accounted for almost 60 percent of New York's total
property value growth between 1879 and 1886.[60]

The elevated lines provided vital additional capacity for New York's
public transit. As Chart 1 indicates, the elevated system was responsible
for most of the traffic growth between 1878 and the early 1890s. Elevated
fares spurted from 2,000,000 in 1876 to 86,000,000 in 1882 and grew
steadily until the adoption of the nickel fare on a full-time basis generated
a second sharp jump in 1886-87. More surprisingly, Chart 1 reveals the
continuous growth of all public transit traffic. As a result, the antiquated
horse railways suffered only slight, temporary declines in fares. In the
late 1880s and early 1890s elevated and surface lines had almost parallel
rates of increase despite the elevated's higher speeds for an equal price.

Behind the street railways' resurgence and the slowing of the elevated
company's growth were several important limitations in New York's
steam-powered elevated railroads. Part of the problem lay with the Manhattan's management. In the 1880s Jay Gould, his son George, and Russell Sage assumed control of the monopoly from Cyrus Field and others
who had directed construction. More concerned with financial manipulation than operation of the now established property, these men made little effort to improve transportation. They showed scant interest in expanding the system except under terms unacceptable to the public, and
they failed to replace steam with a more efficient motive power. Gould
was persuaded to visit an experiment with electric-powered engines, but
when a fuse blew out, the badly frightened speculator would have nothing more to do with electric power. Gould's biographer put it succinctly:
"The Manhattan Elevated was not well run." Nevertheless, the monopoly paid better than 6 percent on heavily watered capital and was considered one of the best financial properties in the nation.[61]

Public hostility was a second limiting factor. The Manhattan's profit-

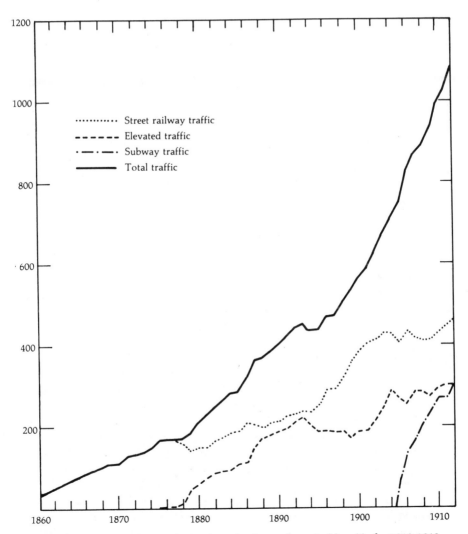

CHART 1. Street railway, elevated, and subway fares in New York, 1860-1912 (in millions). Figures for the Bronx are included after 1897. In all charts "fares" refers to paying passengers; "riders" or "traffic" includes fares and transfers. *Sources: Real Estate Record and Builders Guide,* 50 (November 26, 1892), 683; Public Service Commission for the 1st District, *Annual Report* (1907), II, 25-26, and *Annual Report* (1913), II, 28-29.

able monopoly, the speculator-owners' unsavory reputation and their complacent management contributed much to that opposition. But anger and criticism long predated the arrival of the Goulds and Sage and owed much to the technological limitations of steam-powered elevated railroads. In the 1870s and 1880s court cases, mass meetings, and pamphlets demonstrated determined opposition. Abutting property owners and merchants fought elevated transit as they had fought horse railways, rightly fearing declining property values. Others attacked the system for its noise, dirt, and ugliness, qualities that were especially troublesome in the narrow, building-lined streets downtown.[62] New York courts eventually determined that the elevated companies were liable for damages to the value of abutting property, a decision that cost the Manhattan Company more than $13,000,000 by 1900.[63]

More frustrating was the monopoly's power and permanence despite steady opposition and the limited use of elevated lines elsewhere. John Kellett has shown that the social costs of elevated railroads deterred their adoption in London. John McKay's study of European public transit demonstrates that aesthetic considerations determined or modified forms of transit technology adopted throughout Europe. In contrast he suggests that such considerations were weaker in the United States.[64]

The process was not straightforward. Elevated lines were originally chartered as cable powered single-track roads running above one side of the street. Only afterwards did steam power and the massive structure appear. Indeed the elevated case suggests that other factors did operate. Despite the elevateds' profitability and their superiority to horsecars, five additional rapid transit commissions produced only one short extenstion of New York's steam-powered, high speed lines. In neighboring Brooklyn they were chartered only under the ultimately neglected requirement that a "silent, safety" road be constructed, and few lines were built for local transit elsewhere until electricity replaced steam power.[65]

At the heart of the elevated system's limitations and its restricted use elsewhere were the technology's liabilities. It was expensive to build, costing at least fifteen times the per mile investment of horse railways, and liable to expensive damage suits.[66] More important were the limitations of steam power for the frequent stop and go of urban transit. The locomotive was a unit in the train that took up space but carried no passengers. Size and weight limitations on engines restricted trains to five cars. Longer trains would require heavier engines and a more massive elevated structure.[67] The inability to start and stop quickly limited elevated trains to a twelve miles per hour average, which required forty-five minutes to travel from Harlem to the Battery, a far cry from the popular local definition of rapid transit: "From Harlem to the Battery in 15 minutes."[68] Also serious was the system's meager flexibility to expand with increasing traffic. By the late 1880s trains were badly overcrowded and ran with so little headway during rush hours that any delay by one train held up those behind it. The New York *Times* reported, "It has been a common experience for trains bound down town in the morning to become so crowded by the time they reached Ninety-third street that not another passenger could be taken aboard until room was made by some one leaving the train. And passengers have stood on the platforms at Eighty-third, Seventy-second and Fifty-ninth streets and watched train after train go by, loaded to its limits."[69]

Because of New York's early growth and need for rapid transit in the 1860s, its technological choices were more restricted than they would be a quarter century later. The adaptation of steam locomotives to overhead railroads with their operating limitations, their legal liabilities, and their social and aesthetic costs was not the long range answer to the city's need for high speed lines. Their brief heyday in the 1880s and 1890s suggests a kind of false start in the evolution of an urban transit system— a technology that provided only a stopgap solution. Instead, permanent rapid transit in the center of American cities would be electric rather than steam powered and under rather than above ground. But before the subways came, the Manhattan Company faced fresh competition from rejuvenated surface lines.

2.

Cables and Conduits

NEW YORK's transit in 1880 reflected the fragmented city so well described by Seymour Madelbaum in *Boss Tweed's New York*.[1] Seventeen surface and elevated companies operated independently. To go by horsecar from river to river on 14th Street meant a ride on four different lines, each with a change of cars and another fare. There was no direct route to carry passengers from a West Side ferry to Brooklyn or to Grand Central Station.

Such were the local transit facilities when population began a 69 percent increase and traffic commenced a 122 percent growth in the next two decades.[2] Changes in the location of population exacerbated the difficulty. Encouraged by the advent of elevated lines, uptown growth exceeded the general population increase. In 1880 one third of New York lived above 42nd Street; in 1890 more than one half did.[3] Simultaneously the concentration of business activity downtown grew.

Transporting New York's expanding population in the 1880s involved a complex series of alterations. Municipal government, still relying on a traditional policy of private enterprise in public transportion, failed to act, and the city's elevated and horse railway managers shied from the risks and costs. Entrepreneurship fell to five men without experience in New York transit. They combined financial skills, legal talent, and political connections to resolve the challenges of public transportation. To implement new mechanical technology, they had to raise large sums of capital, to find an adequate legal organization, and to devise a new strategy and structure for operation. And all the while they contended with the continually expanding city and with a transit policy made obsolete by their own innovations.

Conditions and Needs

The steam elevated road's inability to cope adequately with urban growth provoked a search for new technology to move increasing traffic over lengthening distances. Eventually the answer would be the electric-powered subway, but in the 1880s electric power for transportation remained unproven. Instead, tests for noncombustive motive power came quickly on surface lines and as a result they were the next form of technology to meet New York's transit needs.

As Chart 1 reveals, the great jump in the street railways' share of public transit came in the nine years after 1894 when their traffic jumped almost 200,000,000 or 81 percent. The groundwork for the shift, however, was laid in the 1880s when the elevated lines were fast approaching their limits. A New York *Times* analyst observed in 1888 that "the slightly-increased facilities of travel offered from time to time by the elevated roads had been taken advantage of by the traveling public to their utmost."[4] The overburdening of the elevated lines and the increase of short haul traffic downtown not only restored but slowly expanded street railway traffic. Annual per capita street railway fares went from $8.40 in 1880 to $13.50 in 1890 despite rapid transit competition.[5]

Horsecar lines were unprepared for the burden. "Backwardness, stupidity, deterioration . . . [and] an uninterrupted disgrace for thirty years" was Burton Hendrick's summary of the transit situation.

> In 1884 [he continued] there were some thirty independent street railways, owned mostly by established families and estates. They operated largely on perpetual franchises, for which they paid practically nothing into the city treasury. Each company aimed only at cultivating its own traffic, and never considered the convenience of the city as a whole. Transfer privileges were virtually unknown. Even when traveling short distances, one had frequently to take two or three independent lines; and, in crossing the island, New Yorkers sometimes had to follow a zigzag course and pay two or three fares. The cars were small, unventilated, shockingly filthy and broken down. They were lighted by faint kerosene-lamps, and in winter-time a mass of straw or hay, thrown upon the floor, furnished the only warmth.[6]

The most successful companies were those on the north-south avenues. Built under perpetual charters granted by the legislature, their monopolies of the major traffic arteries forced patrons to ignore their filth and pokiness. On those avenues not used by the elevated roads, returns from horsecar operations were good, sometimes exceeding 10 percent on watered securities. The gilt-edged stock of such roads was rarely traded. Complacent with fat profits even in the face of elevated competition (whose fare before 1886 was ten cents, or double that of the horsecar, except during rush hours when it dropped to a nickel), their managements were reluctant to improve operations by installing costly, new mechanical power.[7]

On the newer, crosstown lines the situation was worse. Chartered in the 1870s and 1880s, they were less successful. Many were speculative franchises whose owners delayed construction or merely operated a few cars on a wretched road in order to preserve their grants. The tumble-down 28th and 29th Street line was accused of operating on two streets because it was too ashamed to return along the same route.[8]

The situation clearly was a serious one. As one expert testified in 1883: "The surface roads, which were built from time to time, before the era of the elevated roads, were built by independent companies, as purely business enterprises; they were built not in accordance with any system, not under the auspices of any authorized Commission, not upon any well-devised plan, but rather, as many of our first city sewers were built, namely, in opposition or antagonism to each other."[9] Independent horse-car lines built for the New York of the 1850s simply were unable to meet the needs of the emerging industrial metropolis.

The transit policy of city and state government offered little hope for improvement. In the fifty years after the first horsecar line had appeared in New York, there had been an accumulation of laws and charters without clear direction or force. Government's role was limited primarily to the charter process. At first the city chartered companies as part of its power to regulate the use of its streets. From the outset, graft and favoritism tainted the contests over valuable perpetual grants on major avenues. As noted earlier, one of the city's cyclic reform battles to correct a corrupt and pliant city council had altered transit policy slightly by 1860. The New York legislature continued a tradition that made municipal corporations creatures of the state and assumed a monopoly of the charter process.[10]

But the abuses and flaws remained. Harry Carman concluded that the state's 999-year grants were "so drafted as to invest the grantees with special privilege which they regarded as a private property right subject to little or no public control."[11] A perpetual franchise could be terminated only by condemnation with compensation to the company for its facilities and its right of way. Without control over operation government lacked the means to regulate service in the public interest. Provisions for fares, paving duties, car licenses, and change of power varied with each charter, and in some cases there were no controls. And the absence of financial constraints allowed stock watering while the city was without the power to order improvements or extensions.[12]

This passive public policy left most regulation to company competition and patrons' complaints. Though public protests over the resulting deficiencies dated from the 1850s, no significant change came until 1884, when the city obviously needed more street railways. Even then, reform was designed to eliminate past abuses of graft and favoritism and to insure compensation for the valuable grants. The tradition of private enterprise in transit and the lack of expertise in city government obviated any crusade for a comprehensive policy to coordinate routes and improve service. Past failures could be seen much more clearly than future needs.

Reform in 1884 merely altered a few rules for private enterprise in public transit. An earlier attempt to amend the charter procedure in the legislature had backfired. Reformers had outlawed special grants, which they saw as the source of corruption, but neglected to provide an alternative. After nine years of no new charters, urban growth and the desire of street railway entrepreneurs to build lines on lower Broadway and on crosstown streets led to general incorporation.[13]

The street railway act of 1884 won considerable praise as a reform. It provided for general incorporation by any group of thirteen or more who filed the appropriate articles with the New York secretary of state. The incorporators could obtain a franchise only with the consent of the local authorities and the owners of at least one half of the value of property abutting the line. In lieu of abutter consents permission could be granted by a three-man commission appointed by and subject to the approval of the state Supreme Court.[14]

In cities over 250,000, the road was to compensate the municipality with 3 percent of annual gross receipts for the first three years of operation and 5 percent annually thereafter. Cities could impose snow removal and paving duties, regulate speed, and (along with one half of the abutters) approve the choice of technology. A five-cent maximum fare was established for a continuous ride. Construction was to be completed within three years on pain of forfeiture. No company could build on a street occupied by another without its permission. And at their option, cities could sell franchises at public auction.[15]

The reform was a mixed blessing for public transit. It did supply a badly needed incorporation procedure, set maximum fares, and provide for compensation for valuable franchises. Unfortunately, the law added another layer of regulations to those in existing charters, with confusing and sometimes harmful consequences for both the companies and the public. Despite compensation requirements, there were still no controls over distribution of profits, no mechanism to encourage or compel extensions, and no termination clause for franchises. Thus perpetual franchises, overcapitalization, and decentralized operation continued. The city's representatives still had no active role in transit development. Decisions about routing, extensions, technology, and service remained those of private enterprise and required only the acquiescence of government.

In addition, the reforms created possible barriers to future development. The old policy of passive regulation with free rights of way and no supervision of profits had encouraged entrepreneurs. After 1884 the compensation requirement for new lines left future entrants at a disadvantage vis-à-vis the older operators. But because an extension suddenly subjected the entire revenue of an old line to the new tax, the law also discouraged development of new territory by existing companies. Instead, independent and "dummy" companies proliferated, as did stock watering, fragmentation of operation, and fare charges.[16]

Finally, the law failed to adjust for the innovation of new technology. When in 1887 the Third Avenue Company sought to cable its lines, property owners and the Board of Aldermen delayed implementation for three years. Neither group had the expertise to pass on the question. An important opportunity to mechanize and improve became a political football at the hands of a Tammany-controlled Board of Aldermen. Only after repeated appearances before the board and the courts did the company prevail.[17]

A subsequent change which transferred authority over technology to the State Board of Railroad Commissioners was some improvement but left much to be desired. In the name of local control and protection of property rights, abutters still could delay a change and force a company to consume time and money in court hearings. Otherwise, the Railroad Commission, preoccupied with steam railroads, perfunctorily approved requests with little examination in the public interest.[18] In addition, the franchises for lines on which the new technology was to be installed remained the bailiwick of the Board of Aldermen.

The 1884 law confirmed the tradition of private operation of public transit, as had the 1875 Rapid Transit Act. Local transportation remained closely tied to politics. Government supplied favors and grants but no policy for comprehensive development and mechanization.

The Coming of the New Breed

The advent of new entrepreneurs accompanied the adoption of mechanical power. Population growth and pressure on local transit made it virtually impossible to continue to exempt Broadway, the city's main artery and only diagonal route, from a street railway. A lengthy line on New York's busiest thoroughfare required new motive power, and by the 1880s cable traction had become a feasible alternative to horse-powered railways on major streets in large cities. But the new technology had much higher fixed costs and required more careful coordination of lines.

The process of change in surface transit, then, begins not with actual mechanization, but with the conditions necessary to accommodate that mechanization.

Enterprise was one of those conditions, and the failure of horse railway men to apply the new technology opened the way for outsiders of talent, experience, and influence to enter the field. Jacob Sharp was New York's preeminent horse railway owner. Born in 1817 of humble parentage, he had entered the public transit field in the 1850s after building docks for the city.[19] By 1880 he controlled several lines but never sought to combine them into a system. Nor did he have any use for cable traction. What he sought on lower Broadway was another horsecar line to complement his Broadway and Seventh Avenue Railroad Company on the upper part of the avenue.[20]

But what satisfied Sharp only tantalized others. Broadway intersected most of the major traffic arteries in New York and was "the mouth of a funnel" through which traffic could move downtown in the morning and disperse uptown in the evening.[21] What would be only a profitable horse-car road for old Jake Sharp offered to the bold and far-sighted much greater potential as the trunk of a network of lines. A system would capture not only the traffic of New York's major thoroughfare but would attract even greater numbers of riders and produce larger profits with cable power and free transfers.

Two groups fought Sharp for the Broadway franchise. One was the New York Cable Railway Company, owner of the New York rights to the valuable Hallidie cable patents.[22] Wallace C. Andrews and H. H. Rogers of Standard Oil and banker George Baker, among others, headed the enterprise, which also included two younger men, William C. Whitney, brother-in-law of Standard Oil partner O. H. Payne, and Thomas Fortune Ryan, a protégé of Andrews.[23]

Whitney, a leader in the city's Democratic party and its former corporation counsel, quickly saw the potential profits in street railways. To fight Sharp he allied with company secretary Ryan, whom he described as "the most adroit, suave, and noiseless man he had ever known." Ryan was a young stockbroker who had come from a modest Virginia background to Wall Street where he made valuable contacts with such wealthy, powerful men as Samuel Tilden and Robert Cutting. Like Whitney, the shrewd and taciturn Ryan was very much the man-on-the-make. Both realized that the way to wealth lay in a new field with an opportunity to get in on the ground floor.[24] The pressing transit needs of New York and the availability of the new mechanical traction made street railways just such an industry.

These two became leaders in the Cable Company's affairs. Whitney incorporated the Broadway Railway Company as a construction com-

pany for the cable interests, and he and Ryan held the largest blocks of
the Broadway Company stock. Ryan left his brokerage business and
began to seek the necessary consents from abutters. Aided by counsel
John Parsons, John Cadwalader, and L. E. Chittenden, Whitney and
Ryan set out to fight Sharp with "money, work and energy."[25] To block
the old man, Chittenden organized abutting property owners to influence
Mayor Franklin Edson to veto Sharp's franchise request. But their wily
opponent eluded them when in the summer of 1884 he brazenly bribed
the Board of Aldermen to override the mayor's veto.

The theft of New York's most valuable artery aroused the press and
public. Encouraged by Chittenden, the New York Anti-Monopoly League
exposed evidence of $25,000 payments by Sharp to each alderman. In
addition, Whitney inspired abutters Edward Knox and Horace Thurber
to institute a suit, which successfully vacated the grant.[26] Facing a storm
of protest and injunctions, Sharp turned to new tactics. In November
1884 he offered more favorable terms to counter the Cable Company's
promise of a million dollars and a transfer system in exchange for the
franchise. In addition to the compensation required by the 1884 law of
incorporation, Sharp promised a $40,000 annual payment and a lease to
his uptown line, the Broadway and Seventh Avenue Railway Company,
to provide a continuous ride along the avenue for 5 cents. Again the
obliging Board of Aldermen, popularly known as the "Forty Thieves,"
quickly voted him the franchise as the Broadway Surface Railway Company.[27]

To this point the cable forces had failed despite an impressive array of
weapons and the skillful employment of the public character of local
transit to advance the cause of their private enterprise. The use of political influence to pressure the mayor, public proclamations of tempting
counter-offers, the inspiration of property owner injunctions and tax-
payer suits, and the stirring of protests and investigations from such
groups as the Anti-Monopoly League foreshadowed the tactics employed
in later years by utilities entrepreneurs and appeared to reflect Whitney's
ideas. He countenanced manipulation of public opinion and the judicial
system but drew the line at overt criminal action. Whitney recognized
that blatant theft and the ensuing public outcry paralyzed the politicians
upon whom he and his associates depended for such necessary public
privileges as franchises, extensions, and motive power changes.[28]

After Sharp's success in later 1884, Whitney and Ryan found new allies
and switched tactics. Some of their initial colleagues had failed to pull
their share of the load. In August 1884, John Cadwalder told Whitney
that his allies should help him in the fight or "get out of the way, and let
somebody else come there who will."[29] In addition, Whitney's appointment as Secretary of the Navy threatened to weaken the alliance. Finally,

in early 1885 Whitney and Ryan were approached by three Philadelphians, the second group seeking the Broadway franchise for a cable
company. This trio avoided direct and costly opposition to the unscrupu-
lous Sharp and tried to buy him out. To achieve harmony they sought to
combine with the New York cable interests as well.[30]

The prospect attracted Whitney and Ryan for several reasons. The
Philadelphians William Kemble, Peter A. B. Widener, and William
Elkins, shared the New Yorkers' vision of a mechanized network of lines
with a transfer system to increase traffic. They already had begun to
build such a system in their city, where they had a cable road on Market
Street.[31] Given the inexperience of Whitney and Ryan in street railway
operation and the imminent loss of Whitney, such valuable experience,
leadership, and financial aid could not be ignored.

The Philadelphia promoters explained to Whitney "that a New York
corporation should be created for the leasing of horse-railroads, having
in view the introduction into New York of a general passenger transfer
system such as had become established in Philadelphia."[32] They offered
five shares in their new company with a guaranteed value of $40.00 per
share for each share of Broadway Railway stock.[33]

The offer split the New York cable interests. By early 1885 W. C. Andrews and others, who were allied with a national cable trust being
fought by the Philadelphians, had become enemies.[34] They remained
with the New York Cable Company and struggled unsuccessfully to
implement their own system while Whitney and Ryan joined the Philadelphia contingent and began negotiations to buy Sharp's Broadway
franchise.

The new alliance had a considerable array of talent and experience.
(The terms "group," "syndicate," "combine," and "alliance" refer to action by some or all of the partners. When describing the activities of their
organizations and operating men, company names will be used.) According to his biographer, Whitney contributed a "rapid mind" with "quick,
clear, and astonishingly accurate" judgment. He remained out of the
limelight but enjoyed "matching wits, maneuvering for position, and
playing politics" to achieve "money, . . . reputation, and . . . power."
Through his friendship with Boss Richard Croker of Tammany Hall, his
political work as a Democratic party leader, and his experience as corporation counsel he added ties to local power which the Philadelphians
lacked and which were vital to conduct the public and political side of an
urban transit business.[35]

The sharp-witted Ryan contributed two important qualities: dogged,
untiring industry and the golden gift of silent operation. His tangible
additions to the combine included the consents of Broadway property
owners for a cable line, garnered during the 1884 battle, and a "knack for

making the right contacts" for a growing behind-the-scenes alliance with Tammany Hall.[36]

Like Whitney, Peter Widener and William Kemble had political experience. The fifty-year-old Widener and his mentor Kemble had been prominent members of the Philadelphia Republican machine for a number of years before turning to street railways. Along with the wealthy Elkins, who had joined them in Philadelphia after retiring from the oil refining business, they had ten years' experience in street railways and had overseen the installation and operation of a cable system. Kemble apparently was the leader of the group. Fragmentary correspondence indicates that he knew well the practical side of the business and understood clearly the need for combination and consolidation. Widener was the expansive speculator of the trio, while Elkins played the role of the prosaic, hardheaded businessman.[37]

Thus arrayed, the syndicate embarked on a career that led to the domination of public transit in New York City. The alliance was a blend of experience and new blood, of caution and expansive optimism, of steady industry and imaginative flair. With backgrounds stretching beyond the city and the street railway business, this relatively young combination of men-on-the-make brought new vision and boldness to the field. Whitney, Ryan, Kemble, Widener, and Elkins combined their talents to replace old horse railway men like Jake Sharp and alter radically the nature and operation of New York City street railways.

Combination

The creation of an organized network of lines was another necessary accompaniment to mechanization. With vision and ability the syndicate built New York's first transit system in the last fifteen years of the nineteenth century. In order to implement the new mechanical technology successfully, they borrowed from the railroad system builders and introduced new strategy, organization, and techniques to city transit.

From the outset the syndicate pursued a strategy of combination not grasped by New York horse railway owners and managers. When the Philadelphians studied the situation in the mid-1880s, they were, in the words of the New York Herald, "much impressed with the fact that the different street railroad companies of this city seemed to be acting in a spirit of rivalry, which operated to the injury of the public by limiting their convenience of passage and transfer over the different roads and by increasing the expense of public travel through requiring two fares where only one would be necessary upon a proper system of arrangement between the companies."[38]

The group's aim was not simply to create a monopoly. Rather, it planned to build a network of lines which complemented each other and serviced the important arteries and locations in the city. Such a strategy would increase traffic and make the fullest use of facilities in order to maximize return on the huge investment needed for unification and mechanization.

Each road was supposed to serve a definite purpose. Counsel Francis Lynde Stetson, one of the nation's leading corporation lawyers, drew up a list of acquisitions and specifically defined the usefulness of each for the future network.[39] William Kemble was equally explicit when he wrote William Whitney about the proposed purchase of the Fourth Avenue Company. The line would be an important entree into new territory "because it costs less [than building a new line] and will answer our purpose" to devise "some means by which we can discontinue running so many cars on B[road]way north of 14th."[40] On another occasion Widener approved an extension of the Seventh Avenue road because, "after counting the passengers etc.," the group decided that it could be done "without the expenditure of any money except the cost of four curves," and it would "so strip the business of the Bleeker Street road that they will be compelled to abandon . . . Broadway or sell us [their] 23rd St. [line] at a fair price."[41]

Essential to the strategy was the early acquisition of Jake Sharp's Broadway lines. Widener explained to the public that "in order to make a *system* [my emphasis] as perfect as the one we have in Philadelphia it was necessary to have some one trunk line, as the system could not be perfected with crosstown lines alone, and no trunk line could be used with so much advantage to the system as that of the Broadway and 7th Avenue roads."[42] Following the formation of the alliance in early 1885, negotiations with Sharp went on until the summer. The old man then completed his road on lower Broadway, and its operation skyrocketed the value of his stock. Apparently secure, and aggravated by the opposition of Whitney's friends to his acquisition of the Bleeker Street road, he so raised his price that the syndicate ceased to bargain.[43]

Sharp's action was a fatal mistake. The public indignation aroused by his theft of Broadway had planted the seeds of his destruction. The syndicate carefully cultivated them after Sharp grew recalcitrant. It initiated a stockholder suit to investigate his Broadway and Seventh Avenue Company and its relations with the Broadway Surface line. More damaging for Sharp, the state legislature also began an investigation of his franchises, stimulated at least in part by Ryan. The results were catastrophic. The story of Sharp's brazen bribery of the Forty Thieves became public and aldermen fled the country in panic. In February 1886, less than one month after the investigation commenced, Sharp sold to the syndicate his Broadway and Seventh Avenue road with the franchise for lower Broadway.[44]

But the syndicate was not yet out of the woods. It now learned a valuable lesson about public relations and the use of public opinion which it had striven so hard to stir. The group could stimulate public feeling readily enough but lacked the techniques to control it. The momentum of the investigation produced a recommendation to annul the valuable Broadway franchise. With considerable popular support the legislature revoked the charter of the Broadway Surface line in 1886 and provided for the recapture of its franchise. It also amended the 1884 street railway law to require the sale of franchises at public auction in order to avoid another theft.

A suit by the state of New York to repossess the franchise forced the combine into a two-year court struggle. Finally, in November 1888 the New York Court of Appeals ruled that though the state had the power to repeal the company's charter, it could not confiscate its property, of which the franchise was a part. The right to operate must be sold at auction for the benefit of the company's creditors. Thus, not until August 1889 did the syndicate acquire clear title to the franchise with a bid of $25,000.[45]

The delay was costly but instructive. The combine had to postpone the mechanization of the Broadway road and the acquisition of tributary lines until the franchise was safe. The experience taught the group, especially Whitney, to respect the power of popular feeling.

More so than entrepreneurs in other fields, owners of public transit systems had to be attuned to popular opinion and to politics. Entrepreneurship involved not just questions of strategy and management but also required satisfaction for the public and influence in those areas of government that could affect the system's future. Local government could impose taxes and other obligations on street railways firms and its consent was necessary for new franchises, for extensions, and (until 1889) for change of motive power.[46] To avoid public antagonism the syndicate conducted its future strategy quietly, so that it might better direct events. Appeals to public opinion became a technique of last resort.

The incident also illustrates the limitations of an analogy between street railways and railroad enterprise. As we shall see, the alliance would use many railroad techniques and innovations to combine, finance, and manage its enterprise, but unlike railroad leaders, Whitney and his associates had to confront their competition. Railroad men could either buy or build around competitors. The Whitney-Widener group had to purchase the exclusive franchises of predecessor horse railways in order to complete its system.

Once the allies assured themselves of the control of Broadway, they began their acquisition policy. The New York *Times* explained in 1889 that "they are now the clear possessors of the property and have what they have long aimed to possess—a trunk line from the Battery to Central Park with connecting and crosstown lines. With the trunk line as the basis and their minor lines as a starter in the development of reachers east and west they now have a very good foundation on which to build a street car system which will eventually gridiron the city."[47] Between 1888 and 1893 the group gained control of seven intersecting lines, including such major north-south arteries as Sixth and Ninth Avenues, and such east-west roads as the 23rd Street, Metropolitan Crosstown, and 23rd and Grand Street Ferry Railroad Companies. Within three years after the crash of 1893 darkened the economy, the syndicate controlled all but two of the independent roads which had existed in 1885.[48]

For legal organization the alliance chartered a holding company. The charter was an early use of a device previously employed by a few railroads and would soon become a common method of combining public utilities and manufacturing businesses. The syndicate needed a corporation empowered to purchase, finance, and construct and operate street railway lines. It also wanted secrecy. In the absence of a suitable New York corporation, Counsel Francis Stetson discovered that New Jersey law offered a partial solution. On February 19, 1886, the group incorporated the Metropolitan Traction Company of New Jersey (hereafter called the Traction Company). The Traction Company (reorganized in 1892 as the Metropolitan Traction Company of New York) organized and financed combinations in secrecy and served as a construction firm.

The holding company, which Ryan reputedly likened to "a great big tin box," also offered opportunities for insider profits. Stetson recommended to Whitney that he personally buy the securities of desired companies and then sell them to the Traction Company "at such price as shall seem fair to both of you: You having no part in direction of the Company and each party being free to sell or take as may then appear mutually advantageous." In this questionable proceeding, the Traction Company stockholders were to be advised "as fully as may be that the purchases are from you."[49]

The Traction Company could purchase lines and issue securities, but it had no power to operate New York street railways. In August 1886, Stetson urged the syndicate to get every possible share in the Houston, West Street and Pavonia Ferry Railroad Company, whose New York chartered powers were "almost as valuable to the latter [Metropolitan Traction] Company as would be its adoption with enlarged powers by the Legislature of New York." After buying the Houston road, the syndicate leased the Traction Company acquisitions to it for unified operation.[50]

The syndicate continued its dual organization for combination and operation until it virtually completed its purchases. Finally in 1896, the alliance dissolved the Traction Company and sold its assets to the Metropolitan Street Railway Company (hereafter called the Metropolitan) which had succeeded the Houston Company as the group's operating organization in 1893. Herbert Vreeland, president in 1896 of both the Traction Company and the Metropolitan, explained that "the Directors of the company deemed that the object for which the Traction Company [was formed] as a construction and investment corporation had been attained and concluded that the time had come to distribute its holdings among its stockholders and wind up its affairs. The Street Railway Company is now in a position to operate its roads and can really do better under its franchises and corporate powers than the Traction Company could."[51]

To persuade horse railway owners to part with their properties, the syndicate skillfully mixed a variety of methods with good timing. When it entered the market in 1886, the Manhattan Elevated Company had captured the long haul and some of the medium and short haul traffic from nearby street railways. Widener thought that many operators were "very sick" about the elevated's recent reduction of all fares to a nickel.[52] A director of the Third Avenue Company thought the coming year would be "a very trying one, having to meet a strong competition by the Elevated Road overhead," and in expectation the company stopped payment of the vice president's salary.[53] Faced with the need to invest large sums of capital in a cable system to meet the rapid transit challenge, many horsecar lines were ripe for the plucking. And in later years the improved service of syndicate-owned roads exerted even more pressure on rivals to sell out, as in the Bleeker Street case.

But not all the purchases were voluntary. Occasionally the syndicate was coerced by circumstances or wily competitors. Despite Stetson's injunction not to buy the Wall Street line because of its questionable franchise and poor operation, the group found itself forced to take over the road. Its owners included Anthony Brady, a rising power in Brooklyn street railways and other public utilities, and some of Whitney's friends. More important than friendship, however, was Kemble's and Elkins' desire to keep the Brooklyn street railway people out of Manhattan.[54] The Traction Company bought the line, and each powerful group remained in its own territory.

On another occasion the syndicate felt compelled to absorb two bankrupt crosstown lines, the 28th and 29th Streets and the 34th Street roads, when Edward Lauterbach, counsel for the rival Third Avenue Company, became the receiver of the properties. Fearing that the Third Avenue line might gain control of routes and enter territory controlled by the Metropolitan, the syndicate directed Treasurer Hans Beattie to buy the two roads "even if it costs millions." After considerable expense, the Traction Company controlled both by 1896.[55]

Finance

Though cable cars did not operate on the Metropolitan's lines until the early 1890s the decision to install new technology continued to force changes in New York's surface railway enterprise prior to implementation. Alterations in street railway finance accompanied the appearance of new men and new strategy. While horse railway enterprise had cost thousands of dollars, combination and mechanization required millions and compelled promoters to find new means of funding.

Besides rival coercion other factors made acquisition of many parts of the system costly. The delay due to the Broadway franchise battle was expensive. By 1890 street railway traffic began an upswing from its mid-decade decline. The overcrowding of the elevated and the growth of crosstown and short haul traffic eroded the earlier willingness to surrender. Some valuable north-south lines more remote from the elevated lines scarcely suffered at all. With steady and substantial profits their owners had little incentive to sell. The purchase of such roads required large sums. In the case of a few established firms whose securities were cornerstones of estates, owners were simply unwilling to bargain or placed so high a price as to make purchase impossible.

For such cases the syndicate used an alternative strategy—a lease system. In order to gain operating control, it offered reluctant owners generous annual rentals for 999-year leases. Generally, stockholders received rent at least equal to the average annual earnings of their stock, while the syndicate bore all expenses. For example, the Metropolitan agreed in 1898 to pay the Second Avenue road 8 percent on $1,862,000 capital stock for three years and 9 percent thereafter, and to assume all fixed charges and operating expenses in exchange for a 999-year lease.[56]

The technique conserved capital while giving the syndicate control of roads needed for the system. And, as the earlier letter between Stetson and Whitney indicated, the procedure offered insiders a chance for large profits. They could buy lines cheaply and sell or lease them at higher prices to the Traction Company and split the profits among the alliance. The extent to which this occurred is unknown, but the syndicate members reputedly made large fortunes in their combination and financing.[57]

Though some critics thought the rentals excessive, President Vreeland explained that the increased earnings of the lines as part of a unified network more than justified the leases:

> In order to secure several of our great thoroughfare lines we
> were compelled to give guarantees, the financial wisdom of
> which was much questioned at the time. But the officers of this
> company were not basing their expectations on what those

roads had been doing considered as separate organizations, so
much as on what they could do when run in connection with
our entire system, fed by our lines in all directions, equipped
with the most improved traction, and conducted by a management which made an economy in one branch of its business and
for the benefit of one line felt in every other branch and in every
other line. The wisdom of every lease made has been proved by
experience.[58]

A letter from William Kemble to Whitney demonstrates how the partners planned this strategy. In the early fall of 1887, Kemble thought it
"absolutely essential to the economical operating of the Bway RR that we
devise some means by which we can discontinue running so many cars
on Bway north of 14th." Servicing the areas below 14th Street on Broadway forced the company to run excess cars north of that point for a total
distance of 2,500 miles per day. Kemble figured that at eighteen cents per
mile the annual cost of excess capacity was $164,250.[59]

Rather than turn back the extra cars, he advocated entering new territory to the northeast with a lease of the Fourth Avenue line. "We could
afford to pay as rental all the money *earned on their own business* and a
handsome bonus in addition—depending for our own profit on the new
business brought to the line by the facilities offered by us in addition to
what they now have." Kemble judged that the additional business of 7.5
passengers each way north of 14th Street would produce 9,000 passengers daily, or $164,250 per annum, the amount of the rental. But he
"really believe[d] it would bring to us 30,000 passengers." Thus the group
could pay the Fourth Avenue Company its earnings plus a bonus, count
on the old business of the line to defray operating costs, and rely on the
anticipated additional traffic above 9,000 to finance the bonus and a
profit.

To Kemble the rationale for expansion was clear. According to his best
estimates, traffic growth raised profits faster than expenses. He concluded from his study that an increase of 30,000,000 (or 50 percent of
traffic) annually would require "little additional facilities" and "would
cost us about one cent per passenger additional" for each nickel fare.
Widener's calculation led him to a similar conclusion about the cost of
expansion.[60] Additional traffic on the Broadway line insured greater use
of facilities and a larger return on investment.

While the accuracy of their figures cannot be determined, the calcula-
tions do indicate the basis on which the partners planned for expansion.
Their thinking resembled the strategies that Alfred Chandler has described in the creation of large enterprises in other key industries during
the period.[61] It combined the integration necessary to employ efficiently
a higher fixed-cost technology and to service the high-volume flow in an
expanding market with a defensive desire to shut out competition.

Because the strategy and technology were new and risky, finance was a challenge. Whitney and Ryan started with only modest funds of their own, and though the Philadelphia trio may have provided money from their other operations, not even they could supply the millions needed. To attract capital, the syndicate used the stock watering technique of railroads and elevated railways. They capitalized the system on the basis of anticipated earnings, not on actual assets. As Thomas Fortune Ryan explained, "In those days we generally issued bonds for the property but in the case of common stock and even preferred stock it was not considered necessary to have anything but water behind it—good will."[62]

As Ryan's remark indicates, the practice was neither new nor rare. Many of the horse railways absorbed by the syndicate already had water in them dating from their formation. Because the syndicate had to purchase these already watered lines "at prices then deemed extraordinary— even extravagant," it injected liberal doses of its own water to balance the risk with greater possible returns and to attract other supporters.[63]

The watered (or partially paid for) stock offered the investor a potential bonus. With the success of the enterprise, the value of its stock would rise, hopefully to par or above. The difference between the new value and the amount paid in was a return in addition to dividends. Widener explained to Whitney that the procedure had both long and short range advantages:

> Now as to the policy of increasing the stock. This will not be an inflation, as every Dollar received from the additional stock will be used in construction and paying for Broadway and 23rd St. stock, *all of which will have additional and great earning capacity* [my emphasis]. Then, if you keep your capitalization down and pay what the Public look upon as excessively high Dividends, you arouse the enmity of the Public and the different Legislative Bodies, who will begin to fight on fare reduction. It is better for a corporation to pay a smaller dividend on large capital than a large one on small capital. The Public never look at the amount you are paying Dividends on, but at the amount of Dividend paid; that is what they criticise and fight. All our people understand this and all are anxious that we should increase. We think it better to give each of the present stockholders the right to subscribe to new stock than to call assessments on their present holdings. If they are not financially in condition to take the stock, they can sell their option at a very good premium, which is a privilege we think they should have after waiting all these years.[64]

Stock watering was not just a device to wring quick profits out of the enterprise. Widener declared emphatically to Whitney that "our thought is not to get a large amount of stock to market, but we propose to hold every share of stock we may become the owners of in this corporation, as we believe there is no property we own that will grow so rapidly in value and give the owners so large an annual revenue as this one will. You must not judge the value of this property from the past, . . . but now with all the legal troubles out of the way, we propose to give our personal attention, to the operating of these roads and manage them for every advantgage to the stockholder that is possible."[65]

Widener and his associates were confident that traffic growth and the economies of coordination and mechanization would pay for their profits from combinations and security issues. He reminded Whitney that the Philadelphia contingent's success "has not been made by starting corporations and selling them out but by staying with them and making money by increasing their earning capacity and thereby making them valuable and profitable to all concerned."[66]

Nevertheless, the rentals for leased roads and the interest on bonds issued for purchase of horse railway securities and for mechanization burdened the Metropolitan with high fixed costs. The dividends on watered stock were also a serious drain on annual revenue. And the syndicate's financial techniques further weakened the system by forcing it to depend on continued growth for success.

Consolidation and Mechanization

In the 1890s, however, the technique worked well. By 1896, when the Metropolitan absorbed the Traction Company, the syndicate had created a system which covered most of Manhattan. The Metropolitan owned or leased thirteen lines, including eight of the fourteen major north-south arteries, a belt line and a number of crosstown roads. Daring to compete with the elevated railways for mid- and uptown traffic, it carried almost one third of New York's nearly one half billion annual fares. Consolidation and mechanization transformed once independent companies which had traversed "meandering and circuitous routes" into a gridiron system with Broadway as a diagonal.[67]

The acquisition of new lines and their later mechanization also required innovation in administration. The employment of hundreds to operate cable and electric cars over a hundred miles of track was obviously more challenging than the management of a few dozen men on a five- or ten-mile line. Moreover, the expansion of workforce and area came at just the time when increasing fixed costs demanded careful coordination of schedules and efficient maintenance of complex equipment in order to maximize returns.

The syndicate early recognized the benefits of coordinated operation. In 1886 Whitney explained the group's intention "to lease other lines, and thus, by introducing economy of management and a system of transfers, secure at the same time better returns from the properties and greater accommodations for the public."[68] As noted before, the syndicate leased the Houston line to serve as an operating company for the system, and in January 1889 it hired Daniel Lamont as president "to look after the detail management of our business."[69]

But the actual process of consolidation lagged. Like many entrepreneurs, the allies preferred to concentrate on strategy rather than structure. Only after completion of the cable line on Broadway in 1893 did the syndicate as directors of the Houston Company resolve that "the organization of the operating department of the system of railroads owned and leased by this Company be referred to the Executive Committee, with full power to devise and put in operation economies in administration, with a view to simplyfying and systemizing the management of the various properties conducted by this Company and with full power to employ officers and employees necessary in its judgment to the efficient management of the property."[70]

Through the resulting Metropolitan Street Railway Company the alliance permitted its operating men to rationalize the system. Chart 2 illustrates the company's line-and-staff divisional structure copied from railroad management. At the head was President Herbert Vreeland, responsible to the board of directors and charged with "care for the development of the system in every direction." Unlike his predecessors, political promoter Daniel Lamont and contractor John Crimmins, Vreeland had begun his career as a railroad man, and he was to become an experienced administrator, not a member of the entepreneurial alliance. Beneath him the line—composed of a first vice president and general manager, a general superintendent, and seven division superintendents—ran the transportation business. The president's staff at the central office provided such auxiliary functions as insurance, finance, and accounting. Maintenance of way, power, and construction were the responsibility of a second staff serving the general manager.[71]

Within each division starters in the car barns and inspectors on the streets handled traffic. The inspectors were also charged to train and watch employees (there was a school to teach operators of the mechanized cars), to report on conditions of operation, and to study local traffic conditions. Their reports enabled the company to adjust quickly to hourly needs and to perceive long range changes in traffic patterns. In rush hour traffic the inspectors took charge of loading and moving cars at crowded points to avoid delays and blockades. This force enabled the Metropolitan to maintain its schedules on busy New York streets where cars traveled with as little as fifteen seconds' headway. Using the consolidated operation, the company transported more than half a million passengers daily by 1896.[72]

To complement consolidation the company instituted a transfer sys-

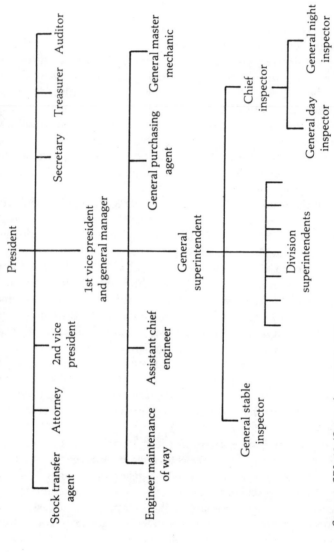

CHART 2. Organization of the Metropolitan Street Railway Company.

Source: SRJ, 12 (September 1896), 515.

tem and rearranged lines. The rerouting offered passengers continuous rides between major points, lessened the inconvenience of car changes and provided faster transportation.[73] Where continuous transit was impossible, the managers established transfer points for free change of cars. The move not only reduced the public's total transit cost but also encouraged more traffic and improved the Metropolitan's competitive position.

Sensing the potential appeal of the free transfer, the syndicate had first offered that privilege as part of its campaign to capture the Broadway franchise in 1885. Widener explained "that with our knowledge of the transfer system, introduced and developed by us in Philadelphia, the same system might be successfully established in New York with great advantage to the community and profit to ourselves."[74] The New York *Herald* told its readers that the group "anticipated that the greater advantage of their system to the public would induce a larger use of roads, and from such larger use and the economies resulting from the saving of unnecessary salaries and organizations they could reasonably expect an advantage from that which would at first seem to be a less profitable operation."[75]

The alliance introduced the technique in early 1887, and by 1888 it issued more than a million transfers annually. Transfers, of course, reduced the real cost of transportation for the rider by offering two rides for the price of one. Quickly popular with the public, the innovation was also apparently profitable to the Metropolitan, which pointed to the rapid rise of its paying fares and estimated that at least half its transfers were riders who would not have boarded at all without the privilege.[76] By increasing traffic, transfers and continuous rides maximized the use of fixed capacity and return on investment.

So successful were the innovations by 1892, that John Crimmins, then president of the system, promised that

> so far as our lines extend it is our purpose to establish a system of transfers which shall take a person patronizing them from any one point to any other point on the lines for a single 5-cent fare. We hope soon to be able to extend our lines so as to reach every one of the ferries on the North and East Rivers, including the ocean ferries—or steamship docks, so that any person coming to the city over the Pennsylvania, or Erie, or Jersey Central, or West Shore, or Long Island, or any other [rail]road, or from Europe by any one of the ocean steamship lines, shall find a ready and comfortable conveyance which will take him to any distant part of the main section of the city for a single fare.[77]

The technique was expanded until by 1896 there was a practically universal free transfer.[78]

The impetus for consolidation was the mechanization that had initiated the process of system building. The substitution of mechanical for horse power demanded large investments for installation and the employment of more skilled personnel to operate and service the new technology. It offered the public greater speed, capacity, and range for the same fare. These benefits in turn attracted more passengers and increased revenues.

The choice of motive power was in part at least an accident of timing and had important consequences for the evolution of New York transit. The lines absorbed in the 1880s and 1890s were horse-powered. As replacements the syndicate could choose steam, compressed air, storage battery, overhead electric, or cable power. The city outlawed the first as too dangerous. The second and third were still only experiments. And in 1888-89 when the alliance was considering mechanization, the West End Street Railway Company, headed by Whitney's brother Henry, had just begun to test overhead electric power on a large scale.

In the 1880s the cable was a clear favorite. The *Street Railway Journal* explained that "it was then generally believed by engineers and street railway managers that for a traffic of such enormous density as that of Broadway and Third Avenue . . . the cable system was far superior to any form of the electric, and would never be superseded."[79] In addition, the Philadelphia contingent had already installed the cable in their city, and the alliance naturally opted for it. Widener enthusiastically wrote Whitney: "I say without fear of successful contradiction that if you place such a cable road on Broadway as we would build it would be the greatest work of your life and one which you could always point to with pride. The work your Brother is doing in Boston whilst good would sink into insignificance when compared with it as I am satisfied it would solve the question of local transportation in New York.[80]

The Traction Company installed its first cable line on Broadway with considerable expense and effort. The jumble of pipes and mains under the street obstructed excavation for the conduit in which the cable ran. Moving these structures at company expense increased the cost and prolonged construction time. Nevertheless by 1893 the completed line stretched from the Battery to 59th Street at a cost of more than one million dollars per mile, twenty times the per mile cost of a horse railway.[81]

Cable power brought cheaper operation and increased revenue. The operating cost of the Broadway road dropped from 66 to 38 percent of gross revenue. Traffic rose 25 percent. Director and former President John Crimmins explained that passenger growth "is one of the invariable features of the substitution." Some came from normal traffic increase, but "a considerable part," he continued, stemmed from "the superior accommodation of mechanically propelled cars."[82]

As described earlier, there were disadvantages. Installation was very

expensive and operation difficult. Crimmins' successor, Herbert Vreeland, estimated the cost of cable and roadbed alone at $125,000 per mile,
quadruple the expense for an electric system.[83] Shredding cables caught
the cable grip and caused runaway cars which sometimes went for blocks
before someone could order the powerhouse to stop the cable in order to
release the grip. The cars handled very awkwardly and dangerously on
curves in congested traffic.[84] As one streetcar historian has described the
operation:

> Longer curves were arranged so that the gripman had to hold
> onto the cable. To negotiate a lengthy reverse curve on New
> York's Broadway line around Union Square, the gripman had
> to choose the best opportunity available in the dense traffic and
> commit himself to the entire crooked stretch; he could not let go
> until he emerged into the straight track beyond. On this hazard-
> ous portion of the run it was the custom for a gripman to set up
> a wild din on his gong, augmented as necessary with profanity
> addressed to persons or vehicles that disregarded his noisy and
> relentless approach. His passengers would be lurched left, then
> right, then left again, and sometimes flung forward by glancing
> collision with a beer wagon or other slow vehicle. The section
> of the line became known, not entirely in fun, as "Dead Man's
> Curve."[85]

The cable's high fixed costs demanded coordinated feeder lines for
maximum return. The acquisition of uptown horsecar lines only partially
resolved the problem, for the horse railways were unable to compete with
the elevated lines to tap the growing traffic of mid- and uptown Manhattan. Consequently the syndicate decided to mechanize two uptown lines
and one crosstown route. A large rectangle of cable lines would carry
traffic up- and downtown and compete with the elevated roads for long
haul traffic.

While the Metropolitan was extending its mechanized lines, the cost
and unwieldiness of a cable system compelled a search for an alternative.
The company hired a brilliant engineer, Fred Pearson, to adapt the electric conduit system then used in Budapest to its needs.[86] In this case electricity was carried from steam generators through a live rail in a trough
between the tracks. A slotted covering protected the public and allowed
streetcars to lower a contact to the rail for power.

An experimental segment on Lennox Avenue proved successful in
1895, and in the late 1890s the Metropolitan began electrification of its
long distance, north-south roads, and some of its crosstown lines. By
1902 some 114 miles were powered by the electric conduit, and shortly
after the turn of the century the company converted its cable lines to the
new technology.[87]

Electric streetcars gave the system greater flexibility and improved service. Capable of faster speeds, they adjusted easily from congested traffic downtown to open streets uptown. The Metropolitan could readily alter the number of cars in a given area to meet demand. With the rapid addition of new and better equipment, the electric streetcar's capacity exceeded both horse and cable cars, and by 1901 the company discovered that electric cars were even cheaper to operate than the cable cars.[88]

But the choice of technology was not simply the result of cost, practicality, and previous experience. A decision to expand the cable system rather than to convert to the trolley in 1892 acquiesced with public opinion. By that time the cable was obsolescent, and the trolley system was widely used. In that same year Widener and Elkins scrapped their Philadelphia cable for the trolley.[89] But Whitney's respect for the strong local antagonism to overhead wires ruled out the overhead system for the Metropolitan. So virulent had been the campaign against the telephone, telegraph, and electric light wires webbing New York's air in the late 1880s that vigilantes, joined by the mayor, had chopped down poles in protest.[90] Not unexpectedly, when President Crimmins rashly proposed a trolley system in April 1892, the press and public rose in spontaneous outrage. Whitney, now sensitive to the danger of an aroused public, quashed the request. Widener later wrote that Whitney felt that "our getting into a fight over a trolley system . . . would work largely to the detriment of our Corporation."[91]

The incident was a significant one. In the short run it committed the company to an additional fifteen miles of costly, outdated cable which would have to be removed in a decade. In the long run it compelled the Metropolitan to adopt the electric conduit, which, though not superior to the overhead wire, was half again as expensive to construct.[92] The result was to saddle the firm with additional high fixed charges. By 1903 the capitalization of New York street railways was almost five times the 1885 figure and fixed payments consumed 50 percent of total revenue.[93] In some cases the heavy charges delayed mechanization of the city's major streets as much as a decade while the Metropolitan tried storage battery and compressed air cars with scant success. Indeed, horsecars operated on some lesser traveled routes until World War I because their traffic would not pay the necessary return on investment in the conduit.

Public Policy and the Political Connection

Whitney's fear of a battle over the trolley again illustrates the very public nature of local transit and suggests the very complex relationship of transit enterprise and policy. The potential effects of the city's power were large. Without a franchise the corporation could not operate; without permission to mechanize it faced stagnation or bankruptcy. Taxes could be used to recapture profits. Duties could be made so onerous as to reduce or eliminate profits. Another serious difficulty was the lack of proper expertise and mechanism for regulation. Controls were badly advised, misapplied, or erratically enforced. Legislation provided a fixed and inflexible set of rules incapable of meeting the needs of a rapidly changing city and transit industry.

The city's control was as ineffective as it was important. As tools to correct abuses, existing laws were blunt instruments which permitted or forbade a certain action but which failed to modify or direct transit development in the public interest.[94] The division of regulatory power between the city and the state fragmented what power there was. And except for the State Railroad Commission, designed primarily to regulate steam railroads, there was nobody experienced in street railway affairs.

What was more, the political machine that dominated New York City's government had no desire or ability to regulate. Instead, it sought favors and support from electric, gas, street paving, and transit companies, whose public character made them subject to local government for contracts and franchises. It interfered only when those favors were not forthcoming, or in extreme cases when public protest made action politically expedient.

Not unnaturally, the syndicate sought to control access to the sources of power for its profit and protection. Its strategy was a dual one. To satisfy the public, service was expanded and improved. The Metropolitan had no public relations officer to trumpet its accomplishments. The improvements—mechanization, continuous rides, and free transfers—were thought to speak for themselves. On the occasions when it sought conspicuous favors, the company relied on press interviews and testimony before public bodies to remind citizens of its progress.

Often the strategy was negative. The Metropolitan strove to avoid confrontations over popular issues and to prevent open clashes with other transit interests. When John Crimmins sparked protest with his trolley proposal, Whitney quickly disavowed the idea on behalf of the Metropolitan. He publicly assured Mayor Hugh Grant that "no method of trolley traction would be compatible with its system at the present time" and that cable power was the "fixed policy" of the company, "already made plain . . . by the investment of millions of dollars."[95]

The Metropolitan also pursued a conciliatory policy toward its largest rival, the Third Avenue Company. Of all the New York horse railway companies, only it competed with the Metropolitan by mechanizing and expanding. Ably led by Albert Elias and long-time horse railway man Henry Hart and closely connected to the state Republican machine through its counsel Edward Lauterbach, the Third Avenue firm ran along the East Side and connected with a Bronx subsidiary, the Union Railway Company, and with crosstown and West Side lines in uptown Manhattan.[96] When the two systems clashed over uptown extensions, the struggle for franchises caused unseemly fights in the courts and before the Board of Aldermen. The Third Avenue firm even inspired a city crusade to recapture two valuable Metropolitan franchises originally granted by the city without compensation. Because the issue fanned the smoldering debate over franchise remuneration, the Metropolitan Company quickly compromised with the Third Avenue line to permit joint expansion and restore peace.[97]

The Metropolitan's relationship with Tammany Hall was in part an extension of its policy to keep the peace. A large enterprise in public transit was quite vulnerable to attacks or blackmail from politicians seeking votes or favors. Whitney was an especially close friend and ally of Boss Richard Croker and through this liaison the company obtained its privileges and immunities. As historian Burton Hendrick explained, "William C. Whitney would not soil his fingers by personal contact with aldermen, but dealt always with one or two men at the top. In return for favors, he did not distribute common bribes, but paid huge lawyers' fees, gave tips on the stock-market, and let favored people in on the ground floor. He and Ryan always cultivated Richard Croker, and that Croker and his associates dealt largely in street-railway stocks they did not themselves deny."[98]

The gains for the system were considerable. Franchises and extensions came with a minimum of disturbance. Jake Sharp spent eight months and thousands of dollars wringing the Broadway franchise out of the local authorities; the syndicate's application for a cable franchise passed in a single day. When interest groups or ambitious politicians threatened to delay vital legislation, an unseen hand brought ready acquiescence.[99]

The alliance with Tammany offered protection from rivals as well as favors. After Whitney informed Mayor Thomas Gilroy that "our mutual friend" (Croker) had agreed that New York should resist an offer by the Manhattan Elevated to extend its lines, negotiations between the city and the Manhattan Company ended, forestalling increased competition for the Metropolitan.[100] When the company fought with the Third Avenue firm, the syndicate skillfully used the Board of Aldermen and the courts to hinder its expansion for several years.[101] Adept use of the courts and the political machine, like business acumen and technological innovation, was crucial to the transit system's evolution.

The Effects

By 1900 the syndicate had completed its strategy to create what Whitney's biographer has called an "Empire on Wheels."[102] In that year the

Metropolitan absorbed its last rival, the Third Avenue Company, which, in its haste to expand and electrify, had overextended itself and gone into receivership. As Map 3 illustrates, the monopoly now offered the city a truly united system of surface transit. In comparison with the many horsecar lines of 1885, it supplied greater speed, range, and capacity at lower cost. And in response to urban growth and better service, street railway traffic (fares and transfers) had almost tripled since 1885. Following a sharp spurt in traffic growth after 1895, the number of public transit riders had increased to 276 fares per capita by 1900 and despite the innovation of the free transfer system, sales of surface fares had grown 77 percent in a decade.[103] Even a severe critic listed the transfer system as an "invaluable convenience," and the New York *Times* judged in 1899 that the Metropolitan "had won great popular favor by the ability of its management and the way it has of giving its passengers the largest measure of accommodation for the minimum cost . . . Every sensible man knows that it would be a public blessing if all the railroads in the city were managed with the ability and the consideration for the convenience of their patrons which is characteristic of the Metropolitan."[104]

Despite the transformation and the praise, all was not well. After 1900 the Metropolitan's monopoly and the inadequacies of its surface transportation network provoked attacks in unprecedented volume. The syndicate's surge to power and the Metropolitan's success evoked countervailing forces, which limited the company's ability to respond to the needs of the fast-growing metropolis.

The rise of the surface monopoly, which by 1902 sold over 60 percent of New York's public transit fares, stimulated as much fear as admiration. Progressive reform groups emerging in the late 1890s looked past the Metropolitan's efficiency to its power and profits and played down past improvements in the face of present and future needs. As reformers began to campaign for more honest and efficient government, the syndicate's close ties with Tammany Hall became a liability rather than an asset. Reformers ascribed its wealth and power to the franchises, favors, and protection granted in exchange for support of the machine.[105]

Simultaneously, the weak financial structure of the system began to crack. Heavy fixed charges for leases, dividends on watered stock, large outlays for electrification, and the acquisition of the Third Avenue system (which was not paying its own way) consumed all the net profits in 1901. And the future was not encouraging. Reformers had enacted a franchise tax that would increase the Metropolitan's taxes by $1,500,000.[106] Work had begun on a subway line which, along with the electrification of the elevated lines in 1902, threatened to rob the surface system of traffic or at least to halt the continuous increase on which its financing was predicated. Chart 3 illustrates that when traffic growth slowed after 1902 the small gains were in transfer rather than revenue

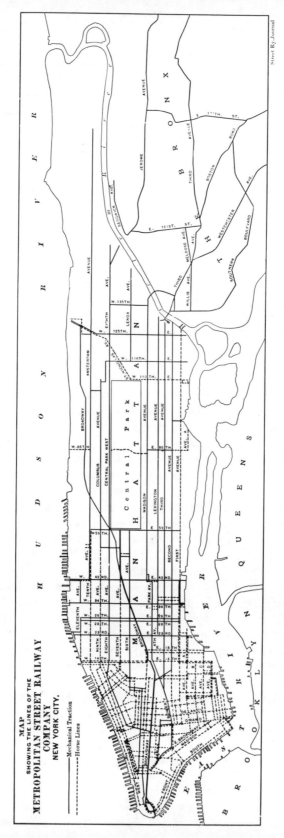

MAP 3. Metropolitan Street Railway Company system, 1901. *Source: SRJ*, 16 (October 13, 1900), 960.

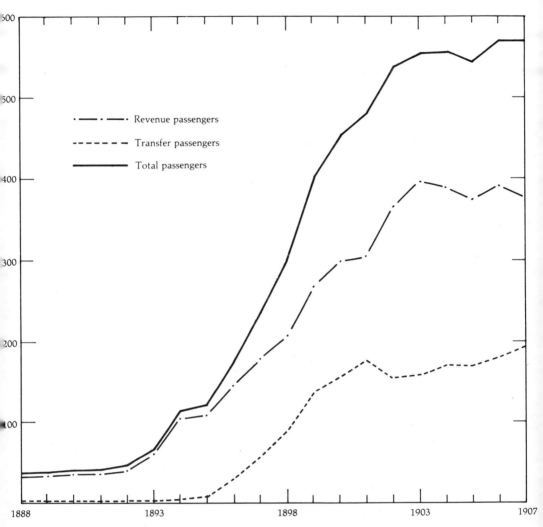

CHART 3. Metropolitan Street Railway Company Traffic, 1888-1907 (in millions). Passenger figures for the 3rd Avenue system in Manhattan are included for 1902-07. *Sources: SRJ*, 18 (October 5, 1901), 484; Public Service Commission for the 1st District, *Annual Report* (1907), II, 25-26.

paying passengers. In fact revenue passengers never equaled the 1903 figure before the company's bankruptcy in 1907. In addition, maintenance charges increased on aging equipment, and inflation pushed up labor and material costs. Caught with a fixed nickel fare which the transfer system had eroded more than 25 percent to 3.5 cents in one decade and faced with the end of revenue growth, the Metropolitan was suddenly in serious financial straits.[107]

The rapid pace of innovation and company accounting techniques caused additional financial problems. Along with many other roads, the Metropolitan had written up assets so that more securities might be issued to pay for expansion and mechanization. To attract investors it had paid out generous dividends and failed to depreciate adequately. Insufficient depreciation reserve and rapid technological change forced the company to finance replacements with new capital issues without writing off the old ones and thus increased the burden of fixed costs.[108]

Ironically, even the transfer system and the Metropolitan's many improvements began to boomerang. The public had become accustomed to them, but they could hardly be sustained without constant revenue growth. The company exacerbated the problem of rising expectations by economizing as revenues stagnated. To increase income it refused to include the Third Avenue lines as part of the transfer system and reduced the number of cars in service.

At the same time urban growth, encouraged in part by improved transit, further congested the streets and swamped the streetcars at rush hour. Overcrowding, straphanging, and platform standing grew. Congestion disrupted schedules and accident costs increased. So close to capacity was the system that on some lines cars operated with only fifteen seconds' headway.[109] However much electrification had bettered street railways, they could not offer sufficient speed or capacity to satisfy New York's needs by 1900.

Moreover, electrification was incomplete. At a time when horse railways had almost disappeared in the nation, New York still had over one hundred miles of horsecar track. Hamstrung by its impecunious circumstances and by its inability to use the cheaper overhead system, the Metropolitan was slow to convert to the electric conduit system on its less traveled routes. As President Vreeland explained: "Our experience in providing underground electric traction for the 59th Street and 23rd Street crosstown lines . . . demonstrated that the removal and replacement of the pipe obstructions along the avenues were so costly as to render underground crosstown building almost prohibitive."[110] The company invested large amounts in compressed air and storage battery experiments before it finally settled on the latter alternative.[111]

As the system began to stagnate, reformers and critics reexamined public transit policy in a search for better service. The syndicate's efforts had vitiated traditional regulation. The gingerbread house of charters, franchise grants, and legislation enacted piecemeal over a fifty-year span —aimed for the most part at the regulation of independent horse railway lines—was no longer adequate. The main feature of that policy, the issue of charters and franchises, failed to touch on the problems central to New York's needs: the supply of satisfactory service at the cheapest possible cost and sufficient planning and development to meet future growth. These responsibilities remained with private enterprise. Only by indirection, with such blunt instruments as franchise recapture or heavy taxation, could city government persuade or coerce the Metropolitan to take desired action. Even more fundamentally, there still was nobody with sufficient expertise and power in city or state government to know what decisions were required and to implement them when made.

Slowly a few experts began to recognize that the changed circumstances of 1900 required drastic revision. Control based on law and fixed grants and predicated on regulation of independent lines by market forces was inadequate for the day of the unified, mechanized system.[112] New franchises were of interest only to the monopoly. As one expert put it, "the value of a franchise depends very largely upon the connections the line makes with other lines." How, then, did one hold a public auction to sell franchises when there was only a single potential bidder?

Ironically, the same expert explained, "the elimination of competition not only renders it more and more difficult to enforce proper control but makes control of some sort more and more necessary." Those charged with regulation had allied with the regulated, and neither had the riding public as its primary concern. Charter provisions and city ordinances "have very well fulfilled their purpose, but experience has shown that if the company is determined to resist, it is very difficult to enforce better service." Increased power for city government did not insure good service, because "it is very easy to levy blackmail, and instances are not rare where a corporation has been placed at the mercy of the party in power." Finally, a return to independent companies with regulation by competition was also inadequate, for "a considerable plant and equipment is required which cannot be easily disposed of, transferred to other localities or put to other uses. The advantages of consolidation, of operation of many miles of road under one system are many and important. The cost of production decreases as the size of the system increases. The passenger finds fares cheaper, transfers more general and passage less frequently broken."[113]

Such insights were rare; state and local governments had only begun to move away from regulation by competition and charter requirements. In the 1884 law the provision for a five-cent fare was one early acknowledgment of change. The removal of the consent power for technology change from the popularly elected Board of Aldermen to the State Board of Railroad Commissioners was another. But for the most part, public transit policy still rested on the old concepts. The 1884 law provided for general incorporation—equal access of all entrepreneurs to the field. The 1886 Cantor law, which called for the grant of franchises by public auction, was a classic statement of market regulation.[114] And charters continued to be perpetual contracts whose fixed provisions did not regulate service.

Once again, technology had provided solutions and generated new problems. Mechanization had multiplied fixed charges in several ways. The rapid obsolescence of the cable and early electric technology demanded rates of depreciation or write-offs so high as to make them unlikely, even had the promoters been farsighted and interested in doing so. The purchase of expensive franchises for implementing mechanization and the adaptation of the conduit system to appease popular concern had still further burdened general revenues. The combination which accompanied mechanization had bankrupted public policy and aroused popular hostility. And mechanization had exacerbated the anger by generating high expectations and by reinforcing the downtown congestion and uptown expansion which limited the trolley's ability to meet those expectations. The evolution of a transit system sufficient for New York's needs would require still another major technological innovation.

3.

From Battery Park
to Harlem
in Fifteen Minutes

As IN THE CASE of the elevated roads, the timing of the street railway's most rapid expansion overshadowed the signals of its inability to meet New York's needs. Despite the advent of mechanized surface lines in the 1890s, the city needed still speedier transit to reach uptown Manhattan and the fast growing Bronx. With the consolidation creating Greater New York in 1898, the pressure for high speed lines to link the new city's boroughs became all the greater. The solution that supplied the requisite rapid transit was the third and completing step in the evolution of New York's public transit system.

As in the past, the application of transit technology yet untried in the United States—subway trains powered by electricity—required financial, legal, and other adjustments for construction and operation. Most striking however, was the new technology's impact on transit policy, making the process of transit system evolution even more complex. The precise role of the city government in the planning, finance, construction, and ownership of the new subways had to be defined amidst the complex swirl of interest groups and politics involved in local transit. And finally the city's new role had to be adjusted to progressive reformers' demands for greater control of public utilities and to the needs of the private operators.

Selecting the New Technology and Policy

The need for further improvement in public transit was quite obvious by the early 1890s. New York was the nation's largest industrial city, seaport, and gateway for the tide of immigraion. In 1898 the five boroughs of the metropolitan area were consolidated into Greater New York—the city boundaries with which we are familiar today. At the decade's beginning the population of Manhattan and the Bronx was 1,530,124; by 1900 the consolidated city contained more than twice that number. Urban growth in the 1890s continued to spread residences outward from southern Manhattan to Brooklyn and New Jersey and up the island toward Harlem and the Bronx. Simultaneously the steel frame skyscraper permitted greater business activity at Manhattan's southern tip.

The numbers of people in the metropolitan area astounded contemporaries. "The crowds upon our streets are incomparable," said one. "Broadway or Fulton Street may have its equal in a few business thoroughfares elsewhere, but no city has anything like the ubiquitous moving throngs that characterize the greater part of Manhattan and Brooklyn from morning to midnight."[1] One historian of the city likened the populace's daily movements to a powerful tide: "In 1890, nearly one and a half million people were living on Manhattan Island, and nearly ninety thousand had moved into the Annexed District beyond the Harlem River. Every morning, almost as many more poured into the city for the day's work. At night, they overflowed into suburban regions to sleep. They herded on cars that crossed the Brooklyn Bridge, on ferries that ploughed across the East and Hudson Rivers, and down the bay to Staten Island, on trains that thundered in and out of Grand Central Station. The evening tide out of New York washed over a vast area."[2]

As the rate of traffic growth jumped upward in the 1890s, the strain on transit facilities was terrific. "Yet every day enlarges the demand," remarked an observer. "On Broadway [he continued] the cars form an almost unbroken procession from Bowling Green to Madison Square, moving at a snail's pace, seriously impeding all other traffic, and almost preventing crossing the street, though there is a policemen at every street-crossing, and special agents of the company at many points. Elevated trains are packed until not another person can be crowded in, and half the weary travelers must stand, swaying precariously and squeezed and jostled by similar unfortunates, often rude and ill tempered."[3]

To meet the challenge required innovation in technology and policy. Selecting the correct technology in turn demanded two interwoven decisions: choosing the proper location for the right of way (surface, elevated, or underground) also hinged on the type of motive power. Street railways received scant consideration. Until the late 1880s they were little more than pokey, horsedrawn embarrassments. When the outcry for rapid transit renewed, the process of combination, consolidation, and mechanization was only just underway. What was more, as the editor of the New York Times commented, "rapid transit cannot be furnished on the surface."[4] Congestion in the business district and frequent stops at intersections precluded any possibility that streetcars could provide the 25 to 30 miles per hour speed that New Yorkers sought. Despite mechanization and combination, rides per capita scarcely increased in the 1890s.

Elevated railroads attracted more serious and extended attention as a proven technology driven by dependable steam power. The prosperous Manhattan Elevated Company had accommodated most of New York's traffic growth since 1880. Its ownership was politically influential and was negotiating for extensions in the late 1880s.

Nevertheless, the Manhattan Elevated's technology and management left it unfit to meet the city's needs. Popular opposition to the elevated road's noise, ugliness, and impact on abutting property helped prevent further construction in the 1880s. An effort to put an elevated line on Broadway failed in a storm of protest. In 1889 only the New York *Sun*, reputed to be the *World's* successor as Jay Gould's pet newspaper, supported a Manhattan proposal for expansion.[5] An 1891 attempt to take Battery Park for additional tracks and a switching yard aroused the ire of groups as disparate as the New York Board of Trade and Transportation, the Knights of Labor, the Citizens' Committee of 100, and the East Side Neighborhood Guild.[6]

Motive power as well as aesthetic considerations disqualified the Elevated Company. As noted earlier, the company's steam engines could provide neither the speed nor the power needed for rapid transit in the 1890s, and the elevated structure precluded larger engines. The use of electricity might have alleviated the problem, but the decisions of George Gould, Jay's successor as head of the Manhattan Company, destroyed that possibility. George delayed electrification, which would have increased the speed and capacity of the elevated, until 1902 "in view of the large expense" and the "uncertainty as to the practicality of electricity as a motive power." The conversion came fourteen years after Frank Sprague developed the trolley and eight years after the first Chicago elevated lines were electrified.[7]

However, although steam-powered elevated roads were inadequate to the task, the Manhattan Company continued to play an active part in the evolution of New York's transit in the 1890s. To uptown residents, real estate speculators, and others who wanted a quick resolution and who were skeptical of an expensive, untried subway, elevated lines were the logical choice. The Manhattan Company and its supporters continued to distract and slow the selection and construction of a subway. Indeed, New York's Rapid Transit Commission did not finally reject the Manhattan Elevated until 1898.

Only a subway system was left. Although New York capitalists had repeatedly rejected this alternative in earlier years because of its cost and the unsuitability of steam power for long tunnels, an 1888 proposal by Mayor Abram Hewitt for an underground railroad reawakened interest. And while Hewitt's plan died in the state legislature for lack of adequate support, it did initiate the drive for a New York subway.[8]

Even more important was the innovation of a new motive power. The development of electric power in the 1880s removed the combustion problem and made the subway more attractive. Electricity offered the possibility of adequate speed and power while removing 99 percent of the pollution found in steam tunnels.[9] And the opening of the electric-powered underground in London in 1890 further facilitated New York's choice of technology.

A city rapid transit commission confirmed the choice in 1891. It ruled out the deep tunnel system used in London, because the depth increased the cost of ventilation, drainage, and movement of passengers to and from the surface. Instead, it settled on the form since used in all American subways—a tunnel built as close to the surface as underground piping and foundations allowed.[10] The road was to be on a single, four-track level, easier to operate, and less likely to be blocked than a two-level tunnel. Furthermore, the bedrock base of the roadbed offered greater safety at high speeds than a manmade, two-tier structure.

For motive power the commissioners, after hearing persuasive arguments from Frank Sprague and after conducting their own investigation, vaguely opted for "electricity, or some other power not requiring combustion within the tunnel."[11] Steam power was barred by law, and the commissioners had little choice, for electricity was the only viable alternative.

Nevertheless, the selection was a risky innovation. Electric power was still in the developmental stage with rapidly changing technology and uncertain costs. Not until three years later did the engineer of a successor commission report that electricity was superior to steam in economy and cleanliness and that it had "long since passed the experimental stage for service of this sort."[12]

Furthermore there was no guarantee of adequate power and speed. In 1891 the city and any prospective investor had only Frank Sprague's testimony that he could develop the necessary motor. Sprague offered to wager $50,000 that he could build an electric system to move a six-car train at 40 miles per hour with either an electric locomotive or a multiple-unit train with motors in each car. Nothing came of the proposal, and Sprague did not invent the multiple unit technique (eventually adopted for all elevated and subway lines) until 1897.[13]

The innovation of a new motive power and a new form of transit complicated the evolution of rapid transit for New York. But while selection of the new technology was troublesome, even more involved and time consuming was the choice of a proper policy for construction. Despite the subway's increasing acceptability, New Yorkers still awaited an entrepreneur who could and would build it. In the 1870s and 1880s at least five groups organized to do just that, but for a variety of reasons none was successful. Besides the motive power problem, squabbles within and between companies over routes and rights, lack of capital, and opposition from abutters and local transit companies combined to stop them all.[14]

In response, New Yorkers turned to the technique used sixteen years earlier: a rapid transit commission to remove roadblocks and aid private enterprise on the public's behalf. In 1891 the state legislature enacted a proposal from Mayor Hugh Grant that modified the old 1875 law to permit the addition of outside experts to a transit commission and to repeal the numerous restrictions on the choice of routes. The act empowered the mayor to appoint a five-man Rapid Transit Commission (RTC) to devise a plan to be approved by the Sinking Fund Commissioners, who would then auction the right to construct and operate. The commission's indefinite tenure instead of the old four-month limit acknowledged the increased complexity of the problem since 1875.[15]

As in 1875 support for the proposal included urban reformers, civic boosters, real estate men, and tax-conscious property owners. Experts on cities described rapid transit as vital to the salvation of the industrial metropolis. Writing in the last decade of the century, Adna Weber argued that "much effort is still needed to make city life what it should be, and that the principal basis of hope lies in the decentralizing forces that have recently appeared." In his judgment "the sole remedy is the multiplication of steam railroads or the building of elevated and underground four-track systems."[16]

At a time when the closing of the frontier seemed to pose a similar threat of concentration on a national scale, New Yorkers were quick to agree. The New York *Times'* real estate analyst observed that only on the city's edges were "to be found those primary essentials to the pleasant home life that has come to be considered peculiarly American—room and pure air."[17] One subway booster argued that rapid transit would allow deconcentration and permit the poor to establish homes in open spaces. Similar pleas were heard from such reformers and civic enthusiasts as Lyman Abbott, Albert Shaw, the New York *Times*, the investment banker Jacob Schiff, and the Chamber of Commerce.[18]

Deconcentration also matched the interests of many groups in the business community which led the drive for rapid transit. Transit expansion's impact on land accessibility and value especially interested uptown property holders and real estate operators. As the New York *Times* commented, "It has doubtless been noticed that every movement for the increase of rapid transit has proceeded from property owners along the west side."[19] Similarly, manufacturers and merchants, mindful of the importance of transportation and desirous of a larger tax base, were vigorous advocates of rapid transit. The proposal for a subway was endorsed by the New York Cotton Exchange, the Produce Exchange, and

the Real Estate Exchange, as well as by those uptown residents and property owners in the Bronx represented in the Property Owners' Association of the 23rd Ward.[20]

So widespread and powerful was popular enthusiasm for rapid transit
that it overcame the opposition of vested transit interests and a home rule
battle between a Democratic city and a Republican state legislature.
When the municipal corporation sought approval from the state legislature, Boss Platt's state Republican machine refused, fearing that a mayor-
appointed commission would offer patronage only to Democrats. The
New York Cable Railway Company (the Andrews group which Whitney
and Ryan had abandoned) sought a rival charter, after reputedly allying
with Boss Platt. At the same time Mayor Hugh Grant and Tammany Hall
were thought to be dragging their feet on behalf of the Manhattan Elevated Company.[21]

Nevertheless, a three-year crusade led by the Real Estate Exchange encouraged local leaders of both parties to hold mass meetings, to form a
Rapid Transit League, and to petition the legislature. Heightened popular
support overwhelmed Tammany foot dragging. Meanwhile public hostility balked the Cable Company's efforts, and Boss Platt's opposition
weakened so that the bill passed.[22]

As in 1875 membership on the bipartisan Rapid Transit Commission in
1891 reflected the strong business flavor of the drive for better transportation. Members of the RTC were William Steinway, Democrat and head
of the piano company; Samuel Spencer, Republican banker at Drexel,
Morgan and Company; John Starin, Democrat and head of local passenger and freight lines operating on the Hudson River and Long Island
Sound; Eugene Bushe, Democrat, railroad lawyer and real estate investor; and Frederick Olcott, mugwump Democrat and president of the
Central Trust Company. Olcott was soon replaced by John Inman, a cotton broker and "one of the best known business men in the Wall Street
district." All five men had railroad interests or experience.[23]

Despite similarities to past boards, circumstances combined to give the
1891 RTC a stronger role than its predecessors. The commission made
several crucial decisions to solve the transit problem, but unlike the 1875
experience, no clear front runner appeared to guide the RTC's deliberations. Thus, in 1891 a public body selected the route, motive power, and
type of rapid transit which a future, unknown bidder would have to
accept.

After opting for an electric-powered subway, the commission designed
a route that served both real estate interests and the city's need for expansion: a line running from the Battery along Broadway and up the West
Side to Yonkers. Concentration of effort on the West Side would help
develop New York's most sparsely populated area. In addition the post-

ponement of construction on the more developed East Side, already served by two elevated lines, the New York Central Railroad and the Third Avenue cable road, would reduce costs.

Nevertheless the choice of route confronted the RTC and the prospective investor with the burden of social overhead investment. Paying for a rapid transit system would precede by a number of years the full benefits of the investment, especially in the thinly settled uptown region. Furthermore, while some of the delayed benefits would eventually be captured as traffic increased with growing uptown settlement, others, such as increasing real estate values, would be profits external to the enterprise. Given the high fixed cost of the subway, then, the problem was to assure sufficient revenue for the operation during its early years.

The solution was the obvious choice of Broadway as the line's backbone. The commission explained that "the existing north and south lines of transit nearest the center of the city absorbed the greater traffic, and . . . the relative pressure upon them was substantially in proportion to their proximity to Broadway."[24] The heavy downtown traffic was expected to balance anticipated losses on the upper West Side until the subway generated uptown settlement and created its own traffic. The 1875 elevated routes had relied on the same strategy. As subway operator August Belmont explained many years later, it permitted rapid transit to develop outlying areas and still return a profit, thus serving both public and private interests.[25]

The 1891 RTC, however, was unsuccessful, for it failed to find a bidder for the subway franchise. The *Engineering News* argued that restrictions in the proposed contract, including a $3,000,000 security bond, a fixed 5 cent fare and a five-year completion deadline on pain of forfeiture, frightened away potential investors.[26] Other critics, including Assistant Engineer William B. Parsons, alleged that the Manhattan Elevated Company, acting through Tammany Hall, influenced the RTC to design a plan which had no chance of success.[27]

Neither argument is especially compelling. Deadlines, security requirements, and fixed fares had not deterred action in 1875. And the scanty available evidence does not support Parsons' claim. The RTC was quite flexible and continually offered to negotiate terms with any prospective bidder.[28] It received no serious offers, not even from the Manhattan Company, which failed to follow up the subway's defeat by obtaining franchises for elevated extensions at easy terms prior to the depression of the mid-1890s.

More important than restrictions or interference were the amounts and risks involved in the use of a new motive power and right of way. The construction of a sixteen-mile system depending on a still uncertain electric power, the possible damages to the foundations of buildings from a near-surface tunnel, and a cost estimated at $50,000,000 (almost double the capitalization of all Manhattan's street railways in 1885)[29] made the risk too great for the expected rate of return. After failing for years to implement its own plan, private enterprise was asked to follow a city plan but with private funds and at personal risk.

The chief difficulty, then, was New Yorkers' inability to adjust to the consequences of new technology. By the mid-1890s New Yorkers clearly wanted better rapid transit, but this time the high fixed cost and the risk of electric-powered subways vitiated the old technique of indirect public aid to private enterprise. The 1891 RTC demonstrated some of the capabilities of an active public role in transit development, but it lacked the means to execute its plan in the absence of private initiative. Building the subway with adequate public controls required more than a simple tightening of old laws. Installation would require a new policy and an agency to implement it.

Innovation in transit policy to meet the needs of the new technology came quickly. In 1894 the state legislature enacted a law to create a new RTC. The eight-man commission included the president of the Chamber of Commerce, the mayor, the city comptroller and five men to be appointed. As in the case of the 1891 commission, the 1894 RTC was to lay out routes, obtain the consent of abutters or of the state Supreme Court, select a technology, and blueprint a specific plan. After obtaining the consent of the mayor and the Board of Aldermen to the plan, the commission was to spell out its terms in a proposed contract for construction and operation. It would then lease the franchise to the highest bidder. New York City would reimburse the contractor for construction costs after the RTC certified the work to be complete. The RTC also was to define the guarantees necessary to insure the builder's good faith. In case of failure to complete the line or to operate it in accordance with the contract, the bidder forfeited the guarantees, the franchise, and if necessary, his equipment to the city, which would be free to lease it again or to operate the line itself.[30]

The act's immediate inspiration was the old 1891 RTC's recognition of its failure and the urgent need for action. In early 1894 the old commission wrote Mayor Thomas Gilroy that its earlier defeat, now reinforced by depressed business conditions, made "doubtful whether any underground road will be built in the near future by private capital alone."[31] It recommended instead legislation to permit city funding for at least part of the project.

When banker R. T. Wilson sought approval from the Chamber of Commerce for just such a scheme, Abram Hewitt objected strenuously and offered a plan that became the basis for the 1894 act. Citing such memorable examples as the Brooklyn Bridge and the Union Pacific Railroad, he argued convincingly against the evils of mixed enterprise and emphasized its unconstitutionality. He reintroduced his 1888 proposal to allow New York City to plan and finance its own enterprise and then to lease it for private construction and operation. His policy required no constitutional amendment for the loan of city credit to private interests. And private construction at a contracted price removed the danger of graft and government inefficiency. Rental based on a percentage of the construction cost and paid annually for a long-term lease would meet interest costs and amortize the city bonds issued to finance the project. There would be no burden on the taxpayers.[32]

Unlike the English origin of the electric subway, the new transit policy was domestically inspired. Certainly Hewitt and other leading subway exponents were familiar with the growing pattern of public ownership in European transit. By the 1890s the German government had built an elevated railway and British cities were operating street railway lines. But when Hewitt first offered his plan in 1888, municipal operation had not yet become a vogue in Britain, and the English subways on which he based his technology were privately financed.[33]

Instead Hewitt reminded New York's Chamber of Commerce that both city and state had successfully completed several major projects vital to the welfare of their citizens. In the absence of private enterprise New York State had built the Erie Canal. New York City had financed and erected the Croton Aqueduct. Finally he recalled that he had served as trustee when New York City and Brooklyn had taken charge of and completed the Brooklyn Bridge, after a disastrous beginning by a private company supported with public funds.[34]

Hewitt's faith in good men acting on behalf of the public welfare was shared by Jacob Schiff of the investment banking house, Kuhn, Loeb and Company. As early as 1891 Schiff doubted that the necessary capital could be found for private development. If so, he thought the bankers would "as compensation for the risks they would have to take, require the creation of a large amount of fictitious capital, upon which [would be paid] as large a return as the growth of traffic shall be expected to permit."[35]

Schiff estimated that private capital would cost 10 percent and public credit could be obtained at 3 percent. The difference would mean profitable operation at a lower fare—hopefully five cents or less. He advocated public finance and construction by a board of trustees composed "of business men of universally acknowledged integrity and capability." And as an example Schiff cited Cincinnati's recent construction of a railroad which the city leased for private operation.[36]

As in the 1875 and 1891 cases, the new proposal's quick enactment resulted primarily from business leadership. In the mid-1890s the need for

rapid transit began to unite the business community—realtors and investors in uptown property, importers and exporters who depended on
transportation in their daily business and who had a considerable stake
in New York and its preeminence, retailers and manufacturers who relied
on transit to bring customers and laborers to their doors, and bankers
who would handle the gilt-edged city bonds.

By early 1893 both the editor of the respected *Real Estate Record and
Buyers Guide* and the board of directors of the Real Estate Exchange had
endorsed public ownership.[37] In 1894 the Chamber of Commerce's vigorous lobby in support of the Hewitt plan generated petitions and support
from influential business and reform groups, including the New York
Board of Trade and Transportation, the Union League Club, the City
Club, and the Council of Confederated Good Government Clubs. Most
of the city's press—the New York *Times, Post, Herald, Tribune, World,*
and *Telegram*—firmly backed the plan.[38]

The desire for cheap rapid transit and frustration over the inactivity of
the Manhattan Company also stimulated support from a wide assort-
ment of other organizations. Labor unions, Christian social groups, the
city's black community, and immigrant associations led by such spokesmen as Samuel Gompers, Henry George, and W. E. B. DuBois joined in
protest against more elevated lines and in favor of a municipally constructed subway.[39] Some seventy labor unions united to form a rapid
transit commission, which lobbied vigorously for municipal construction. The commission twice submitted subway bills to the legislature and
deluged it with petitions containing 55,000 signatures in support of its
proposal.[40] This upsurge in 1893 was the first significant indication of
nonbusiness feeling.

The popular surge was so powerful that even the business community
had to recognize it. Before the RTC could implement the 1894 law, a
trade union sponsored clause provided that the people vote whether or
not to require public development in a November referendum. Though
Hewitt and his associates denounced the idea as "anarchical" and an
unconstitutional delegation of the legislature's powers to the people, the
Chamber grudgingly accepted it to obtain trade union support.[41] For the
first time the public would have a direct voice in transit policy, compelling businessmen to recognize the considerable stake which the entire city
had in local transit. The Chamber of Commerce, the press, reformers,
labor groups, and all spectra of city opinion campaigned so successfully
that New Yorkers voted three to one for public development by the RTC
in the largest turnout in city history.[42] The law's rapid passage and the
referendum testified vividly to the entire public's urgent demand for better rapid transit.

The principle of private enterprise proved to be quite flexible in the face of such need. Few opposed government action strictly because of an abstract belief in laissez-faire capitalism. For many critics the major hindrance was a Tammany-controlled city government which threatened any public project with boodle and patronage. But fear of inefficiency and graft did not preclude an active government role any more than did protests from Tammany and the Manhattan Company. The pressures of urban growth and the absence of private development compelled those interested in transit to adjust their convictions and to find a means to avoid Tammany corruption. As the Board of Trade and Transportation explained: "We believe that an emergency has arisen such as will justify the City of New York in giving the use of its credit to insure the construction and speedy completion of such well-considered plan of rapid transit as shall give the full assurance of meeting the present and future needs of our city in this respect."[43]

As in the elevated case, a major innovation, this time in public policy, looked less radical when introduced by degrees. Tammany had no voice in it, and there was to be no large public payroll to pad. To contemporaries the act of 1894 was not a revolutionary departure but merely a change in policy to meet a particular need. The 1891 act had called for public planning. Its failure pointed out the need to go one step further to city finance and ownership. Viewed in this light, the assumption by municipal government of an active role in transit development was a simple and necessary strategy.

In addition, the 1894 law had much continuity with the past. It maintained former provisions to protect private property by requiring the consent of abutters or of the Supreme Court. And despite the appointment of the mayor and the comptroller to the board, the RTC still had to obtain local consent to the plan for funding and implementation. The contract for construction and operation was a fixed agreement similar to permanent grants between cities or the state and the operators of street and elevated railways. In accordance with the prevalent suspicion of public enterprise, a private company was to equip and operate the line for profit, as had been the case of the surface and elevated roads. The 1894 law did not signal the abandonment of private enterprise in public transit. As in 1875 the policy was to accommodate the needs of the city and the profit-minded operator.

The personnel of the new commission also had some continuity with the past. William Steinway, John H. Starin, and John Inman had been members of the 1891 RTC. The other appointed members, Seth Low, president of Columbia University and a former silk importer; Alexander Orr, head of the Produce Exchange and of the Chamber of Commerce; and John Claflin, a prominent merchant, were reputable, conservative businessmen.[44] If the city was to have a greater role, it would be exercised by businessmen who acted by business methods and principles, just as in 1875 and 1891. And the continuity carried over even to the staff. William Barclay Parsons, who had served as assistant engineer on the 1891 board, became chief engineer. Parsons and the businessmen held similar ideas about the proper role of government, the efficiency of private enterprise, and the urgent need for rapid transit which characterized the old commission.[45]

For the long run, however, the 1891 and 1894 laws did mark a fundamental change in the strategy of public transit. They gave city government an active role in transit development that continues to the present day. They inaugurated a policy of city planning, finance, and ownership of rapid transit facilities that lasted until the 1920s when public operation was added. To implement the new strategy the law created a new city organization. The 1894 commission became the forerunner of the professionally staffed, permanent agency which still controls city transit. And the innovation had ramifications beyond local transportation. Progressive reformers widely used the technique in municipal government to supply the complex and continuous services necessary to govern the modern industrial metropolis.

Implementation: Public Policy

Selecting the proper innovations in technology and policy had required six years since Hewitt's proposal for a city-financed subway in 1888. Execution needed ten years, but the delay's primary cause was not technology, for construction consumed less than four years. Although local transit's public character had always associated it with city and state politics, the determination for municipal ownership now squarely placed the issue in the public arena. Consequently, the implementation of transit policy was quite complex and slow, for supporters now encountered not only the blockades imposed by private interests, but the obstacles mounted by various politicians and government agencies as well.

Popular support was crucial for the success of a city subway, but aroused public opinion was difficult to maintain. It peaked only under the prod of crisis conditions. When it subsided after the 1894 referendum, other forces rose to slow development. Opposition from owners of abutting property, interference by the courts, the machinations of Tammany Hall, and actions by the Manhattan Elevated and Metropolitan Street Railway Companies proved formidable barriers. These groups delayed implementation until 1900 by taking advantage of the novelty of the city's role and its agent, the cautious policy of RTC leaders, and the effects of the consolidation of Greater New York. The frustrations were so great that at times even the RTC seemed ready to abandon the project.

Nevertheless, under the calm and patient guidance of its chairman, Alexander Orr, the RTC persevered. It pioneered successfully the construction of the city's first subway, which except for a single extension, was the only one built before World War I.

The RTC's problems came very quickly. After confirming its predecessor's choice of a near surface, electric-powered subway, the commission made some slight changes in the route. Though not radical, the alterations did compel the board to seek again the consent of abutters.[46] Thus began a long, complicated battle that, more than any other factor, delayed execution of the new policy. Not unnaturally, the commission fought for a Broadway route, since it offered the greatest return to the would-be operator and the greatest convenience to the traveling population. Broadway property owners were just as determined to stop the plan. They favored rapid transit, explained a spokesman, but not where it might injure their property.[47]

The protest was hardly surprising. Broadway landowners had traditionally opposed transit improvement. Led by A. T. Stewart and the Astor family, Broadway merchants and residents had fought and delayed street railway construction for thirty years before 1884. And since the 1860s they had battled the construction of elevated and subway lines.[48] Aided by the prevalent concern for individual property rights, they had been quite successful. Every local transit franchise law after 1875 required that the owners of at least one half the value of abutting property must consent to construction. The 1894 act extended this provision, originally designed to balance the interests of property owners and private transit operators, to public enterprise as well. And once again property owners blocked approval for rapid transit construction on Broadway.

Fortunately, the legislature recognized the power of a comparative few to frustrate a project of paramount importance to the entire city and provided an alternative. Failing to obtain the necessary consents, the developer could apply to the state Supreme Court for the appointment of three commissioners who would take testimony to determine the reasonableness of the project. If they approved and the court agreed, then the project could proceed.[49] In September 1895 the RTC reluctantly petitioned the Supreme Court to appoint commissioners.

There ensued a running struggle between the courts and the commission which lasted until December 1899. After a time-consuming squabble over jurisdiction, the court insisted that its own inexperienced appointees judge plans on which the RTC, aided by its staff and two sets of consulting engineers, had spent a year. The court's commissioners decided not to go behind the RTC's decisions and needlessly duplicate its research, especially since they had no means to do so. Instead they took the detailed testimony of the RTC and its experts on the plan, route, and pro-

jected cost and heard the complaints of the opposition.[50] After delibera-
tion, they accepted the RTC proposal and sent it to the Supreme Court.

In May 1896 a unanimous Supreme Court surprisingly rejected the
RTC petition. It charged that its own commissioners had failed to make
adequate determination of the cost, questioned New York's ability to
spare the necessary funds, and doubted the RTC's capability to complete
the subway without spending double the estimated $50,000,000 cost.
One justice also criticized the project for failure to benefit the entire city,
since it did not extend to the city limits on the East and West Sides.[51]

In effect the court rejected the new purpose and competency of the
city's agent and sought instead to retain the power, which it had exercised throughout the nineteenth century, to shape public policy by the
interpretation of legislative acts. The justices made their own estimates of
the rapid transit problem and reserved for themselves the right to determine what New York should do. And although this behavior suggests
that Tammany politics could have influenced the judgment, there were
no such accusations. The scanty evidence suggests just the opposite.
Judge Morgan O'Brien, an associate of William Whitney, abstained from
voting. Had the court been a Tammany tool to smash the RTC, it certainly could have done a more effective and permanent job.

Once again prominent civic leaders and business organizations rescued
the new policy. Protest was considerable. Among other court critics the
New York *Times* argued that "this whole method of dealing with the subject is an unsatisfactory one. The most competent experts, wholly impar-
tial and disinterested and responsible directly to the city, should have
had the deciding after thorough examination and study, of every technical question involved in the undertaking, and their decision should have
been conclusive."[52] The New York Board of Trade and Transportation,
the Social Reform Club, and the Trades Union Rapid Transit Commission, along with such reformers as Albert Shaw and Lyman Abbott, offered additional encouragement to the RTC.[53] In the face of such reaction, the judicial branch exerted a gradually decreasing role in public
transit development. Nevertheless, until 1900 it continued to complicate
an already difficult task and to delay construction.

The 1896 decision at first so dismayed the RTC that it considered resignation. Counsel Edward Shepard thought that the judgment made rapid
transit impossible, since it simultaneously required several miles of extensions and lower cost.[54] Buoyed, however, by letters and popular support,
the RTC struggled to pick up the pieces. Map 4 illustrates the commission's new route, which extended the system to the city line on both the
East and West Sides. The new plan abandoned Broadway below 42nd
Street for Elm Street and Fourth Avenue to reduce damages and construction costs. The RTC carefully documented for new court-appointed

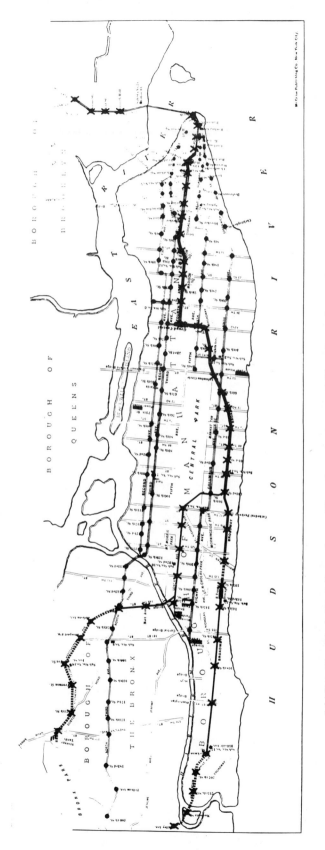

MAP 4. New York City's first subway. The subway is represented by a heavy line with crosses; the elevated system by a heavy line with dots. The crosses and dots mark subway and elevated stations. The decision to extend the subway into Brooklyn was made in 1902. *Source:* Interborough Rapid Transit Company, *Interborough Rapid Transit: The New York Subway, Its Construction and Equipment* (New York, 1904), pp. 24-25.

commissioners a cost estimate substantially less than the $55,000,000 maximum allowed by law.[55]

After a twenty-month delay, the court approved the new plans in December 1897. It recognized the RTC's necessity and popular appeal, and confirmed the legality of its changes. The judges acknowledged that the RTC had determined the cost "with reasonable accuracy" and that the "ability to meet such cost is shown." But the court's mellowing quickly gave way to further meddling. It decided that "in view of the magnitude of the undertaking," the RTC security arrangements were inadequate to protect the city and required instead a permanent security bond from the would-be contractor of $15,000,000 with double sureties.[56]

The RTC argued vainly that it had already established adequate terms as section 34 of the 1894 act specifically empowered it to do, that $15,000,000 was more than double the assets of the largest bonding company in the state, and that the requirement reduced the number of prospective bidders. Two months later the court accepted $1,000,000 as the only permanent bond necessary but still required the additional $14,000,000 during construction. Two years later the RTC, with the aid of the city, finally persuaded the justices to reduce the construction bond to $5,000,000 just before the sale of the franchise.[57]

The struggle for consents and the court's obstruction delayed work for three years. The court's influence also had a more significant result. Its demands compelled the RTC to design an awkward route not adjusted until after World War I. Rapid transit historian James Walker judged it "difficult to estimate the time consumed in adjusting the new [post-1900] lines to this situation, but it is safe to say that rapid transit relief was delayed some years in consequence."[58]

The RTC's battles with the Supreme Court also postponed subway construction by allowing the cyclical pattern of machine and reform administrations in city government to interfere. Less than one month after the court approved the commission's plan in December 1897, Tammany Hall replaced the sympathetic reform administration of Mayor William Strong and regained control of the mayor's office and the Board of Aldermen. Mayor Robert Van Wyck's inaugural address quickly revealed Tammany's hostility to the commission and its project.[59] As an observer remarked in another context, "Corporations from which Tammany is excluded are necessarily evils to be abated. On the other hand, corporations which are leavened by Tammany are necessarily free from those evils and do not need to be interfered with."[60] As Tammany had no influence on the RTC, it soon tried to abolish it. Richard Croker put it baldly: "As to what the Rapid Transit Board will do, I have but slight notion. I am not in the board's confidence. Moreover, I have but little respect for it. In all the years of its existence it has done nothing but talk, talk, talk.

Five bluejays would have done as much. The people have repudiated it at the polls; it has done nothing but talk and waste time and money. It promises nothing but to waste future time and future money. The sooner it gets out the better for the public and the better for its own self-respect."[61]

In an attempt to gain control of the subway project, Croker sought state Republican Boss Thomas Platt's support to replace the RTC with a bipartisan board. Bipartisanship offered Platt's machine some much-sought patronage in New York City while also allowing Tammany access to money and jobs it did not have under the present RTC. The threat aroused the public to stop the maneuver. The Chamber of Commerce, the Retail Grocers Union, the Citizens Union, and an alliance of mug-wumps and organized labor including Bayard Cutting and E. P. Wheeler, the Reform Club, and the Central Labor Union lobbied vigorously against the bill at Albany. Their efforts and Governor Frank Black's veto threat scuttled the proposal.[62]

Quickly Tammany turned to an alternate strategy to block the commission. It protested loudly about the city's inability to finance both this and other necessary capital projects within its debt limit. Part of the confusion was legitimate. The 1898 unification of the five boroughs, including some ninety governmental units, had so obscured the consolidated city's debt responsibilities that a year passed before they were clear. Croker anticipated the problem and soon turned it to his own use. He proclaimed that "the city hasn't the money to build a tunnel. There is only a small margin of credit left to the city. It wouldn't pay for one-quarter of the tunnel. Then again, the tunnel, even if feasible, would take too long. The city hasn't the time or money for tunnels."[63]

By January 1899 a reassessment of property, an accurate determination of the debt, and the approval by the city comptroller of an RTC alternative of subway construction in segments costing $10,000,000, removed any legitimate objection. Nevertheless, Tammany continued to trumpet the debt issue, and Corporation Counsel John Whalen delayed approving the proposed contract with the would-be bidder submitted by the RTC in April 1898. In May 1899, after more than a year's inaction, an RTC letter to Mayor Van Wyck asking his administration's intentions brought no reply.[64]

Tammany's desire to control the largest single capital outlay in the city's history with enormous opportunities for patronage and graft had prompted its bipartisan board proposal. But the long stall over the debt and the contract was unaccompanied by any positive action on its part to usurp the RTC's power. Instead the policy worked to the advantage of a long-time Tammany ally, the Manhattan Elevated Company.

The company already had sought to delay the subway and obtain franchises for itself. An unsuccessful suit by the New York *Sun*, the Elevated Company's constant ally and defender in the 1890s, challenged the constitutionality of the 1894 law and the RTC.[65] Meanwhile the Manhattan proposed to extend its own system. The company asked the RTC for extensions and surface feeder lines in the Bronx and uptown. When the commission pointed out that the 1894 act explicitly forbade it to grant surface roads and asked for specific time limits for elevated construction, the Manhattan broke off negotiations.[66]

In early 1898, after the court's onerous security requirement darkened the subway's future, the company intruded again. This time Richard Croker became its leading booster, seconded by his puppet, Mayor Van Wyck. Croker argued that New York "must have rapid transit relief and have it at once. Aside from that, the elevated road is the better scheme of the two. Wouldn't a man rather ride in the open air than under ground? Another feature of the Manhattan offer which people should not forget is that the railroad furnishes the money. It doesn't cost the city a dollar. We get rapid transit, get it in two years, and get it without bankrupting ourselves."[67]

Despite Tammany's continual harangue on the debt issue, Van Wyck's refusal to cooperate with the board, Croker's vocal enmity toward the RTC, and the eighteen-month delay of the Corporation Counsel, the Manhattan's cautious management refused to seize the opportunity. Negotiations between the company and the RTC dragged on through the first half of 1898 without success. The Elevated Company sought connecting lines in the lower city and extensions up the East and West Sides, but offered no compensation or time limit on construction. After several exchanges the RTC proposed seven franchises for extensions in exchange for annual payments of 5 percent of gross receipts. Manhattan President George Gould dawdled, protested, and counteroffered 0.5 percent. The frustrated RTC finally resolved that "no useful purpose will be served by further delay," and the negotiations ended.[68]

By late 1898 prospects for the subway were dismal. The Manhattan continued its niggardly, cautious policy. Earlier, exploratory talks with such potential bidders as Cornelius Vanderbilt and Chauncey Depew of the New York Central and President Charles Clark of the New York, New Haven and Hartford had proved fruitless. Tammany controlled the city government without whose cooperation action was virtually impossible. Engineer William Parsons left New York for an extended stay in Hong Kong in a bleak state of mind.[69]

With the outlook for public construction so dim, the commission turned to the Metropolitan Street Railway Company. In January 1899 the commissioners asked the legislature to amend the 1894 law to allow private construction and ownership "only . . . in the event of the public credit proving unavailable" and as "additional to their present powers and not a substitute for them." With the nation's recovery from the depression of the mid-1890s, financial conditions were "much more favorable to the successful conduct of such an enterprise than they had been at any time heretofore." Hesitantly the board pleaded with the legislature that "it might perhaps be better to commit the work to a private corporation than that there should be no rapid transit at all."[70]

Suddenly in March 1899, the Metropolitan publicly entered the rapid transit field. It offered to organize a company to build the subway within three years for 5 percent of annual gross receipts as compensation to New York. In exchange it sought a perpetual franchise for operation by the Metropolitan. Fares would be five cents on local and ten cents on express trains with free transfers to streetcars from the express lines and three cent exchanges from the locals. The company guaranteed 30 miles an hour on the express line below 42nd Street and wanted tax exemption until the road paid its cost plus 5 percent.[71]

Whitney's good friend, Richard Croker, who had fallen out with the Manhattan Elevated people in early 1899, had already switched his allegiance to a privately constructed subway.[72] The RTC eagerly memorialized the legislature for additional amendments to carry out the proposal. But it failed to appreciate New Yorkers' desire to control their transit system.

No longer was public transit an issue to be decided by business associations and politicians. The extensive activities of labor unions and reformers in 1893 and 1894 and the overwhelming public support for city development in the 1894 referendum added a powerful collective voice. As the RTC later remarked: "Immediately upon the publication of the terms of the proposed bill, it became manifest that the press, and a large majority of the public, were unalterably opposed to the grant of a perpetual franchise to the Metropolitan Street Railroad Company, or to any other private corporation."[73] So strong was the public protest that Governor Theodore Roosevelt came out flatly against perpetual franchises. In April 1899 the Metropolitan withdrew its offer, citing lack of public support and inability to amend its terms and still make a profit.

Through the spring and summer of 1899, public meetings and proclamations from labor unions, reform groups, and members of the Real Estate Exchange pointedly reminded the RTC and Tammany Hall that they wanted public enterprise and nothing less. When the RTC again pressured Mayor Van Wyck for action on the contract, Tammany had little left to fight for. It had split with the Manhattan Company, and the Metropolitan had retired from the field. The public clearly would not tolerate Tammany control of construction. With no powerful ally and no hope of patronage, Tammany bowed before the rising public pressure.[74]

In the fall of 1899 Corporation Counsel John Whalen approved the contract. Mayor Van Wyck's administration joined the RTC to petition the court successfully to lower the construction bond requirement from $14,000,000 to $5,000,000. With startling suddenness the way was cleared for the sale of the subway franchise, and the RTC opened bids on January 15, 1900.

Implementation: Contract and Construction

Paradoxically, actual construction strained private enterprise more than public administration. By this point the burden of organization and finance had passed to the bidder. Public policy and organization were well established by 1900. Now promoter and contractor faced the challenges of organizing construction and financing working capital for an undertaking as expensive as the consolidation and mechanization of surface lines. Unlike the Metropolitan case, however, the job had to be done in four rather than sixteen years.

The subway contract continued the public transit tradition of regulation by fixed grant. The RTC had the right to inspect books and service, but for the most part operating standards were few. Flexible arbitration procedures were not spelled out. There were no established means to influence operation with appropriate penalties and instruments of inspection. Lack of compliance could be treated only by ignoring the violation or by franchise recapture. The weaknesses did not elicit much criticism; the tradition of regulation by fixed charters had prevailed for half a century in local transit. There was no active system for inspection of service on street railways and no call for one on the subway in 1900. The construction of a subway was uppermost in the minds of the commissioners and New Yorkers.[75] The adjustment of policy to solve the problem of service standards came later with actual operation.

The contract with the successful bidder was supposed to cover all contingencies. It provided for the construction of a 21 mile subway and viaduct system to reach from City Hall at the southern end of Manhattan Island to 225th Street on the West Side, with a branch to Harlem and the Bronx.[76] The city's cost for construction was to be the amount of the successful contractor's bid plus an additional $1,500,000 for real estate and terminals. The bidder was to equip and operate the line at his own expense. The proceeds of municipal bond sales were to reimburse the contractor for the cost of construction after approval of the work by the RTC. The successful bidder agreed to compensate the city with an annual rental at least equal to the interest on its bonds plus 1 percent of the construction cost for the sinking fund to amortize the bonds. The contract had a fifty-year term, plus the bidder's option to renew for another twenty-five years.

The municipality was well protected by a $5,000,000 construction bond, a $1,000,000 permanent performance bond, and a deposit of $1,000,000 in cash or securities during construction to cover damages. As further protection New York had first lien on the equipment, which in any event it was to buy at the expiration of the contract. If the contractor defaulted on construction, the city could recapture and operate or subcontract. Or, it could terminate the contract, sue to enforce the lien, and hold the bidder responsible for any losses. The contract required "sound material," "sound work," and the right of inspection and approval by the RTC's chief engineer, who would settle any dispute about the terms of construction. The job was to be finished in four and one half years, barring strikes, injunctions, or interference by city authorities. The contractor was not to impede the flow of traffic and was liable for damages to abutters. And he was to follow all contract specifications for route, materials, and all parts of the work.

In addition the agreement included some provisions for operation. The bidder agreed to run local trains at least fourteen miles per hour and express trains at least thirty miles per hour for a five-cent fare. He would supply adequate equipment, meet maximum headway requirements for service, and light and heat stations and cars. Finally, the agreement prescribed standards for such duties as control of dampness, construction of restrooms, and ventilation.

Implementation of the contract went more smoothly than its preparation and required a year's less time. Despite considerable apprehension that the route might not pay and that bidders would not appear, the terms were attractive enough to entice two serious bids. The RTC had projected the cost at $35,000,000, an estimate which reputedly included an $8,000,000 profit in construction as incentive to overcome the risk of innovation and the delay for development of traffic along the line.[77] The sale confirmed the attractiveness of their estimate.

John McDonald, an experienced railroad and public works contractor who had constructed a railroad tunnel under Baltimore in the early 1890s, captured the franchise with a bid of $35,000,000 on construction plus $1,500,000 for real estate and terminals. In exchange for the franchise, he offered the city the required minimum rental. His opponent, another contractor named Andrew Onderdonk, bid $40,000,000 and offered the minimum rental plus a percentage of all returns above $5,000,000 per year. The conservative commissioners took the lower bid rather than gamble on returns from operation.[78]

Because the contract called for the bidder to operate as well as construct the road, McDonald was at a disadvantage. He had considerable experience in building railroads but none in running them. In addition the surety companies which had agreed to supply his bond withdrew at the last moment. In a search for a replacement, Andrew Freedman, a

Tammany associate and one of McDonald's backers, took him to August Belmont.[79] Belmont headed the investment banking firm A. Belmont and Company, long the Rothschilds' American representative.

He agreed to support McDonald and quickly assumed leadership. In exchange for control of the franchise, Belmont organized a syndicate to raise the necessary working capital. He chartered the Rapid Transit Subway Construction Company to build the subway under McDonald's direction and provided the necessary money and securities for the bond. To operate the subway he organized the Interborough Rapid Transit Company (IRT) after McDonald signed over the operating portion of the contract.[80]

Belmont was in an excellent position to enter the field of rapid transit. He had access to the large sources of funds for equipment and for the working capital needed in construction and operation. He and his brother Perry, as influential members of the Democratic party, had the political clout so important in public transit. As an experienced banker and shrewd businessman, Belmont had a clear vision of the potential of rapid transit in New York.[81] Even though the uptown portions ran through areas of relatively sparse population, their growth rate was fast, and previous experience along the elevated roads suggested that settlement would expand along transportation lines.[82] The Bronx alone had grown in the 1890s by 126 percent, and by 1910 its population would surpass 400,000.

Belmont appreciated the strategy of combination and consolidation used by the street railway syndicate. He was so confident of success that midway through construction he underbid by $3,000,000, one half of the estimated total cost, for a second franchise to build a subway in Brooklyn. To garner the immense traffic which streamed daily between the two boroughs, he combined the two lines into a single system to be operated by the IRT.[83] Shrewdly visualizing the advantages of coordinated transit, he leased the Manhattan Company at a 7 percent rental in order to attain unified operation of all rapid transit lines in New York.

In the meantime, McDonald efficiently directed construction under the RTC's supervision. To perform its functions, the commission expanded its professional staff to more than three hundred, including six divisional engineers and a corps of auditors, accountants, engineers and testers. Chief Engineer William Parsons organized the staff to oversee, inspect, and approve construction for the RTC, to act as a consultant in negotiations with Belmont, and to plot additional lines. Under McDonald's direction and the vigilant eye of Parsons and his staff, the construction company completed the job efficiently and honestly despite strikes, explosions, and a rock slide.[84]

The opening of the first segment in October 1904 attracted more attention in New York than any event since the Civil War and underscored the public's stake in the project. For several weeks reporters interviewed almost every official involved and reviewed all phases of the engineering, including the electrical work, the artistic aspect of the stations, the waterproof switches, and even the sixty miles of boiler tubes. They overwhelmed the public with statistics: 10,000 men had moved 3,200,000 yards of material to build a twenty-one-mile system with 65,000 tons of steel and 8,000 tons of cast iron.[85] Superlatives crowded the headlines. The "Greatest Engineering Feat of Modern Times" was powered by the "World's Greatest Powerhouse," and had cars whose interior trimmings were the "Hallmark of Perfection." "The largest single contract in the history of civilization" was necessary to build "the Finest Subway in the World," whose completion was "an epoch in the history of New York."[86]

The subway's opening was a "carnival night" in New York with some 125,000 passengers carried in the first five hours. In a fit of ecstasy, the Board of Aldermen voted $50,000 for fireworks and a "collation" for itself and friends, which the mayor quickly vetoed. Like Wall Street, Fifth Avenue, and the Brooklyn Bridge, the subway was expected by New Yorkers to become a distinguishing feature of the city. Eminent speakers described it as a landmark worthy of national attention and wonder. The opening drew coverage in scores of cities from Boston to Dubuque.[87]

The subway was a monument of civic pride and achievement. New Yorkers confidently assumed it would unify the city to make real the geographical expression "Greater New York." Not only did it promise long-needed relief, but it marked a new era in local transit. "As a matter of fact, the new subway is the first system of transportation provided for New York conceived entirely in the public interest and free from the marks of personal scheming or corruption," remarked the New York World perceptively (if with understandable exaggeration).[88]

New Yorkers could afford their pride. They had undertaken a new policy to plan and finance a subway vital to the city. And they had instituted a new organization, the professionally staffed commission, to implement that policy. In the relatively short time of sixteen years, they had overcome inertia, conservatism, and special interests. A new era had arrived to establish "the principle of municipal control or ownership of city railways."[89]

The RTC and New York's Future Transit

The exaggerated newspaper coverage and the widespread popular attention given the new subway suggest how important public transit had become to New Yorkers. By the century's turn local transportation had

become a major issue for the broad coalition of settlement house workers, labor leaders, church spokesmen, muckrakers, political reformers,
and others who participated in the urban progressive movement. The
general recognition of transit's importance to the industrial metropolis
carried the issue beyond the control of the business coalition. Construction of the subway did not stop the process of change. Indeed the high
speed line became a force for change, compelling major adjustments in
both transit enterprise and public policy.

The imminence of further change, however, was not at first recognized. By the early years of the century the business-dominated RTC
appeared to be riding high, though even it could not efficiently handle
the continuing growth and rising expectations. The construction of the
city's first subway had fulfilled ten years' arduous effort. The commission had gradually expanded its actions and responsibilities far beyond
the plan envisioned in 1894. Executing the law made it the spokesman for
rapid transit policy in New York. The RTC was a lobbyist for legislation,
a negotiator with prospective contractors, and a liaison with such city
departments as Health, Parks, and Water when construction affected
them.

In addition to its developmental function, the RTC began to assume a
regulatory role. Responding to the public concern for safety, it made a
careful study to insure the purity of the air in the subway and ordered
improvements of the ventilation system. When complaints arose about
insufficient service, an investigation by the chief engineer and two board
members produced recommendations to the IRT which increased capacity.[90]

The creation of Greater New York in 1898 brought the RTC new and
more complex responsibilities. Originally established as a commission
for Manhattan and the Bronx, it now had to plan for the entire consolidated city. The commission prepared additional plans for Manhattan as
early as 1897, but only after construction began did it become concerned
about Greater New York. Already Brooklynites argued that rapid transit
funds should benefit more than one borough. Soon those living in the
Bronx and other districts joined the chorus.[91] And, to the RTC's dismay,
the coming of the subway led the Pennsylvania Railroad, the Long Island
Railroad, and other companies to map out their own tunnels, which
threatened to preempt prospective subway routes.

In 1902 the commission tardily took a more comprehensive view. In a
review of its functions, counsel for the RTC pointed out that "the interests of the City required that rapid transit problems should be dealt with
by the Rapid Transit Board as a permanent body especially familiar with
the subject and especially equipped to deal with it, all with the idea that
those problems instead of being dealt with by different bodies or by offi-

cers of short tenure should be dealt with in a systematic and far-seeing plan."[92] Chairman Alexander Orr quickly agreed that "it is, therefore, clear that the public now has a right to expect from this Board the preparation of a general and far-reaching system of rapid transit covering the whole City of New York in all its five boroughs."[93]

The now well-accepted RTC quickly obtained powers to oversee all tunnel construction and rapid transit development.[94] Simultaneously the board had Chief Engineer Parsons prepare a comprehensive rapid transit plan for the entire city. Early in 1903 RTC Counselor Edward Shepard, who had been with the commission since 1895, wrote optimistically to board member Charles Stewart Smith: "I am now very hopeful that the good ship Rapid Transit is to have a course not only prosperous (for even last year it was most prosperous) but also without serious trouble."

But a serene voyage was not in store. After the 1902 Brooklyn grant, the RTC never let another contract to construct and operate a subway. In 1907 the state abolished a much criticized RTC and replaced it with a public service commission. Events in the field of surface transit caused the first storm. As we have seen, the Metropolitan found itself in difficult financial straits after swallowing the Third Avenue system and spending several millions to electrify more than one hundred miles of railway. Facing demands to electrify more lines, criticism of its service and a new franchise tax which would increase its annual fixed costs by 25 percent, the syndicate in 1902 reorganized the Metropolitan into the New York City Railway Company. The move brought badly needed capital but only at the expense of converting the Metropolitan dividend into a 7 percent fixed charge.[95] Confronted with the imminent competition of the subway at a time when its strained finances could least afford it, the company faced bankruptcy.

As a solution Thomas Fortune Ryan sought a merger with Belmont's IRT. As the last active member of the syndicate, Ryan and the New York City Railway Company campaigned vigorously for a subway franchise which, when linked by free transfer with the street railway system, would rival the IRT. Privately Ryan threatened Belmont's hold on the IRT. With these tactics he blackmailed Belmont into a merger in December 1905.[96]

The newly created holding company, the Interborough-Metropolitan Company, now controlled all surface, elevated, and subway lines in the Bronx and Manhattan. Belmont turned over management of the lines to President Theodore Shonts, a veteran railroad executive and recent chairman of the Panama Canal Commission.[97] Under Shonts a centralized management was established with a line and staff structure to administer all lines. Thus the general manager, secretary, treasurer and heads of the legal, car and equipment, mechanical, and efficiency depart-

ments held the same position for the subway, elevated, and surface companies, and the formerly separate lines were now part of an integrated
transportation system.[98]

The system was probably the largest single public transit enterprise in
the world. In 1906 it transported over 800,000,000 passengers and operated transit facilities for 60 percent of Greater New York's population.
Along with the Brooklyn Rapid Transit Company, which monopolized
the elevated and surface roads of that borough, it carried almost
1,200,000,000 people annually, or 94 percent of all public transit fares in
the consolidated city.[99]

By this time the widespread popular interest in the subway, which had
allied business, mugwump, labor, and social reform groups during the
1890s, had become part of the progressive movement in New York
City.[100] Urban growth, the unification of the city, and the completion of
the first subway made New Yorkers even more dependent on local transit. By 1902 rides per capita exceeded 300 annually. The creation of the
giant monopoly further accentuated the transit issue so that the *Scientific
American* seriously proclaimed in 1907 that the "transportation problem
is perhaps the most serious that has confronted the city in the whole
period of its existence."[101]

Reformers, city planners, and businessmen and other members of New
York's progressive movement assembled, allied, investigated, reported,
complained, and lobbied. Their criticism focused on the inadequacy of
Greater New York's entire transit system, for despite the subway and
better surface facilities, crowding continued. The search for causes centered on the private operators and the RTC. Soon critics went beyond
documenting complaints about service to strike out at more fundamental
problems: the need to establish greater public controls over transit, to
come to terms with the consolidated city's powerful transit systems, and
to alter policy to satisfy present and future needs.

Agreement was difficult. Most reformers accepted the Board of Trade
and Transportation's statement that "commercial needs and social opportunity outweigh all other considerations. Increase of population without consequent increase of congestion constitutes the crucial City problem. Distribution of population over an ever widening area is the best
solution and adequate and cheap transportation between house and
work the first need to this end."[102] The problem was agreeing on solutions to insure adequate transit. Critics like Samuel Seabury took solace
in a devil theory which emphasized the plunder of the city's interests by
private corporations. Some investigators, like the Merchants' Association, listed specific complaints about service and appealed fruitlessly to
the State Railroad Commission for reform. Others joined the Municipal
Art Society's Committee on the City Plan to point out the failures of old

policies of fixed, piecemeal grants and to emphasize the need for greater public control and planning.[103]

Most analysts advocated greater regulation to protect the public interest, but varied as to its nature and direction. Reformer E. B. Whitney called for municipal ownership and public operation of surface but not subway lines; Samuel Seabury emphasized the subways. The New York Board of Trade and Transportation wanted a continuation of municipal ownership of subways and more control over their private operation through short-term franchises. Transit expert Milo Maltbie compaigned for an indefinite franchise terminable at the city's will with proper compensation to the operators. Politician Bird Coler advised a combined policy of municipal ownership and private operation, with city authority to operate if necessary. The Citizens' Union proposed city transit lines to compete with private companies. Milo Maltbie sought recognition of the monopoly and wanted a flexible regulatory policy in the public interest, while Seabury urged the destruction of the big companies.[104]

The RTC found itself caught in the middle of the public transit maelstrom. It had firmly resolved to pursue a policy of systematic planning and development of rapid transit subway facilities. But the commission's planning procedure and its desire to coordinate routes delayed construction. The RTC's policy compelled it to graft lines onto the existing systems: the IRT, the BRT, and (before the merger) the New York City Railway Company. In its negotiations with the giants the RTC strove for harmony and failed to take an aggressive attitude. As the commission expressed its philosophy in 1902: "It can hardly be doubted that, as from time to time it shall be the interest of the city to itself build any rapid transit railroad, which for public convenience and economic and efficient operation ought to be part of the system of the present Manhattan-Bronx and Brooklyn-Manhattan railroads, enlightened self-interest will dictate to their lessees a willingness or even desire to undertake them upon terms advantageous to the city."[105]

The RTC's strategy, the streetcar company's publicity campaign for a subway franchise, and a reform measure to provide tighter regulation, combined to bring confusion, delay, and inaction. In 1902 and 1903 the commission laid out a comprehensive plan, apparently aimed at the IRT and the BRT. In 1904 it stopped planning to negotiate with the New York City Railway Company when it promised to build a subway. The 1905 merger left the RTC in a quandary. Three years' negotiation had produced no new subways, and the board could no longer play off the IRT against the Railway Company. In 1906, reformers stimulated by the merger pushed through the Elsberg Law, which limited franchises for subway extensions to twenty-five years and grants for new subways to twenty years. The reform removed the stability and attractiveness of long-term contracts. In 1907, when the board opened bidding on its comprehensive system, it received no offers for joint construction and operation.[106]

Meanwhile, the jamming and jostling on the surface and elevated lines grew, and crowds packed the subway. Criticism of the RTC mounted. Its power of self-appointment, originally a technique to prevent Tammany control, suddenly became undemocratic. Reformers, suspicious of big business, criticized the commission as a haven for ex-presidents of the Chamber of Commerce, and in a soon-to-become-familiar theme, attacked the outside contacts of members and staff with those they regulated. "A self-perpetuating body, inbreeding has magnified original weakness," one critic charged.[107] Mayor George McClellan privately described the board as "a group of very worthy old gentlemen of large business experience but extreme old age, who nevertheless seldom died and never resigned."[108] Another critic felt that whatever their intention, the commissioners "have served well the traction interests and have miserably failed to protect the interests of the city."[109]

The RTC had assumed responsibility for comprehensive development of transit and had established useful principles and procedures to execute its functions. But it was undemocratic and slow and lacked adequate power to regulate service. Rapid transit historian James Walker best summarized the commissioners' work with empathy and discernment:

> They were condemned, not because they had not done well with the first subway, but because it was such a great success that they had not multiplied it fast enought to suit those who, now that underground travel was a demonstrated success, clamored for new underground roads all over the city! Because the old board had not ended the crush at the Brooklyn Bridge, because it had not built subways into Brooklyn, and Queens and in other parts of Manhattan, it was denounced by the press, which clamored for its abolition.
>
> [But] giving all due credit to the old Commission, it must be said in fairness that there was some ground for complaint. It procrastinated unduly, deliberating and negotiating when it should have been acting.[110]

Reformers found other city and state agencies just as ineffective, if not more so. The New York Board of Railroad Commissioners' primary interest and responsibility were the state's steam railroads. It was too remote from the local scene and seldom enforced its occasional recommendations.[111] In the past it had generally acceded to the wishes of the local transit companies, and in the case of disputes, played the role of arbiter instead of policy maker.

Nor could a city administration do much about service, even when motivated. Limited reform transferred the Board of Aldermen's consent powers for street railway franchises and RTC contracts to the Board of Estimate and Appropriation. To advise the board, reformers established a professionally staffed Bureau of Franchises. But the bureau could not lay out routes; it could only approve them or make recommendations. Nor did the shift of consent power guarantee harmony and efficiency. The Board of Estimate would be as contentious with the RTC and its successor as the aldermen ever were.[112]

Not surprisingly, when reformer Charles Evans Hughes became governor in 1907, he persuaded the legislature to revamp the regulatory system for public utilities and sweep away the unpopular RTC and the ineffective State Railroad Commission. In its place a state Public Service Commission for the First District (PSC) was created to control all public utilities for Greater New York.[113]

With a staff of 560 and an annual budget exceeding one million dollars by 1909, the PSC's responsibilities considerably expanded the duties of the RTC and the State Railroad Commission. Its greater authority and larger staff required a more carefully defined structure than was the case with the RTC's construction department and ad hoc committees for investigation. Its Bureau of Transportation could fix rates, prescribe equipment, establish forms of reporting and accounting, examine books and records, investigate complaints, order improvements, and regulate leasing and capital issue. To execute these duties the agency could issue orders which, if disobeyed, brought fines as high as five thousand dollars a day. The new commission had the power and expertise to regulate decision making by the transit companies in the public interest, but in line with past practice the PSC's emphasis continued to be the planning and building of transit facilities. Its Bureau for Subway Construction with a staff of six departments consumed 60 percent of the commission's budget.[114]

With some significant additions, the PSC was a fuller development of the public transit policy which had evolved in the 1890s. The PSC followed the pattern established in the laws of 1891 and 1894 for public planning, finance, and ownership of facilities to be leased for private operation. Like its predecessor the RTC, the PSC found itself bogged down in lengthy and time-consuming negotiations with recalcitrant city administrations and with the IRT and the BRT to obtain necessary extensions and new lines. Its techniques—a professional staff, finance by the city at its consent, and negotiation with private interests—paralleled those of the RTC. Its purpose—comprehensive development of coordinated rapid transit facilities for Greater New York—continued the policy set down by the RTC in 1902.[115]

The new comissioners had more varied backgrounds than the old ones.

But like the RTC administrators, they were not professionals. The RTC in 1907 had two politicians and six businessmen; the new commission was headed by two politicians, a businessman, a lawyer who had served as a public official, and an economist who was a utilities expert. There was no wholesale change to professional experts at the top; just a shift in emphasis from businessmen to politicians and public officials. Continuity extended to the staff where Chief Engineer George Rice, successor to William Parsons on the RTC, retained the RTC's divisional engineers.[116]

The advent of the PSC culminated a fifty-year period in the development of New York's public transit. The post-Civil War city's northward expansion had encouraged the innovation of a rapid transit system. Steam technology eliminated subways and instead encouraged entrepreneurs to build elevated railroads with only a slight adjustment in transit policy. Construction, ownership and operation remained the responsibility of private companies while the city ratified their decisions and smoothed their way with the 1875 RTC.

Elevated roads were only an interim solution. Their limitations, the indifference of their managements, and the tradition of passive public policy placed the burden of subsequent development on privately owned street railway lines. Sensing great opportunity, new entrepreneurs entered the field, and in the 1880s and 1890s united numerous horsecar lines into a single system. They substituted mechanical for horse power, rearranged lines, and added a transfer system to furnish the city with faster, cheaper, and more efficient service.

The rise of the new organization bankrupted a public policy which relied heavily on regulation by competition and the terms of perpetual charters. City government was unable to regulate service effectively. More important, its passive policy left it unable to respond to the need for additional rapid transit facilities caused by continued urban growth and the elevated's limitations. The industrial metropolis required an electric-powered subway, but the costs and risks of innovation and the restrictions necessary to protect the public's interest discouraged private development. The city's urgent need and the reluctance of private companies led to a public policy of direct action. To implement the new policy, the old rapid transit commission was transformed. At the city's request the state empowered it to plan and develop a city-financed and city-owned, electric-powered subway to be leased for private construction and operation. To plan and oversee construction the RTC added a professional staff for research, guidance, consultation, and inspection. But the completion of the subway underscored an imbalance in public policy: the city's regulatory role had failed to keep pace with its developmental one. The creation of the powerful PSC finished one cycle and laid the groundwork for future change.

The new active policy, which began in the 1890s and endured until the 1920s, was an accommodation between the profit-minded monopoly and public need. During much of that time local transit remained a strong and growing industry with enough profit margin to allow for adjustment between the public service and private profits. After World War I, conditions changed. The automobile, inflation, and the fixed five-cent fare combined to narrow the profit margin and flexibility for accommodation. The result was to be another major policy shift. Based on its experience and expertise, city government would assume the additional responsibility of operating facilities to protect its large investment in public transit and to insure continuance of a vital service for millions of people.

PART II

Curing Common Congestion:
Transit in Boston

AT FIRST glance the similarities between Boston and New York in the late nineteenth century are many. Both cities had begun as colonial seaports and at the middle of the century their business districts remained a small area near the old waterfront with water boundaries on three sides. Boston's population was fast growing, and by 1880 suburban growth was outracing the city. Within three decades both the city and its metropolitan population had doubled. In both cities the populace had spread out and the urban area had specialized by function. In Boston as in New York the growing number of immigrants, especially the Irish portion of the population, vied with older groups for recognition and power. Here too, an urban machine appeared, catering to immigrant support and coordinating a fragmented city government at odds with a Republican state legislature.

But Boston was not New York City moved to Massachusetts. Specialization and expansion came later. In 1880 its population was less than one third of New York's, and as late as 1910 it had not reached the million mark passed by New York in the early 1870s. Nor did the spokes of the Hub radiate across so large a metropolis as Greater New York. There was no merger comparable to 1898 and no annexation after 1873. Instead, metropolitan Boston, whose 1900 population was only 38 percent of Greater New York, extended across many small cities and towns, including Dorchester and Roxbury (already annexed) to the south, Brookline to the southwest, Cambridge, Belmont, Watertown, and Newton to the west, Arlington, Somerville, and Medford to the northwest and Charlestown and East Boston (already annexed), Everett, Chelsea, and Malden to the north.

The differences go beyond size and timing of growth. There was no Brooklyn to rival Boston, and consequently one transit system serviced the metropolis (excluding a suburban system along the North Shore). And because Boston was truly the area's hub, the evolution of its transit system and policy centered in the city proper. Thus while the system was a metropolitan one, the case focuses on activities and decisions within Boston's political boundaries.

Within Boston the contrasts with New York continued. Boston lacked the Empire City's long, straight avenues. Instead, the sea and the Charles River split the city into several regions linked by winding streets which met in downtown Boston. And just as intricate was the process which permitted the city's Irish political machine to strike an alliance with Boston's Bourbon Democrats.

Such differences distinguish Boston's transit evolution from New York's experience. Topography and timing of growth disqualified certain types of technology, notably steam elevated lines and cable roads, from Boston. Topography also precluded New York's plethora of independent firms and confined the business district to a very small area, making downtown congestion a much greater problem in Boston than in New York. And cooperation between Yankees and Irishmen helped preserve older traditions of public transit policy and sped the implementation of new policies.

Nevertheless, as a rapidly expanding city, Boston had much the same need as New York: mechanization to provide greater speed, range, and capacity in public transit. Once again mechanization raised challenges, not only for implementing new technology, but for innovation in transit enterprise and policy as well.

4.

Witches without Broomsticks

By the 1880s Boston was fast outstripping the capacity of its transit service. Horse railways could not effectively service the growing volume of traffic or the expanding area of the suburbs. Competition among seven lines led to congested streets and chaotic operation. As in other cities, mechanization was the solution. But as of 1885 there was no mechanical technology suited to Boston's needs. Bostonians opposed steam-powered cars as too dangerous, and street railway men rejected them as too expensive to operate. Electric power was still in the experimental stage. The cable system, effective in other large cities, was ill suited to Boston's narrow, curved streets. Furthermore, mechanization was too costly as long as competition produced needless paralleling of lines in some areas and the uncoordinated, joint use of tracks in others. Implementing new motive power would require strategic and structural innovation in enterprise as well as expensive technological change.

Boston and Its Horse Railways

Boston's transformation from the compact merchant city of the 1850s to the sprawling industrial metropolis of 1900 was well under way in 1880. Reclamation of the Back Bay area opened the way for residential dwellings to the southwest. Cambridge to the west and Charlestown to the north sent a stream of commuters into Boston. To the south Dorchester and Roxbury became major suburbs. In two decades their 1880 population more than tripled to 227,000, spread over a twenty-five-square-mile area. By the twentieth century's first decade the 1850 city with its two-mile radius had become a metropolis with a ten-mile radius and a population of more than one million.[1]

As the area of settlement expanded outward, the old city remained the "principal zone of work," to which large segments of the populace moved daily for labor, pleasure, and shopping.[2] The appearance of manufacturing, retailing, and financial centers and the construction of tall iron and steel frame buildings reflected the concentration of business in the central district. Meanwhile the continued specialization of area led to greater separation of home and work.[3]

As the city changed in scale and structure, traffic flows lengthened and grew more complex. The suburban population entered the city each day "along lines which may well be likened to the ribs of a fan," and at night left "along the same lines, but in the reverse direction." But winding rivers distorted and bent the ribs and specialization of area created a web of crosstown and inner city routes.[4]

Until the mid-1880s Bostonians relied on several means of public transit to service the growing traffic. Unlike New York, steam railroads were permitted to enter the business district. As early as 1855 an estimated sixty-five hundred trains ran over Boston's railroads, carrying more than twenty-four million commuters.[5] Nevertheless, steam roads transported only a decreasing fraction of local traffic. Prior to 1860 they had competed with stagecoach or omnibus lines running between Boston and its environs. Afterward they fought a losing battle with the horse railroads which succeeded the omnibus lines. In 1871 steam railroad traffic was one half the horsecar total. By 1890 railroad commuters were only one fifth of local traffic.[6]

Horse railways offered Bostonians cheaper fares and a wider network of routes. First built in Boston in the 1850s, they were a great improvement over the slow, bumpy omnibus lines which they soon replaced. The success of the first lines, the Metropolitan and Cambridge Railroad Companies, attracted numerous imitators. As in New York, each charter required a special act of the state legislature. The people of Massachusetts, who so jealously guarded control of their highways and streets, were unwilling to surrender that power even to cities and towns. In keeping with the generally limited powers of the nineteenth century municipal corporation, dominion over city streets remained with the legislature and the courts.[7]

The dominance, however, did not lead to the kinds of abuses experienced by New York City. As Oscar Handlin has shown, Massachusetts had long insisted on the public character and responsibility of corporations. As a result the regulatory tradition remained strong, even after the period of active state economic development slowed in the 1840s.[8] This power gave the state, and to a lesser extent the city, better control over horse railways. The Massachusetts legislature granted indefinite charters but permitted the mayor and Board of Aldermen to confer locations or franchises, prescribe fares, and regulate speeds, while the charters included such duties as paving, snow removal, and street maintenance. As in New York's early railway history, companies paid nothing for their grants, but neither did they get a franchise in the normal sense of the word. In Massachusetts a franchise was a permit, but not a right, to operate. It was not property and could not be capitalized. It had no definite term and was revocable at the pleasure of the local authorities.[9]

The creation of the Massachusetts Board of Railroad Commissioners in 1869 strengthened the state's role by exercising its power to oversee operation of street railways as well as steam railroads. Authorized to prescribe annual reports, to collect data, to examine corporate records, and to investigate street railway operations if requested by a locality, the board could recommend but not require changes. Instead, publicity and the indefinite franchise gave its recommendations teeth. Promoted and long headed by Charles Francis Adams, the three-man board generally had able and attentive administrators. Though its efforts were mainly directed toward steam railroads, the commission's limited powers, backed by publicity and threats of franchise revocation, provided unusual control of local transit.[10]

Although these policies moderated the abuses of overcapitalization and the misuse of valuable franchises characteristic of New York, they did not always work in the best interests of the public or the roads. To avoid overcapitalization the legislature empowered the Railroad Commission to approve stock and bond issues. Because of its sense of duty to the public and because of the difficulty of documenting costs before construction, the board was reluctant to permit securities issues before building. To avoid the problem, railway companies borrowed the money at short term and issued securities after completion of the work.[11]

The process was more costly but was not too objectionable as long as railways required little capital. After mechanization vastly magnified construction costs, the difficulty of borrowing millions instead of hundreds of thousands of dollars at short term became acute.[12] The practice held down capitalization, and cost figures on Massachusetts lines were considered the most accurate in the nation.[13] But it also increased construction expense and may have impeded extensions or mechanization.

As in other states regulatory policy rested heavily on the competitive forces of the marketplace. An early historian of Boston street railways observed that "the legislature of Massachusetts and the city council of Boston, being imbued with the feeling—almost universally held at that time—that the more competition there was in street transportation the better off the community would be, freely granted rights in the city streets."[14] The state chartered more than twenty companies for the metropolitan area.[15] As in New York the numerous lines meant overconstruction, fragmentation of routes, and more fares.

Fortunately, Boston lacked Manhattan's long, parallel avenues, which encouraged independent companies, for the sea and rivers segmented its topography. Within ten years of the first road's operation in 1856, local companies had combined into four roads to service the major areas of the city. The Middlesex Railroad Company served Charlestown to the north; the Cambridge Railroad Company covered suburbs to the west; the Metropolitan Railroad Company reached Roxbury and Dorchester to the south; and the South Boston Railroad Company extended through Boston's South End to the southeast. A fifth road, the Lynn and Boston, serviced communities along the north shore and entered the city by connecting with the Middlesex at Charlestown.[16]

Each of the four in-town companies established a regional monopoly and fought off or absorbed competitors. Each extended from its portion of the suburbs into the business district, where the four lines met at two common points: Scollay and Bowdoin Squares.[17] There were no crosstown routes, and few (if any) transfers. If the network was fragmented, at least it serviced the major traffic flows between the suburbs and the business district.

Faith in competition as a method of control continued to shape policy. Public complaints against the two most powerful companies, the Metropolitan and the Cambridge, led to the chartering of two rival, parallel roads in 1872 and 1881. Bitterly fought by the older companies as pirate roads, the new lines—the Highland and the Charles River Street Railway Companies—created excess capacity. Although their competition with the established firms brought lower fares and cleaner cars, both companies were shaky enterprises, later absorbed by rivals after years of unprofitable struggle.[18]

Crowded into a compact area one-mile long and one third of a mile wide, the business district illustrated in Map 5 now became the focal point of seven companies—the Cambridge, Metropolitan, South Boston, Middlesex, Lynn and Boston, Highland, and Charles River. Sixteen miles of track lay in crooked streets as narrow as ten feet. In addition, nature and history conspired to limit access to the old city. The harbor to the south and east and the Charles River to the north bounded three sides. Entrance from the west was complicated by steep Beacon Hill and the Boston Common, whose historical, social, and sentimental significance prevented their use. Entrance to the area was by bridge from the north and west and by Tremont and Washington Streets from the southwest. The *Street Railway Journal* explained that when cars "came from all parts of the vast system into the worm like lanes and narrow streets of this 'congested district,' they have to thread their way as best they can."[19]

Under the best of circumstances such conditions required skilled coordination. By the 1880s the fragmentation of transit lines and the jealousy

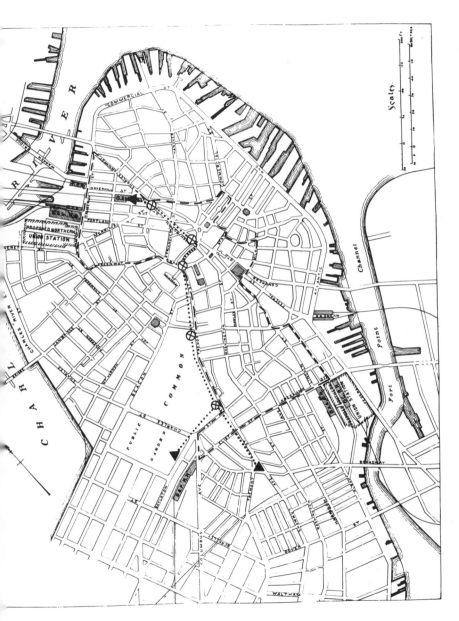

MAP 5. Boston's business district and subway, 1898. The congested area is outlined in a dashed line, and the route of the subway is traced in a dotted line. The circled crosses are subway stations, and the dark triangles are inclines to the surface. *Sources: Report of the Rapid Transit Commission to the Massachusetts Legislature, April 5, 1892, plate 7; BTC, Fourth Annual Report, endpaper map.*

and competitiveness of the roads entering the center city generated a
crisis. Entrance to the district was vital for each road's success, and the
limited number of entry points demanded a type of cooperation that
never existed. The city could and did compel extensive joint use of tracks.
The South Boston line, for instance, used more miles of the Metropolitan's track than its own.[20] Local government, however, could not force
cooperation. The presidents of the roads formed a "We-Are-Seven-Club"
and dined together regularly. Unfortunately, this effort to work for their
"mutual benefit" had little result. One of the participants remembered
that the meals were tasty, but that despite an air of candor, "the whole
truth was not always spoken."[21]

Instead, the combination of topography and competition led to chaos
and congestion. Wherever companies used tracks jointly they fought for
the lion's share of the traffic. As one company president reminisced:

> It is a well-known habit of the public to take the forward of two
> cars running near together, even if it be crowded; and the Met-
> tropolitan and Cambridge roads were at great pains so to
> arrange their time tables as to have a car to lead every car of
> other roads when on their tracks; and the other roads would
> keep shifting their time tables to prevent this . . . There was a
> general practice of racing to get in ahead; and the car that was
> left behind would then fall back and go as slowly as possible in
> order to get passengers from the car in the rear. All this led to
> blockades, accidents, and other serious injury to the service.[22]

What was more, as each company's cars crowded into the business district, they began to clog the tracks and the streets. By the 1880s lengthy
lines of cars crawling slowly along Boston's major arteries formed "blockades" which stretched as much as a half mile or more. Bostonians' complaints persuaded the City Council to limit the number of cars each company operated in the area. But compliance was spotty, for the roads
found themselves unable to live with the ordinance and at the same time
to serve a growing population.[23]

By the 1880s the congestion downtown and the expansion of the suburbs was already exceeding the abilities of Boston's horse railways. The
area's continued population growth and a suburban building boom
promised to exacerbate the situation. The increased speed and coordination necessary to service the emerging metropolis demanded fundamental
changes in public transit. Only combination, consolidation, and mechanization would satisfy the needs of the changing city.

Combination

In the mid-1880s, horse railway men in Boston, as did their counterparts
in New York, fully realized that machinery must replace the horse. The

suburbs grew faster than the city and gradually extended further from the business district, soon stretching beyond a four mile radius and the reach of horsecars. Traffic increased 150 percent in the 1870s to more than sixty-two million in 1879.[24] But because Boston expanded more slowly and reached metropolitan status later than New York, their rates of traffic growth differed. As Chart 4 indicates, Boston surface ridership suffered neither New York's slump in the 1880s nor its spurt in the 1890s. The differences were the result of timing. The saturation point of Boston's horse railways came in the 1880s, almost twenty years after New York, and relatively quick mechanization allowed a steady rate of traffic growth in the next twenty years.

The timing difference also meant that Boston skipped New York's early experience with rapid transit, for as we shall see in a later section, steam-powered elevated railroads were unpopular and ill suited. In addition, by the 1880s there were workable substitutes for the horse on street railways. By 1886 street railway men were examining both cable and electric power. Reportedly the Widener-Elkins group was considering the installation of a cable road in Boston. The presidents of the four established roads applied to the Board of Aldermen for permission to install a cable line on Beacon Street. But after giving "much attention" to the question of motive power, President Calvin Richards of the Metropolitan Company reported that he doubted the utility of cable power for Boston. He awaited instead the practical development of a storage battery system, whose installation would cost much less.[25]

The cable system, which represented the only feasible alternative to horse power in 1886, required an investment of more than $100,000 per mile. High fixed costs demanded maximum use of facilities, which was impossible to achieve with the chaotic scheduling of several companies operating over the same track. As one street railway expert observed, "The joint use of street railway tracks by different companies has become almost as impractical as in the case of steam railroads."[26] As in New York, the desire to mechanize rather than mechanization itself instituted change. Combination was again a prerequisite for the new technology.

By the end of 1886 Boston's transit companies had taken only limited steps. Some operators, like horse railway man Frank Monk, would continue to doubt as late as 1892 "that any metropolitan street railway can operate cheaper by electricity than by horse."[27] Others obtained legislation to permit combination, and two firms absorbed the Charles River and Highland Companies, which paralleled existing roads.[28] But no proposal evolved to unite all roads into a system. Before they developed such a plan, the four established lines were bought by the West End Street Railway Company, a new road chartered by a new man in Boston public transit.

With the backing of a syndicate of friends and associates, Henry Mel-

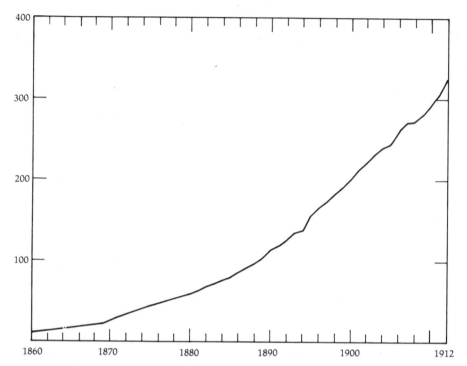

CHART 4. Boston local transit fares, 1860-1912 (in millions). Surface and rapid transit fares are for the Boston Elevated, West End Street Railway, and their predecessor companies. (The figure for 1910 is extrapolated from a report for nine months.) *Sources:* William H. Colcord, *The Rights and Wrongs of a Million: A Story in Four Parts of Street Railroading in Boston* (Boston, 1909), 15; Massachusetts Board of Railroad Commissioners, *Annual Reports* (1872, 1876, 1906-13); Louis M. Hager, *History of the West End Street Railway* (Boston, 1892), 125-126; West End Street Railway Company, *Annual Reports* (1888-97); Boston Elevated Railway Company, *Set of Exhibits Accompanying Statement of the Boston Elevated Railway Company* (Boston, 1916), Exhibit E.

ville Whitney entered the field of street railways without any previous experience. His brother William was already a leader of the group which was to dominate New York street railways, but Henry Whitney was not a member of that enterprise. Similarly, beyond the ownership of a small amount of stock, William apparently had no connection with Henry's Boston syndicate.

Despite his lack of training in local transit, Henry Whitney possessed attributes necessary for success. A friend listed determination, optimism, and vision as his outstanding personal characteristics. The wealthy son of a Jacksonian Democrat who had been collector of the port of Boston,

and a charter patron of the Young Men's Democratic Club of Massachusetts, Whitney rose to an influential role as an *éminence grise* in Massachusetts politics. He also inherited the ownership and presidency of his
father's Metropolitan Steamship Company, which supplied him with
capital and business experience.[29]

Although his character and background equipped him to unite Boston's street railways, Whitney's original reason for entering the local
transit field resulted from a real estate enterprise. He and a syndicate of
friends, including Eban Jordan, founder of a leading Boston department
store, W. W. Clapp, editor of the Boston *Journal*, and Albert Pope, a
bicycle manufacturer, chartered the West End Land Company and purchased five million square feet of land stretching along Beacon Street
from Boston into the town of Brookline. The syndicate planned to develop the tract as part of Boston's suburban building boom. The Land
Company, in which Whitney had half of the 250,000 shares, was established as a trust to manage the enterprise.[30]

To enhance the area's attractiveness the group hired Frederick Law
Olmstead, designer of New York's Central Park, to landscape a wide
boulevard as an extension of Beacon Street from Boston into Brookline.
To provide adequate transportation Whitney and his associates chartered the West End Street Railway as a subsidiary of the Land Company.
The Railway Company was to construct and operate a street railroad
along the boulevard between Brookline and the business district.[31]

At this point the new enterprise's need for mechanization spurred unification. Horse power was inadequate for the long, hilly route. The high
fixed investment for new motive technology demanded efficient operation, but the West End had to run over the tracks of other companies to
reach the business district. The old firms were not inclined to cooperate
in the construction and operation of a new, mechanized road. After having just absorbed the Highland and the Charles River Companies, they
bitterly opposed the West End as another interloper. The two oldest and
most powerful roads, the Metropolitan and the Cambridge, sought to
merge and freeze out the West End.[32]

Despite this powerful opposition, the politically well-connected Whitney obtained locations for his road from the Democratic-dominated
Board of Aldermen, and then discovered that franchises alone were insufficient. A long struggle promised to continue chaotic competition, exacerbate the already critical problem of congestion, and prevent mechanization. Whitney chose instead to absorb Boston's four major lines—the
Cambridge, Metropolitan, South Boston, and Middlesex—and consolidate them into a system. What had begun as an adjunct to a real estate
venture became a major transit enterprise.

In early 1887 Whitney and his associates began to purchase the stock of the established lines, and by June Whitney had control of all four. Simultaneously he used his political connections to overcome opposition to the emerging monopoly and to get special legislation to authorize the combination. The law permitted the West End to issue $12.5 million of 8 percent preferred stock to be exchanged for the stock of the old railways.[33] After several months of negotiation with the horsecar lines, the syndicate consummated the combination, and the West End absorbed all four roads.

Compared to the efforts of the New York syndicate, the West End combination was amazingly quick and simple. In less than a year a single firm without a complex network of overcapitalized subsidiaries replaced the city's quarreling roads. The West End became the largest single street railway system in the world and the first to provide unified operation of public transit in a major American city.[34]

Whitney's astounding success was probably due as much to the circumstances of his operation as to his abilities. Boston's topography eased acquisition by effectively limiting the city to four street railways instead of New York's fifteen, and fewer franchises lessened the combination's capital costs. Topography also confronted horse railway owners with a common problem of congestion on jointly used track. Yet they showed no inclination to assume the burden of change with its attendant costs. They were only too willing to exchange their prospects for fixed returns from preferred stock in the West End while Whitney and his associates as common stockholders assumed the risk and directed operations. As an additional enticement, the stock of the old roads could be exchanged for West End preferred at a bonus of some 20 percent.[35] Finally, credit for the simple structure of the monopoly and possibly for holding down unnecessary fixed charges was due in part to the Massachusetts tradition of public control. The populace and the Railroad Commission would not tolerate the overcapitalization and complex, secret network of corporations that characterized the New York combination.

Nevertheless, considerable credit must also be given to the West End syndicate and especially to Whitney as its driving force. Though he in effect stumbled into the situation, Whitney had the vision and determination to execute a new strategy. Although the precise source of his plan is unknown, the similar efforts of his brother and the Philadelphia group in New York certainly provided a model. Like the New York syndicate, Whitney made skilled use of political connections to overcome the objections of rivals and to obtain the legislation required to permit the combination and a subsequent change of power. He and his associates also financed the combination with a small outlay of actual capital, but, given Massachusetts' indefinite franchise, they used preferred stock with a fixed return in lieu of perpetual leases with fixed rentals to attract the owners of the old lines. Finally, like his New York counterparts, Whitney planned to consolidate his enterprise and mechanize operation for bigger profits and better service.

Consolidation and Electrification

Since combination was a response to the decision to mechanize, the quick merger of Boston street railways was only the initial change in local transit. To operate the acquisitions most efficiently, Whitney and his associates had to rationalize them into a system and build an organization to manage them. At the same time they had to substitute mechanical for horse power, not just on the Brookline route as originally planned, but on the entire system in order to increase speed and capacity and to meet the rapid growth of local transit traffic. Only in this way could they improve productivity, generate sufficient profits to pay returns on the preferred stock, and leave handsome dividends for themselves.

Rationalization began almost immediately. With more than 3,700 employees, 1,700 cars, 8,400 horses, and 200 miles of track, the West End was a gargantuan outfit for its day. Because the company had originally intended to operate only a line between Brookline and Boston, it had no management prepared to administer the new system. Whitney and his associates wisely relied on experienced personnel from the old roads. In November 1887 Prentiss Cummings, president of the old Cambridge Railroad Company, became vice president of the West End. Calvin Richards, who for sixteen years had operated the Metropolitan Railroad, was appointed general manager to oversee the daily administration of the system.[36]

Richards quickly adopted the line-and-staff structure pioneered by steam railroads and earlier used by him on the Metropolitan. He organized company lines into eight divisions, each headed by a superintendent who had held a similar position on the old railways. Each superintendent directed personnel, movement of passengers, and operation of equipment and car houses in his division. He reported to the general manager, whose staff maintained the system. The master mechanic serviced equipment and the roadmaster headed a department charged with building and repairing the lines. In addition there were a store keeper and a department of inspection to oversee and coordinate operations in the streets.[37]

The general manager reported to President Whitney and his staff, which included the vice president, a treasurer, a counsel, and an auditor. Policymaking and major financial decisions rested with an executive committee composed of the president and several members of the board of directors.[38] The system resembled in basic respects the one later adopted by the Metropolitan Street Railway Company in New York.

Along with organizational restructuring, Richards and his successors began to rationalize the West End's operations. They established a system of car color codes to identify routes and installed signs announcing car destinations. They reorganized routes, coordinated schedules, and eliminated blockades. Fares were standardized and some free transfer points established. Previously some of the roads had followed the European zone system with fares ranging as high as ten cents for a single ride. At Whitney's urging, the West End abolished zone fares and established a uniform nickel charge for any ride regardless of length. The flat fare provided a simple method for handling a high volume of traffic moving in diverse directions. It was also a definite saving to long distance passengers at the expense of short haul travelers.[39] Additional conveniences awaited mechanization. Crosstown lines and a universal transfer system only became feasible when a new motive power made longer routes possible.

The choice of technology for mechanization was more difficult for Whitney than for his New York counterparts. Their past experience and New York's topography made the selection of cable power easy. Whitney had no such experience and Boston did not lend itself to cable technology. Besides the high initial expense involved, the city's physical setting threatened even greater costs. Heavy traffic on narrow streets impeded streetcars. There would be problems in building and operating cable lines along curving roads. Boston's bridges also posed a considerable challenge, for no one had yet devised a cable system to cross a drawbridge.[40]

Neither Whitney nor his general manager had much enthusiasm for the costly cable technology, but Calvin Richards was certain that "horses will have to go."[41] To this operating man, even more important than the future demands of heavier traffic and longer routes was the current cost of horse power. His old Metropolitan road had more than four thousand horses, with an annual cost of nearly half a million dollars for maintenance and depreciation, and that figure did not include stables and interest on investment.[42] Now the West End was using twice as many horses as had the Metropolitan.

To cut operating costs, Richards advocated the electric storage battery. Batteries required no great outlay for power plants and conduit construction, and promised to be considerably cheaper to install than the cable. Yet the West End's experiments with the battery were unsatisfactory. Whitney and Daniel Longstreet, who succeeded Richards in 1888, reluctantly began preparations that spring for installation of a cable road.[43]

Whitney's continued skepticism paid great dividends. Still searching for a better alternative, he and Longstreet made an exploratory trip to study experimental electric systems in Alleghany City, Pennsylvania, and Richmond, Virginia. They found that Frank Sprague in Richmond had finally developed a practical electric-powered line: an overhead trolley system.

The advantages of the trolley over the cable were obvious. It was considerably cheaper. Powered by electricity supplied through overhead wires, the trolley required no expensive conduit construction or cable maintenance. It offered greater flexibility of car movement and speed. The operation of electric streetcars on Richmond's muddy streets, around its sharp curves, and up its steep hills convinced Whitney. Longstreet was more suspicious. Probably with the infamous Boston blockades in mind, he questioned whether Sprague could start a string of cars together on one stretch of track. The brash Sprague lined up twenty cars at the end of a day's run, routed Whitney and Longstreet from their hotel beds to witness the experiment, and successfully started each car, one after another.[44]

The Richmond operation excited Whitney and Longstreet to action. After other West End directors had examined that city's traction line, the company contracted with Sprague to build an experimental line in Boston. Its eventual success led to electrification of the entire system. Because of the skepticism born of the cable's expense and its unsuitability for Boston and because of the fortunate timing of Sprague's work, the West End became the world's first big city system to electrify.

Implementing the electric trolley raised more popular opposition than technological challenge. Installation and operation went relatively smoothly. Wherever electrification occurred, traffic increased so fast that the company could hardly keep pace. Though trolleys accounted for only one third of car-miles, operating costs fell from 75.1 percent of gross revenue in 1888 to 68.4 percent in 1891.[45] Study of operating expenses and profits convinced the company that trolleys had moved beyond the experimental stage, and the directors voted to electrify "as rapidly as possible." By 1892 electric cars accounted for two thirds of the firm's total car mileage; by 1894, more than 90 percent.[46]

Opposition stemmed from fear and ignorance, reinforced perhaps by a general suspicion of the powerful monopoly. Whitney's foresight and political connections in the legislature had enabled him to obtain permission to electrify as early as 1887. But Bostonians, including some street railway men, remained unconvinced. One West End director argued as late as 1893 that "it would have been better if it [the West End] had never adopted electricity."[47] Most residents, however, worried that overhead wires threatened fire and electrocution. Whitney wisely avoided confrontation and further unpopularity. Instead he experimented with the Bentley-Knight electric conduit system in Boston and built the overhead lines in the neighboring cities of Cambridge and Brookline. As expected, the failure of the conduit and the success of the trolley soon quieted critics. And in subsequent hearings before the city council and state legislature, the West End brought experts to explain the mysteries of electric operation and to allay fears.[48] By 1890 most Bostonians accepted the new technology.

In the early 1890s the West End offered the populace public transit that was far superior to that provided by the competing lines of 1886. Consolidation and electrification had temporarily ended blockades and increased speed, capacity, and range. The lines, which had carried 86 million in 1886, transported 137 million in 1894, an increase of 59 percent.[49] The company installed larger cars and extended its tracks to keep pace with the dispersal of the population into the suburbs. The high fixed costs of an electric trolley system (eventually about $86,000 per mile) led the West End to institute long crosstown lines to reduce turn-around time. As the growth of crosstown lines multiplied the points of intersection in the system, the company began to expand its free transfer system to generate more traffic and maximum use of facilities. As illustrated by the dark lines on Map 6, a nickel carried a Bostonian to all parts of the metropolitan area by 1896.[50]

The decision to electrify in 1888-1890 had other important consequences. The West End avoided the costly experimentation with cable technology that plagued the New York system and many others. As a result, mechanization proceeded more quickly and more cheaply. The company's fortunate choice of technology and its prudent management (encouraged by the state Railroad Commission's regulation) helped it avoid the rash overcapitalization which toppled the New York operation. By the early 1890s the West End was offering Bostonians faster, cheaper, and better service than could be found in other large American cities.

But even while it gave the metropolis service of unprecedented quality, the West End helped precipitate another transit crisis. As in New York, better local transit only encouraged more population growth and suburbanization. Soon, lengthening lines to the suburbs and increased downtown traffic challenged the capacity of the street railway monopoly.

The Need for Rapid Transit

As in New York City, the need for rapid transit could not be met by even the new technology—the electric streetcar. The alternatives to the trolley —elevated lines or subways—were risky propositions. Rapid transit required much larger amounts of capital than either the old horsecars or the trolley. In the United States of 1890, only New York and Brooklyn had high speed (elevated) lines. Entrepreneurs who wished to imitate the New York elevated roads could not ignore court awards for damages to abutters or the inadequacies of steam power for rapid transit.[51]

MAP 6. West End street railway system, 1895. The West End Company's system is marked by the dark lines. *Source: SRJ,* 11 (April 1895), 209.

Nevertheless, would-be builders like President Charles Powers of the Middlesex Street Railroad Company and New York speculator Moses Field Fowler, rushed to the Massachusetts legislature to get rapid transit franchises for Boston.[52] In 1879 when the first applicants appeared, the New York elevated lines were virtually complete and operating successfully. Their costs were not so readily apparent, and the steam-powered elevated railroads were the model for rapid transit entrepreneurs in Boston.

Through the 1880s Powers, Fowler, and others struggled unsuccessfully to obtain charters, franchises, and capital. The first efforts failed precisely because they were modeled on the New York City system. Since Massachusetts general railroad law forbade steam railroads from running through city streets, special charters were required. Powers and Fowler appeared before the General Court with arguments similar to those of the New York entrepreneurs. They frequently reminded legislators about the race to maintain Boston's place among east coast cities, the need for continued population growth, the advantages of expansion into the healthier suburbs, and the inadequacy of horse railways. And as in New York, entrepreneurs received support from suburbanites.[53]

But proponents quickly found themselves on the defensive. In their annual appearances before the legislature, they fought street railways, property owners, and rival elevated interests. In some cases horsecar owners themselves sought charters in order to prevent construction by others. Conscious of a powerful opposition which included some newspapers, Colonel Henry Lee of the banking firm Lee, Higginson and Company, Charles U. Cotting of the Fifty Associates (a group which had large investments in Boston real estate) and petitions from more than three thousand citizens, legislators were quick to point out the absence of overwhelming pressure for elevated lines in Boston. The city's metropolitan area was only four miles in radius, not nearly so extensive as New York's. Legislators argued that in this case the New York solution was unsatisfactory. In Boston's narrow, crooked streets the noisy, dirty steam trains would operate on massive platforms stretching from curb to curb. The technology acceptable on New York's long, straight avenues was clearly unsatisfactory to Bostonians in the 1880s.[54]

Nevertheless, the New York roads remained a compelling model in the minds of entrepreneurs. As new rapid transit promoters replaced Powers and Fowler, they, too, ignored the subway as an alternative. Instead, proponents of such systems as the Boynton bicycle and Macke overhead rail techniques tried to modify the steam-powered elevated road to make it more palatable. Among the modifiers, the most prominent and successful was Captain Joe Vincent Meigs. An engineer and inventor, Meigs doggedly sought to charter a steam monorail system for more than a decade.[55]

Designed in the late 1870s when steam was the only practical power, the Meigs system had an ungainly engine, tender, and car with both vertical and horizontal wheels running on a single rail. Meigs received a charter in 1884 on condition that he build an experimental line in East Cambridge and obtain approval from Boston's City Council. By 1886 the experiment operated, but with some structural weaknesses and maintenance difficulties. Hampered by a questionable technology and faced with possible damage costs running into hundreds of thousands of dollars, Meigs was unable to obtain the capital to build and his charter lapsed.[56]

Meigs' success in getting a charter was due to his political connections and not his innovation. As in the New York legislature, politics played an important role in Massachusetts railway grants, and Meigs allied with former governor Benjamin F. Butler. Butler's soft money policy and demagoguery were a stench in the nostrils of proper Bostonians, but his spoilsmanship and appeal to immigrant and working class voters generated considerable power in Massachusetts politics.[57] When he became president of the Meigs Elevated Railway Company, the firm got its charter. After its first grant lapsed, the Butler-backed group persistently lobbied for another charter until its second success in 1894.[58]

Butler's influence was not all powerful, however. Between 1887 and 1893 the Meigs interest took a back seat while Henry Whitney and the West End entered the field. As we have seen, Whitney had both money and political connections. A conservative Democrat, he found ready support from fellow party members who abhorred the demagogic Butler. Whitney became an important member of the peculiar Boston political alliance described in Geoffrey Blodgett's *The Gentle Reformers*. He and other wasp Democrats allied with Pat Maguire's city machine to supply top offices to prominent Yankees and "respectable" Irishmen, to provide the machine with recognition, funds, and patronage, and to avoid potential disruptors like Butler.[59]

Whitney's position in this association helped him obtain the legislation required by the West End in the city council and at the statehouse. Thomas Lawson, Boston businessman-turned-muckraker, later commented that Whitney "from his frequent dealings with the Massachusetts Legislature in obtaining franchises, had the reputation of carrying that body in his waistcoat-pocket."[60] Congressman Patrick Collins, Maguire's top lieutenant, was Whitney's close associate. Collins, future Governor William Russell, and former Governor William Gaston lobbied for the West End with the support of the Maguire machine. For further influence Whitney paid for favorable articles in Boston newspapers, and William W. Clapp, editor of the Boston *Journal*, became a stockholder in the West End enterprise.[61]

Along with the horse railway men, Whitney wanted no competition from an elevated road, but he also saw a role for rapid transit as part of an urban transportation system serving the metropolitan area. Like reformers and rapid transit supporters in New York City, he was solicitous for the city's future. Not surprisingly, Whitney's vision of the evolving metropolis dovetailed well with his suburban real estate and transit interests. As did so many contemporaries, Whitney extolled the suburbs as Boston's social safety valve. He explained to the public and the legislature that West End rapid transit lines fed by its streetcars would help prevent "vice and poverty and crime, by giving people a chance to get to the heatlhy suburban districts."[62]

The West End made two proposals for rapid transit. The first—an 1887 tunnel scheme—was quietly dropped after consolidation and electrification began to alleviate temporarily the congestion downtown.[63] But pressure from rivals quickly brought the West End back into the field. After fighting off charter petitions in 1889 from proponents of the Boynton bicycle, Meigs monorail, Macke overhead rail, and other systems, the company offered its own elevated plan to the 1890 legislature. Skillfully using newspapers, lobbyists, and political ties, Whitney and West End Counsel Henry Hyde successfully waged a campaign for an elevated charter. The new charter gave the West End the right to build and operate an electric-powered elevated road and even the right of eminent domain to acquire land necessary for stations and storage. Prior to building, Boston's Board of Aldermen and the state Railroad Commission were to approve all plans, and the latter was to pass on construction.[64]

Once again nothing came of a rapid transit charter. Although the West End began the action defensively, internal records indicate that it seriously planned to build a line. But the unsuitability of elevated technology in downtown Boston threatened high costs. According to Whitney, potential damage awards in the business district were large enough to kill the project. To lessen the expense the company sought to have the city lay out new streets as rights of way for the elevated. This effort, which paralleled R. T. Wilson's plan for mixed enterprise in New York, failed before the complaints of abutters and the protests of those who opposed public aid to a private corporation.[65] By 1891 the West End's elevated plans were dead. Even with electric power, elevated railroads were unsuitable for downtown Boston.

In the early 1890s Whitney and his associates began to realize that to try to provide the evolving metropolis with adequate surface transit was a self-defeating task. Like the New York group, the Boston men implemented new strategy, structure, and technology to create a mechanized transit system. And as in New York the result of their efforts was the reinforcement of the patterns which first created the crisis in local transit. Better transportation permitted greater spread of the population into suburbs and heavier concentration of business activity downtown. As the metropolis grew, the complexity of traffic patterns and the dependency of people on the transit system increased even faster: rides per capita rose at a rapid, steady pace from 118 in 1880 to 175 in 1890.[66]

Whitney's vision of a metropolis with downtown business district and suburban residences was widely shared by Bostonians.[67] His method of attaining that vision was not. As in the New York case, citizens accepted the advantages of a transit system but were suspicious of the monopoly necessary for its achievement. They wanted rapid transit but not the social and economic costs of elevated railways. By the early 1890s it was apparent that in Boston as in New York high speed lines in acceptable form could only come with a new, more active public policy to plan and develop future transit.

5.

Saving the Common
by Going into a Hole

As IN THE New York case, the pressure of continued urban growth in the 1890s quickly reached the limits of the new electric technology and the system created for its implementation. The innovations of private enterprise had provided only temporary amelioration and in the long run had exacerbated the problem. They attracted still more traffic and encouraged more expansion. Furthermore, the monopoly which accompanied those innovations became a vested interest opposing additional change.

Simultaneously with New York but for not quite identical reasons, Boston needed rapid transit. As in the other case rapid transit would compel a series of innovations. First and foremost a new technology was required to reach the expanding suburbs and to avoid downtown congestion. Building the electric-powered subway—the first to be completed and operated in the United States—generated critical problems not only of cost and risk, but also of routing—difficulties which necessitated major alterations in transit policy. Once again the challenges of implementing new technology were the focal point in the evolution of an urban transit system as the failure of private enterprise forced Bostonians to seek government action.

Groping for an Answer

By 1891 the West End Company clearly could not meet Boston's transit needs. Traffic had jumped by fifty-five million passengers or 93 percent in a decade and more than 25 percent since the 1887 formation of the company. Suburban expansion increased the radius of the metropolitan area from four miles in 1887 to ten miles in 1900.[1] The West End had only just begun to convert to electricity at the beginning of the decade, and its lengthening routes eventually exceeded even the one-hour range of trolleys.

But in the early 1890s the primary problem was increased downtown congestion. Trolley blockades .again became familiar occurrences. Particularly crowded were Tremont and Washington Streets, which carried most of the traffic between the business district and the southern and western suburbs. Even when there were no blockades, streetcars and other vehicles fought for space in the cramped streets. Travel through the business district in rush hours could consume a half hour or more.[2]

The West End soon became the target of widespread criticism. By making life hazardous for the pedestrian, the innovation of electric streetcars increased existing hostility to the monopoly. In horsecar days Bostonians had learned to adjust to the pokey cars by skipping across their path or by slowing them with a shake of an umbrella or a cane at the plodding horses. Electric-powered cars, however, failed to shy at waving sticks. A Bostonian often found himself hurrying from the path of one of the new-fangled "witches with broomsticks" (as Dr. Holmes called them), only to jump in front of another going in the opposite direction. Modernization indeed had its price, part of which was a new discipline for the foot traveler. " 'One generation passeth away, and another generation cometh,' and the passing of the first will be considerably hastened by 'this pestilence that walketh in darkness, this destruction that wasteth at noonday,' " wrote one Bostonian, whose own narrow escape was not an uncommon one.

> A few days ago I was so near being mangled or murdered by the broomstick train that even now I shudder at the recollection of my peril. I was crossing Milk Street, my mind busy and my heavy with the prospect of free silver, my eyes focussed upon the future rather than the present, when, presto! the clang of a bell at my elbow startled me.
>
> One leap from the middle to the side of the track saved me from being crunched by this fin de siecle monster gliding swiftly down the inclined plane of Milk Street, out of the control of conductor and motorman, and warranted to crush or kill man or beast in its relentless career.[3]

The West End's failure to build either a subway or an elevated road, after it had lobbied vigorously for each, further aggravated its relations with the public. Bostonians were already suspicious of its monopoly of a vital public service. Now the company's inaction contrasted sharply with Henry Whitney's grandiose rapid transit proposals. Critics overlooked the high costs and risks which discouraged innovation in rapid transit. Instead they accused the West End of acquiring charters in order to prevent competition.[4]

A legislative investigation of the means by which the company obtained its elevated charter reinforced the critics' position. The inquiry exposed the West End's lobby techniques amid charges of bribery and corruption. The company admitted paying newspapers for favorable articles, spending thousands of dollars to maintain a corps of influential lobbyists and financing dinners and meetings to entertain legislators. The investigation also revealed that the West End had bought out at least one of its competitors for an elevated franchise and campaigned for legislation to block the Meigs group.[5] Although the lobby was not unusual for corporations seeking legislative favors, the sensational revelations strengthened opponents' views of the firm as a powerful, grasping monopoly.

As a result of worsening conditions, inaction, and mistrust, critics began to urge a greater public role in transit development. In 1891 the Old South Society (which operated stores along the path of the proposed West End elevated line), together with the Massachusetts Hospital Life Insurance Company, several Boston banks and some of the leading property owners petitioned the legislature

> that the intrusting to a private corporation, or the local government of any one city or town, of the location of the first and necessarily main line [of rapid transit] involves too great a risk to the public interest.
>
> Wherefore, your petitioners pray that a law may be enacted requiring the appointment by the governor, with the consent of the council, of a commission of disinterested and expert persons who shall, after public hearing given to all parties interested, and after full investigation, prepare and report to a subsequent Legislature a plan for a system of elevated or subway railways, or of railways jointly composed of both kinds of railways, or for a system of such other railways as may be found best for the accommodation of public travel to, from and in the city of Boston; and that such further or other provisions of law be enacted as will give proper security to private rights, and promote the public interest and welfare.[6]

In the same year Bostonians elected a new mayor, who acted on this proposal and played a leading role in the decision for a publicly constructed subway. Historian Geoffrey Blodgett described Mayor Nathan Matthews as a "hardheaded, businesslike, and financially stringent" representative of old Boston society. A reputable Democratic lawyer, Matthews had an aura of Yankee respectability which allowed him to carry even Boston's Back Bay Republican district. He was the first mayor to wield effectively the new executive powers established by an 1885 reform charter designed to avoid the inefficiency and corruption of the old council-dominated government.[7]

The mayor was not just a reformer-businessman who represented the "better element." As a Democrat he was a member of the Yankee-Irish alliance mentioned earlier. Matthews owed his successful candidacy to Pat Maguire's machine, and in exchange Maguire required recognition and patronage. The allegiance gave proper Bostonians mayors whom they knew and trusted. Thus Mayor Matthews could urge efficiency in government and also support large public expenditures for rapid transit.[8] With proper leadership an active policy would benefit Boston and its citizens and provide jobs for Maguire's people.

Matthews entered office in January 1891 convinced that the pressing transit issue "should be met at an early date." He argued that city government should grapple with the question rather than leave it to private corporations. The mayor quickly petitioned the legislature for the power to appoint a five-man commission "to devise a plan for rapid transit that shall be permanently useful to the people and profitable to the city."[9]

As in the New York case, a Democratic city government with little power confronted a Republican legislature jealous of its authority. A compromise permitted the governor and the mayor to appoint jointly a commission to study all phases of Boston transportation—streets, railroads, street railways, and rapid transit. It would then report to the legislature specific solutions about locations, probable costs, and methods of implementation. The Rapid Transit Commission (RTC) reflected the Yankee-Irish alliance and the city's prominent business leadership and included Mayor Matthews, Congressman John Fitzgerald from the Maguire machine, financier Henry Lee Higginson, Boston *Herald* editor Osborne Howes, and banker and wholesaler Chester W. Kingsley. It represented a step toward rapid transit after several years of frustrating delay, but the little-noted struggle between the mayor and the legislature over appointments to the RTC was a portent of other home-rule battles which would later influence policy.

Beginning its work in the summer of 1891, the RTC held fifty-one public hearings. It listened to the proponents of numerous rapid transit schemes and showed particular interest in European transportation systems. And later the commission sent Howes and Fitzgerald to inspect the latest technological developments for public transit in such European cities as London, Glasgow, Paris, and Berlin.[10]

The European tour provided information but no simple answers. In choosing between technologies, Fitzgerald and Howes clearly favored American elevated railroads over tunnels (which ran deep underground) and subways (which operated just below the surface). The City and South London Railway, which opened in 1890 as the world's first electric subway, went several hundred feet underground and left Commissioner Fitzgerald with a "buried-alive" feeling in the narrow tunnel or tube. Waves of noise "like the roaring of the ocean after a storm" upset him

and Commissioner Howes. In addition there was a very noticeable temperature change, an alarming factor in a day when pulmonary diseases
were dreaded and little understood killers.[11]

Much older was the steam-operated Metropolitan subway opened in
London in 1863. The world's first public transit underground railway, it
resembled more nearly the line later built in Boston. Running just below
the surface, the Metropolitan was constructed not by tunneling as were
the deep lines but by a cut and cover method somewhat akin to ditch digging. Fitzgerald was not so critical of the Metropolitan, which he described as having more light and fresher air than the deep tunnel, a temperature more equal to that on the surface, and no intensive sound waves.
But as in the New York case, the use of steam power was a strong deterrent. Fitzgerald and Howes also disapproved of subways and tunnels
because of their cost and because of the American public's supposed
reluctance to leave the sunlight and go down into a hole.[12]

The subway was not without its partisans. Bostonian Henry Curtis
Spaulding enthusiastically advocated to the legislature, the RTC, and the
public at large two tunnel plans as solutions to Boston's problems. One
called for the construction of deep tunnels to allow quick passage for
steam railroads through the city. The other scheme provided for a network of subways under Tremont and Washington Streets to carry West
End streetcars under the business district and to permit removal of car
tracks from Boston's most crowded streets.[13] But Spaulding offered no
concrete information about cost or projected return, and no entrepreneur
stepped forward to implement his plan.

The unfavorable impressions of Howes and Fitzgerald and the inadequacy of Spaulding's plans had serious ramifications in the struggle for
better transportation in Boston. Subway proponents constantly had to
defend the practicality of their method and satisfy numerous questions
and fears. Supporters of elevated systems could readily point to roads
operating in this country and to the commissioners' favorable reaction.
In their eyes and in the public's view, elevated roads were both cheaper
and more natural. After all, as one anti-subway man put it, nobody
wanted to go underground before he had to.[14]

The RTC's report in 1892 dealt comprehensively with Boston's transportation problems. It called for the consolidation of steam railroad terminals to two union stations. To ease congestion in the downtown area,
it urged a series of street widenings and extensions. The problem of what
to do with the street railway tracks in the business district was left for
further study. To meet the city's future transit needs, the RTC mapped
out an elevated railroad network, leaving motive power unspecified
while excluding steam. When the line reached the business district, the
commission divided it to form a beltway around the area and recom-

mended that one branch go beneath the Common and the center city for about one mile.[15]

The RTC justified this apparent contradiction of its earlier condemnation of subways by the shortness of the line and "the apparent necessity of the situation."[16] As in New York the costs of a right of way and of damages to abutters in the business district were prohibitive. A subway under the Common and the city streets would have a free right of way, and unlike an elevated line, it would not darken and obstruct narrow streets with numerous posts supporting a massive structure.

In addition to its compromise on the type of transit, the RTC reluctantly explored the possibility of public finance and construction. The commission acknowledged "the dismay which falls upon a great body of intelligent citizens at the mere suggestion of such a thing," but it argued that if Boston built mains to transport water great distances, then it could transport the users of the water.[17] If the city could lay out roads on the surface, then surely it could build roads above or below the surface. If a government could erect a bridge, than it could construct an elevated railroad.

As a precedent and a model the RTC pointed to an 1889 sewage disposal act. By its terms the governor appointed a three-man metropolitan commission to build, maintain, and operate a sewage system for the cities and towns of the Charles and Mystic River Basin. A state bond issue of five million dollars funded construction. Annual fees were collected from the communities using the facility and paid into a sinking fund to service and amortize the bonds. The sewage commission divided operating charges among the municipalities on the basis of population.[18]

Similarly, the RTC recommended the creation of a metropolitan transportation district composed of Boston and its suburbs and placed under a commission appointed by the governor. With approval by the local authorities, the commission could widen and extend streets, purchase rights of way, and construct rapid transit lines to be leased for private operation. If there were no takers, then the commission itself should operate the line. In either case the agency retained control over "fares and all other important matters." As in the case of the sewage commission, a state bond issue was to fund the project. Interest and amortization costs were to be paid by the lessee as a rental fee or by the district communities if the commission operated the facility. District members would receive any surplus and were liable for special taxation to cover shortages.[19]

The RTC's proposal of public ownership was unusual, for municipal ownership of transportation facilities was rare in the United States.[20] As one expert put it, "those best informed believe that in most cases the results have not been satisfactory, and in many instances have proved disastrous."[21] Despite some unfortunate experiences, Massachusetts had a stronger tradition of government aid for public services than most states. Carter Goodrich, historian of public policy and economic development, described the state's experience with public aid as "quite exceptional." In the 1870s Massachusetts had built and operated the Hoosac Tunnel and had made loans to two Berkshire railroads.[22] And in the early 1890s the legislature responded to an increasing demand for urban services and made possible municipal ownership and operation of gas and electric light works.[23] Given such precedents, Bostonians could easily argue that subway building was as much a public service as street construction. This street just happened to run underground.

Furthermore, Massachusetts residents had always jealously guarded the control of their streets. As we have seen, streetcar franchises were a permission but not a right to use the highways. Cities and towns might "for any lawful purpose take up streets or highways traversed by street railways or may alter or discontinue the same as authorized by law, without being liable in damages therefore to a street railway company."[24] Viewed in this light municipal ownership of a subway, but not of the trains which ran through it, simply extended the policy of street control. An 1897 study of the relationship between municipalities and street railways explained that "the essential point . . . is the distinction . . . between the ownership of the pavement, and consequent full control of the street, and the running of the vehicle."[25] Public ownership of the right of way and private operation of the common carriers would insure both proper control and efficiency in local transit.

Finally, government-built systems in Europe were quite impressive. John Fitzgerald thought the Berlin Stadtbahn unsurpassed. It was both well built and well located. He commented enviously that he was "much afraid no private corporation could afford to build such a road here, but if built, no matter by whom, nobody will deny that it would be of inestimable advantage to the people of Boston and its suburbs, and would solve a great part of the rapid transit question with which we have to deal."[26] Though not attracting the fulsome praise of Berlin's viaduct, other government-owned lines were also described as satisfactory and profitable. Fitzgerald even included a description of the British Tramways Act of 1870 which empowered municipal corporations to construct and lease surface lines.[27]

Nevertheless, the tradition of public aid, the incipient trend toward municipal ownership of public services, the strong desire to maintain government control of highways, and the European examples eased but did not inspire the strategy of public construction. Nor was the impetus to be found among the reasons which had generated public support for transportation projects earlier in the century. According to Carter Goodrich the causes of early public promotion were insufficient sources of private capital, inexperience with large-scale corporate organization, and the developmental nature of the project.[28] None of those conditions applied in this case.

Instead it was the crisis in local transportation which forced the RTC to consider city construction as a solution. As in New York, the risks and costs of innovation and the public's hostility toward powerful monopolies made government action the only practical alternative. No businessman stepped forward with sufficient capital and suitable plans. Though capital was certainly available, the risk involved, especially the high cost of damages to abutters, deterred entrepreneurs. In addition, Bostonians' dislike of the West End monopoly was hardly calculated to encourage investors.

The Division of Policy

If Bostonians thought the completion of the Rapid Transit Commission's work was a signal for immediate development, they were sorely disappointed. The crisis was clear but the choice and techniques for solution were not. Most people agreed on the need for rapid transit but few supported the same technology and policy. Innovation of high speed lines was troublesome enough, but accommodating the new technology to Bostonians and their environment was even more difficult. As in New York the final form and route of rapid transit was settled in the public arena amid the swirl of politics and interest groups.

The RTC had clearly favored private enterprise. Its alternate recommendation for development by a metropolitan commission received little consideration. Although the legislature established such commissions to plan and construct parks, sewage systems, and water lines in the same period, these services were unlike public transit.[29] They lacked the opportunity for profits and a strong tradition of private enterprise.

The RTC's plan fragmented in the struggle of interest groups. From the battle among elevated enthusiasts, subway proponents, and supporters of various routes came separate policies. That part of the plan which was cheaper and more profitable—the construction and operation of elevated lines between the center city and the suburbs—was readily sought by private interests. But the building of a subway in the business district involved greater innovation, risk, and expense and promised no greater return. Because private enterprise offered no satisfactory solution, city government planned, financed, and built a subway.

As in New York the very real difficulty of developing a suitable motive power was apparently assumed to be a challenge for the builder. The choice was a complex, technical problem, and much more important in the public mind was the accommodation of rapid transit to the city. To a perceptive onlooker in 1892, the conflicting traditions of Bostonians made the situation appear hopeless. Citizens wanted both to rid the business district of congestion and to retain the convenience of curbside service. Boston's streets were too narrow and crooked to tolerate additional trolley tracks or an elevated road. Yet Bostonians showed no enthusiasm for subways and refused access across the Common for streetcars or elevated trains.

The rock on which comprehensive planning wrecked was the Boston Common. Boston's topography permitted only one inexpensive route—the Common. But at a time when the life and values of the old Boston community were challenged by immigration, expansion, and industrialization, the symbolism of the Common and the attempts to appropriate it to service the evolving industrial metropolis were all the more poignant. Ominously, the first mention of the Common stirred opposition. "A stake may as well be driven here that no such desecration of the 'people's birthright,' the Common, will be permitted under any circumstances," warned the editor of the Boston *Evening Transcript*.[30] Such sentiment was to prove a formidable opponent.

When the General Court convened in January 1893, it quickly submitted the ticklish question to its Committee on Rapid Transit. As the committee moved into public hearings, various suburban groups from Roxbury, City Point, and South Boston lobbied vigorously for rapid transit. For these people the simplest and most direct method was an elevated road from the suburbs through the business district via the Common.[31] As one advocate put it, "the sentiment which was formerly attached to the Common had to a great extent died."[32]

Schemes were soon put forward—one urging the widening of Tremont Street at the expense of the park, another advocating an elevated line along the mall's edge, and still another proposing to lay streetcar tracks straight across the Common and to grass over the ties, leaving only the rails visible. There was talk of repealing the statute which required a referendum for new uses of the Common.

Outrage and protest resounded up and down the eastern seaboard. Led by the *Transcript*, members of old Boston began a crusade. "A man who goes over the common when it is in its best trim, with no uplift in his soul because of what meets his eye," thundered the *Transcript*, "should have no other amusement than counting silver dollars the rest of his natural life."[33] One might as well cut the Bunker Hill Monument grounds into housing lots as submit to "suburbans and others [who] from one cause or another, somewhat coolly, advocate the surrender of the Common to street cars." Prophetically, the editor observed that "it would be cheaper for Boston in the end to spend fifteen millions of dollars for tunnelling than to give up its priceless jewel to the occupancy of shops and street traffic."[34]

"Friends of the Common need bestir themselves without delay" went the cry, and stir they did.[35] Letters poured in, not only from Bostonians but from states as far south as Virginia. One writer suggested that in the event of a referendum only bona fide residents of the original peninsula should vote on the issue. As he construed the debate, the struggle was between the actual residents and the "suburbans."[36]

When the West End Company tactlessly requested that the Committee on Rapid Transit hold a referendum on the operation of streetcars across the Common, the crusade for the defense reached fever pitch. "Distrust and suspicion of the means employed by this corporation to reach its ends are deeply seated in the public mind," accused the *Boston Post*.[37] Petitions of protest came from civic leaders, reformers, and the "women of Boston." The more than twenty-five hundred protestors included Julia Ward Howe and such names as Appleton, Ames, Bradford, Eliot, and Bigelow.[38] After vigorous opposition no one seriously argued that rails run across the Common.

In its efforts to improve service and maintain its monopoly, the West End then further muddied the issue with a preposterous tunnel scheme which played into the hands of those fighting the violation of the Common. The company's plan, as revealed in the *Transcript*, called for a sixty- or seventy-foot cut across the Common from Park Square to the mall at West Street. Here four acres were to be scooped out to accommodate a switching yard and station. From the station two more tunnels were to extend and pass under Park Street Church and the Burial Ground. The entire system was then to be covered with brick or cement, leaving about 330 holes for ventilation. Each hole was to be enclosed with an iron fence around its nineteen-foot circumference.[39] The project would destroy more than one hundred trees and leave the Common resembling a miniature oil field with 330 tiny derricks dotting the landscape. Needless to say, public outcry squelched this idea.

The tactless handling of the Common issue by various transportation interests was more than enough to spark a violent reaction. The West End plan tied the subway to the Common and made a mockery of both proposals. Guided by popular clamor and promoters' expectations of large profits, the legislature's Committee on Rapid Transit shied from the innovation of subways and quickly focused on elevated railroads. To resolve the problems in the business district, it looked to mixed enterprise to provide an alleyway through the business district for an elevated line. A transit commission appointed by the governor was to plan the $11,000,000 viaduct with the mayor's approval and to build it at the city's expense. To recoup the cost, the commission would auction the right to build and operate an elevated road in the alleyway. Since the city was to fund the scheme, Bostonians had to approve the idea in a referendum.[40]

Once again politics and home rule helped defeat a transit plan. Mayor Matthews, the Merchants Association, the Citizens Association (speaking for cost-conscious taxpayers), and a number of leading Bostonians criticized the alleway scheme. They wanted more local control with appointments by the mayor rather than the governor, and they argued that the RTC had rejected the plan in 1892 as too costly and inadequate. A survey by Mayor Matthews disclosed that the cost would be almost double the original $11 million estimate. In November 1893 the voters rejected the proposal by 3,000 votes out of some 50,000 cast.[41]

The closeness of the vote in the face of determined opposition reflected the mounting pressure, especially from suburbanites, to find some solution to the vexing problem regardless of cost. Of the nine wards (from a total of twenty-five) approving the law, six were in Charlestown, Dorchester, and Roxbury. The other three were in the North and South Ends. The proposed elevated line ran through or near eight of the nine wards.[42]

Many Bostonians felt that Matthews, after bringing about the defeat of the alleyway scheme, was responsible for submitting an alternative. Less than two weeks before the referendum, more than eight thousand Bostonians, including business and professional men, women, cabmen, and teamsters petitioned City Hall for the removal of streetcar tracks from the business district in order to end trolley blockades, accidents, and injuries.[43] Led by financier Thomas Livemore and Irish politician Thomas Gargen, the movement was another example of the Yankee-machine alliance that allowed prominent Yankees and "respectable" Irishmen to speak for a wide range of Bostonians.

More perceptive viewers argued, however, that even if the tracks were miraculously removed, nothing could prevent their restoration. Again tradition blocked a simple solution. As one newspaper editor pointed out, "where is the evidence that the people of Boston and its suburbs who so pertinaciously stick to the seats in street cars to the very last inch of the route, will welcome the advent of a new order of things causing them to walk a considerable additional distance in doing their shopping?"[44] Clearly Boston needed a solution that would permit both the removal of the tracks and continued public transit.

The failure of the West End Company and the elevated railroad proponents caused the mayor to turn to a hitherto ignored law. Apparently a backup measure to the alleyway plan, it provided that the mayor with the approval of the Board of Aldermen could appoint three commissioners to lay out and construct a subway under Tremont Street. The subway commission could purchase land and secure rights of way, hire engineers, architects, and other personnel needed to build the facility, and compel the West End streetcars to use the subway for compensation to be determined by the state Railroad Commission.[45]

The act amalgamated Henry Spaulding's subway plan with one proposed by the Boston Merchants' Association. Downtown retailers were especially aware of the transit crisis and were suspicious of the West End monopoly of a service so vital to their own well being. The association recommended a tunnel system under Tremont and Washington Streets (the center of the retail district) for better access to their stores because "our streets cannot be entirely for all the future given up to the tramway."[46] Of more importance, they went beyond Spaulding's vague assertions that somehow private enterprise would supply the required capital and proposed instead that the city alone undertake the construction and then lease the subway for operation by a private corporation.

With the backing of prominent businessmen, public construction aroused little opposition. As in New York, need overcame ideology. The reasons which had led the RTC to list city development as an alternative in 1892 were all the more compelling after eighteen months' frustrating delay. As one civic leader explained, no plan could "be adopted by a majority and the only way is to adopt some drastic measure and leave it to capable, disinterested administrators."[47]

The major drawback, as urban historian Blake McKelvey points out, was that "efforts to by-pass the ineffective city councils by creating bipartisan boards of public works sometimes hastened the development of boss rule."[48] All too often allies of contractors went into municipal service and awarded contracts to friendly firms for kickbacks. Thus local control over the commission and the character of the appointees were vital factors to insure efficiency and honesty.[49] Appointments by the impeccable Mayor Matthews and Bostonians' long experience with public commissions permitted them to support a subway commission with confidence in its success. The peculiar alliance of Yankees with Pat Maguire's machine once again assured that the "best men" would rule.

Bostonians' faith permitted them to go one step further than New Yorkers. Without a political machine as infamously corrupt as Tammany, and with a tradition of public control, they charged their agency with actual construction of the facility. A bill for city development by a locally appointed commission passed the legislature on the last day of the 1893 session.[50]

Mayor Nathan Matthews resorted to this act after the defeat of the alleyway scheme. He received active support from a delegation including Jonathan Lane, president of the Boston Merchants Association, George B. Upham of the Citizens Association, Thomas Livermore and Thomas Gargan of the track removal movement, and about one hundred of Boston's leading citizens and businessmen. As Martin Brimmer, prominent businessman and landholder, put it:

> The large sums which would be laid out on the other plans would be for the destruction of property the public come down

town to enjoy. You would spend these great sums of money in destroying the location of business of the retail trade of the city. This plan involves no destruction. All the money would be spent in construction. It seems to me this subject has been discussed for a sufficiently long time. Every plan has been explained, and the people understand the subject. The time for decision and action has arrived. I suppose the gentlemen present come here as I do to reach a prompt decision and action.[51]

The composition of the group and its concern for the business district made it clear that this gathering was interested primarily in the problem of downtown congestion. The failure to tackle the issue on a metropolitan basis placed the weight of planning on Boston alone. Not unnaturally, Bostonians chose to deal with their most immediate difficulty—transit in the business district. The decision to build a subway for trolley cars rather than high speed trains simplified the question of motive power, and the relatively easy project, involving less than one ninth the cost and distance of the New York subway, would be much less challenging. But, although the end of congestion would speed transportation through Boston, it would not supply a high speed line capable of twenty to thirty miles per hour. Rapid transit to the suburbs was left to private interests seeking elevated railroads. Separation of the subway from the elevated left the latter without a vital link through the business district and threatened to emasculate private development. This split set the subway and elevated groups at odds and delayed coordinated development of a rapid transit system until after the turn of the century.

Implementation of the New Policy

Actual implementation of the new policy by the new professionally staffed agency remained to be accomplished and would require accommodation by Bostonians and planners alike. The subway proposal had received little attention while Bostonians debated the alleyway plan. As in New York innovation meant overcoming inertia, political interests, and opposition from elevated groups. Bostonians' fears of potential health hazards in a subway and of possible irresponsibility by the new transit commission had to be assured. Finally, the 1893 law, which only outlined a policy for city planning, finance, and construction of a subway, required important amendments.

After City Council overwhelmingly approved the 1893 law, Mayor Matthews announced his appointments to the Subway Commission.[52] George B. Swain, a professor of engineering at M.I.T., already had served the state as an inspector of railroad bridges. Charles H. Dalton was a progressive businessman and a former park commissioner. The third member, Thomas J. Gargan, was a respected lawyer and former police commissioner, whose job on the Subway Commission may best be described as public relations and political guidance. Much more than a mere ward heeler, he had become the first Irishman to deliver Boston's Independence Day address and, as we have seen, was coleader of the track removal movement supported by so many prominent Bostonians.[53] His appointment was still another effort to assure the support of the Maguire machine and the Boston Irish for conservative Democratic policies. A local historian judged that Dalton and Swain were "peculiarly qualified for the service they were to render, while Mr. Gargan, a popular politician, was gifted with a variety of abilities which rendered him a practical working member."[54] In contrast to the New York experience, the Yankee-Irish alliance avoided stalling and opposition by the machine.

Since the 1893 law had been passed without serious professional study of routing, cost, or method of construction, the Subway Commission first reviewed the entire project and recommended an amended plan. As the result of a series of alterations and extensions, the estimated cost rose from two million to five million dollars (3.5 million for construction and 1.5 million for land acquisition and damages). City bonds with a maximum of 4 percent interest would fund the project. The rental received from the lessee (expected to be about 4.5 percent of the total cost) would be sufficient to service and amortize the bonds.[55]

In 1894 Mayor Matthews appeared before the legislature to urge passage of the amendments required by the commission's revisions. Before the Committee on Rapid Transit he argued strongly for the subway and the split policy. Millions of dollars spent for street widening had failed to reduce the congestion. The subway would permit the removal of streetcar tracks, end congestion, and provide rapid transit through the business district. Among all the methods proposed, the subway's costs exceeded only the route across the Common—which was politically impossible. Matthews further assured legislators that an elevated railroad could be built by private enterprise at each end of the tunnel. But the great expense, the problem of acquiring a right of way, and the pressure of downtown crowding required that the city build the subway immediately in order to get the trolleys off the streets and under ground.[56]

Subway supporters then paraded a series of professionals to answer the questions of the skeptical legislative committee about the new technology. Engineers testified that the subway would not only take the existing cars off Tremont Street but would increase their average speed and reduce trip time by one third. Furthermore, the subway could be built without permanently affecting the streets—except for the entrances—and without blocking travel at any point. Construction under the mall of the Common would not do any damage other than causing the removal of two rows of trees.[57]

Doctors from Massachusetts General Hospital and Harvard Medical

School testified that the drainage and ventilation systems planned for the tunnel would prevent serious health problems. Indeed, in the winter the subway would provide protection from the elements, and its shallowness would avoid a great contrast in temperature during the summer. Basing their statements not only on theory but on the performance of European systems, the physicians assured the committee that the subway was sanitary and safe.[58]

Finally, the familiar mix of businessmen, civic leaders, professionals, and other prominent Bostonians, including the heads of such local associations as the Municipal League, the Citizens Association, the Board of Trade, the Merchants Association, and the Real Estate Association, spoke for the plan. Letters from many of the merchants doing business on Tremont Street were entered in favor of the proposal. Herbert L. Harding, Secretary of the Citizens Association which had opposed the use of public money for the alleyway plan, appeared in support. The association was concerned not so much with the principle of public construction as with its practicality, he explained. The present scheme "would bring in a large measure of the public benefit and relieve congestion from Tremont St[reet] at the present time; and so far as approving the principle [of public construction] is concerned, they approved the principle to that extent."[59]

Opposition at the hearings was disorganized, misinformed, and often motivated by petty self-interest. Some people protested the construction under the Common, but the tactful handling of the issue by the commissioners, their explanation that there would be no permanent damage and that architects would design the entrances to harmonize with the beauty of the park satisfied all but the most fanatical. A few objected to the subway on principle. One pleaded with the Committee on Rapid Transit not to "have my mother or your mother have to go down in that tunnel with her grey hairs, not knowing where she is going." Another characterized the subway as a place for the West End Company "to put their customers into a long coffin underground for a few rods."[60]

For reasons not clear the West End Company joined the opposition. With a monopoly of local transit it was the obvious lessee, and the subway would resolve its problems of downtown crowding at city expense. Possibly the company resented the rental or the city ownership of the facility. More probably, it feared that some rival might use the subway as a central link for elevated lines to the suburbs. At any rate Counsel Henry Hyde harassed the subway commissioners and other proponents with picayune questions, exaggerated every possible weakness, and deliberately misinterpreted statements by witnesses in order to confuse supporters of the plan.[61] Because Bostonians were already critical of the company's stalling tactics, Hyde had little public influence.

He found ready allies, however, in others who were to cause subway proponents considerable trouble before the system was built. Republican representative Jeremiah McCarthy's Charlestown constituents had strongly favored the 1893 elevated plan which Mayor Matthews had helped defeat. McCarthy saw the subway as a political issue with which to embarrass Matthews and the Democratic party. Throughout the hearings he joined Hyde in agitation and misstatement designed to exploit various local fears. With the aid of elevated railroad proponents, McCarthy skillfully played on the belief that a subway would delay or prevent construction of an elevated line and stirred the opposition of suburbanites already skeptical of the tunnel's benefit to them. He denounced the proposal as a waste of money which would be better spent for relief of the poverty and unemployment resulting from the depression of 1893. McCarthy was joined in his attacks by Thomas L. Hart, a former Republican mayor of Boston. During the 1893 mayoralty election in which Matthews defeated him, Hart had staunchly opposed public construction as beyond the city's power and ruinous to private enterprise.[62]

Another critic who would eventually become very troublesome was Samuel Byrne. He spoke for Tremont Street merchants who feared loss of business during the disruption of the streets for construction and worried that the project would far exceed its estimated cost without popular control of the Subway Commission's expenditures. The danger of lost business during construction began to occur to other businessmen, and Byrne was able to persuade a few to retract their earlier support. As one of the merchants put it, the subway was an expensive folly, which would *"utterly ruin the business of Tremont Street and other valuable portions of the city."*[63] After more than a month of hearings, however, Byrne could gather less than twenty businesses to his side. Subway advocates had more than four times as many firms, plus the eight thousand people who had earlier supported the track removal movement.

But the influence of elevated railroad men and the vagaries of the legislature's Committee on Rapid Transit continued to complicate matters. The committee remained skeptical of underground lines and was much more enamored of the new elevated road it had seen in Chicago. Not a few members distrusted and disliked Mayor Matthews, whom they felt had double-crossed them by urging the defeat of the alleyway plan.[64]

In addition the alliance between the Irish and the conservatives in the Democratic party was coming apart. The depression following the panic of 1893 brought high unemployment to Boston. Politicians appealed to the mayor to create make-work projects. Though Matthews did his best to increase city employment, he refused to spend money freely for relief work. The subway, which would eventually provide hundreds of jobs, offered no immediate solution. As a result neither the project nor Matthews were viewed favorably by the jobless and their representatives.[65]

Meanwhile, Samuel Byrne's group rallied more merchants to its side

142 Curing Common Congestion

and formed the Merchants' Anti-Subway League. On April 30 Boston newspapers reported that the league was forwarding to the legislature a protest signed by three hundred but "understood" to have twelve thousand supporters. Besides complaints about the project's burden on the taxpayers, the petition declared that its signers were "merchants and property owners in the so-called 'congested district,' " and that they were "unalterably opposed to the construction of any subway in any portion of the city of Boston, whether for the alleged purposes of accommodating surface or elevated roads, or both." They were "convinced that such construction would seriously interfere with travel and traffic, proving ruinous to hundreds of merchants and in the end failing to relieve congestion or promote rapid transit."[66]

The combination of these factors plus the vigorous lobby by the Meigs elevated interests temporarily sidetracked the subway bill. Ever since his charter had lapsed in the late 1880s, Joe Meigs and his associates had campaigned before the legislature and the 1892 RTC for a new one. After Henry Whitney left the West End in 1893 to look after some coal mining interests, that company showed little concern for rapid transit. The door was opened for a group of politicians and speculators who used Meigs as a spokesman. The Meigs people exploited the desires of suburbanites for rapid transit and sought a new charter to operate an elevated line from Charlestown to Roxbury. Elevated and subway partisans fought bitterly and reinforced the split in public transit policy.

On the last day of the session, the legislature passed a compromise bill which chartered the Meigs group as the Boston Elevated Railway Company. The law also called for the governor to appoint two additional members to the 1893 Subway Commission, which now became the Boston Transit Commission (BTC). The commission was established for five years to construct the subway, a bridge across the Charles River to Charlestown, and a harbor tunnel to East Boston. The two rapid transit lines were kept separate. The subway was to be built under Tremont Street as planned, while the Boston Elevated line would run along Washington Street as it passed through the business district. Before any work, the entire act had to be approved by Boston voters.[67]

As in the New York case, popular feeling had compelled private interests to accept public action. Meigs still insisted on a steam-powered monorail and ignored the new electric technology. Damages to the Washington Street retail district would be large. Mayor Matthews and most Boston members of the General Court protested loudly, as did many of the same civic organizations previously supporting the subway and all but one of the Boston newspapers. The legislature still insisted on giving the city something it did not want, and the stench of boondoggle filled the air on Beacon Hill. As the Boston *Herald* reported, "It is . . . notorious that the [elevated railroad] bill, in the way in which it has been proposed, is one of the most scandalous pieces of legislation that has ever been brought before the General Court of this Commonwealth."[68] The situation became so ridiculous that Republican Governor Frederick Greenhalge threatened a veto unless a referendum was provided. Facing certain defeat, elevated proponents compromised and added the subway in order to attract enough voters to pass the referendum.

The strategy was successful though no one was entirely happy with the compromise. The Citizens Association refused to support the bill because of the Meigs provisions. But the pragmatic Matthews pleaded that rapid transit had been too long delayed and that "the subway bill simply has nothing whatever to do with the Meigs or any other elevated railway project."[69] In a special vote, the act passed with a thousand-vote majority out of twenty-nine thousand cast. Quickly Governor Greenhalge appointed two additional members of the RTC: George G. Crocker, a prominent Republican and former member of the state Railroad Commission, and Albert C. Burrage, a Republican lawyer and ex-member of the Boston Common Council.[70] On August 15, 1894, the Boston Transit Commission met and chose Crocker as its chairman.

The commission's composition reflected tradition and political compromise. Its three lawyer-politicians, one businessman, and one engineer resembled the membership of the state Board of Railroad Commissioners.[71] And the appointment of Crocker and Burrage acknowledged the state's voice in transit and provided a party balance. The agreement that permitted both city and state representation was probably necessary for passage, but it was nevertheless a partial home rule victory for a city which had only a few years earlier lost all control of its police commission to the state.[72]

Construction

The 1894 act signified the completion of one step in the process of innovation. The new technology had survived the play of interest groups, and the new technique of implementation had been fitted to the network of state and local politics. Now the city's new agency had to define its powers and demonstrate its capabilities.

The BTC's success in implementing the new policy brought the city a subway, convinced Bostonians of the wisdom of public development, and assured the agency's status. During the next four years the commission efficiently handled a number of functions, some specifically granted to it and others assumed as discretionary powers. Besides making preliminary studies, contracting for and overseeing construction, and leasing the line, it fought court battles, lobbied before the legislature, and acted as promotional agent for the subway.

To carry out their duties the commissioners quickly appointed a professional staff headed by Chief Engineer Howard Carson. Though originally only a small group reminiscent of the early canal boards, it expanded with the BTC's work and responsibilities while at times numbering over one hundred.[73] Carson, an M.I.T. graduate and former head engineer of the Charles and Mystic River Basin sewage project, proved to be an outstanding choice. He quickly initiated work for preliminary plans, test borings, and cost estimates. After receiving the staff's research, the BTC formally decided to build a subway.[74]

But before construction could begin, the commission had to fight for its life. Bipartisanship did not end hostility between a Republican legislature and a Democratic city. The BTC's vote for a subway antagonized elevated partisans. Suburban Republican opponents regrouped and almost repealed the subway acts of 1893 and 1894.[75] In response the commissioners conducted a shrewd public relations campaign. With state Senator Francis Kittredge as counsel and lobbyist, they convincingly detailed their progress and the benefits of a subway in appearances before the legislature, reports and pamphlets, and newspaper interviews.[76] Simultaneously they let bids, signed contracts, and broke ground for construction. Their explanations and actions aroused a public desperate for transit relief, and Governor Greenhalge's threat to veto the repeal bill stopped legislative activity.

Enemies of the subway were not halted immediately, but unlike the New York case their delays were brief. The support of Boston's local government for the subway and the commission contrasted sharply with Tammany's hostility to the New York project. Furthermore the Boston plan was much more modest and did not threaten the city's debt ceiling. Finally, although the opposition turned to the courts, the judicial branch in Massachusetts was sympathetic to the city's needs. The courts refused to grant an injunction forbidding the use of the Public Garden as an entrance. The Supreme Court, emphasizing the subway's acceptance by public referendum, unanimously upheld the constitutionality of the new policy and the BTC.[77]

Time spent in the courts and the legislature did not slow the work, which proceeded efficiently under Carson's guidance. The BTC sectioned the construction and contracted it out by bids. To direct, coordinate, plan, and inspect, Carson and his assistant George Rice assembled an enlarged staff of engineers, accountants, and other experts. They kept a tight rein on the contractors, pushed them to stay on schedule, and established a system of fines for violations of the time and space requirements of the contracts. In order to keep Tremont Street open during business hours as required by the act of 1894, the BTC used the London cut-and-cover technique for the near-surface subway. At night workers excavated a series of twelve-foot wide strips across Tremont Street, and covered and shored them with timbers. During the day crews continued the work of digging and construction while traffic moved unhampered above them. They moved materials and dirt through a twelve-foot square shaft at each of the strips, causing only a minimum of dislocation.[78]

With a sensitive eye to public opinion, Carson and the BTC assumed control of the more ticklish jobs. When a contractor slowly and inefficiently excavated a very narrow and busy part of Tremont Street, he forfeited his contract and the job was completed by crews hired and directed by Carson and his staff. When workmen tunneled into a cemetery, the BTC hired Dr. Samuel A. Green, respected ex-mayor of Boston and librarian of the Massachusetts Historical Society, to take charge of the problem. Under his direction workers transferred and reburied the remains of over nine hundred bodies. The commission reported that scrupulous care was taken "so far as is practicable under existing circumstances," and "whenever practicable, [the workmen] placed the bones of one body in a single box" and treated them "as if each bony fragment was now fully identified with the person to whom it formerly belonged."[79]

The staff itself also handled difficult questions about the Common. In the 1896 annual report the BTC proudly described the care taken with the trees and the improvements which resulted from the use of excavated dirt to fill and landscape the low, marshy parade ground.[80] At the completion of the subway in 1898, the commission restored the Common as nearly as possible to its former condition.

The BTC completed the entire project in less than four years. It opened one branch in September 1897 and the remainder a year later. Estimated at $5 million, the actual cost was only $4.2 million. To finance the job the city issued $4.5 million in 3.5 percent bonds maturing in forty years (except for the initial issue, which was at 4 percent). So great was confidence in the commission that the public fully subscribed the bonds, which sold for a small premium.[81]

To operate the facility the BTC negotiated an exclusive contract with the West End Company, the only serious bidder. In an agreement similar to British arrangements mentioned by Howes and Fitzgerald, the company leased the line for twenty years for an annual rental of 4 7/8 percent of the total cost. It agreed to equip the subway and run in it all the electric cars which had operated on Tremont Street above. Fares would remain a nickel, and transfers would continue as before. All equipment was to be safe, convenient, and first rate. Protection of the public's interest rested with the state Railroad Commission and the BTC. The former was to regulate operation while the latter maintained the facility itself. If the West End Company defaulted on the contract, control of the subway reverted to the city.[82]

The project's completion amply fulfilled the expectations for the new policy. The BTC clearly demonstrated its capacity as the city's agent to plan and build a rapid transit line. It finished the line swiftly, efficiently, and honestly, and it negotiated a lease that incorporated the line into the local transit system at a rate calculated to defray the city's cost.

The subway itself was a tremendous success. It doubled the rush hour speed and capacity of the old surface lines. All streetcar tracks were removed from Tremont and Boylston Streets. Blockades disappeared and congestion lessened. Average travel time from Pleasant Street to North Station fell by one third, and Bostonians were quick to use the nation's first subway.[83] Park Street station became one of the busiest railroad stations in the world, handling over twenty-seven million passengers a year. An estimated fifty million people used the line in the first eleven months of operation. Rental receipts averaged just over $200,000 annually—enough to service and amortize the city's bonds.[84]

Opponents and critics soon quieted down. "Croakers [who] predicted that its cool, damp depths would breed colds and pneumonia, [and] that the public would respectfully decline to use it" were clearly wrong.[85] When tested, the air in the tunnels proved purer than that "usually provided in halls, theatres, churches, schools, etc."[86] Skeptical merchants became firm supporters. In 1898 vaudeville impresario B. F. Keith, originally an opponent of the subway, reported happily that there had been no drop in property values as a result of the new line, but there was "on the contrary, a demand for store property from a high class of merchants."[87]

The pioneering facility attracted widespread attention. *Harper's Weekly* thought the subway had "demonstrated at once its value as the key of the rapid-transit problem in [Boston] . . . The effect was like that when a barrier is removed from the channel of a clogged-up river." The *Electrical Engineer* congratulated "everyone, from the transit commissioners, chief engineers, and contractors, down to the laborers toiling in the dirt."[88] Pictures of the subway at the Paris Exhibition were awarded a Grand Prix. And when Lord Kelvin visited Boston, he hurried to the subway before having his dinner and "pronounced it an engineering marvel."[89]

The development of the Boston subway was a remarkable story. At a time when municipal governments in the United States were considered the nation's greatest failure, Boston's government quickly and efficiently built a new form of transit—a subway line that still serves the city. With the new policy came a new, professionally staffed commission as an agent for municipal government. The BTC implemented the new policy which gave Boston a modern transit system, while leaving intact the Boston Common and the values it symbolized for the older community.

The Unification of Policy
As in the previous case, the success of the new technology and policy signaled more action than equilibrium. The first subway solved one prob-

lem and raised several new ones. The suburbs still lacked rapid transit. The split in transit policy prevented adequate coordination for future development. The new subway's success led to demands for funds for more underground lines and for a permanent commission. Finally, the eventual merger of the elevated railroad interests with the West End confronted Bostonians with an even more complete and powerful monopoly of local transit.

Neither the Meigs group, charted in 1894 as the Boston Elevated Railway Company, nor the West End Company attempted to build the proposed elevated line from Sullivan Square in Charlestown via Washington Street in the business district to Dudley station in Roxbury. The former had a weak charter and relied on steam power. Headed by financier Charles Whittier, the Boston Elevated Company remained a speculative enterprise whose hope for profit rested on the sale of its charter rather than on operation. Within a year the group offered the charter to several interests, including the West End, but that company also declined to build an elevated line.[90]

After the departure of Henry Whitney in 1893, the West End lost its previous aggressiveness. As the investment bankers Lee, Higginson and Company gained greater influence, the directors became more cautious. Elevated lines would cost almost ten times as much per mile as street railways.[91] The millions required would decrease dividends to the investors represented by the bankers. In the 1894 subway hearings the company offered opposition but no plan. It became preoccupied with daily operation and public criticism. Management especially feared that popular hostility to trolley wires and the success of the electric conduit in New York might compel the company to abandon the overhead technology for an expensive underground system. The West End directors ignored a Boston Elevated offer to sell for $150,000 and concentrated instead on adjusting trolley routes to the new subway.[92]

The caution of the West End management apparently dissatisfied some of its major investors who recognized the benefits of adding an electric-powered elevated line to their system. The group, which included department store owner Eben Jordan and lawyer William A. Bancroft, allied with investment bankers Kidder, Peabody and Company (which controlled a substantial amount of West End stock) and J. P. Morgan and Company.[93] As in New York the bankers supplied the capital and skills to reorganize the West End Company and finance construction and equipment of the high speed line.

This new syndicate bought control of the Boston Elevated Railway Company from the speculators in 1895 and established a new directorship. William A. Gaston, son of a former Massachusetts governor and adviser to recent Governor William Russell, became president. William Bancroft was made vice president and managing director. Other directors included Eben Jordan, Francis H. Peabody and Robert Winsor of Kidder, Peabody, and Jacob C. Rogers, a banker representing J. P. Morgan.[94]

The new directors moved quickly to implement their charter and establish a monopoly by taking control of the West End Company. They realized from the first the benefits of a unified public transit system. They wanted the Tremont Street subway as a downtown link for the proposed elevated road and the streetcar system as feeder to both the subway and their planned elevated line. When a group of West End directors, backed by Lee, Higginson and Company, proved recalcitrant, a proxy battle in 1896 led to their replacement by men friendly to the Boston Elevated Company. Offering West End stockholders the advantages of consolidation and stock options in the Elevated Company, the Boston Elevated negotiated a twenty-year lease of the West End for a 7 percent return on its common stock.[95]

The Boston Elevated swiftly consolidated its operation. It employed the same line and staff structure and kept most of the West End management. To operate the elevated line it was building from Charlestown to Roxbury, management simply added another division to the structure. It adjusted streetcar operations to feed the rapid transit lines and extended the free transfer system to cover both surface and high speed roads. When the electric-powered elevated opened in 1901, the Boston Elevated was operating a unified streetcar and rapid transit system whose 300 miles of track serviced most of the metropolitan area and transported over 222 million passengers annually, an increase of 33 percent over the West End operation in 1896.[96]

Simultaneously, the company used its political power to strengthen its position. Both Bancroft and Gaston were prominent in local party politics and helped maintain the West End's powerful lobby at the Statehouse. And like so many public service companies, the Boston Elevated's large work force provided jobs for politicians' followers in exchange for needed legislation.[97]

In 1897 the company sought charter amendments to confirm its hold on local transit. It obtained rapid transit franchises for all major locations in the area, explicit permission to substitute electric power for Meigs' steam locomotives, and authorization for its lease of the West End and for rerouting the elevated line into the subway. This amendment to the 1894 act also guaranteed the nickel fare and granted the company immunity from special taxation for twenty-five years. To avoid the vagaries of local politics, the power to revoke franchises was vested in the state Railroad Commission rather than in Boston's Board of Aldermen.[98]

In exchange the development of Boston's rapid transit was clarified. The 1897 act extended the life of the BTC, which would continue to plan and build Boston's rapid transit facilities until replaced by a city transit department in 1918. The law empowered the commission to build one new project and two old ones listed in the 1894 law—a subway to Cambridge, a bridge to Charlestown, and a tunnel to East Boston. As in the case of the first subway, the BTC was to plan, construct, and administer these city-financed facilities. The Boston Elevated agreed to lease and operate them as part of its transit system for annual rentals which would defray the city's cost. The mayor and the Board of Aldermen received the right to approve the route and construction plans for the Charlestown-Roxbury elevated line, at least four miles of which would be built within three years.[99]

As in New York, the rapid rise of the powerful transit monopoly roused serious concern, especially among progressive reformers. Initially the firm fell heir to hostility directed toward the West End Company, which had antagonized Bostonians in several ways. For a decade the West End monopolized local transit but built no rapid transit lines. It fought development of the subway. Its wires webbed the air and its cars blockaded the streets. Finally, it annually returned healthy profits and was suspected of concealing even greater ones.[100]

More immediate was the fear that the 1897 act somehow permitted the Elevated Company to escape the traditional regulation of transit companies. Because the Boston Elevated was established at a time when public transit was booming, Bostonians expected that its guaranteed nickel fare would generate huge profits. The considerable interlocking of stock ownership between the West End and the Elevated convinced many that the lease was a trick by West End owners to avoid public control. Thanks to the provisions of the 1897 law, city government could not tax the Boston Elevated, compel it to reduce fares, or enforce regulation through the threat to revoke company locations.[101] Achieving a total monopoly in less than two years, the company had exclusive rights to all rapid transit lines and operated all surface roads.

In fact, the Boston Elevated's privileges and profits were not excessive. Though exempt from special taxes, the company had to obey all general tax laws past and future. Its nickel fare was standard throughout the nation. As for profits, the West End had returned an ample but unspectacular 7 percent, and with its huge investment in construction and equipment, the Elevated could not be expected to pay more than 7 percent on its own stock.[102]

The transfer of powers for fare setting and franchise revocation from the city to the state Railroad Commission and the company's exemption from special local taxation were not unusual. They were among major reforms recommended by a special state investigation, and in 1898 they became part of general street railway law.[103] Electric technology and mergers increased the complexity of regulation and the range of companies, carrying them beyond the skill and boundaries of local city councils. Only the Railroad Commission had the expertise to regulate stock issues, mergers, accounting, and taxation. With these reforms and the efforts of the Railroad Commission, Massachusetts had the most effectively regulated street railways in the country.[104]

Nevertheless, the Elevated did pose a serious challenge for Boston. Development of public transit was divided between the BTC and the company, and already Bostonians suffered one penalty from this partition. Despite repeated promises that the subway could accommodate elevated trains, the fit was unsatisfactory. Engineer Carson explained lamely that the BTC had thought only streetcars would use the subway. Only after adjustments in platform heights and tolerances between the walls and tracks could the longer elevated cars use the facility. Even then they were slowed by tight fits and sharp curves.[105]

Advocates of local regulation or ownership of urban services sought unification of transit policy under the BTC. They wanted city control of what was clearly a local service. Led by Louis D. Brandeis, then a young and respected Boston corporation lawyer, and by George Upham, a reformer who had advocated the first city-built subway, the group was small at first. It struggled hard to limit the monopoly's increasing power by preventing long term leases, exclusive contracts, and costly agreements that might siphon off excess profits from the public pocket. In 1896 it persuaded the BTC to lease the subway for twenty instead of fifty years. It successfully urged the Railroad Commission to limit the Boston Elevated's lease of the West End to two decades and to reduce the rental from 8 to 7 percent. In 1897 it unsuccessfully fought the charter amendments sought by the Elevated Company.[106]

Reformers' efforts brought only limited success. The company still controlled all three forms of local transit and obtained the amendments it wanted. Public control advocates remained few in number. Most Bostonians, including influential civic leaders, merchants, and other businessmen, remained apathetic about city regulation. What they wanted most was the better transportation promised by the Elevated.

But the inadequacy of the Tremont Street subway for rapid transit, the disadvantages of elevated railways, and a blunder by the Boston Elevated Company reawakened public concern. The Brandeis group built on that anxiety and mounted a campaign that finally unified transit policy and assured city control over the monopoly.

Damage costs for elevated lines and the success of the subway soon convinced the Elevated management of the subway's superiority, particularly in the business district. It built its elevated road only in the suburbs and decided to construct a subway as a central link under Washington Street in the business district. Until the new tunnel was completed, the company used the Tremont Street subway as its downtown link. At the same time it sought to switch streetcar operations from the subway to the surface to make room for the elevated trains.[107]

These decisions antagonized Bostonians. The prolonged four-year battle which ensued between the company and the public ended with the monopoly's acceptance of public control. To Bostonians the return of the streetcar tracks threatened blockades and slow service—the very things that had compelled them to approve a city-built subway. Downtown merchants and other businessmen, prominent citizens, and public control advocates erupted in protest. In a referendum Bostonians voted against the proposal by almost two to one.[108]

Undaunted, the Boston Elevated pushed ahead with its plans for a badly needed Washington Street subway. When the Citizens Association approached it with a proposal for public construction on the Tremont Street model, the company precipitated another battle. It convinced the association to amend the proposition to permit the company to build and own the facility. The revised plan offered better transit without public expense and appealed to that conservative group. For the monopoly it would be cheaper than rental of a city-owned facility, but more important, permanent control instead of a short term lease made the company more secure. Its search for security thus directly challenged the tradition of local regulation based on short tenure, antagonized Brandeis and the public ownership advocates, and aroused the public's latent hostility toward the powerful monopoly.[109]

Brandeis and his associates had little difficulty generating resistance to the Elevated Company's plan. As in New York, various business groups recognized their vital stake in local transportation and fought to control the company. The Associated Board of Trade, the Chamber of Commerce, the Merchants Association, the Produce Exchange, and leading Boston professional men rallied behind Brandeis to form the Public Franchise League. And as in New York, though business and professional men led the movement, they had widespread support from other groups, including reformers, settlement house workers, and representatives from the Teamsters and the Central Labor Union.[110]

Despite the company's considerable influence at the Statehouse and its support from the Citizens Association and Republican Mayor Hart who staunchly opposed city construction on principle, it had to capitulate to its formidable and widespread opposition. By 1902 the Boston Elevated had completed its elevated line to Charlestown and Roxbury. Traffic was increasing by 4 percent annually, and every year of delay confined the company to the inadequate Tremont Street subway. Because profitable operation was more important than absolute control, the Boston Elevated accepted a lease for a new city subway at 4.5 percent for twenty-five years.[111]

The 1897 act and the Washington Street battle fixed the basic outlines of public transit operation and policy for Boston. They essentially guaranteed the position of the private monopoly under public control. They provided for the construction of a rapid transit system which remains the core of Boston's transportation network. And they firmly established a unified policy of public finance, construction, and ownership of rapid transit lines. In sum they marked a formal recognition of the industrial metropolis' need for a coordinated transit system and for an active public role in its development. As Brandeis remarked, "Boston has thus, it is believed, established conclusively the policy of retaining control of its transportation system, and also of securing co-operation (although at present but a small one) for the use of its streets by railway corporations."[112]

In a pattern remarkably similar to the New York case, public transit operation and policy had been radically altered to fit the requirements of the changing city. When the owners of Boston's various horse railway companies proved unable to improve service and meet the city's rapidly growing need for swift, cheap, and efficient transit, a new man stepped in. Henry Whitney implemented the same strategy and structure that was being developed by the New York group. He combined the quarreling horsecar companies into a single enterprise, consolidated lines into a unified network, and replaced horse power with electricity.

A coordinated and mechanized street railway system, however, could not meet all the transportation needs of the evolving industrial metropolis. Its contributions to public transit only reinforced the patterns of population growth, suburban expansion, and increased concentration of business activity in the center city. Crowded streets and lengthening lines of travel necessitated rights of way separate from the streets to allow faster movement.

Because entrepreneurs could not reach a solution both profitable to them and suitable to the public, Bostonians turned to public enterprise. At the request of leading businessmen, professionals, and reformers, the legislature empowered city government to assume a new role. Through the agency of a professionally staffed commission, it implemented a new public transit policy to plan and build a city-financed and city-owned subway.

The success of the new subway, the continued urban growth, the merger of surface and rapid transit interests into a powerful monopoly, and the desire to perpetuate a strong tradition of public control over local transit combined to make a permanent policy of what had been a pragmatic response to particular conditions. As in New York City, the new policy led to public construction of the core of the city's present mass transportation system. Municipal ownership and private operation endured for a quarter of a century until automobile competition and rising prices reduced profit margins and then brought financial losses. Then Boston, like New York, took on the responsibility of operating as well as developing its transit facilities in order to protect its considerable investment and to provide a public service vital to the industrial metropolis.

PART III

Public Transportation
in the Private City:
Transit in Philadelphia

TIMING and topography differentiated the New York and Boston cases. In Philadelphia politics and an unusual dependence on private enterprise had a similar effect. Like New York and Boston, Philadelphia grew in the late nineteenth century, but more slowly. In 1880 the city had almost 850,000 inhabitants and spread across all of Philadelphia County as the result of an 1854 annexation. Thirty years later the same area contained 1,500,000. Perhaps Philadelphia's smaller immigrant influx accounts for part of the growth rate. In 1910 only one in two Philadelphians were of foreign birth or parentage in contrast to three of every four in New York and Boston.

Despite the smaller immigrant base, Philadelphia, like the other two cities, had a political machine, and in this case the machine was even more powerful. Because both state and local machines were Republican, they reinforced one another rather than clashing as was the case in Boston and New York. Philadelphia had neither the reform cycles of New York nor the Yankee-Irish alliance of Boston to ameliorate boss politics. Under Jim McManes, David Martin, and Israel Durham, the machine marched on with only limited interference from the 1870s to the twentieth century's first decade.

The machine's power and the graft and inefficiency that resulted from its control of the city gas plant and other municipal services deterred extension of public ownership and operation. Consequently, when urban growth required new technology for public transit, Philadelphians looked to private enterprise, which responded earlier and more extensively than in the other cases. Mechanization of street railways and the evolution of a transit system began in Philadelphia before either of the other cases, and only here did transit operators proceed to construct an expensive combination of subway and elevated line for rapid transit. The Philadelphia case, then, focuses on the pioneers who conceived, financed, and operated the first mechanized surface system and on their efforts to resist the changes in transit policy which the implementation of rapid transit brought in New York and Boston.

6.

Politics and Enterprise

AFTER THE Civil War, Philadelphia's transportation situation in many ways resembled the New York and Boston experience. In the 1870s private enterprise operated a badly fragmented public transit service, rapidly growing more inadequate with the evolution of an industrial metropolis. Mechanization and the accompanying innovations in strategy and structure fell to a group of entrepreneurs who entered the field through local politics. By 1896 their electric-powered system monopolized public transit, and they fought or ignored demands for rapid transit as the city's growth outstripped the capacity of street railways.

Along with these similarities to preceding cases, however, the evolution of Philadelphia's street railway system raises several interesting questions. Since entrepreneurs began responding to the challenge of urban growth and expansion here before they did in New York and Boston, what were the sources of their innovations? Since they began to mechanize before Frank Sprague's Richmond experiment, how did they settle on cable technology for motive power? Finally, why did the leaders of the transit monopoly, after vigorously opposing rapid transit lines, suddenly decide to build the nation's first privately owned subway at a cost of millions of dollars?

The City and Its Horse Railways

In 1880 Philadelphia was the nation's second largest city. Its population of almost 850,000 had grown 26 percent in the previous decade and would nearly double during the next thirty years. Situated between the Delaware and Schuylkill Rivers, Philadelphia expanded along a north-south corridor until a sufficient number of bridges across the Schuylkill encouraged westward growth at the end of the century.[1] As Map 7 sug-

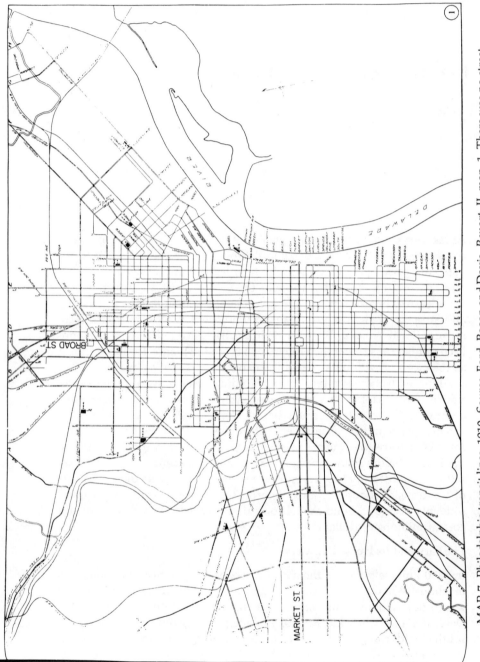

MAP 7. Philadelphia transit lines, 1910. *Source:* Ford, Bacon and Davis, *Report,* II, map. 1. There was no street railway on Broad Street.

gests, the street pattern was the typical grid, centered on Broad Street as a north-south axis and on Market Street as an east-west axis.

Area specialization had begun by the 1850s. Larger segments of the population were moving away from the center city toward the outskirts. The southside was rapidly becoming a sweatshop and slum area. To the north and northwest moved "the skilled and well-paid [who] abandoned the old office and mill districts to seek at the outer, growing edge of the city the amenities of new houses, more light and air, larger yards, new schools and income homogeneity." In the center city and along the Delaware River, manufacturing, finance, and retailing continued to grow as the commercial city became an industrial one.[2]

By the 1860s the trend toward separation of home and work was well established. Historian Sam Warner estimates that perhaps one third of the manufacturing workers commuted to jobs. Philadelphians' avoidance of multi-family dwellings reinforced the dispersal of population. They took pride in Philadelphia's reputation as the "City of Homes." One source claimed that 85 percent of the city's dwellings were inhabited by one family each. Some 84 percent of New York's population lived in buildings with more than ten persons, but only 12 percent of Philadelphians did.[3]

Area specialization and increased distances underlined the dependency on public transit and the inadequacy of Philadelphia's facilities. The city's street grid was ill suited to carry the flood of commuters that flowed daily along radial lines in and out of the business district.[4] Narrow streets constricted traffic, and increasing numbers of passengers overburdened horse railways better fitted to the old commercial city than to the evolving metropolis.

As in New York and Boston, horsecars were the backbone of Philadelphia's public transit. After the first road opened in 1858, its success encouraged considerable imitation. By 1865 more than twenty companies had appeared, and the omnibus—the previous mode of public conveyance—had virtually disappeared.[5] Horse railways were a definite improvement on omnibuses, but they were open to much criticism.

Street railway development was uncoordinated and unsystematic. Competition was thought to be the best regulator of the public interest, and charters were numerous. Routes generally followed the old omnibus lines and the profit expectations of entrepreneurs. Most roads ran from some point in the suburbs to a point in or near the business district. Although a few lines operated east-west between the Delaware and Schuylkill Rivers, the majority extended in the north-south direction in which the city was growing. Because of the uncoordinated routing, most Philadelphians paid at least two fares when traveling between home and work.[6] Tracks and cars crowded already cramped streets. Each narrow avenue held only one track, and companies had to operate on two streets —one going and one coming. As a result, Philadelphia had more miles of street railway than either New York or Boston—an amount equal to one third of the city's total street mileage.[7]

Public opposition and hostility paralleled the experiences of Boston and New York. Criticism initially stemmed from conservative property owners and timid souls opposed to change and fearful of injury. The roads' success quickly silenced these protesters but did not still censure of the charter process. In Pennsylvania as in New York and Massachusetts, municipal corporations were virtually powerless before the state legislature, and Philadelphians had no voice in the conferring of charters. Nor was there a general law for the incorporation of street railways. The legislature freely gave influential entrepreneurs the use of city streets in perpetual, exclusive, and remunerative grants. Their holders often earned 10 percent or more on an investment that, after the initial period of construction, had little risk. Among angry Philadelphians there was a "universal suspicion" that greedy legislators sacrificed the city's interests for bribes, stock options, and other favors.[8]

As in the previous cases, the stench of corruption, the imposition of the state's power on the city, and the gift of city streets for private profit fostered hostility toward street railway companies.[9] Such enmity smoldered for long periods and surfaced when the companies sought special concessions from the city or became embroiled in some local controversy. Furthermore, the public's anger and Philadelphia's limited powers in the face of perpetual, exclusive charters shaped local regulation of horse railways. After failing to obtain a voice in or compensation for the grants, citizens encouraged the city council to enact other kinds of controls. Typically such laws ordered companies to pave and maintain streets, to remove snow, and to pay car license fees and excess profits taxes. One law even permitted the recapture of charters by the city if companies refused to offer adequate service.[10]

These instruments were the only means by which the locality could exert some control over its public transit and receive compensation for its valuable rights of way. The Pennsylvania legislature, always mindful of the powerful Pennsylvania Railroad, did not establish a state railroad commission, which might have provided some regulation as the Massachusetts commission did. And the legislature lacked the time, expertise, and desire to take on the task.

Unfortunately, Philadelphia's sporadically enforced laws furnished more revenue than regulation. Writing in 1930, one expert estimated that the city's street railways "paid a larger return for their privileges during the first half century of their existence than were required, until recent years, by any other American city."[11] The city's paving ordinance eventually forced the companies to replace inferior cobblestone surfaces with more expensive Belgian block and asphalt, and laws for street maintenance and snow removal offered Philadelphia valuable services at no direct cost to taxpayers. But the recapture clause went untested and provided no control over operation. As in the New York and Boston cases, the absence of authority, expertise, and public interest left vital decisions about routes, technology, and schedules to the companies' owners.

While the municipality's policies furnished little regulation, they had a negative effect on performance. Taxes on dividends above 6 percent encouraged watered securities or litigation to avoid payment. License fees of fifty dollars per car brought revenue but discouraged the operators from providing additional capacity. Philadelphia's paving laws were harsher than in most cities. They required companies to pave and maintain the entire width of the streets on which they operated rather than the area between the tracks. The high costs—somewhere between fourteen and twenty million dollars in the first half century of operation—consumed capital and were a potential deterrent to extensions. Another ordinance required that rails be five feet two inches apart—the width of wagons. To avoid rough streets, wagon traffic soon took to the rails and slowed or blocked cars.[12]

Such regulations proved costly for the public and local control. Companies at first ignored or disputed obligations and left streets untended. Application of city ordinances sometimes conflicted with charter provisions, generating slow and expensive court battles. As a result, Philadelphians lamented street conditions while the responsibility for them lay in doubt. Furthermore, the price of the paving eventually performed by the street railway companies became a tax on riders. Fares remained six or seven cents per ride in Philadelphia after dropping to five cents in New York and Boston. Finally, irritation with local regulations spurred the railway companies to persuade the legislature to reduce the city's power still further. The so-called Railway Boss Act of 1868 ordered the city not to regulate street railway companies without specific authorization from the Pennsylvania Assembly.[13]

As in New York, protest over inadequate local control and complaints about influence peddling in charter grants brought limited reform. The new constitution of 1874 forbade special charters for railways. Municipal consent was necessary for any further street railway construction. This sop to local regulation meant little, however, because reformers enacted no general law to permit incorporation of additional lines.[14] Ironically, this failure, prolonged by opportunistic street railway men, prevented new competition and allowed existing companies to consolidate their positions. Not until the legislature enacted a general law in 1889 could new companies enter the field.

Stabilization did not necessarily mean better service, for horse railway operators made little effort to improve accommodations. President John Morton's experiments with steam-powered cars on the West Philadelphia Street Railway failed. The cars' noise, dirt, and clumsiness made them unpopular, and apparently their investment and operating costs were too high. Steam power was adopted on only one line—a suburban route to Frankford.[15]

Owners also made little effort to coordinate operations. As in Boston, they organized a Board of Presidents to "reciprocate information, confer and consult upon subjects of common interest, so as to enable and induce the Companies represented to act in unison and to contribute to expenses for the common benefit of all." The board served as a loose association to regulate fares and avoid rate wars. It forbade free transfers but took no action to coordinate either service or management.[16]

Meanwhile the pressures of urban growth continued in the late 1870s and early 1880s. Philadelphia population neared the 900,000 mark. Real estate development grew in the north and northwest as suburbanization continued. The West Philadelphia Street Railway Company crossed the Schuylkill and began to transport residents from the west bank who streamed toward the center city. Traffic increased and lines lengthened. The need grew for radical alterations in local transit.

New Men and New Strategy

That need promised bountiful profits to entrepreneurs with vision and ability. As before, mechanization and combination required large investment, and the risk was even greater than in the previous cases. In the late 1870s there was no ready substitute for the horse and no model of large-scale street railway enterprise. Once again the source of radical change in street railway development came from men whose business experience began outside the industry.

When William Kemble, Peter Widener, and William Elkins created a new strategy for Philadelphia transit, only one had operated a horse railway. With this limited training, they mechanized and unified city railways into a system which brought large profits for themselves and better service for Philadelphians. Eventually the entrepreneurs' success led them and their imitators to repeat the process in municipal utilities in other cities and to alter fundamentally the organization of urban public services throughout the nation.[17]

All three began their careers as businessmen, and two moved into politics as well. William Kemble, age forty-seven in 1875, was the oldest. New Jersey born and educated at the high school level, he operated a general store, imported lace, and manufactured brushes. After some experience in Pennsylvania Republican politics, he came to prominence as an agent for federal revenue stamps during the Civil War. In 1864 he joined with other Philadelphia politicians to charter the Union Passenger Railway Company, of which he became secretary. Kemble continued to combine business and politics while serving three terms as Pennsylvania State Treasurer after the war. By the 1870s he had become one of the four leaders of Philadelphia's political machine, and as president of the People's Bank of Philadelphia, he controlled state funds deposited with the bank and was an influential source of money for both the state and local machines.[18]

Like Kemble, who was six years his senior, Philadelphia born Peter A. B. Widener mixed business and politics in his early career. After a grade school education he became a butcher and entered ward politics as a Republican. During the Civil War Widener received lucrative contracts from Simon Cameron, secretary of war and boss of Pennsylvania's Republican party, to supply meat to troops in the Philadelphia area. With his profits he opened a chain of meat markets, bought 225 shares of Union Passenger Railway stock, and began to invest in suburban real estate in northwest Philadelphia. Widener also continued his political activities and became city treasurer from 1871 to 1873. But in 1877 he sought and failed to obtain nominations as Philadelphia's mayor and as state treasurer. Thereafter he concentrated on street railways with Kemble and William L. Elkins, a friend who had bonded him as city treasurer and who was an associate in his real estate ventures.[19]

The West Virginia born Elkins, though two years older than Widener, was his junior partner. When oil was discovered in western Pennsylvania in 1859, Elkins left a produce and poultry firm and entered the oil refinery business. After considerable success, he sold out to the Standard Oil Company in 1875. Though reputedly friendly with the Standard Oil people, he did not become active in their organization. Instead Elkins began investing in gas illuminating firms and joined his friend Widener and William Kemble to enter the Philadelphia street railway business.[20]

The three men's business experience, access to capital, and political connections equipped them to dominate the local transit scene. Kemble had allied with the Don Cameron-Matthew Quay Republican organization, which controlled the state legislature, and both he and Widener were influential with the Republican city machine.[21] Their ties were vital to smooth the way for legislation, charters, and franchises and to thwart opponents. Widener's and Elkins' profits in early enterprises and Kemble's position as a bank president provided the capital necessary to enter the street railway business. And finally, all three had managed their own firms and were well known to the Philadelphia business community.

In the absence of precise information, we can only speculate about their reasons for getting into local transit. As in William Whitney's case in New York, urban street railways offered to talented and well-connected men a field free of established and powerful barons. The constitutional reforms of 1874 blocked new competition. Kemble had served as the Union Passenger's secretary for a decade. And like Henry Whitney in Boston, Widener and Elkins had extensive suburban real estate investments which may have attracted them to street railways.[22]

As models for their strategy, Kemble, Widener, and Elkins had two famous examples of earlier efforts to unite independent companies. Closest at hand was the Pennsylvania Railroad, whose management had only just completed the assembly of a self-sufficient interregional system in 1874. To the main line the managers had leased and merged other roads to create a trunk and branch network. They organized the road into three divisions and developed a line and staff structure to administer them. The powerful corporation employed Kemble as a lobbyist, and its history was certainly known to the three men.[23] In addition, Elkins had been a part of John D. Rockefeller's efforts to weld competing firms into a unified organization in the oil industry. But Elkins' part in the creation of Standard Oil was small. The similarity between railroads and street railways and Kemble's apparent leadership in the combine suggest that the Pennsylvania Railroad supplied the model for the pioneer efforts to combine and consolidate Philadelphia transit.[24]

Kemble probably began to develop a strategy of combination while serving as secretary of the Union Passenger Company. Headed by State Treasurer William McGrath and numbering politicians Jacob Ridgway and William Leeds among its directors, the Union was one of the city's most successful roads. With valuable north-south and east-west lines, it connected northern suburbs with the business district at Market Street. Political clout carried the road further in 1873 when its owners compelled the West Philadelphia Street Railway Company to allow the Union to reach Delaware River ferries via the former's Market Street tracks. By 1874 Union patrons could ride to and through the business district for one instead of two fares.[25]

Kemble sought to apply the continuous-ride technique to a larger field. The Union would become the trunk line for a system that ran through the heart of the business district and branched into the northern and western suburbs. When his associates balked, Kemble joined Widener and Elkins to proceed independently.[26] The three men formed the Continental Street Railway Company and set out to capture the Union, whose valuable locations made it an ideal base for the system they envisioned.

To protect themselves from political raids by their opponents and to assure necessary legislation, the trio wove a web of political alliances to the city and state machines. Robert Mackey, former state treasurer and a member of the Quay organization, joined the Continental's board of directors and succeeded Kemble as president in 1877. Matthew Quay himself became a board member along with Widener and Elkins. In 1879 Elkins became aide-de-camp to Pennsylvania Governor John F. Hartranft, while Quay served as president of a subsidiary line. Speaker of the Pennsylvania House William Elliot, another Quay ally, acquired four hundred shares of company stock, and Jim McManes, the boss of Philadelphia, also became a stockholder. The board of directors eventually included representatives for McManes and for William Singerly, head of another faction in city politics.[27]

Kemble, Widener, and Elkins built their road as skillfully as their political base. Using a tactic employed in railroad wars, they constructed the Continental's route parallel to the Union line in the city's heart.[28] Bitter competition ensued with Philadelphia's largest and most powerful road. Shrewdly the three men fought the battle not only in the political arena but in the streets as well. They offered better equipment and more comfortable cars. Their superior service won patronage; by 1880 the group captured control of the Union and leased the Continental to it.[29]

During the struggle Kemble, Widener, and Elkins did not lose sight of their purpose. When they acquired the Seventeenth and Nineteenth Streets line in 1879, the Continental managers recorded in the company *Minute Book* that they acted "with the view of Securing less fare to be charged to the public, and producing a more economical management."[30] In 1881 the group absorbed the West Philadelphia Company, whose line ran west on Market Street from the Delaware River through the business district and across the Schuylkill River into West Philadelphia. As Map 8 illustrates, the trio had a powerful system by the early 1880s. It controlled lines running east-west and north-south through the business district and reaching into the suburban areas in the north and west.

While their network grew, the three men began rationalizing operations to increase productivity and profits. They had purchased or leased various lines on the basis of their previous business. To make money, they had to generate an even larger return—one that would pay the cost of their investment and provide them a profit. Combination would pay only if it lowered costs and attracted new traffic. To achieve·economies of operation, the group united the management of its underliers or subsidiaries in the Union Company. To attract more passengers they offered free transfers within their lines, a new service in local transit. By 1882 their roads carried almost thirty-three million passengers annually, of which one third were transfers.[31] Kemble proudly told Union stockholders that "the very great advantages effected from the combination of the several lines have been fully realized, not only has it increased the receipts and profits of the parent Company, but a profit has been made . . .

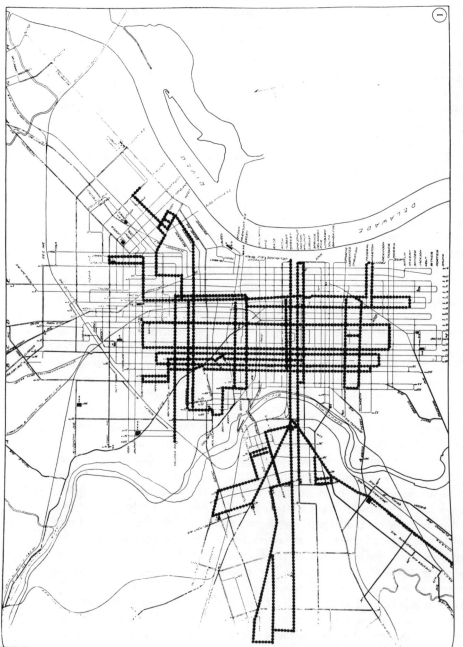

MAP 8. Philadelphia Traction Company system, 1884. The Philadelphia Transit Company system is marked by the dotted lines. *Source: System of Steam-Street Railroads–Railways of Philadelphia* (Philadelphia, 1887); Ford, Bacon and Davis, *Report*, II, map 1.

over all rentals of $8,139. As the rental is stationary the profits should increase with the growth of population and increase of receipts."[32]

Nevertheless, Kemble, Widener, and Elkins could ill affort to stand still. Already banker George Work was attempting to fashion a rival combination with the People's Passenger Company as a base. Furthermore the trio's unification of lines and innovation of free transfers were only a partial solution to Philadelphia's transit requirements. To handle a growing traffic the group's lines needed greater capacity. To service a population expanding farther into the suburbs they needed more speed and power. To increase profits the alliance had to reduce operating expenses. Even as the three entrepreneurs began to build their system, they recognized that the answer to these challenges was the substitution of mechanical for horse power.

Mechanization and Monopoly

In this case, then, the strategy of combination apparently preceded a decision to mechanize, possibly because there was no attractive alternative to the horse when the entrepreneurs embarked on their strategy. But as soon as actual acquisition of additional lines began, the promoters were compelled to replace the horse.

Mechanization was a difficult and far-reaching innovation for Kemble, Widener, and Elkins. They challenged a patent trust, developed new techniques of their own, and made Philadelphia the third city in the United States to adopt cable power. The costs of installation, the trial-and-error institution of a cable system, and its subsequent replacement by a more practical electric system made street railways in Philadelphia (and elsewhere) a big business. High fixed costs meant that efficient operation was even more vital. Competition among lines—possible with horse railways—did not long continue after mechanization. The concern for return on investment encouraged further combination and eventually led to the merger of all city transit lines.

Although the alliance's strategy of system building was new to street railways in 1880, their search for a mechanical substitute for the horse was not. As we have seen, horse railway men in large American cities had tried and discarded steam, compressed air, and other devices. The cable technique used in San Francisco since 1873 had not spread, because street railway men thought it suitable only in mild, constant climates. They assumed that extreme temperatures, ice, snow, and slush would ruin cables and conduits. Only after C. B. Holmes operated a cable line in Chicago in 1881 did local transit men begin to consider it as an alternative.[33]

The Philadelphia group was among the first to follow Holmes' lead.

Widener and Elkins traveled to San Francisco and Chicago to study in-
stallations there. The Chicago visit was particularly influential. As the
historian of cable railways remarked, "Holmes demonstrated that it [the
cable] was economic on absolutely flat terrain, with several pull curves,
and in a climate that ranges from −10° to 100° in the ordinary course of
a year."[34] While Holmes' efforts proved the cable's practicability, growing ridership underlined its need. Chart 5 illustrates that in the fifteen
years after the Civil War, traffic on Philadelphia street railways had
more than tripled, but like New York's street railways, the greatest
growth awaited mechanization. After 1885 the rate of expansion began a
sudden, sharp spurt which would generate a 400 percent increase in two
decades.

The Philadelphians' decision to venture into cable operation required
innovation in three areas: law, finance, and technology. Horse railway
companies lacked the authority to use cables and to raise the large
amount of capital required. In exchange for permission to change power,
city government demanded that companies lower their fare from 6 to 5
cents.[35] Without a law of general incorporation, Kemble, Widener, and
Elkins could not escape this demand by chartering a new street railway
company with expanded powers. Yet they were not anxious to obtain an
incorporation law that might allow more competition.

Aided by shrewd lawyers and their influence at Harrisburg, the three
partners avoided both the nickel fare and more competition by employ-
ing a construction company with expanded powers. In 1883 the Pennsylvania Assembly enacted a motive power law to permit the creation of
"traction companies." Such firms were not street railway companies and
had no right of way, but in the words of the law, they could "construct,
maintain and operate . . . such motors, cables and necessary or convenient apparatus and mechanical fixtures, as will provide for the traction of
the cars" of a street railway company.[36] The Philadelphia Traction Company (PTC), chartered in 1883, became the combine's legal vehicle for
cable construction and operation.

Kemble, Widener, and Elkins also used the PTC as a holding company
to complete consolidation and to facilitate the management of their properties. Because Philadelphia Traction could not own the stock of other
corporations, the group leased their various lines to it. As in the New
York case, the leases were perpetual (999 years) and gave the lessee total
control. In exchange, stockholders in the leased or underlying companies
received a guaranteed rental as a dividend on their stock.[37] Stock in the
underliers then assumed the same character as the preferred stock in
Henry Whitney's Boston system.

Leasing was only an organizational maneuver which conserved capital. A lease gave Kemble, Widener, and Elkins control of a road without

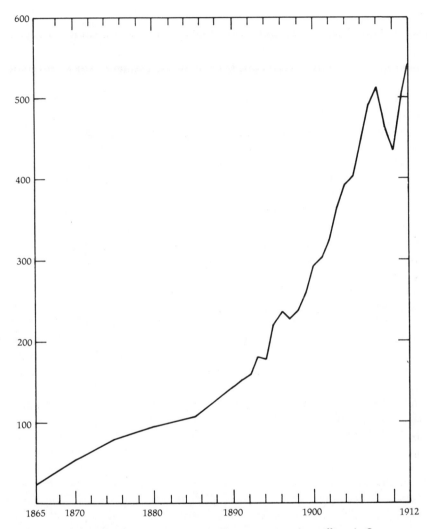

CHART 5. Philadelphia local transit traffic, 1865-1912 (in millions). Sources report only an annual, combined figure for fares and free transfers of surface and rapid transit firms. *Sources:* Chandler Brothers and Company, *Union Traction Company* (Philadelphia, 1899), 12, and *The Philadelphia Rapid Transit Company* (Philadelphia, 1904), 12; *Poor's Manual of the Railroads of the United States* (1898-1911); *Poor's Manual of Public Utilities* (1914).

purchasing large amounts of its stock, but it did not supply the funds needed for construction. At first the Philadelphians apparently furnished capital from their earlier business ventures or sold stock to friends and associates. As in the New York case, they used watered stock to repay themselves handsomely and to attract investors—a custom dating from early horsecar days. By 1887 PTC stock with $25 paid in sold at $68 a share.[38]

In this case, however, the cost of the new technology vastly increased the capitalization and the number of stockholders. The PTC raised $4,000,000 on 160,000 shares compared to the Union's paid-in capital of $616,600 on 20,000 shares. Philadelphia Traction had hundreds of stockholders as against the Union's fifty-six.[39] In this transition to big business, the Philadelphians again benefited from the railroads. Because of horse railways' kinship with steam railroads, their stocks had an organized market before most industrial securities. Horsecar companies in major cities were listed in *Poor's Manual of Railroads* as early as 1868, and their securities were traded on local exchanges at least as early as 1883.[40] By the late 1890s, in Philadelphia as in Boston and New York, thousands held shares in the transit monopoly.[41]

Increased construction costs also sent the PTC to savings institutions. In 1887 the Pennsylvania Company for Insurance of Lives and Granting Annuities loaned the PTC $1,300,000 for thirty years at 4 percent. In return the PTC deposited 10,000 shares of underlier stock valued at $1,950,000. Since the stock represented less than $450,000 actually paid in, the remainder of the loan ($850,000) was capital created by the formation and successful operation of the system.[42]

While they obtained suitable authority, organization, and finance, the partners also sought to implement the cable technology. Control of the patents for standard cable technology belonged to the National Cable Railway Company. Its leaders, including William P. Shinn, former Carnegie partner and ex-manager of the Edgar Thomson Steel Works, and Wallace C. Andrews, the Standard Oil partner who later helped organize the New York Cable Railway Company, demanded $5,000 per mile as a royalty.[43] The Philadelphians decided to create their own cable system. To avoid patent infringements the PTC modified the trust's cable grip and conduit and built an experimental one-mile segment on Columbus Avenue, completed in April 1883. Five months later the company began to build more than twenty miles of cable track.[44]

The work was long, costly, and disappointing. Construction of the ten-mile, double track system consumed five years and almost four million dollars, or about 20 percent of all investment in Philadelphia horse railways before 1891.[45] The trio soon regretted the decision to ignore the cable trust. Pressure buckled the plates of their cheap, bolted conduit, and cold weather contracted the cable slot. The modified grip proved unwieldy and required horses to pull the cars at turns and crossings. Cables snapped or their frayed strands caught the grips. Breakdowns occurred so frequently that the PTC printed special transfer tickets for the occasions. The first segment operated only a month before a two-year shutdown for reconstruction. When longer segments were opened in 1885, the network suffered at least six major failures; one portion was out of order for thirteen months. To avoid the cable cars, passengers reportedly walked as much as half a mile to horsecars.[46] As Dun and Bradstreet's correspondent observed, the management "bought their experience in this bus[iness] at considerable expense."[47]

In 1889, after six years of aggravation, the PTC finally achieved satisfactory operation. After losing a patent infringement suit, the company settled with the trust and adopted the standard cable technology. The cable lines were integrated into the existing transit system, and the three cable roads acted as trunk lines fed by the horse railways. With 147 free transfer points, passengers could now move across much of the city for a single fare. Traffic increased and by 1885 the PTC had more than one third of Philadelphia's total passengers and car mileage. The forty-two million people carried were more than double the system's 1880 figure.[48]

But pressure to improve grew as ridership continued its steep ascent. By 1890 Philadelphia's street railway traffic had increased more than 50 percent in a decade, and the cable system was inadequate to the city's needs. Widener had originally planned to cable all the PTC's lines, but the defects and limitations of cable operation dampened his enthusiasm.[49] Of more importance, the cost of installation restricted cable operation to heavily traveled routes. Horses still powered the lengthening lines to the suburbs, for no other company mechanized before electrification in 1892. Banker George Work's manipulations almost bankrupted the People's Passenger system which controlled 18 percent of local traffic (about half the PTC share). The remaining business was scattered among nine independent companies.[50]

Cautiously Philadelphia Traction turned to the new electric technology. By the early 1890s the day of the cable was waning; electric trolley lines had proved themselves. Their flexibility and relative cheapness made them far superior to cables. They offered greater speed and could be profitably operated on less traveled lines. The company, no doubt chastened by its cable experience and slowed by its four million dollar investment, was not among the first to electrify. However, a visit to Boston convinced Widener, and in 1892 the PTC sought authority to electrify its lines.[51]

Once again implementing new technology required a series of alterations in organization, operation, and policy. Surprisingly, the actual

installation of an electric system provided little challenge. With the experiences of companies in other cities as a guide, conversion to electric
traction was relatively easy. But the widening knowledge of the advantages and profits of electricity extended to the public as well, and popular
interest in the change compelled Philadelphia street railway companies to
make several concessions.

Opposition stemmed, as it had in Boston, from two sources—hostility
to street railways, especially the PTC, and fear and ignorance about
electricity. Ever since the initial grants of francise privileges in the 1850s,
transit firms had enjoyed highly visible and apparently profitable monopolies along public streets. The companies' powerful lobbies and influence peddling in Harrisburg and in city government had thwarted earlier
popular pressure for greater control and lower fares. The limitations of
horsecars and the frequent failure of the cable aggravated public feeling.
One critic complained that "the droves of swine in our cattle cars are not
more cruelly and indecently herded and packed together, than the citizens whose votes had elected the Councilmen, who permit the railway
companies to treat the public as they please."[52]

Among railway owners, Kemble, Widner, and Elkins especially antagonized Philadelphians. They had profitably dominated a vital public service for more than a decade. And in the mid-1880s they added Thomas
Dolan, head of United Gas Improvement Company, to the syndicate.
Together the four controlled three vital city utilities—gas, electricity, and
street railways.[53]

The group's close connections to both city and state machines allowed
it to flout attempts at public control while making large profits. In the
late 1880s city Boss Jim McManes had more than 4,000 shares of PTC
stock and Matt Quay had as many as 3,500 shares on one occasion. In
1883 the syndicate had obtained the vital traction company law to avoid
public demands for a lower fare. In 1887 it secured crucial amendments
to that law to insure the legality of underlier leases to Philadelphia Traction. In 1889 the assembly enacted a law of general incorporation which
enabled the group to charter companies with valuable routes for rationalizing the system. Though the PTC did accept a nickel fare in 1887, its
lobby rode roughshod over the attempts of reformers to obtain better
service and greater public control.[54] And Widener's angry submission to
the reduced charge was hardly calculated to win the company any
friends: "Say! Say! What can I say? Don't the announcements say
enough? I might talk for a week and not say as much as the reduction announcement says. The people wanted five cent fares and we have decided
to give in to them. That's the whole story."[55]

By 1892 a frustrated public supported reformers' efforts to secure valuable concessions in return for city consent to electrify. Concern over the

effects of overhead electric wires reinforced these protests. Anxiety about fires, frightened horses, injury, or even electrocution aroused insurance men, merchants, and the citizenry. As in New York and Boston, local businessmen led protests throughout the city. The Philadelphia Trades League (later renamed the Chamber of Commerce), the Municipal League, the Lumbermen's Exchange, the Fire Underwriters Association, the Master Builders Exchange, and various citizens' committees fought the trolley ordinance. Experts' reassurances and favorable reports from mayors and officials in Boston, Newark, Buffalo, Pittsburgh, Cleveland, Albany, and Cincinnati failed to calm opponents.[56]

Passage came only after the PTC and the other companies compromised with the city. They promised to repave with better materials the entire width of the streets along which they operated. The companies contracted to bury trolley wires at the city's request and agreed not to charge fares above a nickel. Finally, they pledged to build the lines so as not to block the possible construction of elevated railroads.[57]

The concessions were necessary to win the trolley authorization, but the owners and operators rejected any demands for legislation regulating construction and operation. As one trolley man put it: "Which one of you would care to take upon himself the duty and responsibility of saying by an ordinance how it [the overhead system] should be constructed? Where is the ordinance of any of your bodies, your own or your predecessors, in which you put . . . the specifications of construction?"[58] The companies tolerated only mild supervision by the Department of Public Safety. Reformers' goals were vague, city government lacked administrative competence, and the movement for tighter control waned.

Despite the cost of compromising, the expectation of great profits persuaded the companies to yield. Early reports exaggerated the savings of electric traction and underestimated investment and maintenance costs. In Boston a General Electric official prudently warned that "after things have been running a while, I fancy the account of repairs begins to increase. Of course it is impossible to get a true basis for repair expenses on electric railways, except over a series of years."[59] But in Philadelphia Kemble's death in 1891 had removed his restraint on Widener's optimism, and Widener ecstatically embraced the new system. He bought more company stock and advised his friends to do the same.[60]

Widener's decision committed the PTC (and indirectly the other lines) to repave virtually the entire city. By 1900 Philadelphia had been transformed from one of the worst to one of the best paved cities in the United States. But the improvements brought by mechanization and repaved streets came only at considerable cost to both the system and the public. Electrification almost tripled investment in street railways by 1896, and paving expenses between 1892 and 1907 were estimated at nine to fourteen million dollars.[61] As we shall see, Widener's over-optimism eventually boomeranged. Paving expenses and unanticipated costs of electrification eventually weakened the system financially and restricted its ability to serve the city.

Meanwhile technological implementation was rapid and effective. By 1895 the PTC had electrified 75 percent of its 200 miles of track, and other companies converted as quickly. After 1897 both cable cars and horsecars were gone forever. Electricity vastly improved public transit with greater speed, more power, and larger cars, and it encouraged further urban expansion. With more bridges across the Schuylkill and with the advent of trolleys, West Philadelphia grew more rapidly, while suburban population in the north and northwest continued to increase. In 1895 the PTC carried over 100 million passengers, almost triple its 1885 figure, and all Philadelphia lines transported over 220 million, double the city's 1885 traffic.[62]

Electrification also furthered the process of combination and consolidation. The high fixed costs for electric traction encouraged unification and rationalization to increase efficiency and returns. Financiers William Shelmerdine and Robert Carson with the aid of Drexel, Morgan partner John L. Welsh reorganized the old People's Passenger Company as the People's Traction Company and expanded and electrified its lines. Meanwhile banker Jeremiah J. Sullivan combined six horsecar companies into the Electric Traction Company and mechanized its lines.[63] The three traction companies, which by 1894 controlled all but one of the city's lines, began a bitter competition for traffic and routes. But duplication of administrations, power generators, car houses, and tracks reduced possible economies. In some cases three sets of trolley wires stretched along a single street. In their fight against Philadelphia Traction, the People's and the Electric Companies established universal transfers and negotiated for free transfers between their networks.[64]

The costs of competition soon drove the three companies to a merger. In 1895 they secured legislation which permitted the consolidation of traction companies and gave them the full powers of street railway companies. Quickly, the heads of the three firms chartered a new organization, the Union Traction Company (UTC), which in turn leased the old traction companies. The procedure simply repeated the earlier pattern. The new company assumed complete control of the assets and liabilities of the Philadelphia, People's, and Electric Traction Companies. In exchange their stockholders received a guaranteed return on their investment. Voting control in the UTC belonged to the holders of its 600,000 shares of common stock (par value $50).[65] The merger virtually completed the combination of Philadelphia street railways, and within two years the Widener group assumed direction of the new company. Soon after, Union Traction absorbed the remaining independent line, the Hestonville, Mantua and Fairmont Passenger Railway Company, thus uniting the city's street railways into a powerful monopoly.

As in the Boston and New York operations, a professional manager replaced the entrepreneurs as operating head. John Parsons, an experienced street railway man who had trained in the syndicate's Chicago operations, took charge in 1898. Management consolidated the operation of all Philadelphia railways with a modified line and staff organization. It completed the electrification of all lines and so rationalized routes that they were scarcely recognizable to the Philadelphian of 1880.[66] The results were greater efficiency and lower costs. Car mileage dropped while car capacity increased. The ratio of operating expenses to total revenue fell from 47 to 40 percent between 1897 and 1899.[67] By 1900 Philadelphia's street railways were a unified and mechanized system.

The merger did not end entrepreneurial control, for Widener, Elkins, and Dolan remained in power. Widener's and Elkins' sons entered the management and joined the three older men on the UTC's board of directors along with such representatives of People's and Electric Traction as William H. Shelmerdine and J. J. Sullivan.[68] Finance and executive committees made policy decisions and established strategy. Through positions on the boards of directors of Union Traction and its underliers, the trio continued to direct the Philadelphia street railway monopoly.

The Coming of Rapid Transit

THE syndicate's absolute monopoly did not long remain unchallenged. As in New York and Boston, street railways failed to satisfy the rising clamor for rapid transit. The entrepreneurs' reluctance to act and the continued pressures of city growth soon opened the door to outside interests. Unlike the other cases, however, the Philadelphia street railway monopoly used its political power to absorb or defeat challengers, and its owners' eventual decision to build a rapid transit line delayed the need for city construction.

As in Boston, rapid transit proposals in Philadelphia dated from the early success of New York's elevated roads. Proponents, including engineers Lewis Haupt and merchant John Wanamaker, made the familiar arguments about the importance of alleviating congested cities and the healthiness and superiority of the suburban countryside. Their pleas brought little support in the City of Homes. Even elevated supporters recognized that the city's population density fell within the safe limits set by French and English authorities.[69]

Before the turn of the century, rapid transit opponents were far more powerful than supporters. And as in New York and Boston, much of the contest occurred among factions of the business community. Philadelphians, like Bostonians, dreaded steam-powered elevated lines with their noise and dirt. Property owners, merchants, and reformers bitterly battled charter proposals in 1881 and 1892. Meanwhile local transportation interests also fought elevated roads. Especially powerful were the street railway syndicate and the Pennsylvania and Reading Railroads, who feared the loss of local and commuter traffic. Their lobbies helped kill several rapid transit proposals between 1875 and 1893.[70]

Capital and technology needs also generated obstructions. No one came forward with a satisfactory plan and sufficient capital for a subway as an alternative to the elevated. And steam-powered elevated lines, though cheaper to construct than a subway, threatened their owners with millions of dollars for damages to abutting property. Only one line ever went beyond the talking stage; in 1892 the Northeastern Elevated Company actually began construction. But opponents, including merchants, reformers, and local transit lines, quickly stopped the Northeastern and all other efforts in the courts. The Pennsylvania Supreme Court ruled that the company's charter did not permit it to run over streets occupied by street railways, and in a related case, the court found the Quaker City Elevated Company's charter invalid in the absence of a general law of incorporation for elevated railways.[71]

The lack of a concerted public outcry for rapid transit before the end of the century reinforced these obstructions. Mechanization and consolidation improved surface transit considerably in the 1880s and 1890s. The nickel fare and the expansion of the transfer system made travel cheaper, while electric power increased speed and capacity. As a result, there was no public crusade for high speed lines as in New York and Boston in the 1890s.

Public satisfaction and apathy also obviated the policy of public construction chosen in the same period by New Yorkers and Bostonians. Philadelphians strongly relied on private enterprise. The commercial ethic of the businessmen who led reform movements and the success of the new utilities combinations discouraged municipal takeover. In addition, a more orderly and less blatantly corrupt political machine evolved after city charter reform in 1887 and especially after Jim McManes' death in 1897. Under David Martin and Israel Durham a strong, ward-based organization and a careful courting of immigrant votes replaced the election day frauds and chicanery of earlier times.[72]

The combination of better service and quieter government calmed the business-led reform groups that dominated the early public construction movements in New York and Boston. In Howard Gillette's words:

> Following the example set in street railways, a new breed of
> political entrepreneurs combined their assets to use public au-

thority to build their own financial empire. The new syndicate extended its interests to new service industries, gas and electricity, as well as to more traditional kinds of services, such as street cleaning and highway repairs. Respectable and business-like under the [1887] reform charter, the new political machine ruled the city in its own interest, and former reformers resigned themselves to pay the high price of receiving any services at all from their local government.[73]

Or, as Lincoln Steffens so aptly phrased it, Philadelphia was "corrupt and contented."[74]

Philadelphians' experience with a city-operated gas service reinforced their preference for private enterprise. Under Boss Jim McManes the city gas plant had long been a notoriously corrupt and inefficient operation. It supplied citizens with high priced gas and the political machine (called the Ring) with money and patronage. After Philadelphians finally terminated the gas ring and leased the facility for private operation in the mid-1890s, they were in no mood to seek municipal rapid transit. Nor did they have a proven model for city development of transit.[75] At mid-decade the Boston and New York decisions for public construction of subways were still untested.

The eventual success of the subway in both cities, however, quickly awakened a demand for rapid transit in Philadelphians. They saw themselves falling behind in the rivalry among major American cities. Chicago displaced Philadelphia as the nation's second largest city. And New York, Boston, and Chicago all boasted high speed systems built or under construction by 1900.

Philadelphia's traffic growth and its size also encouraged calls for rapid transit. Its large area (129 square miles), elongated on a north-south axis, left the city with surface car lines second only to Chicago in mileage. As the result of suburban expansion and cheaper, faster transit, the doubling of riders in the 1890s heavily burdened an awkward street grid and a streetcar system crammed into narrow streets. The city had only two major thoroughfares to enter the business district. Market Street was already congested with trolleys, wagons, and other traffic, and on Broad Street, the "Fifth Avenue" of Philadelphia, street railways were forbidden.[76]

The narrow streets, their grid pattern and the unplanned development of early horsecar lines meant that the city was laced with tracks. In the words of the transit company: "The topography of Philadelphia was such that its surface travel has been taken care of by a perfect network of tracks, aggregating over 600 miles in length, so that throughout the central part of the city every 400 feet finds a street occupied by a street railway track. The streets are narrow, and with a grade crossing every 400 feet, the rate at which cars could be safely moved was necessarily slower than prevailed in other cities."[77] Philadelphia's growth added to these difficulties over time. Sam Warner notes that "by 1900 every major street in inner Philadelphia carried an electric streetcar line, and traffic jams and slow service plagued the long hauls from West Philadelphia and the northwest."[78]

The city was approaching a transit crisis. As an English observer put it: "No man goes slow if he has the chance of going fast; no man stops to talk if he can talk walking; no man walks if he can ride in a trolley-car . . . There is nothing . . . an American cannot do, except rest."[79] Unfortunately, crowded streets were causing too many Philadelphians to take an unwanted rest on a blockaded trolley or to walk. Congestion and delays increased criticism and reduced the efficiency of surface lines. Passengers demanded speedier service, which could only be achieved by building an expensive rapid transit system.

Because of their preference for private enterprise, Philadelphians looked to businessmen instead of public authority when agitation for rapid transit rose at the end of the century. The nation's recovery from the mid-1890s depression, the success of Boston's subway, and the use of electric power on Chicago's and Boston's elevated lines encouraged private action. In 1901 Tom and Albert Johnson, already operators of transit lines in Cleveland, proposed to extend their Lehigh Valley electric line into Philadelphia via an elevated railroad. In addition, the Widener group was reported to be negotiating with the Pennsylvania Railroad for a tunnel under Broad Street.[80]

The proposal produced little more than public excitement. The Johnsons' elevated line could not run through Philadelphia's narrow streets, and the Widener syndicate was slow to act. It had devoted four years to gain control of and rationalize the monopoly. Not until 1900 did profits exceed the losses suffered during Union Traction's first year of operation. In the absence of suitable enabling legislation, Widener, Elkins, and Dolan refused to be pressured. Unperturbed by the Johnsons' proposal, Widener and Elkins left for a European vacation.[81]

Unfortunately for them, the rapid transit agitation exposed a chink in the syndicate's defenses at a point previously thought to be one of its strongest bulwarks—the political connection. Kemble's death had weakened the group's strong ties to the Quay machine. In 1899-1900 Widener failed to support Quay's bid for election to the United States Senate.[82] The result was to sunder temporarily the link of the state and local machines with the traction combine.

The clamor for rapid transit gave Quay his chance for revenge. He allied with John Mack, a paving contractor with considerable political influence, and arranged for him to acquire thirteen rapid transit franchises in Philadelphia. Under Quay's leadership the Pennsylvania Assembly enacted the requisite legislation in a procedure described by one observer as "a new and hitherto . . . unparelleled record of franchise-looting and defiance of public opinion."[83] With the legislative tracks cleared, the necessary laws highballed through Harrisburg in nine days.

The state issued thirteen charters to Mack and his associates for subway and elevated lines in Philadelphia. With city approval the new companies could build over or under any street. The proposed lines covered every major throughfare in the city, and for five years the grantees had exclusive rights to obtain franchises and build. Any further charters had to be approved by the governor and the secretary of the Commonwealth, both supporters of the Quay machine.[84]

At Quay's urging the machine-controlled city government approved the Mack franchises in five days. In city council all attempts to amend or forestall failed. At the last moment John Wanamaker, the wealthy department store magnate and no mean power in the Republican party, offered the city $2,500,000 for the 999-year franchises it was preparing to give away. Mayor "Stars-and-Stripes-Sammy" Ashbridge, the most notorious of all the Ring's mayors, rejected the offer and immediately signed away the franchises.[85] The entire charter and franchise process required only sixteen days. If the service of the new companies matched that of the legislative bodies involved, Philadelphia would have rapid transit indeed.

A hostile public maintained a well-founded skepticism. The Mack group had little capital actually invested in the scheme and apparently had no plan for construction. Its motive was blackmail. Philadelphia's crowded streets and the success of rapid transit in her east coast rivals, New York and Boston, made the demand for rapid transit imperative. If Union Traction failed to act, the Mack franchises could be sold to an outside rival like the Johnsons. An efficient system of high speed lines would siphon off business from the surface roads which the UTC could ill afford to lose. Though the efficiency of its operation had reduced the large deficit of the first year of operation, earnings had been insufficient to pay any dividends. Serious competition threatened the collapse of the entire system.[86]

The Widener and Mack groups compromised and chartered the Philadelphia Rapid Transit Company (PRT), which leased Union Traction and the Mack companies, and made the monopoly absolute. Already street railway lines occupied "practically every through street" in the city.[87] The thirteen high speed franchises covered all available routes, and the PRT had a five-year right to exploit them. In addition, any future competition had to battle the state and city machines with which the syndicate had again allied.

The combination repeated the patterns of Philadelphia Traction and
Union Traction. The PRT leased the old Union Traction system and the
Mack franchises for 999 years, and assumed all taxes, rentals, and interest charges. In exchange, UTC stockholders accepted a guaranteed return
which would increase from 3 to 6 percent over a six-year period. For his
franchises Mack received an estimated $1,500,000 and 55,000 of the
600,000 PRT shares (par value $50) issued. He and two associates joined
the board or directors, replacing Thomas Dolan. Otherwise, the Widener-
Elkins leadership and their managers continued. Union Traction's operating force simply became PRT employees.[88]

In two decades Philadelphia public transit had been revolutionized.
Unified operation brought increased service, reduced costs, rationalized
lines, and a transfer system. Electricity had replaced the horse to provide
greater speed, capacity, and convenience. Adopting new technology had
made local public transit a big business. The 300,000,000 passengers carried in 1900 more than tripled the 1880 figure.[89] Horsecar companies financed for a few hundred thousand dollars gave way to a system in
which more than fifty million dollars was invested.[90] With the creation of
the PRT, a powerful monopoly controlled Philadelphia's street railways
and the development of its rapid transit. Promoters had worked out the
strategic, financial, and structural implications of the new mechanical
technology, but its impact on policy was still incomplete.

7.

Contract and
Cooperation

AFTER THE New York and Boston experiences, subway construction was no longer a risky innovation. Yet, in the case of Philadelphia as in the others, building expensive high speed lines helped bring important changes in transit operation and policy. As in New York and Boston, the rise of a local traction monopoly seriously disturbed the citizenry of Philadelphia. The urbanization and industrialization of the previous half century destroyed established traditions of small enterprise and local regulation. The growth of population, the increasing pressure for expanded urban services, and the evolution of powerful public utility monopolies raised crucial questions as to how the city's services were to be organized, managed, and controlled. As in other cities, the new technology made obsolete a public transit policy based primarily on regulation by competition among small, independent horsecar lines. Simultaneously, population growth and urban expansion confronted Philadelphians with another problem which their monopoly was slow to solve: the provision of rapid transit.

Despite the Philadelphia Rapid Transit Company's apparently absolute position, its situation was unstable in 1902. The need to plan for growth and rational development, to build complex and costly electric-powered subway lines, and to come to terms with the PRT forced Philadelphians to assume a much more active role in transit development. At the same time the company's internal problems compelled it to moderate its secretiveness and independence, to negotiate with the city, and to recognize its public character and responsibilities. However natural unified operation might seem to the syndicate, a hostile public was yet to be reconciled to monopoly control of a vital service. The rights and responsibilities of the city and the company needed adjustment for their mutual best interests and for future planning and development. In a sense the monopoly process was still evolving. Combination and consolidation were complete, but the new giant now had to be melded with the traditions and institutions of the city.

The condition of Philadelphia transit raised many questions. How could the demand of an expanding city for increasingly expensive transportation facilities be met? Should competition be restored in the public interest or the monopoly be maintained? If retained, should the monopoly be publicly or privately owned? If the latter, then how could the PRT offer desperately needed expansion of service and simultaneously assure its stockholders a fair return on investment?

The situation faced by Philadelphians was clearly unsatisfactory. Unregulated monopoly failed to provide the necessary safeguards for the public interest. The municipalization of the PRT and the construction of a competing municipal system—solutions adopted in other cities—were not seriously considered in Philadelphia, a city that retained a strong tradition of private ownership. In addition Philadelphians exhibited little desire to burden themselves with commitments for expanded service.[1] Private enterprise appeared clearly superior to the pitfalls of public control in 1902.

Induced private competition for the monopoly appealed to a large number of people, especially in that day of strong antitrust sentiment. Yet competition was never forthcoming. The chief hindrance was the solidly entrenched position of the PRT. The enormous capital outlay necessary to build a comprehensive transit system and the alliance of the company with the local and state political machines discouraged aspiring competitors.

To Philadelphians the problems of 1902 seemed intractable in the face of the transit company's awesome power. But within five years four major factors reduced that power and shaped an agreement: the PRT's financial and administrative weaknesses; the company's failure to satisfy demands for increased service amid rising public hostility; the threat of competition and the attempted municipal recapture of the PRT's subway franchise; and the business community's pressure for transit reform.

The PRT's Financial, Administrative, and Public Relations Difficulties

Despite the monopoly's appearance of strength, the PRT was in serious trouble from its inception. It suffered major financial and administrative weaknesses and was vulnerable to public hostility. Each of these problems had a long history. As in the New York case, the syndicate's techniques for funding combination and mechanization created a shaky financial foundation. The Philadelphia group's forte was entrepreneurship

rather than organization; Widener and his associates emphasized manipulation and profit over management.[2] Furthermore, as has been stressed,
the entrepreneurs' political ties and attitudes had irritated Philadelphians
for a quarter of a century. Extraordinarily secretive, they ignored the
very public character of their business. Owners and managers supplied
little information and consistently disregarded or resisted efforts for
greater public control.

Many of the PRT's financial problems stemmed from the costs of
mechanization. The optimistic Widener and his associates were quick to
see the operating economies of electric traction, but they failed to antici-
pate all charges. In common with most of the industry, the group underestimated capital needs and failed to provide adequate depreciation reserves.[3] The continued development of electric technology raised the expense of installation and equipment for one mile of double-track electric
line from $38,500 in 1890 to about $86,000 in 1900. And the cable lines
which electric power replaced represented a $4,000,000 investment on
which the system continued to pay 8 percent. Because the partners failed
to amortize such costs in the face of rapid obsolescence, they had to finance replacements with new security issues while paying interest on
superannuated investments.[4] Increased expenses for more complex equipment and the charges paid on superseded capital created a heavy drain on
revenue in the form of higher fixed charges.

The combine's technique for attracting funds consumed profits from
the enterprise and further increased the burden of fixed charges. As we
have seen, the group used watered or partially paid-in stock to entice
investors and repay themselves. But the dividends paid to themselves and
other stockholders of the underlying lines was based on the nominal
value of shares. Thus the PRT's 6 percent payment to the Union Traction
Company (UTC) was 17 percent on capital actually paid in. Combination pyramided this drainage. In each successive lease the new lessee
assumed all payments to the underliers of the lessor.[5] Thus the PRT paid
rentals (or fixed dividends) not only to the UTC but to the Philadelphia
Traction Company, People's Traction, Electric Traction, and their horse
railway subsidiaries as well. At the close of the company's first year of
operation, these rentals plus bonded indebtedness amounted to more
than $6,800,000 or 44 percent of gross revenue in contrast to the national
average of 31 percent in cities of more than 500,000.[6]

Finally, the syndicate's overoptimistic view of street railway prospects
further aggravated the financial situation. It had anticipated some increase in fixed costs. But because of past experience the group expected
that continued urban growth and an even faster increase in traffic would
combine with the economies of unification to outstrip rising fixed costs.
Meanwhile it attempted to ease the PRT's initial burden of fixed charges

by providing for gradually rising payments to the Union Traction over a six-year span.

The same strategy had apparently worked when the UTC was formed. In its first full year of operation that company lost $850,000. Eventually however, rationalization, the economies of consolidation, and traffic growth improved revenues and lessened the burden of fixed charges. Operating costs fell from 47 percent of gross revenue in 1897 to 42 percent in 1900, and fixed costs dropped from 52 to 42 percent of gross revenue.[7] Traffic grew by almost 30 percent in five years, and by 1901 Union Traction showed a million dollar profit.

But net profits never justified a UTC dividend until after its lease to the PRT. And the new company was in even worse shape, for unlike its predecessor the PRT had little chance to improve its earnings. It would be years before the company received returns on its $1,500,000 investment for the Mack franchises, and the PRT combination offered no opportunities for additional economies to reduce operating costs. The merger did not combine operations; it merely added some franchises to the old Union Traction system.

Trapped with a fixed fare and scant opportunity for economy in a period of sharply rising prices, the PRT's owners watched operating costs rise to more than 50 percent of gross revenue. Congested lines in crowded streets reduced efficiency and raised accident expenses. A secular price rise boosted the cost of labor and materials, and some earlier Union Traction savings resulted from faulty accounting. To reduce operating outlays the UTC had deferred replacements and maintenance, saddling the PRT with increased charges to service aging and often obsolete equipment. As a result the company barely broke even. For the first five years revenue growth scarcely kept pace with increased payments to Union Traction stockholders. Meanwhile the PRT continued a niggardly policy of replacements and renewals, and, like the UTC earlier, it paid no dividends to its own stockholders.[8]

The result was a seriously damaged company. The transit system as a whole returned about 9 percent on paid-in capital.[9] But the syndicate's policies skewed dividends to the underliers and left nothing for repairs or for PRT stockholders. The absence of dividends discouraged additional investment so badly needed to finance new equipment, rapid transit lines, and extensions of surface roads.

The PRT's financial weaknesses and its credit crunch quickly began to reinforce each other. The need for rigid cost-cutting postponed maintenance and replacement of equipment and impaired service—which magnified criticism. The increased public hostility further discouraged investment, thus weakening the company's financial position and further injuring its operation. So depressing were PRT prospects that Widener,

Elkins, and other members of the syndicate were unable to unload the large amounts of PRT stock they held. The Elkins estate had some 50,000 shares at his death in 1903. When John Mack left the PRT in 1906, his associates formed a syndicate to purchase his 55,000 shares. As late as 1907, Widener and his son George had some 35,000 shares.[10] Instead of selling at higher prices the stock they had purchased for a fraction of its par value, the partners were compelled to hold on and gradually pay in the full value in order to keep the PRT afloat.

The PRT's administrative policies further aggravated its condition. In order to save funds in 1896, Union Traction had modified its line and staff structure and reduced the number of personnel—a pattern continued by the PRT. This false economy produced confusion, reduced control and efficiency, and probably raised operating charges. Chart 6 reveals that the relationship between line and staff was vague. Instead of establishing a clear line of authority for the firm's transportation function as the railroads had done, the PRT had divided authority. The second vice president and general manager, who would normally have headed the line, now controlled the staff while the line reported separately to the president through a superintendent of transportation. Communication between line and staff had to pass through the overburdened office of President John Parsons. At the same time, accounting was decentralized so that each department kept its own accounts—a practice that helped conceal deficits and compound confusion.[11]

The strongly entrepreneurial character of the enterprise interfered with its professional managers and operation. Insider manipulation with company stocks antagonized outside investors. Widener and Elkins reputedly acquired lines and used company funds to service real estate speculation. Directors dabbled in operating matters and labor problems. The company even employed a secret service to spy out labor agitators among its low-paid workers.[12]

As serious as the financial and operating difficulties was the PRT's wretched relationship with the public. The benefits of electric trolleys brought only temporary respite from the public suspicion of Philadelphia street railways. In an 1896 attempt to increase revenue, Union Traction abolished many free transfer points. The move outraged Philadelphians, since most passengers had to make at least one change of lines to reach their destinations. The action was essential to shore up company finances, but the secretive UTC directors made little effort to justify their decision. Rejecting any notion of public accountability, they faced the public outcry in stony silence. Then labor troubles arose from protests about low wages and long hours. Again the UTC's need for economy, combined with its apparent indifference to the problems of its employees, antagonized many Philadelphians.[13]

CHART 6. Philadelphia Rapid Transit Company Organization.

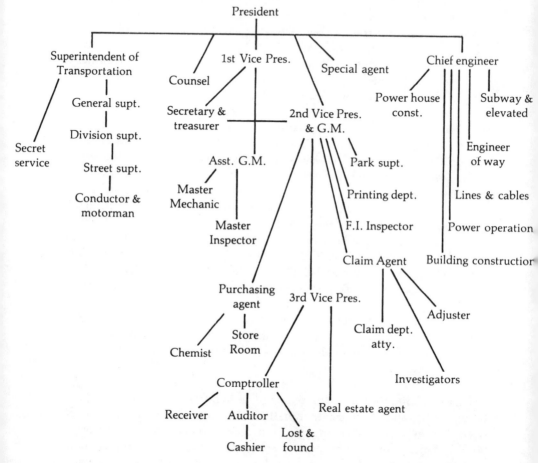

Note: The chart's cluttered look reflects the original. *Source*: *SRJ*, 26 (September 23, 1905), 488.

The public outcry was not without its effects. Protestors rediscovered two ordinances which hung like a pair of Damoclean swords over the system. One, promulgated when the traction companies sought to electrify their lines in 1892, empowered the city to force the companies to bury their wires.[14] If the success of the New York conduit technology ever led to popular demand for the law's enforcement, it would cost the street railway system millions. The other measure dated from the original horse railway laws of 1857 and provided that "the city of Philadelphia reserves the right any time to purchase [the street railways] by paying the original cost of said road or roads and cars at a fair valuation. And any such company or companies refusing to consent to such purchase shall thereby forfeit all privileges, rights and immunities they may have acquired in the use or possession of any of the highways as aforesaid."[15]

This curious piece of legislation, apparently allowing for municipalization of the entire system, had never been used or tested in the courts. And no serious attempt to purchase occurred in 1896 despite a great deal of publicity given the law. Nevertheless, it offered the city a weapon with which to fight a battle for municipal control if it wished, and by directly threatening the monopoly's security, the ordinance posed a further threat to investment.

Finally, the 1901 franchise grab, which led to the PRT's formation, heaped more fuel on the fires of public indignation and hostility. The creation of the company signified a renewed alliance with Philadelphia's notorious political machine or Ring. Even more bothersome to citizens who demanded high speed lines was the Widener-Elkins history of foot-dragging on rapid transit development, for the new monopoly closed out competition from entrepreneurs like the Johnsons of Clevelend.

To concerned Philadelphians the system's evolution was part of a frightening pattern evident throughout the nation at the turn of the century. Big business, more powerful than all other interests, was unduly influencing local, state, and national governments and threatening the democratic process. By 1902 Theodore Roosevelt was in the White House, and progressive reformers in cities and states were calling attention to the evils of the trusts. Into such an atmosphere the PRT was born.

Service and Public Relations

Popular protest provided an important link in the process that radically altered the relationship of the city and the monopoly. Consumer complaints so threatened the company's position that it was eventually compelled to accept public oversight.[16] The monopoly's failure to provide sufficient service weakened Philadelphians' reliance on private enterprise. As in other cities, angry and critical businessmen led a reform movement to secure greater public control of local transportation and insure adequate expansion to meet the needs of the growing metropolis.

By the dawn of the new century a few Philadelphians had begun to join the progressive reform movement found in other cities. The Municipal League led protest against the abolition of free transfers and urged the implementation of the long-neglected municipal purchase ordinance. One prominent member, Clinton Rodgers Woodruff, published a scathing account of the 1901 grab. The Philadelphia *North American* launched a muckraking campaign against the monopoly, exposing the PRT's financial structure and the large returns to Widener, Elkins, and other holders of underlier stock. Led by Rudolph Blankenburg and other reformers, the new City party began to challenge the Republican machine for control of city government in 1903. By 1905 public protest emboldened Mayor James Weaver to break with the Ring and veto Thomas Dolan's attempt to renew his lease of city gas facilities.[17]

More important than the reform movement, however, were consumer protests. Led by businessmen and stimulated by the desire for better service, they fueled efforts to alter the city's relationship with the PRT. After the company's formation in 1902, public opinion, as reflected by newspaper reports and by the statements of local businessmen, reformers, workers, and their organizations, bitterly condemned the PRT and its service. At the same time company officials feared that public criticism of the transit system discouraged potential investors and might lead to municipal recapture or the introduction of competition. By 1907 anxiety over public hostility impelled the PRT to support an agreement drawn up by sympathetic merchants to calm Philadelphians.

Public complaints about service neither began in nor ceased after the 1902-07 period. Nor did they rise in a simple linear progression throughout the five years. Instead they rose and fell in a sequential pattern. They often stemmed from a particular incident, such as unheated cars on a cold day or a rash of trolley blockades. Newspapers and business associations seized on the incidents and magnified them into an issue. Other segments of the populace joined the chorus of protestors with a widening range of complaints until the PRT or happenstance offered some temporary amelioration. A lull then ensued until the next incident. The repetition of the sequence and the swiftness with which hostility arose in each case testified vividly to the inability of the company to satisfy the public's needs.

The controversy over the heating of cars in the winter illustrates the pattern. A 1903 *Street Railway Journal* article calmly observed that none of the city's cars contained heaters. This "distinguishing feature" was due to "an open question among the travelling public whether the discomfort of overheated cars for the greater part of the season does not exceed that of the absence of heat on a few cold days."[18] To the public's mind, however, the only thing open about the question was the car entrance through which cold and wind entered to numb passengers on long, slow rides. Early in the cold, snowy winter of 1904-05, Philadelphians set up a clamor for heated cars. "Transit Company Helped Blizzard in Planting Seeds of Pneumonia" accused the headlines of one newspaper.[19] Investigation soon revealed that cars in other major cities were heated. Why not in Philadelphia? The PRT management pointed out that some (two of every seven) cars were heated and comfortable. Reporters rushed to the scene armed with thermometers, pads, and pencils. The next day the press announced that it had indeed located some heated cars. Temperatures on them ranged from 34° to 41° while the unheated cars measured from 29° to 32°.[20]

Quickly the PRT felt the frigid breath of an icy public, especially in the muckraking Philadelphia *North American*. Daily newspaper columns by physicians lectured on the evils of unheated cars. The doctors asserted that not only cold, but also filth, overcrowding, dampness, and lack of ventilation were health hazards found on the transit system. A schoolmaster publicly advised children that walking was much safer than sitting or standing in the drafty cars. The Central Labor Union, representing 120 labor unions and 62,000 workers, condemned the PRT for disregard of the public interest and was soon joined by unions in the machine, textile, and building trades. Similar criticism followed from the Philadelphia Trades League, an association of more than 2,300 businessmen throughout the city dedicated to "improving the commerce, the business and the manufacturing interests of the port and city of Philadelphia."[21]

The city council, not to be outdone, bravely resolved that all cars should be heated to a minimum of 32°. Although the PRT had again allied with the city's political machine, the Ring's popularly elected councilmen could not afford to disregard completely the public's voices. Furthermore, the machine's hold on city government weakened somewhat when Mayor John Weaver refused to be its puppet.[22]

The PRT could only ride out the storm. Penny pinching had minimized the number of heaters initially installed in the cars. In any event, heaters would do little good on a system woefully short of power. President John Parsons explained that generators had been ordered a year earlier but had not yet been installed.[23] Extra power would not be available until the following summer.

By the winter of 1905-06 all cars were heated, but inadequate power continued to plague the surface lines. With the heaters running full blast, the power supply was so sorely taxed that periodically an overload brought entire sections of the system to a standstill. The nadir came in March 1906 when a fire gutted the largest generating plant in the system

"I have frequently likened these cars, in my mind, to ice cream freezers."
—DR. CHARLES W. KARSNER, OF THE BOARD OF MEDICAL INSPECTORS.

The Pneumonia Rapid Transit Company. *Source:* Philadelphia *North American*, clipping dated December 29, 1904, in PRT Scrapbooks, I (1904), in Cox Collection, Wilkes College Library.

and about three hundred cars had to be pulled off for more than a week.[24]

Even worse, continued service difficulties in 1906 renewed the attacks of the influential Philadelphia Trades League. Led by Thomas Martindale, a wealthy grocer and civic leader, its transportation committee waged a campaign through 1905, 1906, and 1907 for comprehensive transit reform. Martindale's committee, sometimes stirring and sometimes echoing popular protest, daily criticized the company for overcrowded cars; for its failure to meet schedules, expand service, clean cars, and remove snow from the streets; and for its refusal to offer more free transfers.

Martindale's attacks on President Parsons and the PRT were supported in the popular press by businessmen, workers, and shoppers using the lines. The press ridiculed the company in cartoon and doggerel. It labelled the PRT the Parsonsimonious Run Topsy-turvy Company and wondered:

> If a trolley starts from Market Street
>   at 6 o'clock these nights,
> With the car so full that laps and
>   straps and incandescent lights,
> On which to stand are in demand on
>   this cold, bloodless drove,
> How many will show signs of life on
>   reaching Willow Grove?
>
> Jam in ten; there's room for four;
> Oh fudge—I think some one swore.
> Let them shiver—grip's in style,
>   Get hot while they cuss,
> We won't heat a car till they
>   Make it hot for us.[25]

Meanwhile, Martindale's committee steadily gathered figures to support its claims. By 1905 passenger traffic had increased 24 percent over 1902, while the number of licensed cars remained constant. Another study revealed that Philadelphia had a higher passenger-per-car load than other cities. Overcapitalization and inflated rentals were blamed for inadequate service and high fares.[26]

Especially concerned about transit were realtors, whose dependence on transportation was obvious. In September 1903 realtor James D. Winchell complained that "car facilities of this location [in northwest Philadelphia] are far from convenient, and residents throughout the neighborhood have been making inquiry of me relative thereto." General Manager Charles Kruger replied that better service would not be available before the end of the year. A year later Winchell visited President Parsons to repeat his protest and was promised an extension of tracks by winter or early spring. Six months later, in March 1905, he wrote to remind Parsons of his pledge: "The poles, as you are aware, have been up about three years, and I would like to know whether you expect to proceed with this work at any early date." Kruger answered that tracks would be laid "during the coming season." Winchell then asked when cars would operate on the tracks. Kruger replied that he could not say definitely. Four months later Winchell pestered the PRT again to discover when the

DURING YESTERDAY'S BLOCKADE, BRADFORD INSPECTED A RAPID TRANSIT POWER HOUSE, AND PRODUCED THIS PICTURE

The PRT Powerhouse. *Source: Philadelphia* North American, *clipping incorrectly dated February 10, 1905, in PRT Scrapbooks, II (1905), in Cox Collection, Wilkes College Library.*

track laying promised in the previous spring would be completed. The partially finished work had left the streets torn up and "in an extremely bad condition." Kruger disclaimed any knowledge of the condition of the streets. "When these curves will be completed and actually in position, we cannot say." Six weeks later Winchell wearily asked once more when cars would run on the line. Many of his neighbors were inquiring at his office about the promised streetcar operation. Kruger said that he could not give a definite answer. First a crosstrack had to be installed, which would consume two weeks, "after which time the operation of the road will be taken up."[27] When the correspondence broke off at this point, Winchell had spent two years in his quest and still had no concrete answer about service.

The company was not always so impervious to complaints. It added three hundred new cars in the four years after 1902 and overhauled and enlarged existing ones. The PRT improved ventilation and cleaned its cars. It reluctantly complied with routing ordinances and operated night service, which did not pay. A payment of $25,000 was offered the city to help with snow removal, and the company added new snow plows and sweepers. Though declining to expand the free transfer, the PRT did lower the fare. A special rate of six tickets for 25 cents replaced the old nickel fare.[28]

Despite these efforts, numerous problems remained unsolved. The PRT was unable to meet either the demands for improved and extended operation or the requirements of city ordinances clumsily designed to regulate service. Attempts to comply with requests and regulations often backfired and angered some special interest. The PRT industriously plowed the snow from its tracks only to have them blockaded by wagons and delivery vans. When it lobbied for an ordinance to regulate this traffic, the company antagonized teamsters and distributors, who then discovered an ancient law requiring the PRT to plow the entire street.[29] Traffic congestion wrought havoc with schedules and caused violations of an ordinance limiting headway between cars to five minutes.

Extending lines into the suburbs added more cars to the downtown congestion and saddled the system with roads that did not pay. As city growth called for expansion of transit service, the PRT felt obliged to claim the requisite franchises to meet that need and to forestall competition which its shaky financial structure could not face. At the same time the increase in fixed costs for installation and equipment lowered the expected rate of return. In its weak condition the company was slow to act and antagonized the public.

The PRT's clumsiness fueled its critics' fire. Thanks to the directors' and managers' passion for secrecy, outsiders had only an inkling of the company's financial difficulties. A 1905 attempt to acquire more free

trolley franchises totaling 110 miles was perfectly timed to remind Philadelphians of the 1901 grab of rapid transit charters. Attention quickly
focused on the firm's excessive payments to underliers for earlier franchises freely given by the city and partially owned by the same men who
controlled the PRT. The incident so aroused the public that Mayor John
Weaver vetoed ordinances, much to the embarrassment of the Ring and
the company.[30]

Abrupt replies to the Trades League and other critics and the company's seeming indifference to service problems further angered Philadelphians.[31] The tradition of entrepreneurial control and business secrecy
remained strong. Peter Widener sat on the board of directors, and his son
George was first vice president. President Parsons' training in the Widener-Elkins companies and long experience as a tight-lipped executive left
him poorly equipped to handle public relations. The rebuffs alienated
businessmen, who were not only potential allies that best understood the
firm's concern with return on investment, but who, along with lawyers
and politicians, were the core of Philadelphia's leadership as well.[32] The
PRT's isolation made some settlement necessary to regain the sympathy
of the business community and to encourage capital investment in a fal-
tering enterprise.

The Subway and the Threat of Competition

In 1903 President John Parsons publicly announced that "this road is run
on business principles. Before we spend a dollar we make sure it will in
some form eventually come back and bring more with it."[33] The statement bared an inherent contradiction in this private monopoly of public
transit. After 1900 the demands for increased service in Philadelphia
called for extensive investment with limited hope of early return. The
concentration of traffic in the center city required millions of dollars for
rapid transit lines that would parallel surface railways. The better service
would not be profitable for many years, and the financially strapped
company could ill afford the delayed repayment.

Despite this problem the PRT built a rapid transit line. The company's
shaky financial situation, which made large investment ill advised, also
compelled it to construct a subway. It had spent $1,500,000 for the Mack
franchises and could not ignore the need for a high speed line. Failure to
relieve congestion would further antagonize the public. Refusal to build
would forfeit its rapid transit franchises by June 1903.[34] The surrender
would open the door for competition the PRT could not withstand.

Originally the company hoped to build a seven mile elevated line on
busy Market Street from the Delaware River through the business district
to 69th Street in West Philadelphia. But once again elevated technology

was rejected as unsuitable for transit in the center city. Merchants and property owners protested, and the proposed road conflicted with a 15th Street right of way for a Pennsylvania Railroad bridge. As a result, the PRT had to build a subway for the two-mile portion of the line east of the Schuylkill River.[35]

The PRT obtained the necessary amendments from the Pennsylvania Assembly in 1903 and at the same time consolidated five valuable rapid transit franchises, including a subway for Broad Street and an elevated railway to Frankford, under a subsidiary, the Market Street Elevated Passenger Railway Company. By building the Market Street line within the required three years, the PRT would satisfy franchise requirements for the other roads. Construction by the Millard Construction Company began in 1903; by December 1905 part of the line west of 15th Street was open.[36]

But monetary and construction problems plagued the project. To finance the road the transit company issued $10,000,000 of thirty-year, 4 percent bonds on the Market Street Company in 1905. Because of the PRT's financial condition, the bond issue sold very poorly. More important, it fell far short of the $22,000,000 spent for construction and equipment before the line's completion in 1908. Calls on PRT stock raised additional funds. Between 1903 and 1905 three calls supplied $9,000,000 to help finance subway building as well as the expansion and maintenance of the surface system.[37]

Of more immediate importance was the challenge of construction. The city required the PRT to erect its own bridge across the Schuylkill River, to relocate all underground conduits, cables, and mains, and to lay an entirely new sewer within the tunnel walls. The job was not to disturb traffic on Market Street, one of Philadelphia's two main arteries. During the work the construction company successfully overcame quicksand, a gas explosion, and an uncharted tangle of underground pipes.[38] The entire project caused only minimum disturbance to Philadelphians and remained the city's sole rapid transit line for more than a decade.

Because of delays for sewer relocation and a detour around City Hall, the operation could not be finished within the time allotted by the charter. As the April 1906 deadline for the subway's completion approached, the PRT struggled for a time extension in the face of critics' pleas for recapture of the franchise. With Ring support the necessary legislation passed the city council and went before Mayor John Weaver, who seemed disposed to sign it.[39]

Suddenly, on March 16, 1906, Weaver had second thoughts about the bill. The cause of his hesitation was clear. On the previous day, the Philadelphia and Western Railroad (P&W) had applied to the city council to build a subway through Philadelphia on a route near the PRT line. The

P&W was already building an electric system into West Philadelphia. In order to extend its tracks through the city to the Delaware River, it sought a thirty-five year franchise to construct and operate an elevated and subway line in exchange for a rental of 5 percent of its gross receipts. After thirty-five years the city was to buy the line and give the P&W an option to lease it for another forty years for 5 percent of gross earnings and $400,000 annual rental. Construction was to be completed within three years.[40]

The fears of the PRT were materializing. The projected P&W line closely paralleled its system in the heart of the city and threatened ruinous competition. Worst of all, the offer was no fly-by-night blackmail scheme. To create another transcontinental railroad, George Gould was attempting to extend the P&W west to connect with his Wabash system. A subway would provide an eastern entry into Philadelphia, and it was rumored that he planned to tunnel under the Delaware and push across New Jersey to the sea.[41]

The PRT's reaction was at first confused. An initial effort to fight the P&W increased public agitation to veto the time extension for the PRT subway.[42] Quickly the company switched to a fresh strategy voiced by a relative newcomer, George Earle. Earle was a popular Republican businessman who had definite prospects for public office. He was well known in Philadelphia as the "surgeon-general of finance" for his rehabilitation of several banking houses and railroads. After acquiring 40,000 shares of stock, he had become a PRT director in September 1904.[43]

Earle struck a new note of PRT cooperation when he welcomed the P&W enterprise. Proclaiming his loyalty to Philadelphia and his desire to "serve my City [rather] than any corporation," Earle explained that "it is our duty to help him [Mayor Weaver] to get through his [Philadelphia and] Western proposition, in every fair way, for such a proposition was never [before] made to a City, and may not be made again." Skillfully, Earle linked the public quest for PRT competition to the extension of the subway franchise now being held up by Mayor Weaver. Failure to renew it would leave no rival for the P&W, would cost the city $400,000 promised by the transit company for the abolition of grade crossings, and would bring about years of costly litigation between Philadelphia and the PRT. Earle thought both projects should go forward. "The Rapid Transit should build its subway just as fast as possible; the Western its; and anybody else that will another, if possible; and everybody should give them God speed."[44]

If the newspapers are an accurate measure, the public was joyful at the prospect of competition. Here at last was a way to control the PRT. No longer would it be true that "in Mr. Parsons' case there is not competition and if you don't like his goods you walk."[45] Authority could be reasserted by the city over its transit system. Renewed bargaining ensued, and the PRT offered not only to make a $400,000 payment but to surrender all but two of its unused rapid transit franchises to Philadelphia. It also promised not to lay a surface line on hitherto unspoiled Broad Street, the most beautiful boulevard in the city.[46] Critics, led by Martindale's Trades League and other business groups, wanted harsher terms, including the return of all unused franchises and annual rental of 5 percent of gross revenue.[47]

Meanwhile the PRT acquired a potent ally. Powerful retail merchants in the business district desperately wanted the completion of the subway eastward from 15th Street. A petition on behalf of the PRT was presented to the mayor, headed by such names as Clothier, Gimble, Strawbridge, Snellenburg, Lit, and Wanamaker—owners of Philadelphia's biggest department stores. These merchants, though not participants in earlier transit battles, were quick to involve themselves when they believed their economic interests to be threatened.[48] In contrast to the city-wide background of the Trades League and other businessmen's organizations, their point of view was a narrow one. The associations united hundreds of businessmen of different ranks from all parts of the city. The very act of association provided a bond and a more comprehensive view of city problems, while the downtown merchants were a homogeneous group concerned only with their area. This split in the business community aided the PRT in its negotiations with the city and was a major factor in the shaping of the 1907 contract.

The retail merchants' efforts succeeded. Mayor Weaver accepted the PRT offer and signed the extension bill on March 28, 1906. Most objectionable from the critics' point of view was the PRT's retention of the Broad Street subway and Frankford Avenue elevated franchises, which were the crucial arteries for rapid transit between northern sections of the city and the business district. Confidently the PRT made test borings along Broad Street and promised action—a pledge it would never deliver.[49]

Nevertheless, as George Earle had skillfully demonstrated, rapid transit competition would be preserved only by the extension of the PRT franchise. The company was too heavily committed to its subway to abandon the work. Of the two proposals the PRT's line was the one most certain to be completed, and the extension bill was the only way it could be finished.

If the 1906 agreement could be criticized as not wringing the greatest possible concessions from the PRT, it must be remembered that the reformers' position was not unassailable. The April deadline for the PRT franchise demanded immediate decision. Reformers' hopes rested mainly on the P&W's threat of competition, which soon disappeared because of legal and technical flaws. The company's steam railroad charter forbade street railway connections, and its routes through narrow streets threatened serious damage to abutters. Finally, the Pennsylvania Railroad blocked the P&W's westward extension at Strafford, Pennsylvania, and ended the transcontinental scheme.[50]

As a response to reformers' cries for repossession of the Market Street franchise and for burial of the trolley wires, the 1906 settlement was a kind of contract. For the first time since the monopoly existed, city and company seriously negotiated for their best interests. The salutary effect of conciliation to quiet public agitation was certainly not lost on the PRT management.

Meanwhile the pressure of fundamental issues continued. The challenges of urban expansion and downtown congestion remained. Public hostility, though quieted, could resurface at any time. The PRT lost $2,200,000 in 1906 and desperately juggled its accounts to cover the loss. To convert the deficit to a $430,000 surplus, the company borrowed $2,700,000 from Drexel and Company on the day it closed the books for its annual report. The firm credited the loan to revenue under the heading "Open Accounts" and then returned the funds to Drexel with two days' interest.[51] In October the underwriters of the $10,000,000 subway bond were forced to pay the PRT $3,000,000 for the securities they could not sell. In November the PRT made its second $3,000,000 call of the year on its stock. Proceeds from the bond issue were spent or committed, although the eastern half of the subway remained to be built and the surface lines required expensive repairs. To make matters worse, a $300,000 jump in the rental payment to the UTC fell due in the same year.[52]

Evolution of the 1907 Contract

Once again, though for different reasons, the innovation of high speed technology compelled a fundamental shift in transit policy. Ironically, in this case financing the subway—the PRT's greatest effort to improve local transit—brought the company to the brink of bankruptcy. In the words of one expert, the PRT's "credit was practically destroyed, and it was unable to meet the pressing demands of the public for needed extensions."[53] Failure to expand meant the renewal of public hostility and threats of competition. The PRT could not simultaneously face its creditors and an angry citizenry. Some agreement was needed with the city to lighten costly paving obligations, to reduce public wrath, and to improve the company's position in the money markets.

Unlike the Boston and New York cases, Philadelphians' preference for private enterprise and the moral bankruptcy of city government left citizens without a public body to represent their interests. They had no tradition of rapid transit commissions on which to build. In consequence, the Philadelphia settlement had a remarkably private character. Negotiation occurred between the company and factions of the business community. City government played no role except to ratify the agreement reached by private arbitration.

In November 1906 the PRT's financial crunch forced George Earle to announce that the company was abandoning the Broad Street subway plan. Tight money markets and a banker's call on a $3,000,000 note obviated any plans for further rapid transit construction beyond the completion of the Market Street subway.[54] In the subsequent public criticism, Martindale took the lead. He accused Mayor John Weaver of poor bargaining in the previous spring and the PRT of misleading the public with false test borings. A company spokesman's explanation that the Broad Street line meant a large investment with little additional return (it was expected to reduce traffic on nearby surface lines) was lost in the uproar.[55]

Several days later George Earle startled the city by offering his resignation to the board of directors in order "to be free" to speak about transit matters. Parrying the recent renewal of criticism, Earle claimed that the major source of difficulty was public hostility. Severe attacks on the company frightened away the capital necessary for expansion. The PRT refused to build the second subway for fear of "socialist soakers" demanding a nickel fare. Admittedly the company was wrong to keep franchises it was not going to use and certainly the high rentals to underliers and the water in the capital structure were problems. But, Earle smoothly explained,"the best remedy for past evils is not to frighten capital from giving additional accommodations imperatively needed. After all, the public should be joint owners in these enterprises; they should share in the profits, not management, and so be contented and happy over the growth that others benefit by."[56] Cooperation, then, was the key to Philadelphia's transit problems.

Not surprisingly, Earle's statement was derided by men like Martindale, who had labored so long for reform. But reaction was not entirely negative. The powerful retail merchants again came to the company's aid. Taking Earle's hints about cooperation and partnership literally, they proposed an agreement between Philadelphia and the PRT. Addressing the public "as citizens interested in fair play to both investors and the public, and as representatives of large material interests dependent for their prosperity upon the welfare of the city," the merchants advocated a plan of cooperation which would concede the position of the underliers and protect a 6 percent return on investment in the PRT. In exchange the PRT was to make the city and the people "full, equal participants in all the net profits of the enterprise." All existing charges and duties would be capitalized and met by an annual charge on the company. The city would be free of any liability but be represented on the board of directors. Such an agreement, they believed, would bury the hatchet, help the PRT's quest for capital, and provide service for the people.[57]

Led by Morris Clothier of Strawbridge and Clothier, the retailers' group probably numbered less than a dozen but included the heads of Philadelphia's largest department stores. In aggregate their annual sales totaled $100,000,000, and all did business along the route of the subway extension. Quickly they organized as the Retail Merchants' Association (RMA) and drew up a more concrete plan. After consultation with George Earle and President Parsons, the RMA set forth its specific proposals in January 1907.[58]

Its suggestions called for the city to repeal the 1857 municipal recapture ordinance (thus guaranteeing the position of the underliers) and the wire-burial law. In exchange the PRT agreed to a contract with Philadelphia which gave the city three places on the board of directors, provided it annually with half of all profits after a fair return (6 percent cumulative) had been paid to the stockholders, permitted an annual audit of the PRT books, returned the Broad Street subway franchise to the municipality, and provided for city approval of future leases, mergers, and securities' issues. All fare changes were to be agreed on by both parties. Philadelphia received the right to purchase the property after fifty years for an amount equal to the par value of the stock, which was to be paid in full within two years. The PRT was to make annual payments into a city sinking fund which in fifty years would pay for the purchase of the company. In lieu of the old car tax and snow removal and paving duties, the company was to pay annually a sum equal to their value. The route of the Frankford elevated line was to be redrawn to make practical its possible construction by the PRT. In addition the city agreed to offer the company a ninety-day option on all future transit franchises. These RMA recommendations became the basis for the subsequent debate and were essentially the provisions of the contract as finally enacted.[59]

Reaction to the plan by the Trades League and the various business associations was predictably negative. Though invited to participate in planning the contract, they remained skeptical of the idea from the time of the RMA's initial announcement. Their objections to the agreement were numerous. First, it did not guarantee the necessary service reforms. Since neither party could alter the rates of fare unilaterally, there was no chance for lower fares or universal transfers. The ninety-day option clause would prevent the entry of future competition. The major weapons of city control over the PRT—municipalization and the trolley wire law—were forfeited. Payment on the basis of profit sharing rather than gross receipts might mean that the city would never receive a penny. The revocation of the 1857 ordinance secured the perpetual franchises of the underliers. In fifty years Philadelphia could purchase only the leases of the PRT and whatever was built by the company; at the same time it would assume the rentals to the underliers.[60]

Mayor John Weaver also was quick to condemn the plan, and his criticism paralleled those of the businessmen. He pointed out that no city official had participated in its formulation. Furthermore, the PRT was giving away very little in Weaver's estimation. Stock calls were needed in any event to complete the subway, and Philadelphia's representation on the board of directors was only an inconsequential minority.[61]

As an alternative the Trades League, supported by the United and the Sectional Businessmen's Associations, offered its own plan. It proposed a limited franchise to be determined by the city council. With the expiration of the agreement the city was empowered to purchase all the companies in the system. Philadelphia would suspend the 1857 ordinance only for the life of the contract and the trolley wire law for ten years. The underliers should make the requisite concessions to permit proper operation of the transit lines by the PRT. In turn the PRT should perform such specific improvements in service as were agreed upon. The company would also complete the calls on its stock and surrender all franchises which it could not construct to be auctioned to the highest bidder.[62]

The PRT swiftly chose the RMA proposal. Parsons told Martindale that the Trades League plan was impractical. There were over fifty underlying companies and more than twenty thousand stockholders represented by the leases, and the PRT had no way of making them come to terms.[63] After PRT acceptance, enactment of the compact with the aid of the Ring and its newly elected mayor, Joseph Reyburn, was fairly simple. The measures necessary to insure the agreement's constitutionality soon passed the state legislature. Governor Edwin S. Stuart, the former Republican mayor of Philadelphia who had vetoed the 1892 trolley ordinances, signed the bills authorizing the 1907 contract.

Following this defeat, much of the opposition apparently felt that further struggle was futile and withdrew from the fight. Belatedly, several civic organizations spoke out against the contract. The Citizens' Municipal Organization and the Women's Civic Club vainly protested before the city council. With the Ring's cooperation the agreement sped through committee and passed both houses. Mayor Reyburn, who had at first opposed the scheme, suddenly saw the light. On July 1, 1907, he hurriedly signed the agreement, scarcely even bothering to consult the city solicitor about it.[64]

The contract was enacted "under conditions which were characterized at the time as 'indecent haste' and without due consideration."[65] Yet to dismiss it as a gigantic fraud designed to bilk the city, as some critics suggested, goes beyond the evidence. The agreement received more than six months' thorough publicity and discussion and had considerable support from city newspapers, which bridled only at minor provisions. As they saw it, though the compact aided the company's financial position, it also would end the continuous haggling and substitute badly needed cooperation for the old adversary relationship.[66]

Neither Martindale of the Trades League nor Edmund Stirling, the shrewd editor of the Philadelphia *Public Ledger* who knew as much about the PRT as anyone outside the company, made any claim of fraud.[67] George Earle, who started the procedure with his plea for cooperation and who was a confirmed believer that "if you be right, in the long run you are the gainer," was not a conspirator or a swindler.[68] For Earle, what was best for the company was also best for the city. As he wrote privately to Parsons:

> For the first time since I have been in the Company, there begins to be an appreciation that something better can be done than attack the Rapid Transit Company.
>
> If I get this into a situation where both the public and our Company can co-operate to meet the almost insoluble problems ahead of you, I will feel more than compensated for the abuse and annoyances to which I knew I would be subjected by forcing a sane consideration of this subject upon the public attention. That so much could be accomplished in seven days was beyond my wildest dream, but I do not want to force this matter.
>
> Of course you understand that I am taking no part in the criticisms made. It is relief, not criticism, that interests me.[69]

To President John Parsons, whose loyalty resembled the company allegiance of nineteenth century railroad leaders, the contract was neither collusion nor fraud, but a badly needed respite. As he explained to another director: "I do not believe for a minute that the City can take the property of the Company, but, for the sake of peace, so far as the future is concerned, we would be in favor of a reasonable arrangement, but not otherwise."[70]

A period of calm to recover and finance the subway's completion was for Parsons a vital, if not the overriding, goal. Peace would not come as long as the city could threaten municipal recapture. Despite his worries there never was any overt threat of a city takeover. The PRT's most caustic critic admitted as much.[71] But the company's financial needs and the rising movement for city ownership of public services throughout the nation made the 1857 ordinance a critical factor in determining investment. PRT support for the RMA plan averted potentially more radical settlements which might have discouraged investors.

Parsons and Earle, the RMA, and the Trades League represented various interest groups. None can be truly said to have stood for the general public's needs for a better planned and better serviced city.[72] But in the private city of Philadelphia with its machine-dominated government, the off-the-record interplay of special interests determined issues of public welfare. The Trades League and the various business associations came closest to representing the public, while the RMA spoke for itself and apparently for the PRT. The RMA was not the company's puppet. The two organizations worked for a mutual best interest: the finance and completion of the subway. As early as 1905 Lit Brothers pledged to do "all that is in our power . . . toward giving you space [for a subway station] and in any other way assisting you." In response to the RMA's help, the PRT acknowledged "the very great obligations we are under to your Association, and every member of the Board is desirous of doing everything possible to meet your wishes."[73]

Ironically, the RMA plan did not differ so radically from the Trades League alternative. The PRT and the city benefited little more from the one than the other. If the first plan failed to guarantee service reforms, the second left them to some vague negotiation process with no provision for enforcement. Both plans provided for the suspension of the recapture and wire-burial ordinances. Both called for the surrender of unused franchises and complete payment for PRT stock. In the crisis that faced the city and company in 1907, the essential requirement was an agreement to resolve short range problems and to permit planning and cooperation for the long range ones. The need to obtain such a compact and the similarities between the two proposals helps account for the business associations' early withdrawal and subsequent silence and for the favorable reaction of the city's newspapers.

Implementation

The 1907 contract marked the beginning of a new era of cooperation. It defined the basic relationship between Philadelphia and the company for almost sixty years to come and signified the city's assumption of a more active role in local transit. At first that role was limited to participation via membership on the PRT's board of directors. But as the settlement suggested, the company had surrendered its leadership for development of rapid transit. Within a few years Philadelphia would follow the successful examples of New York and Boston and assume that responsibility. Once again a changing city's needs had outstripped the abilities of its private transit monopoly to meet them. As in the other cities, municipal funding and public development by a professionally staffed commission were necessary to service the new industrial metropolis.

In the long run the contract had much to offer both the city and the company. Writing in 1926, one perceptive observer stated that the agreement was "neither all good nor all bad. It has not accomplished all that it was designed to do, but neither has it failed to accomplish substantial results for the benefit of both parties to the agreement."[74] Elimination of the PRT's snow removal and paving duties reduced its nontransportation costs, and Philadelphia resumed direct responsibility for the care of its own streets. No longer would needed repairs and extensions be delayed while the city and the company haggled over the obligation for them. In addition the abolition of car licenses removed an impediment to service which penalized the PRT for every additional car used.

The settlement also helped guarantee the PRT's monopoly and strengthen the city's regulatory role. The ninety-day option meant that the company would not have to seek rapid transit franchises it could not use in order to protect its position. With PRT control over the surface system and the subway, profitable operation of a rival, isolated rapid transit line was unlikely. In addition, the PRT's right of first refusal and its influence in city and state politics made successful incursion by a competitor improbable.[75] The examples of Boston and New York suggested that Philadelphia would soon build its own high speed lines for operation by the monopoly. At the same time, local government's representation on the board of directors, its right to examine the books, and its power to approve all future mergers, leases, and capital issues offered controls absent before 1907. Despite the city's minority position on the board, its new voice and its right to audit represented an important recognition by the PRT that street railways were public transit subject to municipal oversight and direction.

The 1907 contract involved a significant retreat from the secretiveness that had previously characterized the syndicate's operations. No longer could speculators and financiers manipulate the system as in the past. Disagreements between Philadelphia and the company over service, fares, and profits continued until the public takeover in the 1960s. But the city now had a much clearer picture of the company's operations and level of profits. At least some of the causes for suspicion and hostility on both sides had been removed. The two parties could negotiate from this point as partners in an endeavor, one primarily concerned with profit and the other with service.

However, these long range benefits were not so readily apparent in 1907. Indeed, both parties found little to rejoice over in the short run. Most disturbing to Philadelphians was the failure to receive better service. The remaining stock calls (totaling nine million dollars) were required to finance the subway. Since the PRT ran deficits throughout the period, there were no funds left to improve operation. No new trolley cars were added from 1906 until after a 1911 reorganization. By 1910 complaints were so loud that a reluctant state Railroad Commission conducted an investigation which confirmed many of the criticisms.[76]

Accusations that the 1907 ordinance was a swindle continued. Special ire was reserved for the unconditional surrender of the trolley wire and underlier condemnation ordinances instead of a limited suspension during the contract's term. The actual implementation of either law was doubtful, but the acts were an important part of Philadelphia's limited leverage over the monopoly. Skeptics challenged the agreement's constitutionality, only to be defeated before the state Supreme Court in 1911. Suspected PRT and Ring cooperation was confirmed by the appointment of machine members Clarence Wolf and William Carpenter as the city's board representatives along with Mayor Reyburn.[77] The Ring shoved their nominations through city council before the ink dried on the contract.

Initially at least, the machine and the PRT were doing business at the same old stand. In the words of one bitter critic: "The era of readjustment in the relations between municipalities and public service corporations has brought no good to Philadelphia. A general wave of dissatisfaction with old conditions in the operation of street railways swept over the city but instead of providing a better system of control, it carried with it all the safeguards and protections of old franchises and laws. It left in its wake a city bereft of all control over its transportation system and bound for at least fifty years under a contract that has no counterpart in municipal history."[78] For such men the agreement "was essentially a company proposition." "From a municipal point of view it was a stupendous blunder" which could "not be defended."[79]

Ironically, even the PRT, which pushed so hard for the contract, profited only after the syndicate relinquished control. The company's condition did not immediately improve, and public hostility abated only temporarily. In 1908 and 1909 Philadelphians rose in anger when the need for additional revenue drove the company to abolish strip tickets and its remaining transfer points. With shaky finances and a critical public, the PRT was not an attractive investment. In 1908 company stock was selling for $12.50 even though $42.50 was paid in, and the PRT soon encountered antagonism of another sort.[80] In 1909 and 1910 it suffered two major strikes. The second lasted over two months and virtually crippled the company, causing a two million dollar loss.[81]

The source of these troubles was obvious: the continued need for money to rebuild and expand. In 1908 the PRT's rentals to the UTC reached a maximum of $1,800,000 and annual interest payments of $400,000 on its subway bonds began. This increase plus a major overhaul of the track (costing $870,000) forced the company deeper in debt.[82] Renewed public anger and strikes exacerbated the PRT's financial problems. With aging equipment and rising costs the company again found itself on the verge of bankruptcy.

Recovery came only with reorganization under new management. Banker E. T. Stotesbury, a Morgan partner and head of Drexel and Company in Philadelphia, insisted on control of the system before advancing the necessary capital. To avoid bankruptcy and the probable loss of their own investment in the PRT, Widener and his associates accepted a stock trust directed by Stotesbury. He then financed a ten million dollar bond issue guaranteed by Union Traction. To reorganize and operate the system he hired Thomas E. Mitten, a professional manager who had previously headed the Chicago City Railway Company.[83]

The Stotesbury-Mitten reorganization allowed the PRT to implement its half of the 1907 contract. It brought in badly needed capital to purchase new equipment and supply more power. Mitten ended the period of entrepreneurial control. He instituted a more open policy with the press and public and standardized and reformed operating procedures. He consolidated and rerouted lines, centralized accounting, and installed an adequate depreciation reserve. Finally, Mitten established a cooperative wage plan which ended labor protests. Within five years the new management expanded capacity, improved service, reduced public suspicion, and began to pay the first dividends in PRT history.[84]

Simultaneously, the company acquiesced in city leadership for future rapid transit lines. The PRT's financial constraints, its concentration on reorganization, and its surrender of all but one of its unused franchises in the 1907 contract indicated that the company had abdicated its control of rapid transit development. Subsequently, Philadelphia's next reform administration assumed responsibility for building high speed lines with little public debate or company protest. After reformer Rudolph Blankenburg's election as mayor in 1912, he established a Department of City Transit to oversee rapid transit construction. The professionally staffed department planned, built, and administered all additional subway and elevated facilities.[85] As provided under the 1907 contract, the monopoly used its option to lease and operate the city-owned lines as part of the local transit system. By 1913 Philadelphia's public transit policy conformed to the pattern established earlier in Boston and New York.

The 1907 agreement and the successful reorganization of the PRT signified the completion and acceptance of the monopoly process. As one observer said in 1907: "Competition was possible among parallel horsecar lines, but with nearly every available route occupied by one great system the idea of a competing surface line is clearly visionary. The development of the system to elevated and underground lines only emphasizes the advantage of consolidation."[86] Acceptance brought greater stability and permitted both city and company to plan with greater certainty. The time for entrepreneurship and speculation had passed. The new era of the industrial metropolis and comprehensive transit system called for rationalization, administration, and cooperation.

The rise of the commercial city of the mid-nineteenth century had called forth horsecar lines to meet its transit needs. Industrialization, the changing city, and the advent of new mechanical technology with its high fixed costs brought the big electric traction system to Philadelphia. Finally, the 1907 contract rationalized relations between the municipality and its transportation monopoly. Together these two would cooperate to build and operate a rapid transit system. The demands of urban growth compelled even the "privatized" Philadelphians to abandon their reliance on private enterprise. As in the Boston and New York cases, Philadelphia's city government had to come to terms with the traction monopoly and assume an active role for transit development suitable to the large industrial metropolis.

Conclusion:
The Consolidated System
and the Policy
of Public Development

THE CHANGE in urban transit enterprise followed a clear and familiar pattern.[1] In the last half of the nineteenth century businessmen in industries with expanding markets and complex, costly production and distribution processes adopted new strategy and structure. In established industries entrepreneurs with the aid of investment bankers merged small, competing firms into large combinations. A new class of professional managers rationalized operations and established a bureaucratic framework to administer the new, large firms.

Similarly, in urban transit growing populations and expanding areas demanded new motive technology. The introduction first of cable and then of electric traction quintupled investment between 1890 and 1902.[2] Higher fixed costs and the rapidly growing volume of traffic compelled the merger of formerly independent horsecar lines into large systems with coordinated schedules, crosstown lines, free exchanges, and a line and staff divisional structure adopted from the railroads.

The work of such entrepreneurs as Peter Widener, Henry Whitney, and William Kemble paralleled the efforts of men like Cornelius Vanderbilt and Tom Scott in railroading, John D. Rockefeller in oil, and Andrew Carnegie in steel. The coming of Herbert Vreeland, John Parsons, Thomas Mitten, and others reflected the rise of a new class of professional managers to rationalize and operate the new, large enterprises. Finally, the roles of August Belmont, Kidder, Peabody and Company, and Drexel and Company exemplified the need for investment bankers who supplied capital and financial skills for the great merger movement of the late 1890s.

A comparison of the cases illustrates that this process of innovation was not simply a mechanistic response. The strategy of combination and consolidation began first in Philadelphia, whose rate of population increase lagged behind New York. Mechanization came last in New York, which had the greatest rate of accretion, and Boston with its steady rate was the first to have a subway. Nor does the pace and timing of change correlate well with rates of traffic gain. Boston, which lacked the spurts of New York and Philadelphia, was the first to have an electrified street railway monopoly and the first to implement the new policy of public development and ownership of high speed lines. In Philadelphia the advent of the new policy trailed well behind the 1890s jump in traffic.

The differences in pace and timing among the cases lay in the variations of the markets themselves. A configuration of local factors, including size and rate of growth, city and state politics, urban leadership, and the law and traditions of public control of transit, shaped the system's evolution. The differences also demonstrate the limitations of paralleling the experience of urban transit with other industries in the late nineteenth century. Public policy was much more a part of the process of change in such utilities as local transit. Politicians sat on boards of directors, abutters stymied construction in the name of local control, popular excitement and machine politics delayed or influenced technology choices, and legislatures set rates. Even more than railroad men, transit operators depended on political connections and influence. Though railroad leaders might hire lobbyists to further their interests, transit firms required their promoters to possess political skills and ties. Railroads could choose among alternate routes; a transit system required control of all major thoroughfares.

The complex interaction of policy and local transit also suggests that despite their influence and connections, the power of transit leaders was restricted. John McKay's study of urban transit development in late nineteenth century Europe points out sharp contrasts with the American experience.[3] In Europe but not in America, he found that aesthetic considerations shaped technology adoption. Thus transit firms beautified poles, buried wires, and mixed conduit and overhead systems.

McKay, however, says little about the possible link between beautification and economics, especially when aesthetic improvements affected the property values of abutting landholders and retail merchants. Furthermore, the three cases studied here suggest that the contrast between Europe and the United States was not so sharp as indicated. Combinations of local groups influenced the adoption and operation of technology for rapid transit. Coalitions prevented the construction of ugly, steam-powered elevated lines in Boston and Philadelphia and successfully opposed repeated attempts to expand them in New York. In all three cities subways substituted for elevated railroads in downtown areas, and Bostonians and New Yorkers carefully specified subway station design and lighting. Furthermore, until the nickel charge became standard, New Yorkers compelled elevated lines to offer low fares during workingmen's hours just as in Europe.

The same influences were true of surface transit. New Yorkers forced local transit companies to build conduits rather than overhead systems. In Boston the overhead wires came only after popular protest necessitated a test which demonstrated the overhead's superiority. Even in privatized Philadelphia, contending groups required policy modifications in exchange for electrification ordinances. Finally, while overhead wiring triumphed with less control here than in Europe, its rapid adoption may owe much to different patterns of urban growth. As David Ward and McKay have pointed out, suburbanization was much further advanced in the United States.[4] The resulting pressure of already large suburban populations for quick transit expansion was greater here than in the traditionally concentrated cities of Europe.

The importance of public policy in nineteenth century transit, however, did not insure efficient planning or regulation. Inadequate or ill-conceived legislation, lack of expertise and information, and perhaps most important, the sudden and rapid pace of technological innovation and urban growth prevented adequate arranging and coordination. Transit policy reflected the political battle among contending groups of varying interest and power.

Nowhere was the complex relationship of technology and policy more clear than in the implementation of rapid transit. The extension of public power to the planning, finance, construction, and ownership of high speed lines by a public agency was not simply the result of delayed or external benefits requiring social overhead investment. Certainly such investment was a dynamic in the development of an urban economy. The support of large sections of the business community, including suburban real estate operators, downtown retailers and city-wide business associations, suggests that businessmen understood transit's impact on growth. Yet the explanation is incomplete for it fails to account for the actions of many key participants. For example, mechanization of surface railways and innovation of rapid transit lines may well have increased costs faster than entrepreneurs could profit from those expenses. If such were the case, the beneficiaries should have fought for construction by any means, and operators should have pushed for public construction. Nevertheless, in all three cases, major beneficiaries ignored the advantages of social overhead investment. In Boston and New York abutting merchants and landowners opposed the advent of subway lines. And in each city private operators built or fought to build subways despite the possibility of public construction. The bitter Washington Street battle in Boston, the Metropolitan's proposal for private construction in 1899, August Belmont's willingness to assume at least one half of the cost of a Manhattan to

Brooklyn subway in 1902, and the PRT's decision to dig its own subway in Philadelphia illustrate the eagerness of private operators to assume the burden of subway building.

The decision for municipal construction suggests two other important points. If municipal enterprise did not result solely from a need for social overhead investment, neither was it the conscious effort of transit men to pass on costs to the public. In all three cities transit men genuinely resisted efforts for public control. In New York, the Whitney-Widener group and the Gould-Sage elevated interests sought to slow or stop municipal subway construction through their Tammany alliances, and August Belmont took advantage of public construction only after the decision was made, the contract awarded, and the contractor in serious financial straits. In Boston, the efforts of Brandeis and other reformers for public construction of the Washington Street subway and for greater local control of the transit monopoly provoked bitter resistance by the Boston Elevated Company. And in Philadelphia, the apparently pro-company 1907 contract in fact represented a considerable modification of the PRT's pre-1907 power and was accepted reluctantly by the company in order to stave off bankruptcy. In all three cities policy alterations represented genuine efforts by merchants, other businessmen, and reformers to improve transit and to impose tighter controls over private enterprise in public service.

Likewise, the three cases illustrate that public aid for local transit had only limited similarity to public enterprise in early nineteenth century transportation projects.[5] Efforts by states and localities to support the building of bridges, turnpikes, and especially canals did set some precedents for later public action. State governments provided special charters and special powers including eminent domain. They cleared away legal barriers and provided financial aid. In many cases boards of state commissioners used public funds to build and operate canals with the help of an engineer who drafted plans and oversaw construction and maintenance.

The parallels with late nineteenth century transit, however, fail in one important respect. Many early transportation projects were what Carter Goodrich has called developmental efforts.[6] In other words they represented social overhead investment to encourage development of a region by private enterprise. In contrast rapid transit construction was designed to both exploit and develop. Subways in the business district and inner suburbs were expected to tap existing demand and generate profits while traffic grew along the outlying lines.

The shift to public enterprise for subway building depended on timing, innovation, and policy. In New York and Boston the pressure for subway construction coincided with the panic and depression of the mid-

1890s, which severely and temporarily hampered private enterprise. In both cases construction required risky innovation. Electric technology was still evolving in the early 1890s, and there was genuine uncertainty about Americans' propensity to "go down into a hole." The addition of that risk to an initial fixed investment of millions of dollars makes quite understandable the early hesitancy of private enterprise and its subsequent enthusiasm after the subway's success and the return of prosperity.

Finally, the interaction of transit and policy contributed to the evolution of a system. Increased demands for municipal control of what had become a vital service in the evolving metropolis of the 1890s initially discouraged private enterprise. But the subsequent continuation of popular antipathy to public service monopolies encouraged operators to protect their positions by building their own lines or by assuming long term franchises in order to incorporate high speed lines into the transit system of large metropolitan cities.

The Public Transit System

The appearance of unified, centrally controlled transit systems was not confined to the three cities under study. By the turn of the century local transit in most large American cities adhered to the same pattern. Independent horsecar lines proved to be inadequate to meet the pressure of urban growth. Promoters like Widener and the Whitneys were quick to see the need for better service and to recognize the potential of new mechanical technology for the public and for themselves. In Washington, Baltimore, Pittsburgh, and elsewhere they gained control of individual lines and combined them into large units. They and their operating managers rationalized organization and mechanized operation. According to the United States Census Bureau, one firm came to dominate local transit with a comprehensive network of lines in seventeen of the nation's twenty largest cities by 1902.[7]

The process was only slightly altered in Chicago, the other industrial metropolis comparable in size to our case studies. Once again the innovation of mechanical technology and its impact on policy shaped the evolution of a transit system. The early horse railways were soon organized into regional companies, as in the Boston case. In the 1890s financier Charles Yerkes, with the backing of Widener and Elkins, built an empire including 479 miles of streetcar lines and 40 miles of electric-powered elevated railways. The opposition of reformers angered by his financial manipulations and deception stopped Yerkes short of complete unification. Eventually, however, a city board united all street railways in 1913 and all elevated railway lines were unified by 1917. Subways were not so necessary in a younger, more open city, and Chicago did not build its first underground line until the 1930s.[8]

The advent of a mechanized transit system and its widespread impact on city life did not escape contemporary comment. Writing shortly after World War I, muckraker Burton Hendrick thought that "the streets of practically all American cities, as they appeared in 1870 and as they appear today, present one of the greatest contrasts in our industrial development," and the biggest change of all "was the mechanism of city transportation."[9] Hendrick marvelled at the trolley's "enormous influence . . . in extending the radius of the modern city, in freeing urban workers from the demoralizing influences of the tenement, in offering the poorer classes comfortable homes in the surrounding country, and in extending general enlightenment by bringing about a closer human intercourse. Indeed, there is probably no single influence that has contributed so much to the pleasure and comfort of the masses as the trolley car."[10]

Historians echo the point. Charles Glaab and Theodore Brown hold that "changes in urban transportation were fundamental in creating the spatial expansion and the specialization characteristic of the modern city."[11] And Sam Bass Warner's *Streetcar Suburbs* shows how essential were street railways to the pattern of Boston's growth.[12]

The implementation of mechanical power and the rationalization of operation by private enterprise offered urbanites cheaper transit with greater speed, capacity, and range. Though the impact may not have been as sharp as in Europe where there was little suburban development before the coming of the electric system, the change was striking. For the first time in American history, inhabitants could travel throughout their city on a coordinated transit network. Suburban growth outstripped the growth of the city proper and followed the patterns of transit lines.[13]

In addition, the flat, nickel fare promoted expansion by subsidizing long hauls at the expense of short haul, inner city traffic. Possibly as important were the virtually universal free transfers, which allowed riders to make several car changes and which along with the flat fare considerably reduced the rider's transportation costs.[14] Finally, flat fares and free transfers also contributed to overall urban development. Along with through lines and coordinated schedules they permitted more flexible adjustment from traditional radial transit routes to the complex patterns of inter- and intra-district travel in the central city.

The system's overall importance to the metropolis can be best measured in rides per capita, and though the figures in New York, Boston, and Philadelphia do not equal the revolutionary change John McKay found in Europe, they are impressive. As noted in Chart 7, rides per person quadrupled in European cities between 1890 and 1910. A similar ratio, measuring all fares divided by the population of the area in which the system operated, demonstrates increases of 200 percent in New York and Greater New York and 250 percent in Boston and Philadelphia between 1880 and 1910.

CHART 7. Fares per capita in New York, Boston, Philadelphia, and several European cities, 1880-1910

City	1880	1890	1900	1910		Increase (percent)	
British	-	56	-	226		406	
German	-	56	-	203		363	
Vienna	-	43	-	175		407	
Greater New York	152	218	246	321		211	
New York	174	267	276	359		206	
Boston	118	175	232	280[a]	(479)[b]	237[a]	(406)[b]
Philadelphia[c]	111	137	226	280	(331)[d]	252	(298)[d]

a. Based on the year ending June 30, 1911 because the figures reported for 1910 were for nine months.
b. Combined fares and transfers for the year ending June 30, 1911.
c. Philadelphia figures include fares and transfers because separate statistics for fares were not available in most cases.
d. Figures for 1908.
Sources: For European data, see McKay, Tramways, 197. For New York and Greater New York, see New York State, Public Service Commission for the First District, Annual Report (1913), II, 28-29. For Boston, see Chart 4 and Massachusetts Board of Railroad Commissioners, 43rd Annual Report (1911), 611. Boston population figures include the cities and towns serviced by the Boston Elevated in 1900: Arlington, Belmont, Boston, Brookline, Cambridge, Everett, Malden, Medford, Newton, Somerville, and Watertown. Because the company had only one terminus in Chelsea and most of that city was serviced by the Lynn and Boston, Chelsea was omitted. For Philadelphia, see Chart 5. Philadelphia population base was Philadelphia county.

Impressive though the American figures are, they still understate the rate of change in two cases. Philadelphia's street railway strikes severely crippled traffic in 1909 and 1910. Ridership in 1908 was 331 fares per capita, triple the 1880 figure, and the numbers for 1911 (326) and 1912 (347) indicate that the 1908 measure is an accurate one.[15] In Boston an extremely liberal policy permitted almost two thirds as many transfers as fares, a far higher ratio than in New York or Philadelphia in 1910.[16] As a result a significant number of riders who would have been recorded as fares in the other two cities became transfers in Boston. If transfers and fares are combined, Boston had 479 rides per capita in 1910, quadruple its 1880 figure. Finally, New York's lower rate of increase is another reminder of its earlier growth. Nevertheless the doubling or tripling of rides per capita to 300 or more in all three cities is clear evidence of the transit system's vital contribution to the industrial metropolis by the twentieth century's second decade.

Despite their advantages, the mechanical technologies and the systems created to exploit them were not without questionable side effects. The continued increase of population and the spreading of residences encouraged by transit innovations quickly overstrained the capacity of surface systems. As a result, cities' limited resources had to be allocated to urban transit. Perhaps more important were the social costs. Warner has suggested how the growth encouraged by electric streetcars contributed to social fragmentation and stratification in suburban development.[17] In addition, suburban expansion spread the city across political divisions, which disrupted comprehensive planning and administration in the metropolis. Finally, for better or worse, the pace of life quickened. Streets became more congested and accidents more frequent. Better traffic control became imperative. The increased burden of traffic regulation, at first assumed by streetcar companies, eventually became a public cost.

The social impact of the new transit technology has received at least moderate study, but the process of adopting the new motive power and forms of transit and its consequences for enterprise have been less closely examined. Analysts have emphasized changing technology but slighted organizational and operational innovations. System building was an entrepreneurial and managerial response to urban growth and the development of cable and electric power.

The efforts of such promoters as Widener and the Whitneys produced mixed results. They and their lawyers devised sophisticated but risky techniques for finance and merger. With their operating men they developed organizational structures and operating techniques for efficient management, but to insure necessary legislation they allied with city machines. Their systems were integrated with city-built rapid transit lines and became the basis of present big city mass transit, and their strategy was widely copied in other public utilities as well as in transportation. By 1910 the Public Service Corporation of New Jersey, which Thomas Dolan had helped found, operated gas, electric power, and transportation services in 187 communities.[18]

But entrepreneurs' tactics eventually weakened public transit financially and politically. For their work promoters took millions of dollars. Their haste for personal profit, their techniques of finance, and their underestimation of capital costs saddled city transit systems with excessive fixed charges. These actions in turn drained funds, discouraged additional investment, and contributed significantly to the collapse and reorganization of many transit systems shortly after World War I and again in the 1930s. Refinance reduced the fixed charge burden, but the preceding period of marginal operation and bankruptcy weakened service and left the systems ill prepared for further expansion and for competition in the automobile age.[19]

The huge profits of organizers and the political alliances they negotiated created long-standing public distrust. When operating costs and competition from gasoline driven vehicles rose after World War I, few citizens showed any inclination to support fare hikes or provide subsidies to maintain or expand local transit systems. The absence of support further damaged public transit and encouraged greater reliance on automobiles.[20]

Despite such burdens public transit remained a vital service in all three cities. Buses replaced trolleys on city streets. Rapid transit lines continued to operate. But as profit margins disappeared between 1918 and 1940, management of those lines became a public enterprise in Boston and New York partly because of their crucial importance and partly as an extension of the policy of municipal construction and regulation of local transit.

The Policy of Public Control and Development

Beginning in the 1890s, city construction of subways inaugurated a new policy for urban transit. In our three cases, surface lines operated by private enterprise failed to meet the growing needs of these large cities. Just as entrepreneurs sought to end the fragmentation of local transit in response to the pressures of urban growth and the advent of new technology, so did the advocates of policy reform seek to strengthen public regulation.

The reformers' motivation was not always conscious or direct. Indeed, in each case the initial decision for public construction was an ad hoc response to the metropolis's need for better transit. Though supporters cited previous government actions as precedents, the present and future well-being of the city was clearly the stimulus. Nor was city construction a wholesale abandonment of the traditional reliance on private enterprise. Rather, it was a mix. Public enterprise was to meet the transit challenge to the point that private enterprise could reassume responsibility. Thus the transit commissions planned and built high speed lines financed and owned by the city, but the facilities were leased to private operation.

In view of the traditional preference for private enterprise, such a compromise is not surprising. Provided that controls were established, Americans continued to rely on the profit motive as the best incentive for efficiency. The leading advocates of the new urban transit policy were especially firm in that belief. Investigations by Robert Wiebe, Samuel Hays, and Gabriel Kolko, among others, have emphasized the important part businessmen played in the Progressive Era.[21] As we have seen, their role was not a new one. After the Civil War businessmen shaped the development of local transit and transit policy in New York, Boston, and Philadelphia. Some, particularly realtors and downtown merchants, had an overt self-interest in the building of the subways. Others, as individuals or members of business associations, spoke as civic boosters and reformers for what they believed to be the city's and their best interest. Of course they were not acting alone. Referenda in Boston and New York and popular protest against the PRT in Philadelphia indicated the city-wide support for publicly built rapid transit.

The very breadth of interest soon removed rapid transit development from business sponsorship. Such costly, complex services as transportation, heat, and light were essential for the industrial metropolis. Stricter urban transit regulation and the advent of public commissions to build city subways reflected that importance. As David Thelen has shown, the increased consumer demand for and dependency on such utilities led to greater public control and was at the heart of the progressive movement.[22]

Transit was, after all, important to many segments of the expanding metropolitan population. High speed lines offered many urbanites greater geographic and social mobility by making available the environment and status of suburban life. Reformers saw in rapid transit an opportunity to reshape the city. Settlement house workers like Robert Woods and Joseph Eastman hoped that city-built, cheap rapid transit would allow tenement dwellers to evade urban squalor. Good government advocates expected public development to offer greater control over the transportation monopoly. City construction of transit and tighter government regulation of franchising and operation would not only improve service but would also eliminate the entrepreneur's alliances with the city machine.

As the cities began to build lines, the advent of complex technology and the evolution of monopoly helped centralize transit regulation formerly divided among state legislatures, municipal governments, state railroad commissions, and the forces of the market. Policing surface and high speed operation became the task of a professionally staffed public body—the state railroad commission or its successor, the public service commission.

Reformers and urban experts expected government-constructed rapid transit and professionally staffed commissions to serve several necessary functions in the new industrial city. The agency would be a nonpartisan instrument of government. It would furnish the expertise to plan, supply, and administer facilities and services required in the metropolis. The new policy and the new commission created to execute it would permit orderly development and control of what historian Robert Wiebe has called the "fragmented and confused city."[23]

Not surprisingly, neither the policy nor the agency satisfied these anticipations. Wiebe has pointed out the limitations of the reformers'

philosophy and technique.[24] Sanguine and optimistic, they fostered expectations their policy could not fulfill. In some respects reformers
strengthened the very organization they wished to control, for regulation
of the transit monopoly signified its acceptance. And finally, discretionary regulation was no guarantee of olympian neutrality and infallibility.
In New York the building of high speed lines would be delayed for a
decade during the wrangling of the Public Service Commission, the transit companies and the representatives of city government. And in both
New York and Boston commissioners postponed the politically unpopular move of raising the nickel fare while inflation and rising costs reduced
returns and investment.[25]

Glaab and Brown argue that local transportation has never kept pace
with city needs: "There has been a consistent technological lag—or what
might be more properly termed a socio-technological lag—in that certain
theoretical possibilities in urban transportation required changes in cus-
tomary living patterns too drastic to be accepted and the movement of
large numbers of people back and forth through the space of the city has
never been efficient."[26] Sam Bass Warner has gone even further, to criti-
cize the facilities that were built. He argues that in Philadelphia "too
much was spent" on transit by a city "starved for funds." "The transit
effort . . . constituted a costly misallocation of the city's scarce resources
in favor of the downtown and inner city."[27] As we have seen, New York
also came close to its debt limit in order to finance subway construction,
and both the Boston and New York transit commissions at first favored
the downtown area at the expense of metropolitan considerations.

Nevertheless, the policy of public construction and the rapid transit
commissions were surprisingly successful. At a time when municipal
government was called America's greatest failure, New Yorkers and Bostonians generated the organizational and technological innovations that
allowed them to build quickly, honestly, and efficiently what were probably the most expensive and complex projects in their history.[28] Within
two decades after electric power became feasible for local transportation
all three cities had electric-powered subways—two of which were city
built. In Boston the process of innovation and construction required
seven years. In New York it was sixteen years, and in Philadelphia ten
years elapsed between adoption of the new transit policy and completion
of the first line.

Admittedly these new lines did not solve the transit needs of each metropolis. Indeed, they led to expanded demand. Overwhelming growth
and expansion coupled with the quick acceptance of the subway appear
to have been as troublesome as "technological" or "socio-technological"
lag. Nevertheless, both the technology and the technique were and are
important. In each case the city-built system quickly became and remains

today the core of public transit. And whatever the limitations and mistakes of early planners, such systems have made a significant difference in traffic patterns. A 1960 study revealed that rapid transit lines transported more than 50 percent of the rush hour traffic in the business districts of Boston, Philadelphia, and New York. The 5 percent of their central districts devoted to nonproductive storage of autos contrasts sharply with the 40 percent in Los Angeles.[29]

Furthermore, in all three cases transit commissions continued to plan and build (or oversee construction of) additional city-financed lines. And in later years, when inflation, urban expansion, and automobile competition boosted costs, lessened traffic density, and decreased the profit margin, those agencies assumed an additional important function. To salvage Boston's, New York's, and Philadelphia's large investment and to maintain a vital urban service, they became operators as well as builders. Today their successors, the Massachusetts Bay Transit Authority, the New York Transit Authority, and the Southeast Pennsylvania Transit Authority plan, build, and operate regional public transit systems crucial to the functioning of each industrial metropolis.

The techniques used to build the first subways were applied to other areas of city life as well. The planning and construction of highways, and the regulation of city bus, electric power, and gas companies also became the duty of professionally staffed public agencies. In addition, progressives made wide use of the nonpartisan, bureaucratic technique to administer parks, recreation, police, and other urban services—a legacy which continues today.

Finally, developments at the municipal level paralleled similar efforts in state and national government. As Robert Wiebe has shown, the expansion of government activities and of the professionally staffed organizations needed to administer them was the backbone of the search for order that characterized the age.[30] Despite the antibusiness rhetoric of the insurgents, the results of the search were not so much a repudiation of the pattern established by businessmen as a supplementing of that order with imitation in government and regulation of private enterprise.

Whatever its shortcomings, the bureaucratic framework was broadly disseminated both in private enterprise and government to service a complex society. Succeeding generations have elaborated the structure to provide expertise, regulation, administration, and development. As Alfred Chandler has suggested, it is a fundamental part of the change in organization and decision making that separates the urban, industrial society of the twentieth century from the agrarian, commercial world of an earlier age.[31]

Notes

Introduction

1. For descriptions of the American city in this period, see Arthur M. Schlesinger, *The Rise of the City, 1878-1898* (New York, 1933); Charles N. Glaab and A. Theodore Brown, *A History of Urban America* (New York, 1967), chapters 5-8; Blake McKelvey, *The Urbanization of America* (New Brunswick, New Jersey, 1963); and Sam Bass Warner, *The Urban Wilderness: A History of the American City* (New York, 1972), especially chapters 2, 4, 6, 7.

2. U.S. Bureau of the Census, *Twelfth Census of the United States: 1900. Population*, I, lxix.

3. Warren Simpson Thompson, *Population: The Growth of Metropolitan Districts in the United States: 1900-1940* (Washington, D.C., 1947), 33-45.

4. For early urban public transit, see George Rogers Taylor, "The Beginnings of Mass Transportation in Urban America," parts I and II, *Smithsonian Journal of History*, I (Summer and Autumn 1966), 35-50 and 39-52; and John A. Miller, *Fares Please* (New York, 1960), 1-34.

5. U.S. Bureau of the Census, *Eleventh Census of the United States: 1890. Social Statistics of Cities*, 50.

6. Taylor, "Beginnings," I, 40-48; Miller, *Fares*, 1-15.

7. Taylor, "Beginnings," II, 39-52; Miller, *Fares*, 16-34; William D. Middleton, *The Time of the Trolley* (Milwaukee, Wisconsin, 1967), 12-27; and Frank Rowsome, Jr., *Trolley Car Treasury* (New York, 1956), 17-34.

8. Taylor, "Beginnings," II, 43, 46-47; Miller, *Fares*, 16-21.

9. For example, see Harry James Carman, *The Street Surface Railway Franchises of New York City* (New York, 1919); and Frederick W. Speirs, *The Street Railway System of Philadelphia: Its History and Present Condition* (Baltimore, 1897), 12-16, 73-76.

10. Carman, *Franchises*, 39-78; Speirs, *System*, 11-13, 16, 53; and Oscar and Mary Flugg Handlin, *Commonwealth, A Study of the Role of Government in the American Economy: Massachusetts, 1774-1861* (New York, 1947), 255.

11. For examples see Carman, *Franchises*, 39-78; and Speirs, *System*, 53-76.

12. Anthony Sutcliffe, *The Autumn of Central Paris; The Defeat of Town Planning, 1850-1970* (London, 1971), 79-86; William B. Parsons, *Report to the Board of Rapid Transit Railroad Commissioners in and for the City of New York on Rapid Transit in Foreign Cities* (New York, 1894), 41-42; Theodore C. Barker and Michael Robbins, *A History of London Transport: Passenger Travel and the Development of the Metropolis* (London, 1963), I, 34-35, 66-67, 178-197.

13. John P. McKay, *Tramways and Trolleys: The Rise of Urban Mass Transport in Europe* (Princeton, New Jersey, 1976), 19.

14. Rowsome, *Treasury*, 35-38; Taylor, "Beginnings," II, 47; Miller, *Fares*, 31; Middleton, *Time*, 23. The estimated range coincides with Miller's judgment and with the approximate limit of horse railways in Boston at the end of the horsecar era. Sam Bass Warner, *Streetcar Suburbs: The Process of Growth in Boston, 1870-1900* (Cambridge, Massachusetts, 1962), 22.

15. U.S. Bureau of the Census, *Eleventh Census of the United States: 1890. Report on the Transportation Business in the United States*, I, 699; Miller, *Fares*, 27.

16. McKay, *Tramways*, 29-34.

17. George W. Hilton, *The Cable Car in America* (Pasadena, California, 1970), 29-48; Miller, *Fares*, 35-53. For purposes of clarity cable cars, even though powered by steam, will be referred to as "cable-powered" to distinguish them from cars run directly by steam.

18. Hilton, *Cable Car*, 29-48.

19. U.S. Bureau of the Census, *Eleventh Census of the United States: 1890. Bulletin 55*, "The Relative Economy of Cable, Electric and Animal Motive Power for Street Railways," 4-6; *Street Railway Journal* 18 (October 5, 1901), 489; and 16 (October 13, 1900), 1001.

20. Census, *Report on Transportation*, 699.

21. Charles B. Fairchild, *Street Railways: Their Construction, Operation and Maintenance* (New York, 1892), 133-134; Augustine W. Wright, *American Street Railways: Their Construction, Equipment and Maintenance* (Chicago, 1888), 68; Census, *Report on Transportation*, 697; Miller, *Fares*, 39-41. The estimate in Wright for horse railway construction was $6,300 for one mile of single track. I doubled that figure (which probably overstates the cost) to get a measurement comparable to the cable figure.

22. Mark D. Hirsch, *William C. Whitney, Modern Warwick* (New York, 1948), 426-427; Middleton, *Time*, 50; Rowsome, *Treasury*, 55-57; Hilton, *Cable Car*, 32.

23. Census, *Report on Transportation*, 682.

24. Miller, *Fares*, 54-69; Harold C. Passer, *The Electrical Manufacturers, 1875-1900* (Cambridge, Massachusetts, 1953), 242-247.

25. The remainder was steam, compressed air, and miscellaneous. U.S. Bureau of the Census, *Twelfth Census of the United States: 1900. Abstract*, 387.

26. Passer, *Electrical Manufacturers*, 216-217, 242-247; Rowsome, *Treasury*, 110-111, 114.

27. U.S. Bureau of the Census, *Special Reports: Street and Electric Railways, 1902* (Washington, 1905), 45. Data on investment and construction and equipment costs are waterlogged and unreliable. But since this is true for both

cable and electric lines, the ratio is probably not far off. In fact the most accurate data on cost of electric lines ($86,000 per mile of track) and the most expert study of cable construction ($350,000 per mile of track) indicate that the ratio is even higher. *SRJ*, 14 (September 1898), 488, 492; Hilton, *Cable Car*, 153.

28. Census, *Special Report, 1902*, 11, 82.

29. *SRJ*, 18 (October 5, 1901), 489; and 16 (October 13, 1900), 1001.

30. Census, *Special Report, 1902*, 6, 120-121.

31. Frederick Lewis Allen, *The Big Change: America Transforms Itself, 1900-1950* (New York, 1952), 14.

32. Census, *Special Report, 1902*, 11, 46-49, 120-121.

33. Barker and Robbins, *London Transport*, I, 99-177; John R. Kellett, *The Impact of Railways on Victorian Cities* (London, 1969), 316-318.

34. James Blaine Walker, *Fifty Years of Rapid Transit* (New York, 1918), 71-86; Robert C. Reed, "Charles T. Harvey and the New York Elevated Railway," *Railroad History*, no. 130 (Spring 1974), 23-41.

35. Walker, *Fifty Years*, 111-113; Elnathan Sweet, *Report on the New York Elevated Roads* (Albany, 1880), 9, 14, 19, 22, 26-27, 33.

36. The review of the telegraph's history is based on the survey in Alfred D. Chandler, *The Visible Hand: The Managerial Revolution in American Business* (Cambridge, Massachusetts, 1977), 197-200. See also Robert L. Thompson, *Wiring a Continent: The History of the Telegraph Industry in the United States, 1832-1866* (Princeton, New Jersey, 1947).

37. For a discussion of the evolution of railroad management practices, see Chandler, *Visible Hand*, 94-121, 175-185.

38. The review of the telephone's history is based on the survey in Chandler, *Visible Hand*, 200-203. See also Robert V. Bruce, *Alexander Graham Bell and the Conquest of Solitude* (Boston, 1973), and John Brooks, *Telephone: The First Hundred Years* (New York, 1976).

39. For the gas industry, see Louis Stotz and Alexander Jamison, *History of the Gas Industry* (New York, 1938), chapters 2-9; and for the electric industry see Passer, *Electrical Manufacturers*.

40. The ensuing summary of gas and electric utilities is based on a survey of the following company and city utility histories: Leonora Arent, *Electric Franchises in New York City*, Columbia University Studies in History, Economics and Public Law, vol. 83 (New York, 1919); George T. Brown, *The Gas Light Company of Baltimore: A Study of Natural Monopoly*, The Johns Hopkins University Studies in Historical and Political Science, vol. 54 (Baltimore, 1936); Charles M. Coleman, *P. G. and E. of California: The Centennial Story of Pacific Gas and Electric Company, 1852-1952* (New York, 1952); Frederick L. Collins, *Consolidated Gas Company of New York: A History* (New York, 1934); Thomson King, *Consolidated of Baltimore, 1816-1950* (Baltimore, 1950); Forrest McDonald, *Let There Be Light: The Electric Utility Industry in Wisconsin, 1881-1955* (Madison, Wisconsin, 1957); Raymond C. Miller, *Kilowatts at Work: A History of the Detroit Edison Company* (Detroit, 1957); and Nicholas B. Wainwright, *History of the Philadelphia Electric Company, 1881-1961* (Philadelphia, 1961).

41. The quotation is from Collins, *Consolidated of New York*, 322.

42. Miller, *Kilowatts*, 94.

43. Glaab and Brown, *Urban America*, 97, 174-178; Roger Lane, *Policing the City: Boston, 1822-1885* (Cambridge, Massachusetts, 1967), chapters 3-5; James B. Richardson, *The New York Police: Colonial Times to 1901* (New York, 1970), 48-50, 79-80; John Duffy, *A History of Public Health in New York City, 1625-1866* (New York, 1968), 569-570; M. N. Baker, "Water-Works," in Edward W. Bemis, *Municipal Monopolies* (New York, 1899), 18, 187-188; and Nelson M. Blake, *Water for the Cities* (Syracuse, New York, 1956), 140, 173-177, 268-288.

44. Edward W. Bemis, *Municipal Ownership of Gas in the United States*, Publications of the American Economic Association, vol. 6 (Baltimore, 1891), and Morton Keller, *Affairs of State: Public Life in Late Nineteenth Century America* (Cambridge, Massachusetts, 1977), 341.

45. See, for example, Gustavus Myers, "History of Public Franchises in New York City," *Municipal Affairs*, 4 (March 1900), 71-206.

46. Brown, *Gas Light of Baltimore*, 61-62.

47. McDonald, *Light*, 109-111.

48. Investment for roadbed and overhead construction in Boston's West End Company (whose capitalization had very little water) was $27,700 per mile. One mile of well constructed telegraph line cost $200. *Total* investment (including plants and all other costs) for Massachusetts gas companies ranged from $2,000 to $11,000 per mile with the average in the $4,000-$7,000 range. For street railway cost, see *SRJ*, 14 (September 1898), 488; for the telegraph's cost, see Thompson, *Wiring*, 243; and for gas costs see the Massachusetts Board of Gas and Electric Light Commissioners, *26th Annual Report* (1910), cciii-cciv.

49. Robert D. Weber, "Rationalizers and Reformers: Chicago Local Transportation in the Nineteenth Century," Ph.D. dissertation, University of Wisconsin, 1971.

1. Getting Up in the World

1. Real Estate Record and Builders Guide, *A History of Real Estate Building and Architecture in New York City during the Last Quarter of a Century* (New York, 1898), 58-63; Bayrd Still, *Mirror for Gotham* (New York, 1956), 205-206; Wirt Howe, *New York at the Turn of the Century, 1899-1916* (Toronto, Canada, 1946), 10.

2. Thomas D. Crimmins, ed., *The Diary of John Crimmins* (n.p., 1925), 1058-62; Samuel B. Ruggles, *Letters on Rapid Transit* (New York, 1875), 9.

3. Charles N. Glaab and A. Theordore Brown, *A History of Urban America* (New York, 1967), 159.

4. Alexander B. Callow, Jr., *The Tweed Ring* (New York, 1965), 48-49.

5. *Regional Survey of New York and Its Environs*, II: *Population, Land Values and Government* (New York, 1929), 43. For economic growth before 1870, see Robert G. Albion, *The Rise of New York Port, 1815-1860* (New York, 1939).

6. U.S. Bureau of the Census, *Tenth Census of the United States. 1880: Report on Social Statistics of Cities*, I, 531-532; *Regional Survey*, II, 71.

7. New York *Herald*, October 2, 1864, 4, also quoted in James Blaine Walker, *Fifty Years of Rapid Transit* (New York, 1918), 7.

8. Harry James Carman, *The Street Surface Railway Franchises of New York City* (New York, 1919), 78-79; George Rogers Taylor, "The Beginnings of Mass Transportation in Urban America," part II, *Smithsonian Journal of History* (Autumn 1966), 43, 47, 50.

9. Taylor, "Beginnings," II, 52; New York State: Public Service Commission for the First District, *Annual Report* (1913), II, 28-29.

10. Carman, *Street Railway Franchises*, 85-86, 103, 108.

11. PSC, *Report* (1913), II, 28.

12. New York *Herald*, October 2, 1864, 4, also quoted in Walker, *Fifty Years*, 7-8.

13. Henry Collins Brown, ed., *Valentine's Manual of Old New York* (New York, 1926), 4; Seymour J. Mandelbaum, *Boss Tweed's New York* (New York, 1965), 14; Daniel Van Pelt, *Leslie's History of Greater New York* (New York, 1898), I, 457.

14. Carman, *Street Railway Franchises*, 25-26; Taylor, "Mass Transportation," II, 34.

15. Record and Guide, *History of Real Estate*, 58-60.

16. New York *Daily Tribune*, February 2, 1866, 4.

17. West Side Association of the City of New York, *Proceedings of Public Meetings* (New York, 1871), v-vi.

18. Mandelbaum, *Tweed's New York*, 12; W. H. Rideing, "Rapid Transit in New York," *Appleton's Journal*, 19 (May 1878), 393; West Side Association, *Proceedings*, Document I, 15, 28.

19. Mandelbaum, *Tweed's New York*, 12.

20. John I. Davenport, *Letter on the Subject of Population of the City of New York, Its Density and the Evils Resulting Therefrom* (New York, 1884), 11.

21. See, for example, John P. McKay, *Tramways and Trolleys: The Rise of Urban Mass Transport in Europe* (Princeton, New Jersey, 1976), 107, 206-207; Clay McShane, *Technology and Reform: Street Railways and the Growth of Milwaukee, 1887-1900* (Madison, Wisconsin, 1974), 16-17, 25, 94, 101; and Geoffrey Blodgett, *The Gentle Reformers: Massachusetts Democrats in the Cleveland Era* (Cambridge, Massachusetts, 1966), 122-124.

22. See for example Church's speech on the construction of the New York Elevated Railroad in *Rapid Transit Assured: A Feast of Thanksgiving* (New York, 187?), 19-25. For his later career, see New York *Times*, January 15, 1890.

23. Simeon Church, *Rapid Transit in the City of New York* (New York, 1872).

24. New York City Health Commissioner Charles F. Chandler quoted in Davenport, *Letter on Population*, 15.

25. New York *World*, March 31, 1868, 4.

26. Walker, *Fifty Years*, 10-14.

27. Ibid., 10-104.

28. Ibid., 15-16, 22; A. P. Robinson, *Report on the Contemplated Metropolitan Railroad* (New York, 1865), 22, 28-29, 32-34; New York State. Legislature: Senate, *Report of a Special Commission Designated by the Senate to Ascertain the Best Means for Transportation of Passengers in the City of New York*, January 31, 1867 (document 28), 5-6, 27-29; New York *Daily Tribune*, January 11, 1879.

29. Walker, *Fifty Years*, 28; New York State: Public Service Commission for the First District, *Investigation of Interborough Metropolitan Company and Brooklyn Rapid Transit Company* (New York, 1907), I, 425-468. The ratio is actually much higher. The horsecar figure is based on the New York and Harlem Company for 1870, which included some steam railroad construction.

30. Sam Bass Warner, *The Urban Wilderness: A History of the American City* (New York, 1972), 26-27.

31. Mandelbaum, *Tweed's New York*, especially chapters 6-7; and Callow, *Tweed Ring*, chapter 7.

32. Carman, *Street Railway Franchises*, 85-86, 103, 108.

33. Attempts to use the commission in New York City government in the 1860s failed because of tangled jurisdiction, local hostility, and graft. Callow, *Tweed Ring*, 4, 76-78; American Society of Civil Engineers, *Rapid Transit and Terminal Freight Facilities* (New York, 1875), 31-32.

34. New York Senate, *Report, 1867*. The quote is from page 5.

35. New York State: Public Service Commission for the First District, *The History of State Regulation in New York* (Albany, 1908), 7.

36. Julius Rubin, "An Innovating Public Improvement: The Erie Canal," in Carter Goodrich, ed., *Canals and American Economic Development* (New York, 1961), 15-66; Carter Goodrich, *Government Promotion of American Canals and Railroads, 1800-1890* (New York, 1960), 52-61. Alfred D. Chandler, *The Visible Hand: The Managerial Revolution in American Business* (Cambridge, Massachusetts, 1977), 81-82.

37. Walker, *Fifty Years*, 79-80; William F. Reeves, *The First Elevated Railroads in Manhattan and the Bronx in the City of New York* (New York, 1936), 13; Robert C. Reed, "Charles T. Harvey and the New York Elevated Railway," *Railroad History*, no. 130 (Spring 1974), 23-41.

38. Van Pelt, *Leslie's History*, I, 459.

39. Walker, *Fifty Years*, 106-107, 115; Jose DeNavarro, *Sixty-Six Years Business Record* (New York, 1904), 39-41; Reeves, *First Elevated Railroads*, 16-19; Elnathan Sweet, *Report on the New York Elevated Roads* (Albany, 1880), 20. The quotation is from New York Laws of 1872, chapter 885.

40. Walker, *Fifty Years*, 126-127; Simeon Church, *Shall the City Build a Railroad?* (New York, 1873); *An Act to Create a Board of Commissioners of City Railways and to Provide Means of Rapid Transit in the City of New York* (Copy of proposed bill in New York City Public Library); New York *Daily Tribune*, January 30, 1873.

41. West Side Association, *Proceedings*, document 3, 11-38; document 2, 56; New York *Daily Tribune*, January 30, 1873, February 2, 1877; New York *Times*, January 30, 1873; Walker, *Fifty Years*, 126-127.

42. ASCE, *Rapid Transit Facilities*, 31.

43. Ibid., 33.

44. Ibid.; Testimony of William H. Morrell in New York State Assembly: Municipal Ownership of Street and Elevated Railroads Committee, *Report and Testimony* (Albany, 1896), II, 1358; New York *Daily Tribune*, March 5, 1875.

45. New York Laws of 1875, chapter 606.

46. New York *Daily Tribune*, July 2, 1875.

47. New York City: Board of Commissioners of Rapid Transit, *Minutes of Proceedings, July to December, 1875.*

48. Ward Burnett to Mayor William H. Wickham, February 6, 1875, and Thomas C. Campbell to Mayor Wickham, February 14, 1875, in Mayors' Papers, Box 6187 at New York City Municipal Archives; RTC, *Minutes,* 9-13.

49. RTC, *Minutes,* 72, 104, 114, 119-127, 130, 352-360; New York *Daily Tribune,* October 30, 1875.

50. In the Matter of the New York Elevated Railroad Company, 70 N.Y., 327 (1877); In the Matter of the Gilbert Metropolitan Elevated Railway Company to Acquire Title to Lands in the City of New York, 70 N.Y., 361 (1877).

51. Henry W. Broude, "The Role of the State in American Economic Development, 1820-1920," in Hugh G. J. Aitken, ed., *The State and Economic Growth* (New York, 1959), 11.

52. RTC, *Minutes,* 280-309.

53. Mandelbaum, *Tweed's New York,* 23, 126, 182-185.

54. The press's major concern was fear of further delay before implementation of the plans. New York *Herald,* July 2, September 5, and October 5, 1875; New York *Post,* September 7 and October 7, 1875; New York *World,* October 5, 1875; New York *Evening Telegram,* September 6, and October 4, 1875; New York *Evening Mail,* October 7, 1875; New York *Journal of Commerce,* September 8, 1875; New York *Evening Express,* October 8, 1875; New York *Times,* July 2, October 7, 1875.

55. For Field see *Dictionary of American Biography,* VI, 357-359; and Samuel Carter, *Cyrus Field: Man of Two Worlds* (New York, 1968), chapter 25. For DeNavarro see *National Cyclopedia of American Biography,* XV, 246-247; and Jose DeNavarro, *Sixty-Six Years Business Record* (New York, 1904), 39-48. For Garrison see *National Cyclopedia of American Biography,* VII, 262-263.

56. Elnathan Sweet, *Report on the New York Elevated Roads* (Albany, 1880), 2-5.

57. For New York Elevated Company finance, see Box 6 of the Cyrus Field Papers at the New York Public Library for letters and telegrams between Field and Secretary Phillip Harris in the spring of 1879 and for "Memorandum of Agreement Between Messrs. Drexel, Morgan and Company and Mr. Cyrus W. Field," dated May 14, 1878. For the Metropolitan Elevated see Jose F. DeNavarro, *Sixty-Six Years,* 46.

58. Sweet, *Report,* 23-34.

59. Ibid., 2-5; William F. Reeves, *The First Elevated Railroads in Manhattan and the Bronx of the City of New York* (New York, 1936), 23-24.

60. New York *Times,* March 15, 1891. For property value increases in the 12th, 19th, and 22nd Wards, see "Annual Increase in Assessments of Real Estate in New York City" in Manhattan Elevated Railway Company Papers, Bound File 1175, Thomas Watson Library, Columbia University.

61. For the Gould-Sage operation of the elevated railroads, see Julius Grodinsky, *Jay Gould: His Business Career, 1867-1892* (Philadelphia, 1957), 288-317. The quotation is from page 21.

62. Walker, *Fifty Years,* 118-121; *Report of Meeting at Chickering Hall, June 21, 1877 to Protest Against the Destruction of Property by Elevated Rail-*

roads without Compensation to the Owners (New York, 1877).

63. George Gould to New York Rapid Transit Commission, May 6, 1898, in RTC, *Rapid Transit Documents, 1897-1904* (n.p., n.d.).

64. John R. Kellet, *The Impact of Railways on Victorian Cities* (London, 1969), 50-52, 57; McKay, *Tramways*, 84-106.

65. Walker, *Fifty Years*, 275. There was a steam-powered interurban line composed of elevated, tunnel, bridge, and street railway, which linked Kansas City, Missouri, to Kansas City, Kansas, in the late 1880s. Chicago lines built in the 1890s were quickly electrified. Theodore S. Chase, ed., *History of Kansas City, Missouri* (New York, 1888), 415-416.

66. Cost of road and equipment for the elevated was estimated at $700,000 to $800,000 per mile, while similar figures for horse railways in 1890 range from $31,000 to $51,000 per mile. Walker, *Fifty Years*, 113; *Engineering News*, 25 (May 23, 1891), 488, and 26 (October 24, 1891), 394; U.S. Bureau of the Census, *Eleventh Census of the United States, 1890: Report on the Transportation Business in the United States*, I, 697.

67. Harold C. Passer, *The Electrical Manufacturers, 1875-1900* (Cambridge, Massachusetts, 1953), 241, 271-272.

68. New York *World*, April 8, 1893, October 2, 1904; *Railroad Gazette*, 26 (November 2, 1894), 752; New York *Times*, October 23, 1904.

69. New York *Times*, January 5, 1890.

2. Cables and Conduits

1. Seymour J. Mandelbaum, *Boss Tweed's New York* (New York, 1965).
2. See above Chart 1.
3. New York *Times*, March 15, 1891.
4. New York *Times*, December 26, 1888, 8.
5. Ibid., December 26, 1888, and October 9, 1896.
6. Burton J. Hendrick, "Great American Fortunes and Their Making," *McClure's Magazine*, 30 (November 1907), 34. Hendrick's count of roads is incorrect. The State Board of Railroad Commissioners reported only seventeen. *Third Annual Report of the Board of Railroad Commissioners of the State of New York, 1885* (Albany, 1886), I, 409-443.
7. Burton J. Hendrick, *The Age of Big Business* (New York, 1919), 142; Charles Edward Russell, "Where Did You Get It, Gentlemen?" *Everybody's Magazine*, 18 (January 1908), 122; New York *Times*, September 29, 1892; Mark David Hirsch, *William C. Whitney, Modern Warwick* (New York, 1948), 208-209. For returns of various street railway lines from 1860 to 1906, see New York State: Public Service Commission for the First District, *Investigation of the Interborough Metropolitan Company and the Brooklyn Rapid Transit Company* (New York, 1907-09), I, 425-502.
8. Wirt Howe, *New York at the Turn of the Century, 1899-1916* (Toronto, Canada, 1946), 38; New York *Times*, April 2 and October 28, 1892.
9. New York City: Board of Rapid Transit Commissioners [of 1883], *Proceedings before the Rapid Transit Commission* (New York, 1883), 15.
10. Harry James Carman, *The Street Surface Railway Franchises of New*

York City (New York, 1919), 24, 40, 49, 85-86.

11. Ibid., 24.

12. Delos F. Wilcox, "Elements of a Constructive Franchise Policy," *Proceedings, National Conference for Good City Government* (n.p., 1910), 4-5.

13. Ibid., 6-7; Carman, *Street Railway Franchises*, 154-158.

14. New York Laws of 1884, chapter 252.

15. Ibid.

16. Carman, *Street Railway Franchises*, 157-158; Wilcox, "Elements," 6.

17. New York *Herald*, January 18, 1887, and February 24, 1888; New York *Times*, November 15, 1888, January 12 and October 3, 1889, and June 18, 1890.

18. New York City Merchants Association, *Passenger Transportation Service of New York* (New York, 1903), *viii*; Charles A. Higgins, *City Transit Evils: Their Causes and Cure* (Brooklyn, 1905), 91.

19. *Appleton's Cyclopedia of Biography*, V, 483.

20. For the battle for the Broadway franchise see Carman, *Street Railway Franchises*, 78-107, 159-172; Hirsch, *Whitney*, 210-223; and Hendrick, "Fortunes," 37-43.

21. John Parsons to John Cadwalader, August 20, 1884, volume 16 of the William C. Whitney Papers, Library of Congress (hereafter cited by volume, WP).

22. See page 5.

23. Hirsch, *Whitney*, 210-212; Hendrick, "Fortunes," 38; Arthur Pound and Samuel Moore, eds., *More They Told Barron* (New York, 1931), 181; Henry Hall, *America's Successful Men* (New York, 1895), I, 561.

24. Hirsch points out that Whitney's family had a background in transportation. His father and brother ran a steamship line, and Whitney himself had dabbled in railroad investments. Hirsch, *Whitney*, 207, 214; "Thomas Fortune Ryan," *DAB*, XVI, 265-268. The quotation is from Hendrick, *Age*, 133-134.

25. The quotation is from John Cadwalader to George Henry Warren, May 31, 1884, 16, WP. For distribution of stock see "To the Owners of Property between Union Square and South Ferry May 8, 1884," 16, WP.

26. L. C. Chittenden to Whitney, August 2, 1884, September 21, and October 31, 1884; Broadway Railway Company to Mayor Franklin Edison, August 12, 1884, 16, WP.

27. John Parsons to Cadwalader, August 20, 1884, 16, WP.

28. For an example of Whitney's thinking see the letter from Whitney to Hubert O. Thompson, late August, 1884, quoted in Hirsch, *Whitney*, 214.

29. Cadwalader to Whitney, August 22, 1884, 16, WP.

30. P. A. B. Widener to Whitney, January 10, 1885, 17; Whitney to H. R. Low, March 3, 1886, 31, WP.

31. Frederick W. Speirs, *The Street Railway System of Philadelphia: Its History and Present Condition* (Baltimore, 1897), 31-36; Hendrick, "Fortunes," 34-37.

32. Whitney to Low, March 3, 1886, 31, WP.

33. Undated offer to the shareholders of the Broadway Railway Company, 31, WP.

34. Widener to Whitney, January 10, 1885, 17, WP.

35. Hendrick, *Age*, 130-131; Alfred Lewis, "Owners of America, II: Thomas F. Ryan," *Cosmopolitan Magazine*, 45 (July 1908), 142-144; Widener to Whitney, February 1, 18, 1888, 51; January 24, 1889, 58; Chittenden to Whitney, September 16, 1884, 16, WP. The quotations are from Hirsch, *Whitney*, 1, 51.

36. Hendrick, "Fortunes," 38-39; Hirsch, *Whitney*, 465; New York *Tribune*, January 17, 1886. The quotation is from "Ryan," *DAB*, XVI, 265.

37. Hendrick, "Fortunes," 34-36; Kemble to Whitney, September 23, 1887, 48, October 15, 1889, 60; Widener to Whitney, March 2, 4, 1889, 59; March 14, 1890, 60, WP. For additional information on the Philadelphia trio see below pages 162-63.

38. New York *Herald*, February 19, 1886, 10.

39. Stetson to Whitney, August 4, 1886, 36; April 8, 1887, 38, WP.

40. Kemble to Whitney, September 23, 1887, 48, WP.

41. Widener to Whitney, February 1, 1888, 51, WP.

42. Widener quoted in the New York *Herald*, February 20, 1886, 3.

43. Hirsch, *Whitney*, 217-218; Whitney to Low, March 3, 1886, 31, WP.

44. Carman, *Street Railway Franchises*, 166-168; Hirsch, *Whitney*, 218-221.

45. The People . . . v. John O'Brien as Receiver, 111, N.Y. 1 (1888). The bid was unopposed and therefore low. The syndicate already had partial title to the property through ownership of the Broadway and Seventh Avenue Company.

46. New York Laws of 1884, chapter 252.

47. New York *Times*, August 31, 1889, 8.

48. "Organization and Operating Methods of the Metropolitan Street Railway Company of New York," *Street Railway Journal (SRJ)*, 12 (September 1896), 514, 517; Hirsch, *Whitney*, 224-225, 423-424, 430-433.

49. Stetson to Whitney, August 4, 1886, 36, WP. The Ryan quotation is in Hirsch, *Whitney*, 244.

50. Stetson to Whitney, August 4, 1886, 36, WP; Hirsch, *Whitney*, 226.

51. Herbert H. Vreeland quoted in the New York *Times*, November 18, 1896, 11.

52. Widener to Whitney, October 21, 1886, 38, WP.

53. Third Avenue Railroad Company, *Minute Book*, December 13, 1886.

54. *Dictionary of American Biography*, I, 581-582; Kemble to Whitney, August 26, 1891; Elkins to Whitney, August 27, 1891, 65, WP.

55. New York *Times*, March 12, 1901, 16.

56. *Statement of President H. H. Vreeland at Stockholders' Meeting May 17, 1900* (n.p., 1900), 1, 3-5; New York City: Board of Estimate and Appropriation, "Report . . . of the Investigation . . . into the New York Railways System," *Minutes*, CCIX, 3032.

57. For example see Hendrick, *Age*, chapter 5.

58. *Statement of Vreeland, May 17, 1900*, 5.

59. Kemble to Whitney, September 23, 1887, 48, WP. The quotations in the next paragraph are also from this letter.

60. Ibid.; Widener to Whitney, August 14, 1890, 62, WP.

61. Alfred D. Chandler, Jr., "The Beginnings of Big Business in America,"

Business History Review, 33 (Spring 1959), 1-31.

62. Ryan quoted by Henry L. Stimson in *Diary of Henry L. Stimson*, entry of May 21, 1924, from Philip C. Jessup, *Elihu Root* (New York, 1938), I, 186.

63. New York State. Assembly: Special Committee to Investigate . . . Municipal Ownership of Street and Elevated Railroads, *Report and Testimony* (Albany, 1896), I, 1022-24, II, 1-33; Russell, "Where Did You Get It?" 122. The quotation is from "Transportation Earnings and Profits on Manhattan Island," *SRJ*, 15 (December 1899), 876.

64. Widener to Whitney, August 14, 1890, 62, WP.

65. Ibid.

66. Widener to Whitney, January 30, 1891, 63, WP.

67. "Organization and Operating Methods," *SRJ*, 513-516. The quotation is from American Institute of Electrical Engineers, "The Metropolitan Street Railway System," *New York Electric Handbook* (New York, 1904), 165. For traffic data see above Chart 1 and below Chart 3.

68. Letter from William C. Whitney in the New York *Tribune*, March 3, 1886, 5.

69. Widener to Whitney, January 8, 1889, 58, WP.

70. Houston, West Street and Pavonia Ferry Railway Company, *Minute Book*, June 13, 1893 (privately held). For the Philadelphians' inattention to organization see Whitney to Widener, January 24, 1891, 63, WP.

71. "Organization and Operating Methods," *SRJ*, 514-516. The quotation is from page 514. When it absorbed the Third Avenue system in 1900, the Metropolitan reorganized its divisions into two districts, each under a district superintendent who reported to the Superintendent of Transportation. American Institute of Electrical Engineers, "The Metropolitan Street Railway System," 161-163.

72. "Organization and Operating Methods," *SRJ*, 514-518.

73. Ibid., 518.

74. New York *Herald*, February 20, 1886, 3.

75. Ibid., February 19, 1886, 10.

76. "The Street Railways of New York," *Railroad Gazette*, 26 (1894), 865-866. Precise calculation of the transfer's impact is impossible in the absence of adequate data. We cannot verify what portion of revenue increase resulted from the attractions of the free transfer. Certainly, however, the net effect of traffic growth in the 1890s was profitable, since each additional passenger's revenue more than covered the one cent per passenger cost estimated by William Kemble. For Kemble's estimate see above page 54, and for fares see below Chart 3.

77. John Crimmins quoted in the *Real Estate Record and Builders Guide*, 49 (April 30, 1892), 682.

78. *SRJ*, 18 (October 5, 1901), 403.

79. "Transportation Earnings," *SRJ*, 876.

80. Widener to Whitney, March 4, 1889, 59, WP.

81. George Hilton, *The Cable Car in America* (Pasadena, California, 1970), 309. For estimate of horse railway cost per mile, see chapter 1, note 66.

82. *The Metropolitan Traction Company, December 17, 1896* (n.p., 1896). This is a message to stockholders whose claims may be exaggerated. The quotation is from the New York *Times*, August 31, 1895, 1.

83. For an estimate of the cost of an electric road in a large city, see introduction, note 48.

84. New York *Times*, December 8, 1896, and February 15, 1888; Special Committee to Investigate Municipal Ownership, *Report and Testimony*, II, 137-138; New York *Herald*, July 6, 8, 1893, and April 1, 1894; Frank J. Sprague, *The Solution of Manhattan's Rapid Transit* (New York, 1891), 7-8.

85. Frank Rowsome, Jr., *Trolley Car Treasury* (New York, 1956), 56.

86. Stearns Morse, "Slots in the Streets," *New England Quarterly*, 24 (March 1951), 9-11.

87. "Street Railway Franchises in New York," *Municipal Affairs*, 6 (March 1902), 68-69.

88. *SRJ*, 18 (October 5, 1901), 489, and 16 (October 13, 1900), 1001.

89. Hilton, *Cable Car*, 29-48; Speirs, *Street Railway System of Philadelphia*, 61-62.

90. For example, see New York *Times*, March-July, 1899.

91. *Record and Guide*, 49 (April 30, 1892), 682; New York *Times*, July 1, 6, 8, 1892. The quotation is from Widener to Henry Robinson, January 18, 1895, in Peter A. B. Widener letter-book, privately held.

92. Charles B. Fairchild, *Street Railways* (New York, 1892), 132-134, 424-425. Fairchild, editor of the *SRJ*, thought construction of conduit, roadbed, and track on a cable line cost $111,000 per mile of double track—an estimate which probably understates the cost of electric conduit in New York. He estimated the cost of a similar amount of overhead line at $61,000 per mile which is more than double the figure reported by the West End Street Railway Company of Boston. *SRJ*, 14 (September 1898), 488.

93. By 1902 the capitalization of the Metropolitan system was at least $125,000,000, while seventeen years earlier the book value of all New York horse railways was $27,696,000. Board of Estimate, "Report," 3038; *In the Matter of the Petition of the New York Cable Railway Company* (New York?, 1885), chart labeled "New York Horse Railroads." For fixed charges in 1903, see "The Metropolitan Street Railway Company System" in Metropolitan Street Railway Company File 2223, Scudder Collection at the Thomas Watson Library, Columbia University.

94. Wilcox, "Elements," 4-9.

95. Whitney to Mayor Hugh Grant, October 5, 1892, in Mayors' Papers, Box 6143 at New York City Municipal Archives.

96. Carman, *Street Railway Franchises*, 62-71; Hirsch, *Whitney*, 441.

97. "Agreement between Metropolitan Street Railway Company, *et al.* and the Third Avenue Railroad Company, *et al.*, December 21, 1897," in Third Avenue Railroad Company, *Minute Book*, December 31, 1897; Hirsch, *Whitney*, 442-454. Hirsch mistakenly dates the agreement as late 1898.

98. Hendrick, "Fortunes," 44. Whitney was among the first to greet Croker upon his return from England to resume control of the city administration in 1898. Other Tammany men are known to have been involved in Whitney-Ryan deals. See Thomas D. Crimmins, ed., *The Diary of John Crimmins* (n.p., 1925), entry for February 28, 1899, 104.

99. Hendrick, "Fortunes," 44; Hirsch, *Whitney*, 225-226, 424-426.

100. Whitney to Mayor Thomas Gilroy, May 15, 1893, volume I, series II of Whitney letterbooks, WP; New York *Times*, May 16, June 8, 9, 20, 1893.

101. Third Avenue Railroad Company, *Minute Book*, December 31, 1897; Hirsch, *Whitney*, 442-451; Hendrick, "Fortunes," 44-48.

102. Hirsch, *Whitney*, 468.

103. For rides per capita in New York, see Chart 7. For impact on growth of traffic, see above Chart 1 and Chart 3.

104. New York *Times*, July 1, 1899, 6. The first quotation is from *Outlook*, XC (September 5, 1908), 7.

105. Russell, "Where Did You Get It?" 118-127; *Outlook*, 84 (November 5, 1901), 281; New York *Times*, March 21, 1902; Hirsch, *Whitney*, 512-514, 516-518; A. C. Bernheim, "A Chapter of Municipal Folly," *Century Magazine*, 50 (May 1895), 149-152. For the Metropolitan's control of traffic, see Chart 1 and Chart 3.

106. "Street Railway Franchises," *Municipal Affairs*, 78.

107. The decline in the real value of fares between 1891-95 and 1901-05 was calculated by multiplying total paying passengers for each five year period by five cents and dividing by the total number of passengers (paying and transfer) for each period. For fares and total passengers see the sources cited in Chart 3.

108. PSC, *Investigation*, II, 993-1037.

109. Ibid., I, 117-118; IV, 1966-2154; *SRJ*, 18 (August 31, 1901), 225; 12 (September 1896), 117.

110. *Statement of Vreeland, May 17, 1900*, 10-11.

111. Whitney to Widener, January 10, 1900, volume 7, series II, Whitney letterbooks, WP.

112. Milo Maltbie, "A Century of Franchise History," *Municipal Affairs*, 4 (March 1900), 194-206. The next quotation is from page 198.

113. Ibid., 205-206, 199.

114. New York Laws of 1886, chapter 271.

3. From Battery Park to Harlem in Fifteen Minutes

1. Ernest Ingersoll, "Getting About in New York," *Outlook*, 58 (April 2, 1898), 834.

2. Lloyd Morris, *Incredible New York: High Life and Low Life of the Last One Hundred Years* (New York, 1951), 197.

3. Ingersoll, "New York," 836.

4. New York *Times*, April 12, 1888, 4. For rides per capita, see Chart 7.

5. New York *Times*, March 22, 1889; New York *Commercial Advertiser*, June 15, 1891.

6. New York *Times*, April 19, 21, 23; May 10, June 25, and July 30, 1891.

7. *To the Stockholders of the Manhattan Elevated Railway Company, February 20, 1899* (n.p., 1899), 2; Harold C. Passer, *The Electrical Manufacturers, 1875-1900* (Cambridge, Massachusetts, 1953), 242-247, 270-275.

8. Allan Nevins, *Abram S. Hewitt, with Some Account of Peter Cooper* (New York, 1936), 497-503.

9. William B. Parsons, *Report to the Board of Rapid Transit Railroad*

Commissioners in and for the City of New York on Rapid Transit in Foreign Cities (New York, 1894), 60-63.

10. RTC, *Report . . . to the Common Council of the City of New York, October, 1891* (New York, 1891?), 2-3.

11. Ibid., 12.

12. New York City: Board of Commissioners of Rapid Transit, *Minutes*, I, October 2, 1894, 53. See also Parsons, *Report*, 60-63.

13. Frank J. Sprague, *The Solution of Municipal Rapid Transit* (New York, 1891); "Ideal Rapid Transit," New York *Commercial Advertiser*, February 16, 1891; New York *Evening Post*, June 13, 1891; Passer, *Electrical Manufacturers*, 270-275.

14. James Blaine Walker, *Fifty Years of Rapid Transit* (New York, 1918), 87-104.

15. New York Laws of 1891, chapter 4.

16. Adna Ferrin Weber, *The Growth of Cities in the Nineteenth Century: A Study in Statistics* (New York, 1899), 437, 471.

17. New York *Times*, July 22, 1888, 6.

18. John I. Davenport, *Letter on the Subject of Population of the City of New York, Its Density and the Evils Resulting Therefrom* (New York, 1884); New York *Times*, March 24, 1889; New York City Chamber of Commerce, *36th Annual Report, 1893-94* (New York, 1894), 91; John Martin, *Rapid Transit and Its Effects on Rents, Living Conditions and How to Get It* (New York, 1909).

19. New York *Times*, February 19, 1888, 15.

20. Ibid., February 8, 11, 19, and March 7, 1888; Property Owners Association of the 23rd Ward, "Memorial to Mayor Hewitt, May 9, 1888," in Mayors' Papers, Box 6187 at New York City Municipal Archives.

21. New York *Times*, April 11, 22; May 10, 1889; January 22; May 31, 1890; Herbert J. Bass, *I Am a Democrat: The Political Career of David Bennett Hill* (Clinton, Massachusetts, 1961), 154-155.

22. New York *Times*, April 10; May 15, 1890; January 14, 25, 31, 1891; Bass, *Democrat*, 155, 175.

23. New York *Times*, January 6, 1891, 9; Walker, *Fifty Years*, 131. Daniel Van Pelt, *Leslie's History of Greater New York* (New York, 1898), 132, 361.

24. RTC, *Report*, 2.

25. August Belmont's statement is in New York State: Legislature, *Minutes and Testimony of the Joint Legislative Committee Appointed to Investigate the Public Service Commission* (Albany, 1916), VI, 545-546.

26. *Engineering News*, 28 (November 24, 1892), 492-494.

27. Walker, *Fifty Years*, 136.

28. New York *Times*, January 18, 1893.

29. For horse railway capitalization in 1885, see chapter 2, note 93.

30. Copy of the Chamber of Commerce bill in New York *Times*, March 16, 1894.

31. RTC to Mayor Thomas Gilroy, January 30, 1894, in Mayors' Papers, Box 6187.

32. Chamber of Commerce, *36th Annual Report*, 84-89, 91-105, 112-125, 135-138.

33. John P. McKay, *Tramways and Trolleys: The Rise of Urban Mass Transport in Europe* (Princeton, New Jersey, 1976), 184. For New Yorkers' knowledge of European transit see, for example, New York *Times*, November 1, 1890; December 26, 1890; February 3, 1891; *Engineering News*, 28 (November 24, 1892), 486-488.

34. Nevins, *Hewitt*, 570-571. The apparent paradox of Hewitt's castigation and praise of the Brooklyn Bridge project is easily explained. As a mixed enterprise the bridge was a disastrous failure, but when government took complete control, it was successfully completed. For Hewitt's part in the bridge's construction, see Alan Trachtenberg, *Brooklyn Bridge, Fact and Symbol* (New York, 1965), chapters 6-7.

35. Jacob Schiff to Mayor Hugh Grant, March 16, 1891, in Mayors' Papers, Box 6187.

36. Ibid. See also Cyrus Adler, *Jacob Schiff: His Life and Letters* (Garden City, New York, 1928), I, 345-349.

37. *Record and Guide*, 50 (September 17, 1892), 344; New York *Times*, January 4, 1893.

38. New York *Times*, March 8; April 3, 13, 17, 18, 19, 26, 1894; New York *Telegram*, April 11, 1894; New York *Post*, February 16, 1894; New York *Herald*, March 2, 1894; New York *Tribune*, March 3, 1894; New York *World*, March 16, 1894. Only the New York *Sun*, ever the apologist for the Manhattan Company, opposed the plan. New York *Sun*, January 30, 1894.

39. New York *Times*, January 17, 21, 1893.

40. John DeWitt Warner, "New York Subways, the Rapid Transit Commissioners and the People," *The Independent*, 58 (March 9, 1905), 527.

41. New York *Times*, April 6, 1894.

42. The vote was 132,647 to 42,916. RTC, *Minutes*, I, December 4, 1894, 79.

43. The New York Board of Trade and Transportation, quoted in New York *Times*, March 8, 1894, 8.

44. Walker, *Fifty Years*, 140-141.

45. For Seth Low's views, see Low to Alexander Orr, March 27, 1894, in Chamber of Commerce, *36th Annual Report*, 137-138. Both Inman and Orr initially opposed the Hewitt scheme as too naive and open to Tammany graft. Ibid., 120-121. For Steinway's and Inman's views on public construction see New York State. Assembly: Special Committee to Investigate Municipal Ownership of Street and Elevated Railroads, *Report and Testimony*, (Albany, 1896), II, 1332-37. For William Parsons' beliefs, see Parsons to Edward M. Shepard, February 26, 1899, in Edward M. Shepard Papers owned by Columbia University.

46. New York *Times*, November 14, 1895.

47. Ibid.

48. Harry James Carman, *The Street Surface Railway Franchises of New York City* (New York, 1919), 78-107.

49. New York Laws of 1891, chapter 4, and Laws of 1894, chapter 752.

50. RTC, *Minutes*, I, February 18, 1896, 328; Edward Shepard to Alexander Orr, January 14, 1896, in Mayors' Papers, Box 6187; "Report of the Commissioners, In the Matter . . . to Determine Whether a Rapid Transit Railway . . .

Ought to be Constructed," quoted in New York *Times*, March 8, 1896.

51. *In the Matter of Rapid Transit Commissioners*, 5 NY App. Div. 290 (1896).

52. New York *Times*, January 22, 1896, 4.

53. Ibid., June 5, 11, 1896. For protest by the press, see volume 18, May 23-30, 1896, of J. J. R. Croes' scrapbooks of clippings at the Engineering Societies Library in New York City.

54. Edward Shepard to R. R. Bowker, May 23, 1896, Shepard Papers.

55. "Copy of Route and General Plan," RTC, *Rapid Transit Documents, 1897-1904;* Walker, *Fifty Years,* 147-150; New York *Times,* November 9, 1897.

56. *In the Matter of Rapid Transit Commissioners,* 23 NY App. Div. 472 (1897).

57. "Report of Committee on Contract to the Rapid Transit Commission, November 17, 1898," in *Documents, 1897-1904; In the Matter of Rapid Transit Commissioners,* 26 NY App. Div. 608 (1899); Walker, *Fifty Years,* 160-161.

58. Walker, *Fifty Years,* 149.

59. *Messages of Robert A. Van Wyck, Mayor, to the Municipal Assembly* (New York, 1898-1901), January 3, 1898, 19.

60. *Municipal and Railway Record,* 4 (April 15, 1899), 146.

61. Croker interview quoted in New York *Times,* February 3, 1898, 6.

62. Theodore Lothrop Stoddard, *Master of Manhattan: The Life of Richard Croker* (New York, 1931), 180-182; "Rapid Transit and Politics," *Outlook,* 58 (January 22, 1898), 212-213; New York *Times,* March 16, 20, 22, 23, 1898.

63. Croker interview quoted in New York *Times,* February 3, 1898, 6.

64. Walker, *Fifty Years,* 157-160; "Memorial to the New York Legislature, January 19, 1899," in *Documents, 1897-1904.*

65. RTC Counsel Shepard wrote confidentially of the *Sun's* suit that it stemmed from its "having the sort of inspiration it does and especially [from] the profound dislike of us reformers." Shepard to George Foster Peabody, October 14, 1896, in Shepard Papers; New York *Times,* December 12, 1895; March 24, 1897; *Sun* vs. Mayor, 8 NY App. Div. 230 (1896) and 152 NY 257 (1897).

66. New York *Times,* June 12, August 16, September 18, 1896; "Letter of George Gould, President of Manhattan Elevated Railroad Company, to Rapid Transit Commission, June 11, 1896," and "Report of Contract Committee," in *Documents, 1897-1904;* William Parsons, *Manhattan Elevated Railway: Collection of Documents and Reports . . .* (New York, 1898).

67. Croker interview quoted in New York *Times,* February 3, 1898, 6. See also *Message of Robert Van Wyck to Municipal Assembly, January 3, 1898.*

68. RTC, *Report of the Board of Rapid Transit Railroad Commissioners of the City of New York, 1900-1901* (New York, 1902), 41, 52-55. The quotation is on page 52. See also "Gould to RTC, May 6, 1898," in *Documents 1897-1904;* Parsons, *Manhattan Elevated Railway,* entries for January 31 and March 17, 1898.

69. Parsons to Shepard, October 15, 1898, in Shepard Papers; RTC, *Report, 1900-1901,* 56, 65.

70. RTC, *Report, 1900-1901,* 62-65. The Metropolitan had approached the RTC as early as December 1897 but elected to await the Manhattan's decision.

71. "Root, Howard, Winthrop, Stimson, Jay and Chandler, Counsel of the Metropolitan Street Railway Company to RTC, March 27, 1899," Defendants Exhibit F, Continental Securities Company v. Belmont, 83 NY Misc. 340 (1913) and 168 NY App. Div. 483 (1915), case record on appeal.

72. Croker's statements favoring the subway are quoted in the New York *Times*, December 17, 1898, and April 2, 1899. For Croker's break with the Manhattan Company, see J. J. R. Croes, "Scrapbooks," 26 and 27, January-February 1899.

73. RTC, *Report, 1900-1901*, 65.

74. New York *Times*, April 3, 10; May 4, 8; September 10, 1899.

75. Walker, *Fifty Years*, 162.

76. RTC, *Contract for Construction and Operation of a Rapid Transit Railroad* (New York, 1900).

77. Testimony of Andrew Freedman in Continental Securities v. Belmont, Case Record, 595-596, 598, 617. Belmont later testified that cost of construction was in excess of $35,000,000. New York State: Legislature, *Investigation of the PSC*, V, 608.

78. Walker, *Fifty Years*, 171-172, 164; *National Cyclopedia of American Biography*, V, 481.

79. John Hettrick, "The Reminiscences of John T. Hettrick," 77-83 in the Oral History Project of Columbia University, hereafter cited Hettrick, OHC.

80. Ibid.; Testimony of August Belmont and Andrew Freedman, Continental Securities v. Belmont, Case Record, 305-308, 496, 595-598, 617; Walker, *Fifty Years*, 164-172.

81. Perry Belmont, *An American Democrat: The Recollections of Perry Belmont* (New York, 1940), 460; Walker, *Fifty Years*, 167-168; *NCAB*, XXXVIII, 25-26.

82. See New York *Times*, March 15, 1891, for analysis of population growth by ward, 1860-90.

83. Walker, *Fifty Years*, 178-179, 182, 186.

84. Ibid., 181-186; William B. Parsons, "Diary" (3 volumes of typescript in Columbia University's Special Collection); Hettrick, OHC, 96-107; RTC, *Minutes* (1901), 905, 948-983.

85. John Hettrick, "New York's New Underground World," *The Independent*, 57 (October 20, 1904), 896-902; Earl Mayo, "New York's Subway in Operation," *Outlook*, 78 (November 5, 1904), 565; New York *Herald*, Sunday supplement, October 2, 1904; New York *Evening World*, October 27, 1904.

86. New York *World*, Sunday supplement, October 2, 1904; New York *Sunday Herald*, September 11, 1904; New York *Sunday Sun*, October 23, 1904.

87. Brooklyn *Eagle*, October 29, 1904; New York *Evening Sun*, September 27, 1904; New York *Herald*, October 28, 1904. See also Volume VI of Belmont collection of newspaper clippings at the Museum of the City of New York.

88. New York *World*, Sunday supplement, October 2, 1904, 3.

89. *Outlook*, 78 (November 5, 1904), 561.

90. Walker, *Fifty Years*, 204-206.

91. Ibid., 152, 173, 176-177.

92. RTC, *Minutes*, March 20, 1902, 1431.

93. Ibid., May 15, 1902, 1520. See also RTC, *Report, 1902*, 13, 30-31.

94. New York Laws of 1902, chapter 584. The following quotation is from Shepard to Charles S. Smith, February 2, 1903, in Shepard Papers.

95. "Street Railway Franchises in New York," *Municipal Affairs*, 6 (March 1902), 68-86; E. B. Whitney, "Public Ownership in New York," *International Quarterly*, 12 (October 1905), 11-12; *Outlook*, 84 (November 5, 1901), 281; Mark David Hirsch, *William C. Whitney, Modern Warwick* (New York, 1948), 525-528, 538.

96. Burton Hendrick, "Great American Fortunes and Their Making," *McClure's Magazine*, 30 (June 1908), 333-338; Hettrick, OHC, 120-126; Walker, *Fifty Years*, 192-199; Testimony of August Belmont in New York State: Legislature, *Investigation of the PSC*, VI, 533-542.

97. "Theodore Perry Shonts," *DAB*, XVII, 123-124.

98. New York State: Legislature, *Investigation of the PSC*, III, 39, 176, 197, 205, 216, 235, 362-363.

99. New York State: Public Service Commission for the First District, *Annual Report* (1909), III, 420-421.

100. For a similar movement from public service to progressivism, see David P. Thelen, *The New Citizenship: Origins of Progressivism in Wisconsin, 1885-1900* (Columbia, Missouri, 1972); For progressivism in New York City, see Richard Skolnick, "The Crystallization of Reform in New York City, 1890-1917," Ph.D. dissertation, New York University, 1964.

101. *Scientific American*, 96 (May 18, 1907), 406. For ridership, see Chart 7.

102. New York Board of Trade and Transportation, *Passenger Transportation Franchises and Their Control: Report by the Executive Committee of the New York Board of Trade and Transportation, Adopted by the Board, September 27, 1905* (New York, 1905), v-vi.

103. Samuel Seabury, *Municipal Ownership and Operation of Public Utilities in New York City* (New York, 1905); New York City Merchants Association, *Passenger Transportation Service in the City of New York, September, 1903* (New York, 1903?); Municipal Art Society: Committee on City Plan, *Bulletin*, no. 3 (1903), *Bulletin*, no. 20 (January 12, 1905).

104. Milo Maltbie, "A Century of Franchise History." *Municipal Affairs*, 4 (1900), 194-206; E. B. Whitney, "Public Ownership," Seabury, *Municipal Ownership*; New York Board of Trade and Transportation *Report*; Bird Coler, "New York's Transit Merger," *Electric Magazine*, 146 (March 1906), 187-191; New York City Citizens Union, *Suggestions for Improvement of City Transit* (New York, 1903).

105. RTC, *Report, 1902*, 13.

106. Some contracts were awarded for construction only, with the expectation of future negotiations with potential operators. Walker, *Fifty Years*, 199-203.

107. John D. Warner, "New York's Subways," 528.

108. Harold Syrett, ed., *The Gentleman and the Tiger: The Autobiography of George B. McClellan Jr.* (Philadelphia, 1956), 245.

109. Seabury, *Municipal Ownership*, 105. See also Ray Stannard Baker, "The Subway 'Deal': How New York City Built Its New Underground Railroad,"

McClure's Magazine, 24 (March 1905), 458, 464-465; Coler, "Transit Merger," 189-191.

110. Walker, *Fifty Years*, 207.

111. Charles A. Higgins, *City Transit Evils: Their Causes and Cure* (Brooklyn, 1905), 91; West Side Citizens Transit Reform Committee of One Hundred, *Report of the Executive Committee, May 20, 1903* (New York, 1903?), 5-9; Merchants Association, *Passenger Transportation, viii.*

112. New York City: Franchise Division, *Reports, 1905-1908;* Walker, *Fifty Years*, 199, 202, 214-220.

113. Robert F. Weser, *Charles Evans Hughes: Politics and Reform in New York, 1905-1910* (Ithaca, New York, 1967), 153-171; Merlo J. Pusey, *Charles Evans Hughes* (New York, 1951), I, 200-209.

114. Henry Bruere, "Public Utilities Regulation in New York," *Annals of the American Academy of Political and Social Science*, 31 (May 1908), 1-17; Augustus Cerillo, Jr., "Reform in New York City: A Study of Urban Progressivism," Ph.D. dissertation, Northwestern University, 1969, 235. Even with expanded powers, the PSC discovered the difficulty of the regulation of service in the complex transit business. See Frederick W. Whitridge, *The Public Service Commission's Correspondence with the Receiver of the Third Avenue Railroad* (New York, 1910).

115. Louis Roth, "History of Rapid Transit Development in the City of New York" (typescript in New York City Municipal Reference Library), 15-61; Walker, *Fifty Years*, 213-241.

116. Pusey, *Hughes*, I, 207; Walker, *Fifty Years*, 208-210.

4. Witches without Broomsticks

1. Sam Bass Warner, *Streetcar Suburbs: The Process of Growth in Boston, 1870-1900* (Cambridge, Massachusetts, 1962), 1, 43, 153; Arthur M. Schlesinger, *The Rise of the City, 1878-1898* (New York, 1933), 85; George Rogers Taylor, "The Beginnings of Mass Transportation in Urban America," part I, *Smithsonian Journal of History*, I (Summer 1966), 37-38; Leo F. Schnore and Peter R. Knights, "Residence and Social Structure: Boston in the Ante-Bellum Period," in Stephen Thernstrom and Richard Sennett, *Nineteenth Century Cities: Essays in the New Urban History* (New Haven, Connecticut, 1969), 248-249.

2. Warner, *Suburbs*, 1.

3. Ibid., 1-3, 153; David Ward, "The Industrial Revolution and the Emergence of Boston's Central Business District," *Economic Geography*, 42 (1966), 152-171.

4. Taylor, "Mass Transportation," II, 34; Warner, *Suburbs*, 49-52. The quotation is from Abraham E. Pinanski, *The Street Railway System of Metropolitan Boston* (New York, 1908), 5. See also Walter S. Allen, "Street Railway Franchises in Massachusetts," *Annals of the American Academy of Political and Social Science*, 27 (January 1906), 103.

5. Charles J. Kennedy, "Commuter Services in the Boston Area," *Business History Review*, 36 (Summer 1962), 153-170; Taylor, "Mass Transportation," II, 32-33; United States Bureau of the Census, *Eleventh Census of the*

United States: 1890. Social Statistics of Cities, 50; Louis P. Hager, *History of the West End Street Railway* (Boston, 1892), 125-126.

6. Taylor, "Mass Transportation," II, 50; Hager, *West End,* 125-126; "The Boston Rapid Transit Situation," *Engineering News,* 29 (March 16, 1893), 252.

7. Allen, "Franchises," 92-93; Taylor, "Mass Transportation," II, 47.

8. Oscar and Mary Flugg Handlin, *Commonwealth, A Study of the Role of Government in the American Economy: Massachusetts, 1774-1861* (New York, 1947), 55, 261.

9. Allen, "Franchises," 92-94; Louis D. Brandeis, "The Experience of Massachusetts in Street Railways," *Municipal Affairs,* 6 (Winter 1902), 721-723.

10. Robert H. Whitten, *Public Administration in Massachusetts* (New York, 1898), 114-116; Allen, "Franchises," 94-95; Brandeis, "Experience," 722.

11. Brandeis, "Experience," 723-725; Allen, "Franchises," 95.

12. Brandeis, "Experience," 723-725; Allen, "Franchises," 95.

13. *Street Railway Journal (SRJ),* 14 (September 1898), 492.

14. Allen, "Franchises," 103.

15. William H. Colcord, *The Rights and Wrongs of a Million* (Boston, 1909), 15.

16. Prentiss Cummings, "Street Railway System of Boston," *Professional and Industrial History of Suffolk County, Massachusetts* (Boston, 1894), III, 88-90; Allen, "Franchises," 103-107; Boston Elevated Railway Company, *Fifty Years of Unified Transportation in Metropolitan Boston* (Boston, 1938), 15.

17. Cummings, "System," 288-290.

18. Ibid., 290-292.

19. *SRJ,* 10 (May 1894), 299.

20. Cummings, "System," 291.

21. Ibid., 292-293.

22. Ibid., 292.

23. B. Leighton Beal, "Boston Municipal Subway," *Municipal Affairs,* 4 (March 1900), 219; Linus M. Child, *Shall the Metropolis of New England Have an Elevated Railway?* (Boston, 1879), 7; Charles E. Powers, *Shall the Metropolis of New England Have an Elevated Railroad?* (Boston, 1880), 7; Boston *Herald,* February 10, 1882.

24. Colcord, *Rights,* 15; Warner, *Suburbs,* 22; Schnore and Knights, "Residence," 248-249.

25. George W. Hilton, *The Cable Car in America* (Pasadena, California, 1970), 471-472; William Glasgell, "West End Street Railway: Factors in Its Early Development," senior paper, Harvard University, 1970, 11. Calvin Richards' statement is in Metropolitan Railroad Company, *Annual Report for the Year Ending November 30, 1886,* 10-11.

26. Whitten, *Administration,* 118.

27. Arthur Pound and Samuel Moore, *More They Told Barron* (New York, 1931), 42.

28. Moody Merrill, *Argument of Honorable Moody Merrill . . . on the Petition of the Highland Street Railway Company for Authority to Lease . . . , February 24, 1886* (Boston, 1886), 3; Cummings, "System," 293.

29. Samuel L. Powers, *Portraits of a Half Century* (Boston, 1925), 197-203; Geoffrey Blodgett, *The Gentle Reformers: Massachusetts Democrats in the Cleveland Era* (Cambridge, Massachusetts, 1966), 85, 113. For the limited relationship between Henry and William Whitney see Mark D. Hirsch, *William C. Whitney, Modern Warwick* (New York, 1948), 551; and "William Whitney Account Sheet" (with J. S. Metcalf and Company for December 1889) in volume 61 of the William C. Whitney Papers, Library of Congress.

30. West End Land Company, *Deed of Trust, December 19, 1886*, in Corporate Records Division of Baker Library, Harvard Business School; Hager, *West End*, 12-13.

31. Cummings, "System," 293-294; Charles Sergeant, "Early Experiments in Boston," *SRJ*, 24 (October 8, 1904), 534-535.

32. Hager, *West End*, 21-22, 29-30; Cummings, "System," 294; Boston *Journal*, September 7, 1893; "To the Stockholders of the West End Land Company, October 1, 1889," in West End Street Railway Company File in Corporate Records Division, Baker Library, Harvard Business School.

33. Hager, *West End*, 21-22, 29-30; Cummings, "System," 294-295; "The Street Railway System of Boston," *SRJ*, 11 (April 1895), 207-208; Lewis Stackpole Dabney, *Arguments of L. S. Dabney for the Remonstrants against the West End Street Railway Company's Bill . . .* (Boston, 1887); Massachusetts Statutes of 1887, chapter 413; Pinanski, *Street Railway System*, 15-17; Chronology of Boston street railway development prepared by Bradley Clarke of Cambridge, Massachusetts.

34. *SRJ*, 4 (January 1888), 18.

35. Hager, *West End*, 22.

36. "Street Railway System," *SRJ*, 207-232.

37. Ibid., 223-224; H. W. Putney, comp., *Officials Engaged in Conducting Transportation upon the Boston Elevated Railway and Its Predecessor the West End Street Railway* (Pamphlet in MBTA Library, Boston, Massachusetts); Hager, *West End*, 156-157. When the road began electrification, it added an engineer to the general manager's staff to direct the work. Stearns Morse, "Slots in the Streets," *New England Quarterly*, 24 (March 1951), 5-9.

38. "Street Railway System," *SRJ*, 222-225.

39. Hager, *West End*, 26; Massachusetts Public Service Commission, *Report of the Public Service Commission and the Boston Transit Commission Acting as a Joint Commission under Chapter 108, Resolves of 1913* (Boston, 1914), 14-15; Edward S. Mason, *The Street Railway in Massachusetts* (Cambridge, Massachusetts, 1932), 118-119; "They Paid Four Fares to Four Railways to Go to Boston in the Old Days," *Cooperation*, 27 (October 1948), 55-58.

40. For the cost and operating problems of cable systems, see above pages 6, 60-61.

41. "Views of C. A. Richards of Boston," *SRJ*, 3 (December 1887), 1048.

42. Ibid.

43. Metropolitan Railroad Company, *Annual Report for 1886*, 10-11; Henry M. Whitney to William W. Clapp, September 24, 1887, W. W. Clapp Papers, Houghton Library, Harvard University.

44. Frank J. Sprague, "Birth of the Electric Railway," *SRJ*, 78 (September

15, 1934), 320-321; Frank J. Sprague, "The Electric Railway," *Century Magazine,* 70 (August 1905), 519; Harold C. Passer, *The Electrical Manufacturers, 1875-1900* (Cambridge, Massachusetts, 1953), 242-247.

45. Operating and accounting sheets in West End Street Railway File at the Manuscript Division, Baker Library, Harvard Business School.

46. West End Street Railway Company, *Fifth Annual Report* (1892), 3; and *Seventh Annual Report* (1894), 4. The quotation is from the company's *Third Annual Report* (1890), 4.

47. Nathaniel Thayer, quoted in Pound and Moore, *More Barron,* 43-44.

48. Boston: Board of Aldermen, *Report of Adjourned Hearing before the Committee of the Whole on West End Petition for Use of Overhead Electric System* (Boston, 1889), 66, 71; Hager, *West End,* 121-122.

49. See above Chart 4.

50. Massachusetts Public Service Commission, *Report under Chapter 108,* 14-15; Mason, *Street Railway,* 118-119; Interview with Bradley Clarke, President of Boston Street Rail Fans Association, January 15, 1975.

51. For the experience with elevated railroads in New York, see above pages 8, 30-31, 35-39.

52. Massachusetts: General Court. Committee on Street-Railways, *Not Wanted: Elevated Railways in the City of Boston* (Boston, 1879).

53. *Railroad Gazette,* 12 (November 5, 1880), 580-582; Linus M. Child, *Speech before Commission [on elevated railroads], March 13, 1880* (Boston, 1880), 15, 26-27, 36-38; Boston *Herald,* March 17, 1889; February 10, 1882; Woodward Emery, *Summary of the Closing Argument of Woodward Emery . . . for a Charter to Build an Elevated Railway in Boston* (Boston, 1890), 4, 6-7; Powers, *Shall the Metropolis;* Somerville *Journal,* February 15, 1879; Malden *Mirror,* February 18, 1882.

54. Henry Muzzy, *Remarks on the "Act to Permit Joe V. Meigs and Associates to Build an Elevated Railway," March 7, 1882* (Boston, 1882); Moody Merrill, *Elevated Railways. Opening Arguments for . . ., February 25, 1880* (Boston, 1880); Child, *Speech,* 28-33, 35-37; Committee on Street-Railways, *Not Wanted,* 2, 5-7, 9, 161-164; Boston *Evening Transcript,* February 13, 1880; April 9, 1889; Edward P. Brown, *Elevated Railroads. Closing Argument of . . . , February 12, 1883* (Boston, 1883), 1-11; Boston *Daily Advertiser,* March 3, 1879; Boston *Journal,* March 2, 1880; "Remonstrances against Elevated Railroads, 1881-1882" (Petitions in Massachusetts Statehouse Library).

55. Francis D. Donovan, "Meigs Elevated Railway Ran in East Cambridge," in Scrapbook 18, no. 25 at Massachusetts Statehouse Library; Massachusetts: General Court. Committee on Street Railways, "Hearings on the Macke System of Elevated Railways" (typescripts in Massachusetts Statehouse Library).

56. Joe V. Meigs, *The Meigs Elevated Railway System* (Boston, 1887); Donovan, "Meigs Elevated."

57. John A. Garraty, *The New Commonwealth, 1870-1890* (New York, 1968), 238, 241; Matthew Josephson, *The Politicos, 1865-1896* (New York, 1938), 54, 89, 92, 111. See also R. S. Holzman, *Stormy Ben Butler* (New York, 1954).

58. Meigs, *Elevated Railway,* 1-6; Boston *Journal,* June 21, August 4, 1894; Boston *Herald,* June 29, 1894.

59. Blodgett, *Gentle Reformers*, especially pages 141-145.

60. Thomas W. Lawson, *Frenzied Finance* (New York, 1905), 134.

61. Blodgett, *Gentle Reformers*, 53-55, 110, 113; Massachusetts: General Court, *Report of the Committee to Investigate Methods Used for and Against Legislation Concerning Railroads. Investigation into the Conduct of Members of the House in Connection Therewith* (Boston, 1890), 209-210, 410, 439-440; Henry M. Whitney to W. W. Clapp, January 17, August 27, 1887, Clapp Papers.

62. Boston *Journal*, February 20, 1893, 4. See also Boston *Herald*, March 26, 1891, and Blodgett, *Gentle Reformers*, 123-124.

63. Massachusetts Statutes of 1887, chapter 413; Thomas Wigglesworth et al., *Shall the Citizens of Boston Be Taxed to Furnish a New Highway Solely for the West End Street Railway Company?* (Boston, 1890?), 39-40.

64. Massachusetts Statutes of 1890, chapter 454.

65. Whitney to Clapp, October 4, 1890, Clapp Papers; West End Street Railway Company, *Records of the Executive Committee*, September 29, 1890 (privately held); Hager, *West End*, 124; Wigglesworth, *Shall the Citizens?* 2-8.

66. See Chart 7.

67. Warner, *Suburbs*, 8-9, 157-158.

5. Saving the Common

1. Sam Bass Warner, *Streetcar Suburbs: The Process of Growth in Boston, 1870-1900* (Cambridge, Massachusetts, 1962), 153. For traffic, see above Chart 4.

2. B. Leighton Beal, "Boston Municipal Subway," *Municipal Affairs*, 4 (March 1900), 219; Robert A. Woods and Joseph B. Eastman, "The Boston Franchise Contest," *Outlook*, 82 (April 14, 1906), 835; Abraham E. Pinanski, *The Street Railway System of Metropolitan Boston* (New York, 1908), 20; Louis P. Hager, *History of the West End Street Railway* (Boston, 1892), 59, 77; Boston *Evening Transcript* [hereafter *Transcript*], October 8, 9, 1891.

3. *Transcript*, November 28, 1893, 4.

4. Goeffrey Blodgett, *The Gentle Reformers: Massachusetts Democrats in the Cleveland Era* (Cambridge, Massachusetts, 1966), 110-113; *Transcript*, January 3, 1890; Thomas Wigglesworth et al., *Shall the Citizens of Boston Be Taxed to Furnish a New Highway Solely for the West End Street Railway Company?* (Boston, 1890), 2-8, 39-40. For similar hostility toward the West End's successor, see Richard M. Abrams, *Conservatism in a Progressive Era: Massachusetts Politics, 1900-1912* (Cambridge, Massachusetts, 1964), 72, 79.

5. Massachusetts: General Court, *Report of the Committee to Investigate Methods Used for and against Legislation Concerning Railroads. Investigation into the Conduct of Members of the House in Connection Therewith* (Boston, 1890), *viii-xix*, 208, 214, 309-310, 410-411, 439-440; Blodgett, *Gentle Reformers*, 110-113.

6. *Transcript*, December 16, 1890, 4.

7. Blodgett, *Gentle Reformers*, 159-160.

8. Ibid., 141-145, 159-160.

9. Mayor Matthews quoted in *Transcript*, January 5, 1891, 2.

10. Massachusetts: General Court. Rapid Transit Commission, *Report of the Rapid Transit Commission to the Massachusetts Legislature, April 5, 1892,* 138-222.

11. Ibid., 154-157, 187-189. The quotations are from pages 162 and 155.

12. Rapid Transit Commission, *Report,* 5-6.

13. Henry Curtis Spaulding, *Local Transportation at Boston* (Boston, 1891).

14. Massachusetts: General Court. Joint Special Committee on Transit, "Hearings on Subways in Boston before the Joint Special Committee on Transit, 1894" (typescript at Massachusetts Statehouse Library), IX, 64.

15. Rapid Transit Commission, *Report,* 14-94.

16. Ibid., 6.

17. Ibid., 98-99.

18. Massachusetts Statutes of 1889, chapter 439.

19. Rapid Transit Commission, *Report,* 101-102.

20. Frank Parsons, *The City for the People* (Philadelphia, 1901), 115; Jacob H. Hollander, *The Cincinnati Southern Railway: A Study in Municipal Activity* (Baltimore, 1894).

21. Charles A. Snow, *Snow on Corporations: Quasi Public and Other Corporations* (n.p., n.d.), 1095.

22. Carter Goodrich, *Government Promotion of American Canals and Railroads, 1880-1890* (New York, 1960), 232-234; Edward C. Kirkland, *Men, Cities and Transportation: A Study in New England History, 1820-1900* (Cambridge, Massachusetts, 1948), I, 387-432. For the roots of the state's developmental and regulatory role, see Oscar and Mary F. Handlin, *Commonwealth, A Study of the Role of Government in the American Economy: Massachusetts, 1774-1861* (New York, 1947).

23. Frank Parsons, "Legal Aspects of Monopoly," in Edward W. Bemis, ed., *Municipal Monopolies* (New York, 1899), 449.

24. Snow, *Corporations,* 997.

25. Massachusetts: General Court. Special Committee to Investigate the Relationship between Cities and Towns and Street Railway Companies, *Report of the Special Committee Appointed to Investigate the Relations between Cities and Towns and Street Railway Companies, February, 1898* (Boston, 1898), 30.

26. Rapid Transit Commission, *Report,* 163.

27. Ibid., 177-184.

28. Goodrich, *Government Promotions,* 7-8.

29. James A. Merino, "A Great City and Its Suburbs: Attempts to Integrate Metropolitan Boston, 1865-1920," Ph.D. Dissertation, University of Texas at Austin, 1968, 55-62.

30. *Transcript,* April 5, 1892, 4.

31. Ibid., February 1-3, 1893; Boston *Herald,* February 2, 1893.

32. *Transcript,* February 1, 1893, 1.

33. Ibid., April 9, 1892, 12.

34. Ibid., February 2, 1893, 4.

35. Ibid., February 1, 1893, 4.

36. Ibid., February 3, 1893.

37. Boston *Post*, February 12, 1893, 4.

38. Boston *Herald*, February 10, 1893.

39. *Transcript*, March 4, 1893.

40. Massachusetts Statutes of 1893, chapter 481.

41. *Herald*, October 27, November 8, 1893.

42. *Herald*, November 8, 1893.

43. *Transcript*, October 25, 1893.

44. Ibid., February 9, 1893, 4.

45. Massachusetts Statutes of 1893, chapter 478.

46. *Transcript*, November 21, 1891, 5.

47. Letter of George S. Hale to *Transcript*, March 1, 1893, 4.

48. Blake McKelvey, *The Urbanization of America* (New Brunswick, New Jersey, 1963), 88.

49. See Boston *Herald*, February 25, 1893, for a statement by Herbert L. Harding, Secretary of the Citizens Association, expressing faith in a commission of the "best men of the community," whose actions were to be approved by the mayor.

50. Massachusetts Statutes of 1893, chapter 478.

51. *Transcript*, December 18, 1893, 8.

52. The Board of Aldermen voted 11 to 1 and the Common Council voted 62 to 2. *Herald*, December 19, 22, 1893.

53. Blodgett, *Gentle Reformers*, 144-145.

54. Edwin M. Bacon, *The Book of Boston* (Boston, 1916), 113.

55. Boston Transit Commission, *First Annual Report of the Boston Transit Commission* (Boston, 1895), 58-62.

56. Committee on Transit, "Hearings on Subways," I, 2, 13-15.

57. Ibid., I, 21; II, 34-36.

58. Ibid., V, 34-60; VI, 3-5.

59. Ibid., VII, 76.

60. Ibid., IX, 67, 35.

61. Ibid., I, 31-41; VIII, 93-110; XIV, 7-41.

62. Ibid., IV, 34; V, 29; VI, 35, 75; X, 60-63, 92; *Transcript*, November 21 and December 13, 1893.

63. Committee on Transit, "Hearings on Subways," X, 37.

64. Boston *Herald*, June 23, 1894.

65. Blodgett, *Gentle Reformers*, 164-165.

66. Boston *Herald*, April 30, 1894, 7.

67. Massachusetts Statutes of 1894, chapter 548.

68. Boston *Herald*, June 29, 1894, 4.

69. *Transcript*, July 3, 1894, 1.

70. *Herald*, July 27, 1894.

71. Kirkland, *Men, Cities and Transportation*, II, 243.

72. Roger Lane, *Policing the City: Boston, 1822-1885* (Cambridge, Massachusetts, 1967), 213-219.

73. BTC, *Third Annual Report* (1897), 25-61, passim. For a discussion of an early canal board, see Ronald E. Shaw, *Erie Water West: A History of the Erie Canal, 1792-1854* (Lexington, Kentucky, 1966), 86-88.

74. BTC, *First Annual Report* (1895), 10-12.

75. An April 10 meeting of subway opponents was supported by twenty-two members of the Massachusetts House of Representatives. Of this number twenty were Republican and at least sixteen represented suburban wards of Boston. Boston *Herald*, April 11, 1895.

76. For example see BTC, *The Boston Subway* (Boston, 1895); and *The Subway: What the Commission Has Done* (Boston, 1895); Boston *Herald*, April 11, 1895.

77. BTC, *First Annual Report* (1895), 20; *Second Annual Report* (1896), 3-4; Prince v. Crocker, 166 Mass., 347 (1896).

78. BTC, *Second Annual Report* (1896), 32; *Fourth Annual Report* (1898), 4, 63.

79. BTC, *First Annual Report* (1895), 65, 67.

80. BTC, *Second Annual Report* (1896), 57.

81. BTC, *Sixth Annual Report* (1900), 24; *Fifth Annual Report* (1899), 17. Little, if any, of the efficiency can be attributed to falling costs during the 1890s depression, for the cost estimates were made in 1894 and 1895, the nadir of the depression.

82. BTC, *Legislation, Court Decisions, Contract for the Use of the Subway, Contract for the Use of the New Tunnel and Subway, Lease of the East Boston Tunnel* (Boston, 1911), 149-164. For the lease's similarity to British arrangements, see John Fitzgerald's comments on the 1870 Tramways Act in Rapid Transit Commission, *Report*, 138-141, and John P. McKay, *Tramways and Trolleys: The Rise of Urban Mass Transport in Europe* (Princeton, New Jersey, 1976), 168-169, 174, 184.

83. BTC, *Fifth Annual Report* (1899), 7-8, 10; William H. Colcord, *The Rights and Wrongs of a Million* (Boston, 1909), 17.

84. BTC, *Fifth Annual Report* (1899), 8-9; *Sixth Annual Report* (1900), 14.

85. Woods and Eastman, "Franchise Contest," 835.

86. BTC, *Fifth Annual Report* (1899), 32.

87. *Transcript*, March 27, 1899, 14.

88. "Opening of the Boston Subway," *Harper's Weekly*, 41 (September 18, 1897), 934; H. W. Weller, "Opening of the Boston Subway for the West End Trolley Cars," *The Electrical Engineer*, 24 (September 2, 1897), 197.

89. Bacon, *Book of Boston*, 114.

90. Boston *Journal*, August 4, 1894; Kidder, Peabody and Company to Henry M. Whitney, January 10, 1895, volume 5 of the Kidder, Peabody and Company letterheads, Baker Library, Harvard Business School.

91. The ratio is based on Walker's estimate of the cost per mile of New York's elevated railroad ($700,000-$800,000) and on the West End's report of total investment per mile of electric street railway ($85,800). James Blaine Walker, *Fifty Years of Rapid Transit* (New York, 1919), 113; *SRJ*, 14 (September 1898), 488.

92. Boston *Herald*, November 10, 1896; *Transcript*, October 21, 1896; untitled circular dated October 16, 1896, and signed by Walter Hunnewell, F. L. Higginson, and others, in the West End Street Railway Company file, Corporate Records division, Baker Library.

93. George A. Kimball, "The Boston Elevated Railway," *New England Magazine*, 24 (July 1901), 458; West End Land Company, *Deed of Trust, December 19, 1886*, in Corporate Records Division, Baker Library; *SRJ*, 14 (February 1898), 105. For Kidder, Peabody's prominence in West End affairs, see Kidder, Peabody to Henry Whitney, May 24 and November 7, 1892, in volume 5 of Kidder, Peabody letterbooks; and Benjamin Orne to Frank G. Webster of Kidder, Peabody, March 27, 1895, in West End file in Manuscript Division, Baker Library.

94. Albert E. Pillsbury, *Argument of . . . in Support of The Bill of the Boston Elevated Railway Company, April 29-30, 1897* (Boston, 1897), 5-8.

95. Ibid.; *Lease of West End Street Railway Company to Boston Elevated Railway Company, December 9, 1897*.

96. Boston Elevated Railway Company, *Fifty Years of Unified Transportation in Metropolitan Boston* (Boston, 1938), 51, 53-55; "Street Railway Conditions and Financial Results in Metropolitan Boston," *SRJ*, 14 (September 1898), 474-477; H. W. Putney, comp., *Officials Engaged in Conducting Transportation upon the Boston Elevated Railway and Its Predecessor the West End Street Railway* (pamphlet in MBTA Library, Boston, Massachusetts), 15-16. For traffic data, see Chart 4.

97. Abrams, *Conservatism*, 68; *SRJ*, 14 (February 1898), 105; Richard Herndon, *Men of Progress* (Boston, 1896), 49-50.

98. Massachusetts Statutes of 1897, chapter 500.

99. Ibid.

100. For examples of the suspicion see Pinanski, *Street Railway System*, 33; Abrams, *Conservatism*, 65; Melvin I. Urofsky and David W. Levy, *Letters of Louis D. Brandeis*, I: *Urban Reformer* (Albany, 1971), 128-130; *Transcript*, February 1, 1893.

101. Massachusetts: Board of Railroad Commissioners, "Special Reports on Street Railway Matters: West End Leases," *Twenty-ninth Annual Report* (1898), 140-141; Abrams, *Conservatism*, 72-73.

102. Massachusetts Railroad Commissioners, "West End Leases," 144.

103. Walter S. Allen, "Street Railway Franchises in Massachussetts," *Annals of the American Academy of Political and Social Science*, 27 (January 1906), 94-97; Robert H. Whitten, *Public Administration in Massachusetts* (New York, 1898), 114-118; Special Committee to Investigate the Relationship between Cities . . . and Street Railways, *Report*, 118-119. Boston had surrendered ultimate control of the West End franchises to the state Railroad Commission as early as 1887. Massachusetts Statutes of 1887, chapter 413.

104. Louis D. Brandeis, "The Experience of Massachusetts in Street Railways," *Municipal Affairs*, 6 (Winter 1902), 722; "Street Railway Conditions," *SRJ*, 492.

105. BTC, *Fourth Annual Report* (1898), 64.

106. Urofsky and Levy, *Urban Reformer*, 129-130; Brandeis, "Experience," 727-728; Sylvester Baxter, "Street Railway Consolidation," *Annals of the American Academy of Political and Social Science*, 11 (January 1898), 120; Leo S. Rowe, "Street Railway Lines," *Annals of the American Academy of Political and Social Science*, 11 (March 1898), 142-143; BTC, *Second Annual Report* (1896),

12; Massachusetts Railroad Commissioners, "West End Leases," 140-155.

107. Brandeis, "Experience," 728; Pinanski, *Street Railway System*, 32-33; Woods and Eastman, "Franchise Contest," 836-837.

108. Woods and Eastman, "Franchise Contest," 837.

109. Ibid., 837-839; Abrams, *Conservatism*, 66-67; Albert E. Pillsbury, *The Washington Street Subway: "Before the Committee on Metropolitan Affairs," March 28, 1901*; Urofsky and Levy, *Urban Reformer*, 143-144.

110. Woods and Eastman, "Franchise Contest," 838-841; Abrams, *Conservatism*, 67-69; Alpheus T. Mason, *Brandeis: A Free Man's Life* (New York, 1956), 111; Urofsky and Levy, *Urban Reformer*, 160-173, 183.

111. Herbert L. Harding, *The Washington Street Subway* (Boston, 1900); Thomas N. Hart, *Boston Subways: Remarks Before the Committee on Metropolitan Affairs* (Boston, 1901); Abrams, *Conservatism*, 71-72.

112. Brandeis, "Experience," 729.

6. Politics and Enterprise

1. United States Bureau of the Census, *Twelfth Census of the United States: 1900. Population*, I, 430-433; Chandler Brothers and Company, *Union Traction Company* (Philadelphia, 1899), 12; Thomas Conway, "Street Railways in Philadelphia since 1900," *Annals of the American Academy of Political and Social Science*, 24 (September 1904), 354.

2. Sam Bass Warner, *The Private City: Philadelphia in Three Periods of Its Growth* (Philadelphia, 1968), 58-61, 63-78, 169-171; Conway, "Street Railways," 354. The quotation is from Warner, *Private City*, 171.

3. Warner, *Private City*, 61; Lincoln Steffens, *The Shame of the Cities* (New York, 1957), 134; *Evolution of Philadelphia's Street Railway Systems* (Philadelphia, 1909), 1; John Russell Young, ed., *Memorial History of the City of Philadelphia* (New York, 1895), I, 555.

4. Warner, *Private City*, 53; Chicago City Council: Committee on Local Transportation, *Report on the Transportation Subway Systems of Boston, New York, Philadelphia, Paris, London* (Chicago, 1909), 88.

5. George Rogers Taylor, "The Beginning of Mass Transportation in Urban America," part II, *Smithsonian Journal of History*, 1 (Autumn 1966), 46-47, 49; Edmond Stirling, Articles on the history of Philadelphia local transit printed in the Philadelphia *Public Ledger*, February 10-March 13, 1930 (typescript in the Harold Cox Collection at Wilkes College Library, Wilkes Barre, Pennsylvania. Hereafter referred to as Stirling articles), 5-6.

6. Chicago City Council, *Report*, 87; Stirling articles, 5-9, 34-35; New York News Bureau: Philadelphia Local Service, *1854-1904, Fifty Years with Passenger Railways in Philadelphia* (Philadelphia, n.d.), 5; Frederick W. Speirs, *The Street Railway System of Philadelphia* (Baltimore, 1897), 11-17, 28.

7. Speirs, *System*, 13-16; Taylor, "Mass Transportation," II, 47, 49; Stirling articles, 10-11; Chicago City Council, *Report*, 87.

8. Stirling articles, 10-11, Harold E. Cox and John F. Myers, "The Philadelphia Traction Monopoly and the Pennsylvania Constitution of 1874: The Prostitution of an Ideal," *Pennsylvania History*, 35 (October 1968), 408-410.

9. Stirling articles, 10, 13; Speirs, *System*, 73-77; Cox and Myers, "Traction Monopoly," 408-409.

10. Speirs, *System*, 71, 80.

11. Stirling articles, 12-22, 54. The quotation is from page 18.

12. "Philadelphia Rapid Transit Company, Union Traction Company History, 1895-1921" (typescript apparently prepared by the PRT and in the Cox Collection), 18; Stirling articles, 15-22, 29.

13. Cox and Meyers, "Traction Monopoly," 409-410; Speirs, *System*, 52-67.

14. Cox and Meyers, "Traction Monopoly," 410-412.

15. *Steam on Street Railways*, reprint from the *Journal of the Franklin Institute* (June 1877); *Railroad Gazette*, 8 (September 22, 1875), 414; 9 (May 18, 1877), 223-225, 255; 10 (March 29, 1878), 165; Frank Rowsome, *Trolley Car Treasury* (New York, 1956), 35; Stirling articles, 26-27.

16. Board of Presidents of the City Passenger Railways, *Minutes Books, 1859-1873, 1874-1899*. The quotation is from the entry for November 27, 1860. Stirling articles, 23-24; Speirs, *System*, 28-30.

17. Burton J. Hendrick, *The Age of Big Business* (New York, 1919), chapter 5.

18. New York *Times*, September 28, 1891; Burton J. Hendrick, "Great American Fortunes and Their Making," *McClure's Magazine* 30 (November 1907), 36-37; Frank B. Evans, *Pennsylvania Politics, 1872-1877: A Study in Political Leadership* (Harrisburg, Pennsylvania, 1966), 64-68, 13-14.

19. Hendrick, "Fortunes," 34; New York *Times*, November 7, 1915; Harry P. Mawson, "The Magnates of the Philadelphia Traction Company," *Leslie's Weekly*, 74 (May 5, 1892), 233; *Dictionary of American Biography*, XX, 185-186; Union Passenger Railway Company, *Minute Book, 1864-1926: Stockholders,* May 9, 11, 1864 (Cox Collection).

20. *Dictionary of American Biography*, VI, 84-85; Mawson, "Magnates," 233; Hendrick, "Fortunes," 34-36.

21. Evans, *Leadership*, 13-14, 64-68; Howard F. Gillette, "Corrupt and Contented: Philadelphia's Political Machines, 1865-1887," Ph.D. dissertation, Yale University, 1970, 215, 219. Gillette insists on calling the three men politicians, although Elkins was clearly a businessman. He shows no evidence that either Kemble or Widener pursued politics as a profession after 1880. Instead, their street railway activities expanded in Philadelphia and elsewhere, and they became entrepreneurs who maintained bipartisan political connections vital for their business.

22. Mawson, "Magnates," 233; Gillette, "Corrupt," 209.

23. Hendrick, "Fortunes," 36. The Pennsylvania Railroad's strategy is discussed in Alfred Chandler, *The Visible Hand: The Managerial Revolution in American Business* (Cambridge, Massachusetts, 1977), 151-156.

24. In the late 1870s Tom Johnson initiated a similar strategy in Indianapolis and Cleveland, but there is no evidence of any connection with the changes in Philadelphia. Tom L. Johnson, *My Story* (New York, 1915), 19-24.

25. Gillette, "Corrupt," 185-186, 192-200.

26. New York News Bureau, *Fifty Years*, 11; Stirling articles, 37-38.

27. Continental Passenger Railway Company, *Minute Book, 1873-1926,* November 8, 1873; February 5, June 14, 25, 1879 (Cox Collection); Gillette, "Corrupt," 208, 213, 215, 217-219.

28. Stirling articles, 38.

29. Ibid.; Union Passenger Railway Company, *Minute Book, 1864-1894: Directors,* January 12, 1880 (Cox Collection).

30. Continental, *Minute Book,* June 11, 1879.

31. Board of Presidents, *Minute Book,* November 18, 1879; Continental, *Minute Book,* November 2, 1881; Union, *Stockholders' Minute Book,* January 8, 1883. The trio was not the sole pioneer of the free transfer system, for Tom Johnson was introducing the technique in Indianapolis at almost the same time. Michael Massouh, "Innovation in Street Railways before Electric Traction," *Technology and Culture,* 18 (April 1977), 209-212.

32. Union, *Stockholders' Minute Book,* January 10, 1881.

33. George W. Hilton, *The Cable Car in America* (Pasadena, California, 1970), 14-31.

34. Ibid., 31.

35. Stirling articles, 53.

36. Pennsylvania Laws 108, Act of June 13, 1883. See also Stirling articles, 41; Cox and Meyers, "Traction Monopoly," 412-413.

37. Stirling articles, 38-39; typescript of Philadelphia street railway history, headed E. A. Ballard (Cox Collection), 5-6.

38. *Dictionary of American Biography,* XX, 185-186; Hendrick, "Fortunes," 35; Union, *Stockholder Minute Book,* January 8, 1883; Credit Ledger 153 State of Pennsylvania, in R. G. Dun and Company Collection at Baker Library, Harvard Business School, 408, 470.

39. Philadelphia Traction Company, *Stock Ledger No. 1* (Cox Collection); Union, *Stockholder Minute Book,* January 8, 1883; Philadelphia Traction Company, *Minute Book, 1884-1925: Stockholders,* June 20, 1893; June 20, 1894; March 20, 1895 (Cox Collection).

40. *The Manual of Statistics,* 5 (January 1, 1885), 210, 213-214, 222; Henry Poor, *Manual of the Railroads of the United States, 1868-69* (New York, 1868), 185. For the development of an industrial securities' market see Thomas R. Navin and Marian V. Sears, "The Rise of a Market for Industrial Securities, 1887-1902," *Business History Review,* 29 (June 1955), 105-138.

41. Philadelphia *Evening Bulletin,* February 25, 1907.

42. R. G. Dun and Company, Ledger 153, 470; Stirling articles, 49. The PTC deposited 7,500 shares of West Philadelphia stock ($50 paid in), and 2,500 shares of Union Passenger stock (average $30.83 paid in).

43. National Cable Railways Company, *System of Traction Railways for Cities and Towns* (New York, 1883?), 3; Joseph Frazier Wall, *Andrew Carnegie* (New York, 1970), 353-358; Hilton, *Cable Car,* 32.

44. Hilton, *Cable Car,* 251; Philadelphia *Public Ledger,* September 18, 1883; *Railroad Gazette,* 15 (September 2, 1883), 620.

45. Robert M. Feustel, *Report on Behalf of the City of Philadelphia on the Valuation of the Property of the Philadelphia Rapid Transit Company. City of Philadelphia vs. Philadelphia Rapid Transit Company, Pennsylvania Public Service Commission,* Docket No. 5304, 98.

46. Hilton, *Cable Car*, 155, 251-253.

47. R. G. Dun and Company, Ledger 153, 470.

48. Speirs, *System*, 31-32; Union, *Stockholders' Minute Book*, January 10, 1881; *System of Steam-Street Railroads-Railways of Philadelphia* (Philadelphia, 1887). The Philadelphia *Evening Bulletin*, March 1, 1887, reports the 147 free transfer points.

49. Hilton, *Cable Car*, 251; Chandler Brothers, *Union Traction*, 12. For operating problems with a normal cable system, see pages 6, 60-61.

50. People's Passenger Railway Company, *Minute Book #2, 1882-1886*, January 9, 1883 (Cox Collection); Speirs, *System*, 31; Feustel, *Report*, 93.

51. "Growth of Leading American Electric Railways," *Brill Magazine*, 12 (November 1924), 197-198.

52. Charles Richardson, *The City of Philadelphia: Its Stockholders and Directors* (Philadelphia, 1893), 6.

53. *Dictionary of American Biography*, V, 355-356; Gillette, "Corrupt," 301-305; PTC, *Stock Ledger, #1*.

54. Stirling articles, 41, 56-57; Cox and Meyers, "Traction Monopoly," 413-414; Speirs, *System*, 5, 33; Philadelphia Traction Company, *Stock Ledger, #1*.

55. Philadelphia *Evening Bulletin*, February 25, 1887, 6.

56. *Street Railway Journal*, 8 (April 1892), 250; Philadelphia *Public Ledger*, March 31, April 1, 1892; Philadelphia City Councils: Railroad Committee, *The Trolley System. Stenographic Report of Testimony of Experts and Arguments of Rufus E. Chapley, Esq. and John C. Johnson, Esq.* (Philadelphia, 1892), 90-106.

57. Speirs, *System*, 61-62, 81-82; Stirling articles, 54; PTC, *Stockholder Minute Book*, March 5, 1892.

58. Philadelphia Councils, *Trolley System*, 121-122.

59. Arthur Pound and Samuel Moore, eds., *More They Told Barron* (New York, 1931), 91-92.

60. Widener to Henry W. Palmer, February 20, 1894, and to Matthew Quay, March 15, 1894, Widener letterbook (privately held).

61. Stirling articles, 54; Feustel, *Report*, 19, 98.

62. Ibid., 55; Speirs, *System*, 32, 34; Chandler Brothers, *Union Traction*, 12.

63. Philadelphia *Evening Bulletin*, August 15, 1919; Stirling articles, 42; "Philadelphia Rapid Transit Company: Corporate History" (volume of charters and other data in Cox Collection).

64. "The System of the People's Traction Company, Philadelphia," *SRJ*, 11 (June 1895), 1-14; Albert A. Bird, "Philadelphia Street Railways and the Municipality," *The Citizen*, 1 (February 1896), 288; Stirling articles, 56; Speirs, *System*, 33-35.

65. Pennsylvania Laws of 1895, Act of July 23, 1895; *Lease: Philadelphia Traction Company to Union Traction Company, October 1, 1895; Lease: Electric Traction Company to Union Traction Company, July 1, 1896; Lease of People's Railway Company and the People's Traction Company to Union Traction Company, July 1, 1896.*

66. "Organization and Operating Methods of the Union Traction Com-

pany of Philadelphia," *SRJ*, 14 (November 1898), 691-700; Philadelphia *Evening Bulletin*, August 15, 1919; Stirling articles, 42-43; Chandler Brothers, *Union Traction*, 12, 14; and *The Philadelphia Rapid Transit Company* (Philadelphia, 1904), 9.

67. Union Traction Company, *Annual Report of the Union Traction Company of Philadelphia, June 30, 1897*, 5; *Annual Report, June 30, 1899*, 4.

68. Union Traction Company, *Minute Book, 1899-1908* (Cox Collection); Stirling articles, 39.

69. Lewis W. Haupt, *Rapid Transit* (Philadelphia, 1884); and *Rapid Transit in Cities*, a reprint from the *Journal of the Franklin Institute* (June 1888); C. W. Buchholz, "Some Reasons Why Elevated Railroads Are a Necessity to Philadelphia," *Railroad Gazette*, 24 (December 2, 1892), 893.

70. Buchholz, "Reasons," 893; Philadelphia *North American*, June 2, 3, 1881; Philadelphia *Public Ledger*, February 18, 20, 1892; Gillette, "Corrupt," 204-205, 295.

71. Potts v. Quaker City Elevated Railway Company, 161 Pa. 395 (1894); Commonwealth *ex rel.* Attorney General, Appellant v. Northeastern Elevated Railway Company, 161 Pa. 409 (1894); Cox and Meyers, "Traction Monopoly," 419; Philadelphia *Public Ledger*, February 18-20, August 20, 1892; Stirling articles, 87-88.

72. Warner, *Private City*; Gillette, "Corrupt," 6-8; George Morgan, *The City of Firsts: A Complete History of the City of Philadelphia* (Philadelphia, 1926), 283-286; Rudolph Blankenburg, "Forty Years in the Wilderness; or Masters and Rulers of the 'Free Men' of Pennsylvania," *The Arena*, 33 (January-August 1905), 15-16, 459.

73. Gillette, "Corrupt," *i*.

74. Steffens, *Shame*, 134.

75. Blankenburg, "Forty Years," 572; Morgan, *City*, 283.

76. Ellis Paxon Oberholtzer, *Philadelphia: A History of the City and Its People: A Record of 225 Years* (Philadelphia, n.d.), II, 420; Speirs, *System*, 7; "Philadelphia: The Convention City," *SRJ*, 26 (September 23, 1905), 473-475.

77. Philadelphia Rapid Transit Company, *Philadelphia's Rapid Transit* (Philadelphia, 1908), 1.

78. Warner, *Private City*, 191-192.

79. Beckles Willson, *The Story of Rapid Transit* (New York, 1903), 195.

80. Philadelphia *North American*, March 10, 1902; Clinton R. Woodruff, "Recent Street Railway Legislation in Pennsylvania and Philadelphia," *Municipal Affairs*, 5 (June 1901), 421; Stirling articles, 62.

81. Stirling articles, 62.

82. Cox and Meyers, "Traction Monopoly," 416.

83. Clinton R. Woodruff, "Philadelphia Street-Railway Franchises," *American Journal of Sociology*, 7 (1901-02), 216.

84. Pennsylvania Laws 523, Act of June 7, 1901; Pennsylvania Laws 572, Act of June 19, 1901; Pennsylvania Laws 577, Act of June 20, 1901.

85. Steffens, *Shame*, 156-157.

86. Stirling articles, 66-68; Cox and Meyers, "Traction Monopoly," 419-420.

87. Chicago City Council, *Report*, 88.

88. *Lease: Union Traction Company to Philadelphia Rapid Transit Company, July 1, 1902*. Estimates of the payment to Mack varied from $1.5 million to $2.5 million. President John Parsons later said that $1.5 million was the correct amount. Philadelphia *Public Ledger*, March 7, 1906. For Mack's stock holding, see *Commercial and Financial Chronicle*, 83 (September 22, 1906), 688.

89. Chandler Brothers, *Union Traction*, 12. See also Chart 5.

90. Feustel, *Report*, 5, 19.

7. Contract and Cooperation

1. For reformers' failure to demand city recapture of Union Traction Company franchises in an 1896 transit battle, see Frederick W. Speirs, *The Street Railway System of Philadelphia* (Baltimore, 1897), 88.

2. For example, see William C. Whitney to P. A. B. Widener, January 24, 1891, vol. 63 of Whitney Papers, Library of Congress.

3. The tendency to underestimate capital costs was a common error among American railroad and street railway men as a result of their accounting techniques. In one of the better regulated states, Massachusetts street railways failed to face the problem of proper charges for maintenance and depreciation until 1914. Edward S. Mason, *The Street Railway in Massachusetts* (Cambridge, Massachusetts, 1932), 101. For a more general discussion see Alfred Chandler, *The Visible Hand: The Managerial Revolution in American Business* (Cambridge, Massachusetts, 1977), 111-115.

4. Edmund Stirling, articles on the history of Philadelphia local transit printed in the Philadelphia *Public Ledger*, February 10-March 13, 1930 (typescript in the Harold Cox Collection at Wilkes College Library, Wilkes Barre, Pennsylvania. Hereafter referred to as Stirling articles), 48-49, 54-55, 78; U.S. Bureau of the Census, *Eleventh Census of the United States: 1890. Census Bulletin 55*, "The Relative Economy of Cable, Electric and Animal Motive Power for Street Railways," 697; *Street Railway Journal*, 14 (September 1898), 492.

5. Stirling articles, 48-50; Charles C. McChord, *Report of C. C. McChord to the Public Service Commission of the Commonwealth of Pennsylvania in re Philadelphia Transit Situation* (Philadelphia, 1927), 8-14, 21-22; *Lease: Union Traction Company of Philadelphia to Philadelphia Rapid Transit Company, July 1, 1902*.

6. U.S. Bureau of the Census, *Special Reports: Street and Electric Railways, 1902* (Washington, D.C., 1905), 59. Figures for the UTC's and PRT's operation on this and the next page come from *Poor's Manual of the Railroads of the United States, 1898-1911*.

7. Chandler Brothers and Company, *The Philadelphia Rapid Transit Company* (Philadelphia?, 1904), 9. For traffic data, see chart 5.

8. Stirling articles, 62, 72-73, 89; Ford, Bacon and Davis, *Pennsylvania State Railroad Commission in the Matter of the Complaints against the Philadelphia Rapid Transit Company. Report to the Commission by Ford, Bacon and Davis, March 7, 1911* (Philadelphia, 1911), I, 1-9, 17-19, 30-34.

9. Robert M. Feustel, *Report on Behalf of the City of Philadelphia on the*

Valuation of the Property of the Philadelphia Rapid Transit Company. City of Philadelphia vs. Philadelphia Rapid Transit Company. Pennsylvania Public Service Commission, Docket No. 3504, chart 14.

10. For Elkin's holdings see *Commercial and Financial Chronicle,* 79 (September 17, 1904), 1024; for Mack's holdings, *Commercial and Financial Chronicle,* 83 (September 22, 1906), 688; and for Widener's holdings see Box 16, File 5004, Charles Kruger to George Widener, November 8, 1906, and March 1, 1907, in Philadelphia Rapid Transit Company Correspondence in Harold Cox Collection, Wilkes College Library, Wilkes Barre, Pennsylvania (hereafter cited PRT, box, file).

11. *SRJ,* 13 (September 1897), 556; "Organization and Operating Methods of the Union Traction Company of Philadelphia," *SRJ,* 14 (November 1898), 691-692; "Philadelphia Rapid Transit Company, Union Traction Company History, 1895-1921" (typescript apparently prepared by the PRT and in the Cox Collection), 6. See Vollum, Fernley, Vollum, and Rorer, *Report of Examination of the Books, Accounts and Vouchers of the Philadelphia Rapid Transit Company for the Year Ending June 30, 1908,* 8-9.

12. "PRT, 1895-1921," 3-4, 7-8; Stirling articles, 51. For owner interference with operations see Charles Kruger to George Elkins, PRT, XIV, 1213; Charles Kruger to George Widener, PRT, XVI, 5004; and Charles Kruger to Henry and John Phipps, PRT, XIV, 1205.

13. Stirling articles, 58.

14. Speirs, *System,* 81.

15. Philadelphia Ordinances, Chapter 168, Ordinance of July 7, 1857.

16. For an analysis of consumer progressivism, see David P. Thelen, *The New Citizenship: Origins of Progressivism in Wisconsin, 1885-1900* (Columbia, Missouri, 1972), especially 1-3, 82-84, 250-289.

17. Clinton R. Woodruff, "Philadelphia Street-Railway Franchises," *American Journal of Sociology,* 7 (1901-02), 216-233; George Morgan, *City of Firsts: A Complete History of the City of Philadelphia* (Philadelphia, 1926), 289-291; Rudolph Blankenburg, "Forty Years in the Wilderness; or Masters and Rulers of the 'Free Men' of Pennsylvania," *The Arena,* 33 and 34 (January-August 1905), 133-136; Speirs, *System,* 87-88; Clinton R. Woodruff, "The Municipal League of Philadelphia," *American Journal of Sociology,* 11 (November 1905), 336-358.

18. W. W. Wheatley, "The Philadelphia Rapid Transit System—I," *SRJ,* 21 (March 28, 1903), 477.

19. Philadelphia *North American,* January 28, 1905.

20. Philadelphia *Evening Bulletin,* January 26, 1905.

21. Philadelphia *North American,* December 19-25, 1904; January 19-20, 1905; Martindale to Parsons, May 12, 1905, PRT, XIV, 1228. The quotation is taken from the heading of the Martindale-Parsons letter.

22. Harold Zink, *City Bosses in the United States* (Durham, North Carolina, 1930), 202, 212-217.

23. Philadelphia *Record,* February 3, 1905.

24. Philadelphia *Public Ledger,* March 24, 1906.

25. Philadelphia *North American,* February 9, 1905.

26. Martindale to Parsons, May 12, 1905, PRT, XIV, 1228; Philadelphia *Public Ledger*, January 21, 1905; PRT, II, 1003; Stirling articles, 72.

27. PRT, XXIII, 5159B.

28. Philadelphia *Public Ledger*, January 2, 1905; PRT, II, 1003; Stirling articles, 72.

29. Philadelphia *Press*, November 24, 1904; Philadelphia *North American*, December 12, 14, 1904.

30. Stirling articles, 71.

31. For example, see Philadelphia *Press*, June 7, 1905, and Philadelphia *Public Ledger*, June 9, 1905. For a discussion of railroad leaders' attitudes toward public relations in the nineteenth century, see Thomas Cochran, *Railroad Leaders, 1845-1890* (Cambridge, Massachusetts, 1953), 185-188, 200-201.

32. Sam Bass Warner, *The Private City: Philadelphia in Three Periods of Its Growth* (Philadelphia, 1968), 175.

33. Wheatley, "System," 472.

34. Pennsylvania Laws, 523, Act of June 7, 1901.

35. Stirling articles, 68.

36. Pennsylvania Laws, 523, Act of March 25, 1903; Stirling articles, 68-69.

37. Stirling articles, 70; Philadelphia Rapid Transit Company, *Philadelphia's Rapid Transit* (Philadelphia, 1908). The figure for the subway's cost is from a statement headed "Original Cost: Market Street Subway Elevated Books," in the Cox Collection.

38. Philadelphia *Evening Bulletin*, October 22, 1906, July 23, 1906; Philadelphia *Public Ledger*, July 23, 1906.

39. Philadelphia *Telegraph*, March 2, 1906.

40. The P&W story can be found in Harold E. Cox, "The Philadelphia and Western Story," *Traction and Models*, 3 (October 1967), 6-10, and in the daily newspapers of March and April 1906.

41. Philadelphia *Press*, March 31, 1906.

42. Ibid.; Philadelphia *Public Ledger*, March 18, 1906.

43. Herman L. Collins and Wilfred Jordan, *Philadelphia: A Story of Progress* (Philadelphia, 1941), IV, 529; Earle to John Parsons, May 2, August 29, 1904; Parsons to Earle, September 13, 1904, PRT, XII, 1191.

44. Typescript of statement by George Earle to the press, April 1906, PRT, XV, 1324.

45. James W. Brooks to Thomas Martindale, April 27, 1905, PRT, XIV, 1228.

46. Philadelphia *Telegraph*, March 22, 1906.

47. Philadelphia *North American*, March 21, 1906.

48. Philadelphia *Public Ledger*, March 17-18, 1906.

49. Philadelphia *North American*, March 28, 1906; Philadelphia *Evening Bulletin*, June 11, 1906.

50. Cox, "P&W," 8; Philadelphia *Public Ledger*, March 18, 1906; Philadelphia *Evening Bulletin*, March 31, June 23, 1906.

51. PRT, *Annual Report, 1906*, 7; Charles Kruger to Drexel and Company, June 30, 1906, PRT, III, 1011; Meyer Goldsmith, "Expenses of the Phila-

delphia Rapid Transit Company Assumed by the City," Box 571, Philadelphia City Archives.

52. *Commercial and Financial Chronicle*, 83 (October 6, 1906), 818; Kruger to Parsons, December 3, 1906, PRT, X, 1163.

53. Stirling articles, 73.

54. Philadelphia *Evening Bulletin*, November 12, 1906.

55. Philadelphia *Telegraph*, November 13, 1906; Philadelphia *Public Ledger*, November 13-14, 1906.

56. Philadelphia *Public Ledger*, November 16, 1906, 2.

57. Ibid., December 7, 1906, 2.

58. Philadelphia *North American, Record, Press*, and *Public Ledger*, December 7, 1906. For an estimate of the group's size, see its first petition in Philadelphia *Evening Bulletin*, March 17, 1906.

59. Philadelphia *Evening Bulletin*, January 22, 1907.

60. United Business Men's Association, *The Philadelphia Rapid Transit Question: The Retail Merchants Plan* (n.p., n.d.); Trades League of Philadelphia, *Extract of Minutes, Board of Directors Meeting*, February 14, 1907.

61. Philadelphia *Evening Bulletin*, January 29, 1907.

62. Ibid., January 11, February 15, 1907.

63. Ibid., February 19, 1907.

64. Philadelphia *Public Ledger*, July 2, 1907.

65. Stirling articles, 75.

66. Philadelphia *Public Ledger*, June 18, 1907; Philadelphia *Record*, July 1, 1907; Philadelphia *North American*, June 19, 1907; Philadelphia *Press*, June 21, July 2, 1907; Philadelphia *Inquirer*, June 22, July 1, 1907; Philadelphia *Evening Bulletin*, July 2, 1907.

67. Stirling articles, 75; Trades League of Philadelphia, *Argument before the Governor* (reprint from the *Financial Bulletin*, n.p., n.d.).

68. Earle to Parsons, September 23, 1907, PRT, XII, 1191.

69. Earle to Parsons, November 23, 1906, PRT, XII, 1191.

70. Parsons to Director Henry Phipps, January 29, 1907, PRT, XIV, 1205.

71. Philadelphia *North American*, November 28, 1906.

72. See Warner, *Private City*, 206-209, for a critique of business-oriented groups as planners.

73. Lit Brothers to John Parsons, March 1, 1905, and Parsons to RMA, July 10, 1908, PRT, XX, 5057A.

74. Philadelphia *Public Ledger*, October 30, 1926, 12.

75. For example see story of the defeat of the Philadelphia and Suburban Railway Company's attempt for an elevated subway line in Stirling articles, 88.

76. Stirling articles, 78; Harold E. Cox, *Early Electric Cars of Philadelphia, 1885-1911* (Forty Fort, Pennsylvania, 1969), 134; Ford, Bacon and Davis, *Report*.

77. Philadelphia *Evening Bulletin*, July 2, 1907.

78. Edwin C. Lewis, "Philadelphia's Relation to the Rapid Transit Company," *Annals of the American Academy of Political and Social Science*, 31 (May 1908), 600.

79. Ibid., 603, 610.

80. Chandler Brothers and Company, *Traction Investment of the Philadel-*

phia Rapid Transit Company: Bankers' Advice to Purchasers (Philadelphia?, 1908), 7.

81. John MacKay Shaw, "Mitten," (typescript 1930 biography in Philadelphia Free Library), 247-248.

82. A. B. Loeb, Maintenance of Way Committee, to PRT Board of Directors, January 23, 1908, PRT, XIII, 1200.

83. *Dictionary of American Biography*, XIII, 71-72; *Second Supplement*, 634-635; PRT, *Annual Reports*, 1910, 1911; Stirling articles, 89-90.

84. PRT, *Annual Reports*, 1911-18; Stirling articles, 92-99; "PRT, 1895-1921," 3-10.

85. City of Philadelphia: Department of City Transit, *Statement of A. Merritt Taylor, Director of Department of City Transit, City of Philadelphia, Submitted to the Public Service Commission of the Commonwealth of Pennsylvania, July 26, 1915* (Philadelphia, 1915), 3-13; *Report of Transit Commissioner, City of Philadelphia, July, 1913* (n.p., n.d.), I, 1-12; McChord, *Report*, 32-34.

86. Philadelphia *Public Ledger*, June 18, 1907, 8.

Conclusion

1. The best work in this field has been done by Alfred Chandler. See his *The Railroads: The Nation's First Big Business* (New York, 1965); "The Railroads: Pioneers in Modern Corporate Management," *Business History Review*, 39 (Spring 1965), 16-40; "The Beginnings of 'Big Business' in American Industry," *Business History Review*, 33 (Spring 1959), 1-31; *Strategy and Structure: Chapters in the History of the Industrial Enterprise* (New York, 1962); and *The Visible Hand: The Managerial Revolution in American Business* (Cambridge, Massachusetts, 1977).

2. U.S. Bureau of the Census, *Special Reports. Street and Electric Railways, 1902* (Washington, D.C., 1905), 6.

3. John P. McKay, *Tramways and Trolleys: The Rise of Urban Mass Transport in Europe* (Princeton, New Jersey, 1976), 84-107.

4. David Ward, "A Comparative Historical Geography of Streetcar Suburbs in Boston, Massachusetts, and Leeds, England," *Association of American Geographers Annals*, 54 (December 1964), 477-489; McKay, *Tramways*, 201.

5. For example see Carter Goodrich, *Government Promotion of American Canals and Railroads, 1800-1890* (New York, 1960); Carter Goodrich, ed., *Canals and American Economic Development* (New York, 1961); Harry N. Scheiber, *Ohio Canal Era: A Case Study of Government and the Economy, 1820-1861* (Athens, Ohio, 1969); Oscar and Mary Handlin, *Commonwealth*; Louis Hartz, *Economic Policy and Democratic Thought: Pennsylvania, 1776-1860* (Cambridge, Massachusetts, 1948); Milton S. Heath, *Constructive Liberalism: The Role of the State in the Economic Development of Georgia* (Cambridge, Massachusetts, 1954); and "Public Railroad Construction and the Development of Private Enterprise in the South before 1960," *Journal of Economic History*, supplement 10 (1950), 40-53; Robert A. Lively, "The American System: A Review Article," *Business History Review*, 29 (March 1955), 81-96.

6. Goodrich, *Government Promotion*, 7-11.

7. The top twenty included all cities of 200,000 in the 1900 Census, counting Brooklyn and Manhattan separately. Sixteen had outright monopolies and San Francisco had one dominant firm. Chicago and Washington each had two strong systems, and Manhattan was still divided between elevated and surface systems in 1902. U.S. Bureau of the Census, *Special Reports, 1902*, 120-121.

8. Robert D. Weber, "Rationalizers and Reformers: Chicago Local Transportation in the Nineteenth Century," Ph.D. dissertation, University of Wisconsin, 1971; Sidney I. Roberts, "Portrait of a Robber Baron: Charles T. Yerkes," *Business History Review*, 35 (Autumn 1961), 344-371; Theodore C. Barker and Michael Robbins, *A History of London Transport: Passenger Travel and the Development of the Metropolis* (London, 1974), II, 61-62.

9. Burton J. Hendrick, *The Age of Big Business* (New York, 1919), 119.

10. Ibid., 122-123.

11. Charles N. Glaab and A. Theodore Brown, *A History of Urban America* (New York, 1967), 147.

12. Sam Bass Warner, *Streetcar Suburbs: The Process of Growth of Boston, 1870-1900* (Cambridge, Massachusetts, 1962).

13. Ibid., 49-64.

14. Edward S. Mason, *The Street Railway in Massachusetts: The Rise and Decline of an Industry* (Cambridge, Massachusetts, 1932), 119-120; Glen E. Holt, "The Changing Perception of Urban Pathology: An Essay on the Development of Mass Transit in the United States," in Kenneth T. Jackson and Stanley K. Schultz, eds., *Cities in American History* (New York, 1972), 333-334.

15. The figures were calculated by dividing Philadelphia's 1910 population into the traffic figures for 1908, 1911 and 1912 found in Chart 5.

16. For the year ending June 30, 1911, in Boston, fares were 305,098,665 and transfers were 198,314,000. Massachusetts Board of Railroad Commissioners, *43rd Annual Report* (1911), 611. In 1910 transfers were only 21 percent of fares in Greater New York and 16 percent in New York. New York State: Public Service Commission for the First District, *Annual Report* (1910), III, 20-21, 265. In Philadelphia transfers were only 19 percent of fares in 1911. *Poor's Manual of Public Utilities, 1914*, 401.

17. Warner, *Streetcar Suburbs*, 153-166.

18. Public Service Corporation of New Jersey, *Public Service Review, 1928: 25 Years of Public Service* (n.p., n.d.); and *Fortieth Anniversary, 1903-1943* (n.p., n.d.).

19. A. V. Woodworth, "Some Street Railway Reorganizations," *Harvard Business Review*, 4 (January 1926), 187-195; Holt, "Pathology," 334.

20. See, for example, Paul Barrett, "Public Policy and Private Choice: Mass Transit and the Automobile in Chicago Between the Wars," *Business History Review*, 49 (Winter 1975), 495-496.

21. For example, see Robert Wiebe, *Businessmen and Reform: A Study of the Progressive Movement* (Cambridge, Massachusetts, 1962); Samuel P. Hays, *Conservation and the Gospel of Efficiency: The Progressive Conservation Movement, 1890-1920* (Cambridge, Massachusetts, 1959); and Gabriel Kolko, *The Triumph of Conservatism: A Reinterpretation of American History, 1900-1916* (New York, 1963).

22. David P. Thelen, *The New Citizenship: Origins of Progressivism in Wisconsin, 1885-1900* (Columbia, Missouri, 1972).

23. Robert H. Wiebe, *The Search for Order, 1877-1920* (New York, 1967), 13.

24. Ibid., 154-155, 298-301.

25. James Blaine Walker, *Fifty Years of Rapid Transit* (New York, 1918), 217-240; Mason, *Street Railway in Massachusetts*, 139, 157-159; Holt, "Pathology," 335-336.

26. Glaab and Brown, *Urban America*, 147.

27. Sam Bass Warner, *The Private City: Philadelphia in Three Periods of Its Growth* (Philadelphia, 1968), 193-194.

28. For a recent study which focuses on municipal failure, see Ernest S. Griffith, *A History of American City Government: The Conspicuous Failure, 1870-1900* (New York, 1974).

29. American Municipal Association, *Collapse of Commuter Service* (Washington, D.C.?, 1960?), 2, 7.

30. Wiebe, *Search*, 293-302.

31. Alfred D. Chandler, "Decision Making and Modern Institutional Change," *Journal of Economic History* 33 (March 1973), 2-3.

Bibliography

General

Nineteenth century urban transportation and transit policy have received less attention from scholars than they did from trolley car enthusiasts and contemporaries. One splendid exception is John P. McKay, *Tramways and Trolleys: The Rise of Urban Mass Transport in Europe* (Princeton, New Jersey: Princeton University Press, 1976), a fine study of the interaction of transit technology and policy. For the United States, historian George Rogers Taylor's "The Beginnings of Mass Transportation in Urban America," parts I and II, *Smithsonian Journal of History*, 1 (Summer-Autumn 1966), 35-50, 31-54 (which stops in 1860), is the starting point for research in local transit. Unfortunately, there is little to follow it. George Hilton and John Due, *The Electric Interurban Railways in America* (Stanford: Stanford University Press, 1960) covers the street railways outside the city, and Glen E. Holt, "The Changing Perception of Urban Pathology: An Essay on the Development of Mass Transit in the United States," in Kenneth T. Jackson and Stanley K. Schultz, eds., *Cities in American History* (New York: Alfred A. Knopf, 1972), 324-343, provides a brief summary of urban transit. A contrasting view of the decline of mass transit can be found in Paul Barrett, "Public Policy and Private Choice: Mass Transit and the Automobile in Chicago between the Wars," *Business History Review*, 49 (Winter 1975), 473-497. John A. Miller, *Fares, Please* (New York: Dover Publications, 1960), is the best industry account from omnibus to motor bus; Frank Rowsome, Jr., *Trolley Car Treasury* (New York: Bonanza Books, 1956), and William D. Middleton, *The Time of the Trolley* (Milwaukee, Wisconsin: Kalmbach Publishing Company, 1967), are mostly pictorial descriptions whose strength is the technical side of their accounts. Even better is Harold C. Passer, *The Electrical Manufacturers, 1875-1900* (Cambridge, Massachusetts: Harvard University Press, 1953), an outstanding study of the development of electric technology and the electric equipment industry. Also very helpful for technology is George Hilton, *The Cable Car in America* (Pasadena, California: Howell-North Books, 1970). Burton Hendrick, *The Age of Big Business* (New Haven: Yale University Press, 1921), chapter 5, offers a general study of private enterprise in local transit which can be supplemented by the

Miller and Hilton books cited above. There are no general works on transit policy in nineteenth century cities; studies on particular cities will be cited below.

Primary materials are plentiful for the technology, organization, and operation of street railways. Two industry journals, *The Street Railway Review* and especially *The Street Railway Journal*, are invaluable starting points for research for the industry as a whole and for local systems. Surveys by the U.S. Census Bureau, including the *Eleventh Census of the United States: 1890. Bulletin 55*, "The Relative Economy of Cable, Electric and Animal Motive Power for Street Railways"; *Report on Transportation Business in the United States at the Eleventh Census, I: Special Reports: Street and Electric Railways, 1902* (Washington: Government Printing Office, 1905); and *Special Reports: Street and Electric Railways, 1907* (Washington: Government Printing Office, 1910), are vital sources of aggregate data for costs and returns as well as for discussions of changing technology and patterns of organization in city transit. Also helpful for construction costs are Charles B. Fairchild, *Street Railways, Their Construction, Operation and Maintenance* (New York: Street Railway Publishing Company, 1892), and Augustine W. Wright, *American Street Railways, Their Construction, Equipment and Maintenance* (Chicago: Rand, McNally and Company, 1888). Primary materials for public policy will be found in the three cases discussed below.

Cities Studies

Because of the nature of the subject and the materials, local transit is usually treated in studies by cities. In addition to the cases examined here, there are numerous works of varying quality for other cities. Among the better ones is Robert David Weber, "Rationalizers and Reformers: Chicago Local Transportation in the Nineteenth Century," Ph.D. dissertation, University of Wisconsin, 1971. Sidney I. Roberts, "Portrait of a Robber Baron: Charles T. Yerkes," *Business History Review*, 35 (Autumn 1961), 344-371 is a chattier, less analytical account. Forrest McDonald, "Street Cars and Politics in Milwaukee, 1896-1901," *Wisconsin Magazine of History*, 39 (Spring-Summer 1956), 166-170, 206-212, 253-257, 271-273, is flawed by a narrow concern with good guys and bad guys. Much better are David P. Thelan, *The New Citizenship: Origins of Progressivism in Wisconsin, 1885-1900* (Columbia, Missouri: University of Missouri Press, 1972), and Clay McShane, *Technology and Reform: Street Railways and the Growth of Milwaukee, 1887-1900* (Madison, Wisconsin: State Historical Society of Wisconsin, 1974). Other city studies include Graeme O'Geran, *A History of the Detroit Street Railways* (Detroit, Michigan: Conover Press, 1931); Dallas M. Young, *Twentieth Century Experience in Urban Transit: A Study of the Cleveland System and Its Development* (Cleveland: The Press of the Western Reserve University, 1960); and William Tindall, "Beginnings of Street Railways in the National Capital," *Columbia Historical Society Records*, 21 (1918), 24-86.

Major primary and secondary sources for each case are discussed below. In addition there are valuable and extensive records of major street railways systems in the Corporate Records Division of Baker Library at Harvard Business School. Local newspapers are also an important source to determine the attitudes of various interest groups and the outlines of system and policy development. Finally, for each city there is a considerable body of pamphlets, magazine articles, local histories, biographies of relevant figures, legislative reports, and court proceedings cited in the text.

New York

For a view of New York in the last third of the nineteenth century, Seymour J. Mandelbaum, *Boss Tweed's New York* (New York: J. Wiley and Sons, 1965), and Bayrd Still's *Mirror for Gotham* (New York: New York University Press, 1956) are most helpful. The best secondary sources for transit are James Blaine Walker, *Fifty Years of Rapid Transit* (New York: The Law Printing Company, 1918), and Mark David Hirsch, *William C. Whitney, Modern Warwick* (New York: Dodd, Mead, and Company, 1948). The former is a well researched account of rapid transit policy and development, and the latter provides a richly detailed if sometimes confusing and unfocused story of street railways in New York. Harry James Carman, *The Street Surface Railway Franchises of New York City* (New York: Columbia University Press, 1919) is a disappointingly narrow policy study which does at least detail the companies and their routes. Robert C. Reed, "Charles T. Harvey and the New York Elevated Railway," *Railroad History*, no. 130 (Spring 1974), 23-41, and Julius Grodinsky, *Jay Gould: His Business Career, 1867-1892* (Philadelphia: University of Pennsylvania Press, 1957), supplement the Walker book for the elevated railroads. Burton Hendrick, "Great American Fortunes and Their Making," *McClure's Magazine*, 30 (November 1907-January 1908), 33-48, 236-245, 323-328, is a vivid though sometimes biased and inaccurate account of the New York syndicate.

Primary materials are particularly rich in the New York case. The William C. Whitney Papers at the Library of Congress offer a rare view of entrepreneurial operation. Other valuable sources for street railway enterprises are New York State: Public Service Commission for the First District, *Investigation of Interborough Metropolian Company and Brooklyn Rapid Transit Company*, 7 vols. (New York: Law Reporting Company, 1907-09) and the oral memoirs of John T. Hettrick at the Columbia Oral History Project. The latter is not always accurate and should be used carefully. For the public side of local transit, the minutes, reports, and documents of the rapid transit commissions are the single best source. The most complete collections are in the New York City Public Library and in the city's Municipal Reference Library. The Edward Shepard Papers and the William Parsons Papers owned by Columbia University offer some inside views of the 1894 RTC by its counsel and its chief engineer. The Mayors' Papers at the New York City Municipal Archives contain some correspondence with private citizens and with the city's transit commissioners. Finally, the writings of Milo R. Maltbie and Delos F. Wilcox offer valuable contemporary summaries and analyses of public transit policy. Especially useful are Maltbie's "A Century of Franchise History," *Municipal Affairs*, 4 (March 1900), 194-206, and Wilcox's "Elements of a Constructive Franchise Policy," *National Conference for Good City Government Proceedings* (n.p., 1910), 170-189.

Boston

Among secondary sources Sam Bass Warner's *Streetcar Suburbs: The Process of Growth in Boston, 1870-1900* (Cambridge, Massachusetts: Harvard University Press, 1962) provides a point of departure for studying the city of the 1880s and 1890s. Geoffrey Blodgett, *The Gentle Reformers* (Cambridge, Massachusetts: Harvard University Press, 1966), and Richard M. Abrams, *Conservatism in a Progressive Era* (Cambridge, Massachusetts: Harvard University Press, 1964), contain valuable information on the politics of local transit. The Boston Elevated Railway Company, *Fifty Years of Unified Transportation in Metropolitan Boston* (Boston, 1938), and Abraham E. Pinanski, *The Street Railway System of Metropolitan Boston* (New York: McGraw Publishing Company, 1908), are general histories of city transportation.

Primary sources are plentiful. Prentiss Cummings, "Street Railway System of Boston," in the *Professional and Industrial History of Suffolk County, Massachusetts* (Boston: Boston History Company, 1894), III, 286-302, is a rare account of street railways by a former company president. Louis P. Hager's company history, *History of the West End Street Railway* (Boston, 1892), contains important speeches by Henry Whitney. The Massachusetts Bay Transit Authority Library has two large scrapbooks on street railways and subways as well as other company materials. Unfortunately, the Frank Sprague Papers at the New York City Public Library have little information about the West End Company's decision to electrify. More helpful are the 1887 and 1888 issues of the *Street Railway Journal* and Charles S. Sargent, "Early Experiments in Boston," *SRJ*, 24 (October 8, 1904), 534-535. For transit and politics, Massachusetts General Court: Committees, *Report of the Committee to Investigate Methods Used for and against Legislation Concerning Railroads* (Boston, 1890), is very revealing. Walter S. Allen, "Street Railway Franchises in Massachusetts," *Annals of the American Academy of Political and Social Science*, 27 (January 1906), 91-110, and Louis D. Brandeis, "The Experience of Massachusetts in Street Railways," *Municipal Affairs*, 6 (Winter 1902), 721-729, are important public policy histories and analyses by two contemporary experts. The best sources for the evolution of the new, active policy are Massachusetts General Court: Rapid Transit Commission, *Report of the Rapid Transit Commission to the Massachusetts Legislature, April 5, 1892* (Boston, 1892), and Massachusetts General Court: Hearings. Street Railroads, *Hearings on Subways in Boston before the Joint Special Committee on Transit* (Boston, 1894), at the Massachusetts Statehouse Library. Finally, the plans and activities of the local transit commission can be found in the reports and documents published by the Boston Transit Commission and located in the Massachusetts Statehouse Library and in the Boston Public Library.

Philadelphia

Sam Bass Warner, *The Private City: Philadelphia in Three Periods of Its Growth* (Philadelphia: University of Pennsylvania Press, 1968), provides the best background for the nineteenth century city. Helpful for politics and policy are Harold

E. Cox and John F. Meyers, "The Philadelphia Traction Monopoly and the Pennsylvania Constitution of 1874: The Prostitution of an Ideal," *Pennsylvania History*, 35 (October 1968), 406-424, and Howard F. Gillette, "Corrupt and Contented: Philadelphia's Political Machine, 1865-1887," Ph.D. dissertation, Yale University, 1970. Frederick W. Speirs, *The Street Railway System of Philadelphia* (Baltimore: The Johns Hopkins University Press, 1897), is a dated and sometimes biased but still informative account of street railway history, organization, and policy. The Hendrick article listed in the New York section also supplies biographical information about the still obscure Kemble, Widener, and Elkins. And George Hilton's book on cable cars cited earlier includes a brief but instructive description of the Philadelphia trio's struggles with cable technology.

The best primary sources on Philadelphia street railways can be found in Harold E. Cox's collection at Wilkes College, Wilkes-Barre, Pennsylvania. His materials include over seventy volumes of newspaper clippings compiled by the PRT and by Edmund Stirling, editor of the Philadelphia *Public Ledger*; numerous company minute books and records; and the correspondence files of the UTC and the PRT for the years 1896-1912. Another important source is Edmund Stirling's history of Philadelphia street railways in the *Public Ledger*, February and March 1930. Rudolph Blankenburg, "Forty Years in the Wilderness; or Masters and Rulers of the 'Free Men' of Pennsylvania," *The Arena*, 33 and 34 (January-August 1905), is a lively if often biased account of politics and transit, while reformer Clinton R. Woodruff's "Philadelphia Street-Railway Franchises," *American Journal of Sociology*, 7 (1901-02), 216-233, is a tart description of the incredible 1901 franchise grab. Finally, a series of public reports including Ford, Bacon, and Davis, *Pennsylvania State Railroad Commission in the Matter of the Complaints against the Philadelphia Rapid Transit Company*, 2 vols. (Philadelphia, 1911); Robert M. Feustel, *Report on Behalf of the City of Philadelphia on the Valuation of the Property of the Philadelphia Rapid Transit Company. City of Philadelphia vs. Philadelphia Rapid Transit Company* (Pennsylvania Public Service Commission, Docket No. 3504); and Charles C. McChord, *Report of C. C. McChord to the Public Service Commission of the Commonwealth of Pennsylvania in re Philadelphia Transit Situation* (Philadelphia: B. S. Adams, 1927), are informative studies of local transit conditions and policy.

The following list contains some of the sources used in this work. Though by no means complete, it does include the more relevant materials. Additional information can be found in the notes.

I. Transit Bibliographies

Blaisdel, Ruth. *Sources of Information in Transportation*. Evanston, Illinois: Northwestern University Press, 1964.

Boston: City Planning Board. *A Compendium of Reports and Studies Relating to the Commerce and Industries of Boston*. Boston: Boston Printing Department, 1924.

Boston Elevated Railway Company. *Reference List of Literature on Electric Railway Transportation in Boston as of February, 1927*. Boston: Boston Elevated Railway Library, 1927.

———— *Urban and Electric Railways: A Selected Reference List of General Literature*. Boston: Boston Elevated Railway Library, 1930.

Brooks, Robert Clarkson. "A Bibliography of Municipal Problems and City Conditions," *Municipal Affairs*, 5 (March 1901).

Bureau of Railway Economics. *Electric Railroads—History: A List of Selected References in the Bureau of Railway Economics Library*. Washington, 1961.

"Check List of Works Relating to Street Railways, Rapid Transit, etc., in the City of New York," *Bulletin, New York Public Library*, 5 (April 1902), 160-162.

Haase, Adelaide R. *Index of Economic Material of the States of the United States: New York, 1789-1904*. Baltimore, 1907.

Holt, Glen E. "Urban Mass Transit History: Where We Have Been and Where We Are Going," in Jerome Finster, ed., *The National Archives and Urban Research*. Athens, Ohio: Ohio University Press, 1974, 81-105.

Jaboolian, Arax. "Rapid Transit: An Annotated List of Selected References, 1927-1940," *Municipal Reference Library Notes*, 26 (June 19, 1940), 49-69.

Massachusetts General Court: Committees. Boston Elevated Railways, 1925. *Reference List of Literature Pertaining to the Transportation System of Metropolitan Boston, 1910-1924*. Boston, 1925.

Massachusetts: Public Service Commission and others. *Bibliographies, etc., on Street Railways in Massachusetts*. Boston: Wright and Potter Printing Company, 1919.

McReynolds, James Bronson. *Civic Bibliography for Greater New York*. New York?, 1911.

Metcalf, Kenneth N. *Transportation Information Sources*. Detroit, Michigan: Gale Research Company, 1966.

New York City Public Library. *Catalogue of the William B. Parsons Collection*. New York: The New York Public Library, 1941.

Northwestern University Transportation Center. *A Reference Guide to Metropolitan Transportation*. Evanston, Illinois: Northwestern University Press, 1964.

Palmer, Foster M. "The Literature of the Street Railway," *Harvard University Bulletin*, 12 (Winter 1958), 117-138.

Stevens, Don Lorenzo. *A Bibliography of Municipality Regulation and Municipal Ownership*. Cambridge: Harvard University Press, 1918.

"Subways in the City of New York: An Annotated List of Selected References, 1910-1927," *Municipal Reference Library Notes*, 13 (May 18, 1927), 89-111.

II. Primary Sources

A. Manuscripts and Company Records.

August Belmont Papers. New York City Public Library.

Boston Local Transit Companies. Annual reports, financial and other documents of the Boston Elevated Railway Company, the West End Street Railway Company, and Boston horse railways. Corporate Records Division of Baker Library at Harvard Business School.

——— Scrapbooks and miscellaneous data. Massachusetts Bay Transit Authority Library.

William W. Clapp Papers. Houghton Library, Harvard University.

R. G. Dun and Company Credit Ledgers. Baker Library, Harvard Business School.

Cyrus W. Field Papers. New York Public Library.

Rufus Henry Gilbert Papers. New York Historical Society.

Reminiscences of John T. Hettrick. Oral History Project of Columbia University.

Kidder, Peabody Company Papers. Baker Library, Harvard University.

Seth Low Papers. Columbia University Library.

New York City Local Transit Companies. Annual reports, financial and other documents of the IRT, the Metropolitan Street Railway Company and others. Corporate Records Division of Baker Library at Harvard Business School.

——— Minute books of the IRT and miscellaneous papers of other companies. New York Transit Authority Library.

——— Minute books and other documents of street railway companies. Privately held.

——— Primary and secondary materials of the IRT, the Manhattan Elevated, the Metropolitan and other companies. Scudder Collection at Columbia University.

New York City Mayors Papers. New York City Municipal Archives.

William Barclay Parsons Collection. Pamphlets, broadsides and other documents of New York local transit companies. New York City Public Library.

William Barclay Parsons Papers. Columbia University Library.

George Herndon Pegram Autobiography. New York City Public Library.

Philadelphia Local Transit Companies. Annual reports, financial and other documents of the PRT and UTC. Corporate Records Division of Baker Library at Harvard Business School.

——— Minute books, stock ledgers, account books, and other materials of the PRT, UTC, PTC, and horse railways. Harold E. Cox Collection at Wilkes College Library.

Edward Morse Shepard Papers. Columbia University Library.

Frank J. Sprague Papers. New York City Public Library.

West End Street Railway Company. Minute books, privately held.

——— Miscellaneous records. Manuscript Division of Baker Library at Harvard Business School.

William C. Whitney Papers. Library of Congress.

B. Public Documents

Boston: Board of Aldermen. *Report of Adjourned Hearing before the Committee of the Whole Board of Aldermen* [on West End Company petition for overhead system]. Boston, 1889.

Boston Transit Commission. *Annual Reports, 1895-1918.*

——— *The Boston Subway.* Boston, 1895.

——— *Legislation, Court Decisions, Contract for the Use of the Subway, Con-*

tract for the Use of the New Tunnel and Subway, Lease of the East Boston
Tunnel. Boston, 1911.

────── Statement of the Subway Commission: Subway Act of 1893. Boston,
1894.

────── The Subway. What the Commission Has Done. Boston, 1895.

Chicago: City Council. Committee on Local Transportation. Report on the
Transportation Subway Systems of Boston, New York, Philadelphia, Paris,
London. Chicago, 1909.

Continental Securities Company and others v. August Belmont et al. 83 NY
Misc. 340 (1913) and 168 NY App. Div. 483 (1915), Case Record on Appeal.

Feustel, Robert M. Report on Behalf of the City of Philadelphia on the Valuation
of the Property of the Philadelphia Rapid Transit Company. City of Philadelphia vs. Philadelphia Rapid Transit Company. Pennsylvania Public Service Commission, Docket No. 3504.

Ford, Bacon, and Davis. Pennsylvania State Railroad Commission in the Matter
of the Complaints against the Philadelphia Rapid Transit Company. Report
to the Commission by Ford, Bacon and Davis, March 7, 1911. 2 vols. Philadelphia, 1911.

Isador Wormser v. the Metropolitan Street Railway Company and the Interurban Street Railway Company. 98 NY App. Div. 29 (1904), Case Record
on Appeal.

Massachusetts. Board of Railroad Commissioners. Annual Reports, 1880-1913.

────── General Laws of Massachusetts Relating to Street Railway Companies.
Boston, 1896.

────── An Indexed-Digest of the Reported Decisions, Precedents and General
Principles Enunciated by the Board of Railroad Commissioners, 1870-1911.
Boston, 1912.

────── "Special Reports on Street Railway Matters: West End Railway Leases,"
Twenty-ninth Annual Report (1898), 140-55.

Massachusetts General Court: Committee on Street Railways. Evidence before
the Massachusetts Committee of Street Railways as to the Safety of Overhead Electric Wires. Boston, 1889.

────── Not Wanted: Elevated Railways in the City of Boston. Boston, 1879.

Massachusetts General Court: Committees. Report of the Committee to Investigate Methods Used for and against Legislation Concerning Railroads.
Investigation into the Conduct of Members of the House in Connection
Therewith, with Evidence Taken at the Hearings before the Committee. Boston, 1890.

Massachusetts General Court: Joint Special Committee on Transit. Hearings on
Subways in Boston before the Joint Special Committee on Transit. Boston,
1894.

Massachusetts General Court: Rapid Transit Commission. Report of the Rapid
Transit Commission to the Massachusetts Legislature, April 5, 1892.

Massachusetts General Court: Special Committee to Investigate the Relationship
between Cities and Towns and Street Railway Companies. Report of the
Special Committee Appointed to Investigate the Relations between Cities
and Towns and Street Railway Companies, February, 1898. Boston, 1898.

268 Bibliography

Massachusetts Public Service Commission. *Report of the Public Service Commission and the Boston Transit Commission Acting as a Joint Commission under Chapter 108, Resolves of 1913.* Boston, 1914.

McChord, Charles C. *Report of C. C. McChord to the Public Service Commission of the Commonwealth of Pennsylvania in re Philadelphia Transit Situation.* Philadelphia, 1927.

New York City: Board of Estimate and Appropriation. "Report . . . of the Investigation . . . into the New York Railways System," *Minutes,* CCIX, 3024-49.

New York City. Board of Rapid Transit Railroad Commissioners. *Documents, 1897-1904.*

—— *Minutes of Proceedings of the Board of Commissioners of Rapid Transit in the City of New York from July to December, 1875.* New York, 1877.

—— *Minutes of Proceedings of the Board of Commissioners of Rapid Transit Appointed on the Second Day of April, 1879 by Honorable Edward Cooper, Mayor of the City of New York.* New York, 1880.

—— *Minutes of Proceedings of Commissioners of Rapid Transit, December 12, 1883-June 19, 1884.* New York, 1884?

—— *Minutes of the Proceedings of the Board of Rapid Transit.* New York, 1890.

—— *Minutes of Proceedings of the Board of Rapid Transit Railroad Commissioners . . . June 8, 1894-June 27, 1907.* 8 vols. New York, 1894-1907.

—— *Report of the Board of Rapid Transit Railroad Commissioners in and for the City of New York to the Common Council of the City of New York in Pursuance of the Provisions of Section 5 of Chapter 4 of the Law of 1891, Together with the Documents, Maps and Plans Attached Thereto, October 20, 1891.* New York? 1891?

—— *Reports, 1901-1906.* New York, 1901-07.

New York State: Legislature. *Minutes and Testimony of the Joint Special Legislative Committee Appointed to Investigate the Public Service Commissions.* 6 vols. Albany, 1916.

New York State: Legislature. Assembly. *In Assembly, February 1874 Introduced by Mr. Eastman. Rapid Transit for the City of New York. Synopsis of the Provisions of the Bill.* Albany, 1874.

—— *Report and Testimony of the Special Committee to Investigate the Desirability of Municipal Ownership of Street Railroads.* 2 vols. Albany, 1896.

New York State: Legislature. Senate. Special Committee to Ascertain the Best Means for the Transportation of Passengers in the City of New York. *Report of a Special Commission . . . to Ascertain the Best Means for the Transportation of Passengers in . . . New York, January 31, 1867.* Albany, 1867.

New York State: Public Service Commission for the First District. *Documentary History of Railroad Companies.* Vol. V of Public Service Commission, *Report, 1913.*

—— *History and Description of Rapid Transit Routes in New York City Adopted Under the Rapid Transit Act.* New York, 1910.

—— *The History of State Regulation in New York.* Albany, 1908.

—— *Investigation of Interborough Metropolitan Company and Brooklyn Rapid Transit Company.* 7 vols. New York, 1907.

New York State: Supreme Court. Trial Term, part I, Criminal Branch. *Metropolitan Investigation: Presentment, April 20, 1908.*

Parsons, William Barclay. *Report to the Board of Rapid Transit Railroad Commissioners in and for the City of New York on Rapid Transit in Foreign Cities.* New York, 1894.

Philadelphia: Councils. *Agreement Authorized by Ordinance of Councils. Approved July 1, 1907.*

Philadelphia: Councils. Railroad Committee. *The Trolley System. Stenographic Report of Testimony of Experts and Arguments of Rufus E. Shapley, Esq., and John G. Johnson, Esq.* Philadelphia, 1892.

Philadelphia. Department of City Transit. *The Rapid Transit Problem, October 1, 1913.* Philadelphia, 1913.

—— *A Report and Discussion upon the Proposals of the Philadelphia Rapid Transit Company.* Philadelphia, 1919.

—— *A Study and Review of the Problem of Passenger Transportation in Philadelphia by a Unified System of Lines.* Philadelphia, 1916.

Philadelphia: Transit Advisory Committee. *Report of the Transit Advisory Committee to General Conference on Transit Situation in Philadelphia, May 24, 1930.*

Philadelphia: Transit Commissioner. *Report of Transit Commissioner, City of Philadelphia, July, 1913.* 2 vols.

U.S. Bureau of the Census. *Eleventh Census of the United States. 1890. Bulletin 11.* "Transportation—Rapid Transit in Cities."

—— *Bulletin 55.* "The Relative Economy of Cable, Electric and Animal Motive Power for Street Railways."

—— *Report on the Transportation Business in the United States, 1890.*

U.S. Bureau of the Census. *Special Reports. Street and Electric Railways, 1902.* Washington, 1905.

—— *Special Reports: Street and Electric Railways, 1907.* Washington, 1910.

U.S. Federal Electric Railways Commission. *Proceedings of the Federal Electric Railways Commission.* Washington, 1920.

Vollum, Fernley, Vollum, and Rorer. *Report[s] of Examination of the Books, Accounts and Vouchers of the Philadelphia Rapid Transit Company for the Year[s] Ending June 30, 1908-1910.*

—— *Report of the Examination of the Books, Leases, etc., of the Philadelphia Rapid Transit Company from July 1, 1902 to December 31, 1910 and Reconstruction of the Books as of December 31, 1910.*

C. Newspapers and Periodicals

Boston *Evening Transcript*, 1890-1905.

Boston *Globe.* Clippings file. 1900-05.

Boston Newspapers. Clippings file in the Massachusetts Statehouse Library. 1890-1900.

—— Charles E. Powers' collection of clippings in the Massachusetts Statehouse Library about elevated railroads in Boston and New York. 3 vols. 1878-82.

New York *Commercial and Financial Chronicle*, 1901-07.
New York Newspapers. August Belmont clippings collection on New York transit in the Museum of the City of New York. 20 vols. 1904-10.
———— John J. R. Croes' clippings collection on New York street transportation in the Engineering Societies Library in New York City. 27 vols. 1879-99.
New York *Times*, 1888-1900.
Philadelphia *Evening Bulletin*, 1906-07.
Philadelphia Newspapers. Clippings on Philadelphia transit gathered by the PRT and located in the Cox Collection at Wilkes College. 37 vols. 1904-12.
Philadelphia *Public Ledger*. Clippings on Philadelphia transit collected by Edmund Stirling and located in the Cox Collection at Wilkes College. 37 vols. 1905-35.
Railroad Gazette, 1875-84.
Real Estate Record and Builders Guide [for New York], 1891-94.
Street Railway Journal, 1884-1907.
Street Railway Review, 1891-1906.

D. Books, Pamphlets, and Articles

Allen, Walter S. *Opinion of an Expert on the West End Street Railway*. Boston?, 1895.
———— "Street Railway Franchises in Massachusetts," *Annals of the American Academy of Political and Social Science*, 27 (January 1906), 91-110.
American Institute of Electrical Engineers, "The Metropolitan Street Railway System," *New York Electrical Handbook* (1904), 125-169.
American Society of Civil Engineers. *Rapid Transit and Terminal Freight Facilities*. New York, 1875.
Belmont, Perry. *An American Democrat: The Recollections of Perry Belmont*. New York, 1940.
Bemis, Edward W., ed. *Municipal Monopolies*. New York, 1899.
Bird, Albert A. "Philadelphia Street Railways and the Municipality," *The Citizen*, 1 (January-February 1896), 256-261, 286-290.
Blankenburg, Rudolph. "Forty Years in the Wilderness; or Masters and Rulers of the 'Free Men' of Pennsylvania," *The Arena*, 33 and 34 (January-August 1905).
Boston Associated Board of Trade. *Report of the Transportation Committee*. Boston, 1893.
Boston Elevated Railway Company. *Statutes, Surface Railway Leases, Contracts, etc., 1887-1916*. Boston, 1916.
Breen, Matthew P. *Thirty Years of New York Politics Up-to-Date*. New York, 1899.
Brandeis, Louis D. "The Experience of Massachusetts in Street Railways," *Municipal Affairs*, 6 (Winter 1902), 721-729.
———— *The Washington Street Subway*. Boston, 1902.
Bruère, Henry. "Public Utilities Regulation in New York," *Annals of the American Academy of Political and Social Science*, 31 (May 1908), 1-17.
Chandler Brothers and Company. *The Philadelphia Rapid Transit Company*. Philadelphia?, 1904.

—— *Traction Investments of the Philadelphia Rapid Transit Company*. Philadelphia?, 1908.

—— *Union Traction Company*. Philadelphia, 1899?

Church, Simeon E. *Shall the City Build a Railroad?* New York, 1873.

Clarke, Thomas C. "Rapid Transit in Cities," *Scribner's Magazine*, 11 (May-June 1892), 568-578, 743-758.

Clarke, Thomas W. *Elevated Railroads. Arguments of Thomas William Clarke, Esq., Before the Street Railway Committee, January 24, 1884*. Boston, 1884.

Crimmins, Thomas D., ed. *The Diary of John D. Crimmins*. n.p., 1925.

Cummings, Prentiss. "Street Railway System of Boston," *Professional and Industrial History of Suffolk County, Massachusetts*. 3 vols. Boston, 1894.

Dabney, Lewis S. *Arguments of L. S. Dabney for the Remonstrants against the West End Street Railway Company's Bill, and for the Preservation of the Boston Common*. Boston, 1887.

Davenport, John J. *Letter on the Subject of the Population of the City of New York, Its Density and the Evils Resulting Therefrom*. New York, 1884.

Demarest, Theodore F. C. *The Rise and Growth of Elevated Railroad Law*. New York, 1894.

DeNavarro, Jose F. *Sixty-Six Years Business Record*. New York, 1904.

Dillon, John F. *Commentaries on the Law of Municipal Corporations*. 5 vols. Boston, 1911.

Easton, Alexander. *A Practical Treatise on Street or Horse-Power Railways*. Philadelphia, 1859.

Edison General Electric Company. *Economy of the Electric Railway*. New York, 1891.

Evolution of Philadelphia's Street Railway Systems. Philadelphia, 1909.

Fairchild, Charles B. *Street Railways, Their Construction, Operation and Maintenance*. New York, 1892.

Hager, Louis P. *History of the West End Street Railway*. Boston, 1892.

Hale, Edward E. "The Congestion of Cities," *The Forum*, 4 (1887), 527-535.

Harding, Herbert L. *The Washington Street Subway*. Boston, 1900.

Hart, Thomas N. *Boston Subways: Remarks before the Committee on Metropolitan Affairs*. Boston, 1901.

Haupt, Lewis M. *Feasibility of Underground Railroads in Philadelphia*. Philadelphia, 1888.

—— *Rapid Transit*. Philadelphia, 1884.

Higgins, Charles M. *City Transit Evils, Their Causes and Cure*. Brooklyn, 1905.

Howe, Wirt. *New York at the Turn of the Century, 1899-1916*. Toronto, Canada, 1946.

Ingersoll, Ernest. "Getting About New York," *Outlook*, 58 (April 2, 1898), 829-839.

Interborough Rapid Transit Company. *Interborough Rapid Transit: The New York Subway, Its Construction and Equipment*. New York, 1904.

Lewis, Alfred H. "Owners of America, II: Thomas F. Ryan," *Cosmopolitan Magazine*, 45 (May 1908), 141-152.

Lewis, Edwin O. "Philadelphia's Relation to the Rapid Transit Company," *Annals of the American Academy of Political and Social Science*, 31 (May 1908), 600-611.

—— The Street Railway System in Philadelphia: Brief Argument of Edwin O. Lewis, Common Councilman for the 27th Ward, in Opposition to the Proposed Philadelphia Rapid Transit Company Ordinance, June 20, 1907.

Maltbie, Milo R. "A Century of Franchise History," Municipal Affairs, 4 (March 1900), 194-206.

—— "Rapid Transit Subways in Metropolitan Cities," Annual Report of the Smithsonian Institution (1904), 759-772.

Meigs, Joe Vincent. The Meigs Elevated Railway System. Boston, 1887.

—— Rapid Transit Made Plain. Lowell, Massachusetts, 1894.

Merrill, Moody. Argument . . . on the Petition of the Highland Street Railway Company for Authority to Lease, Purchase and Consolidate with Other Street Railway Companies and to Adopt the Cable System of Motive-Power . . . , February 24, 1886. Boston, 1886.

New York Chamber of Commerce. Rapid Transit in New York City. New York, 1905.

New York Citizens Union: Bureau of City Betterment. Suggestions for Improvement of City Transit, February, 1903. New York, 1903.

New York City Merchants Association. Passenger Transportation Service in the City of New York. New York, 1903.

New York Municipal Art Society: Committee on City Plan. Bulletin No. 3. New York, 1903.

—— Bulletin No. 14. "Report on Rapid Transit in New York." New York, 1904.

—— Bulletin No. 24. (May 11, 1905). New York, 1905.

—— Subway Transit, January 12, 1907. New York, 1907.

New York Rapid Transit Association. The Great Need. A City Railroad as a City Work. Rapid Transit for the People at Cost and No Tribute to Monopolies. New York, 1873.

New York Transit Conference, 1906. Provisional Report: Means of Making Effective Municipal Control of Passenger Transportation within the City of New York. New York, 1906.

Philadelphia Rapid Transit Company. Philadelphia's Rapid Transit. Philadelphia, 1908.

Pillsbury, Albert Enoch. Argument . . . in Support of the Bill of the Boston Elevated Railway Company, April 29-30, 1897. Boston, 1897.

—— Argument . . . in Behalf of the Boston Elevated Railway Company before the Committee on Metropolitan Affairs, March 28, 1901. Boston, 1901.

Rapid Transit Assured: A Feast of Thanksgiving. New York, 187?.

Rapid Transit Meeting, Chickering Hall, Tuesday Evening, June 5, 1877. New York, 1877.

Report of Meeting at Chickering Hall, June 21, 1877, to Protest against the Destruction of Property by Elevated Railroads without Compensation to the Owners. New York, 1877.

Richardson, Charles. The City of Philadelphia: Its Stockholders and Directors. Philadelphia, 1893.

Rideing, W. H. "Rapid Transit in New York," Appleton's Journal, 19 (May 1878), 393-408.

Robinson, A. P. *Report upon the Contemplated Metropolitan Railroad.* New York, 1865.

Seabury, Samuel. *Municipal Ownership and Operation of Public Utilities in New York City.* New York, 1905.

Sergeant, Charles S. "Early Experiments in Boston," *Street Railway Journal,* 24 (October 8, 1904), 534-535.

Shaw, Charles P. *Cable Railways vs. Horse Railroads for Intramural Transit in the City of New York.* New York, 1885.

Spaulding, Henry Curtis. *Local Transportation at Boston Comprising Swift Transit by Tunnel Railways Connecting Together the Tracks of All the Steam Railroads and Rapid Transit by the Aid of Subways.* Boston, 1891.
——— *Swift Transit by Tunnel Railways.* Boston, 1891.

Sprague, Frank J. "The Electric Railway," *Century Magazine,* 70 (July-August 1905), 434-451, 512-526.
——— *Rapid Transit Situation in New York. An Address Before the Electric Club, February 26, 1891.* New York, 1899.

"Street Railway Franchises in New York," *Municipal Affairs,* 6 (March 1902), 68-86.

Sweet, Elnathan. *Report of the New York Elevated Roads.* Albany, 1880.

Syrett, Harold C., ed. *The Gentleman and the Tiger: The Autobiography of George B. McClellan, Jr.* Philadelphia, 1956.

United Business Men's Association of Philadelphia. *The Philadelphia Rapid Transit Question: The Retail Merchants Plan.*

Urofsky, Melvin I., and David W. Levy. *Letters of Louis D. Brandeis.* Vol. I: *Urban Reformer.* Albany, 1971.

Van Wyck, Frederick. *Recollection of an Old New Yorker.* New York, 1932.

Warner, John deWitt. "New York's Subways, the Rapid Transit Commission, and the People," *The Independent,* 58 (March 9, 1905), 525-537.

West Side Association of the City of New York. *Proceedings of Public Meetings.* New York, 1871.

West Side Citizens' Transit Reform Committee of One Hundred. *Report of the Executive Committee, May 20, 1903.* New York, 1903.

Whitney, Edward B. "Public Ownership in New York," *International Quarterly,* 12 (October 1905), 1-12.

Whitney, Henry M., and Prentiss Cummings. *Additional Burdens on Street Railway Companies.* Boston, 1891.

Whitney, Travis H. "New York City Public Service Commission," *Proceedings, American Political Science Association,* 5 (1908), 96-110.

Whitridge, Frederick W. *The Public Service Commission's Correspondence with the Receiver of the Third Avenue Railroad.* New York, 1910.

Wigglesworth, Thomas, and others. *Shall the Citizens of Boston Be Taxed to Furnish a New Highway Solely for the West End Street Railway Company?* Boston, 1890.

Wilcox, Delos F. "The Crisis in Public Service Regulation in New York," *National Municipal Review,* 4 (1915), 547-563.
———"Elements of a Constructive Franchise Policy," *Proceedings, National Conference for Good City Government* (1910), 170-189.

———— *Municipal Franchises.* 2 vols. New York, 1911.

Woodruff, Clinton R. "Philadelphia Street-Railway Franchises," *American Journal of Sociology,* 7 (1901-02), 216-233.

Woods, Robert A., and Joseph F. Eastman. "The Boston Franchise Contest," *Outlook,* 82 (April 14, 1906), 835-841.

Wright, Augustine W. *American Street Railways: Their Construction, Equipment and Maintenance.* Chicago, 1888.

Wright, Henry C. "Development of Transit Control in New York City," *Annals of the American Academy of Political and Social Science,* 31 (May 1908), 17-41.

E. Miscellaneous

Goldsmith, Meyer. "Expenses of the Philadelphia Rapid Transit Company Assumed by the City," Box 571 in Philadelphia City Archives.

———— "The Philadelphia Rapid Transit Company: Summary of Street Paving Repairs," Box 571 in Philadelphia City Archives.

Parsons, William B. (collector). "Manhattan Elevated Railway. Collection of Documents and Reports Submitted to the New York City Rapid Transit Railroad Commissioners Board and the Manhattan Railway Company on the Plans for Improving the Rapid Transit Facilities in New York City," in New York City Public Library.

Stirling, Edmund. Articles on history of Philadelphia local transit printed in the Philadelphia *Public Ledger,* February 10-March 13, 1930. Typescript copy of Cox Collection at Wilkes College.

III. Secondary Sources

A. Articles

Barrett, Paul. "Public Policy and Private Choice: Mass Transit and the Automobile in Chicago between the Wars," *Business History Review,* 49 (Winter 1975), 473-497.

Broude, Henry W. "The Role of the State in American Economic Development, 1820-1920," in Hugh G. J. Aitken, ed. *The State and Economic Growth.* New York: Social Science Research Council, 1959, 4-25.

Brown, Burton G. "The Boston Subway: 1897," *Bulletin, National Railway Historical Society,* 38 (1973), 18-27, 43-46.

Cox, Harold E. "The Philadelphia and Western Story," *Traction and Models,* 3 (October 1967), 6-10.

Cox, Harold E., and John F. Meyers. "The Philadelphia Traction Monopoly and the Pennsylvania Constitution of 1874: The Prostitution of an Ideal," *Pennsylvania History,* 35 (October 1968), 406-424.

Evans, Harold. "Philadelphia's Street Railway Problems," *National Municipal Review,* 17 (October 1928), 1-8.

Foxcroft, Frank. "The Boston Subway and Others," *New England Magazine,* 13 (October 1895), 193-210.

Hancock, John L. "Planners in the Changing American City, 1900-1940," *Journal of the American Institute of Planners*, 33 (September 1967), 290-304.

Hendrick, Burton J. "Great American Fortunes and Their Making," *McClure's Magazine*, 30 (November 1907-January 1908), 33-48.

Holt, Glen E. "The Changing Perception of Urban Pathology: An Essay on the Development of Mass Transit in the United States," in Kenneth T. Jackson and Stanley K. Schultz, eds. *Cities in American History*. New York: Alfred A. Knopf, 1972, 324-343.

Kennedy, Charles J. "Commuter Services in the Boston Area," *Business History Review*, 36 (Summer 1962), 153-170.

McLain, Frank D. "The Street Railways of Philadelphia," *Quarterly Journal of Economics*, 22 (February 1908), 233-260.

Morse, Stearns. "Slots in the Streets," *New England Quarterly*, 24 (March 1951), 3-12.

Myers, Gustavus. "History of Public Franchises in New York City," *Municipal Affairs*, 4 (March 1900), 71-206.

Reed, Robert C. "Charles T. Harvey and the New York Elevated Railway," *Railroad History*, no. 130 (Spring 1974), 23-41.

Roberts, Sidney I. " Portrait of a Robber Baron: Charles T. Yerkes," *Business History Review*, 35 (Autumn 1961), 344-371.

Skolnick, Richard. "Civic Group Progressivism in New York City," *New York History*, 51 (July 1970), 411-439.

Smerk, George M. "The Streetcar: Shaper of American Cities," *Traffic Quarterly*, 21 (1967), 569-584.

Taylor, George Rogers. "The Beginning of Mass Transportation in Urban America," parts I and II, *Smithsonian Journal of History*, 1 (Summer-Autumn 1966), 35-50, 31-54.

White, Leonard D. "Origin of Public Utilities Commission in Massachusetts," *Journal of Political Economy*, 29 (March 1921), 177-197.

Wolf, Andrea, and Dita Mantegazza. "Transit Expansion and Growth of the Bronx," *Bronx County Historical Society Journal*, 7 (January 1970), 12-24.

B. Books and Pamphlets

Abrams, Richard M. *Conservatism in a Progressive Era: Massachusetts Politics, 1900-1912*. Cambridge, Massachusetts: Harvard University Press, 1964.

Adler, Cyrus. *Jacob H. Schiff: His Life and Letters*. 2 vols. Garden City, New York: Doubleday, Doran and Company, 1928.

Andrews, James Henry Millar. *A Short History of the Development of Street Railway Transportation in Philadelphia*. Philadelphia, 1945.

Bacon, Edwin M. *The Book of Boston*. Boston: The Book of Boston Company, 1916.

Barger, Harold. *The Transportation Industries, 1889-1946*. New York: National Bureau of Economic Research, 1951.

Barker, Theodore C., and Michael Robbins. *A History of London Transport*. 2 vols. London: Allen and Unwin, 1963 and 1974.

Blodgett, Geoffrey. *The Gentle Reformers: Massachusetts Democrats in the*

Cleveland Era. Cambridge, Massachusetts: Harvard University Press, 1966.

Boston Elevated Railway Company. *Fifty Years of Unified Transportation in Metropolitan Boston.* Boston, 1938.

Brown, Henry Collins. *Valentine's Manual of Old New York.* New York: Valentine's Manual, Inc., 1925.

Callow, Alexander B. *The Tweed Ring.* New York: Oxford University Press, 1965.

Carman, Harry J. *The Street Surface Railway Franchises of New York City.* New York: Columbia University Press, 1919.

Carosso, Vincent P. *Investment Banking in America: A History.* Cambridge, Massachusetts: Harvard University Press, 1970.

Carter, Samuel. *Cyrus Field: Man of Two Worlds.* New York: Putnam, 1968.

Collins, Herman L., and Wilfred Jordan. *Philadelphia: A Study of Progress.* 4 vols. Philadelphia: Lewis Historical Publishing Company, 1941.

Cox, Harold E. *Early Electric Cars of Philadelphia, 1885-1911.* Forty Fort, Pennsylvania, 1969.

Crocker, George G. *From the Stage Coach to the Railroad Train and the Street Car.* Boston: W. B. Clarke Company, 1900.

Cudahy, Brian J. *Change at Park Street Under: The Story of Boston's Subways.* Brattleboro, Vermont: S. Greene Press, 1972.

Evans, Frank B. *Pennsylvania Politics, 1872-1877: A Study in Political Leadership.* Harrisburg, Pennsylvania: Pennsylvania Historical and Museum Commission, 1966.

Fairlie, John A. *Essays in Municipal Administration.* New York: The Macmillan Company, 1910.

Glaab, Charles N., and A. Theodore Brown. *A History of Urban America.* New York: The Macmillan Company, 1967.

Glaeser, Martin G. *Public Utilities in American Capitalism.* New York: The Macmillan Company, 1957.

Grodinsky, Julius. *Jay Gould: His Business Career, 1867-1892.* Philadelphia: University of Pennsylvania Press,1957.

Harkness, LeRoy T. *The Dual System Contracts in Their Relation to the Rapid Transit History of New York City.* New York, 1913.

Hendrick, Burton J. *The Age of Big Business.* New Haven: Yale University Press, 1921.

Hilton, George W. *The Cable Car in America.* Pasadena, California: Howell-North Books, 1970.

Hilton, George W., and John F. Due. *The Electric Interurban Railways in America.* Stanford, California: Stanford University Press, 1960.

Hirsch, Mark D. *William C. Whitney: Modern Warwick.* New York: Dodd, Mead, and Company, 1948.

Jenkins, Stephen. *The Greatest Street in the World: The Story of Broadway, Old and New.* New York: G. P. Putnam's Sons, 1911.

Jessup, Philip Caryl. *Elihu Root.* 2 vols. New York: Dodd, Mead, and Company, 1938.

Judson, Isabella. *Cyrus W. Field: His Life and Work.* New York: Harper and Brothers, 1896.

Kellet, John R. *The Impact of Railways on Victorian Cities.* London: Routledge and K. Paul, 1969.

King, Clyde L. *The Regulation of Municipal Utilities.* New York: D. Appleton and Company, 1914.

Kurland, Gerald. *Seth Low: The Reformer in an Urban and Industrial Age.* New York: Twayne, 1971.

Langtry, Albert P., ed. *Metropolitan Boston: A Modern History.* 5 vols. New York: Lewis Historical Publishing Company, 1929.

Madelbaum, Seymour J. *Boss Tweed's New York.* New York: J. Wiley and Sons, 1965.

Mason, Alpheus T. *Brandeis: A Free Man's Life.* New York: Viking Press, 1956.

Mason, Edward S. *The Street Railway in Massachusetts: The Rise and Decline of of an Industry.* Cambridge, Massachusetts: Harvard University Press, 1932.

McKay, John P. *Tramways and Trolleys: The Rise of Urban Mass Transit in Europe.* Princeton, New Jersey: Princeton University Press, 1976.

McKelvey, Blake. *The Urbanization of America.* New Brunswick, New Jersey: Rutgers University Press, 1963.

McShane, Clay. *Technology and Reform: Street Railways and the Growth of Milwaukee, 1887-1900.* Madison, Wisconsin: State Historical Society of Wisconsin, 1974.

Middleton, William D. *The Time of the Trolley.* Milwaukee, Wisconsin: Kalmbach Publishing Company, 1967.

Miller, John A. *Fares, Please!* New York: Dover Publications, 1960.

Morgan, George. *The City of Firsts: A Complete History of the City of Philadelphia.* Philadelphia: The Historical Publication Society, 1926.

Morris, Lloyd. *Incredible New York: High Life and Low Life of the Last Hundred Years.* New York: Random House, 1951.

Nevins, Allen. *Abram S. Hewitt with Some Account of Peter Cooper.* New York: Harper and Brothers, 1935.

New York News Bureau: Philadelphia Local Service. *1854-1904, Fifty Years with Passenger Railways in Philadelphia.* Philadelphia, n. d.

Oberholtzer, Ellis P. *Philadelphia: A History of the City and Its People: A Record of 225 Years.* 4 vols. Philadelphia: S. J. Clarke Publishing Company, n. d.

Owen, Wilfred. *Cities in the Motor Age.* New York: Viking Press, 1959.

——— *The Metropolitan Transportation Problem.* Washington: Doubleday and Company, 1956.

Passer, Harold C. *The Electrical Manufacturers, 1875-1900.* Cambridge, Massachusetts: Harvard University Press, 1953.

Pinanski, Abraham Edward. *The Street Railway System of Metropolitan Boston.* New York: McGraw Publishing Company, 1908.

Pusey, Merle J. *Charles Evans Hughes.* 2 vols. New York: The Macmillan Company, 1951.

Real Estate Record and Builders Guide. *A History of Real Estate, Building and Architecture in New York City during the Last Quarter of a Century.* New York: Real Estate Record Association, 1898.

Reeves, William F. *The First Elevated Railroads in Manhattan and the Bronx of the City of New York.* New York: New York Historical Society, 1936.

Regional Survey of New York and Its Environs. Vol. II: *Population, Land Values and Government.* New York, 1929. Vol. IV: *Transit and Transportation.* New York, 1928.

Rodgers, Cleveland, and Rebecca Rankin. *New York: The World's Capital.* New York: Harper and Brothers, 1948.

Rowsome, Frank. *Trolley Car Treasury.* New York: Bonanza Books, 1956.

Schlesinger, Arthur M. *The Rise of the City, 1878-1898.* New York: The Macmillan Company, 1933.

Scott, Mel. *American City Planning since 1890.* Berkeley, California: University of California Press, 1969.

Smerk, George M., ed. *Readings in Urban Transportation.* Bloomington, Indiana: Indiana University Press, 1968.

Snyder, George Duncan. *Notes on City Passenger-Transportation in the United States.* London: The Institution, 1913.

Soloman, Richard J., and others. *History of Transit and Innovative Systems.* Cambridge, Massachusetts: M.I.T. Press, 1971.

Speirs, Frederick W. *The Street Railway System of Philadelphia: Its History and Present Condition.* Baltimore: The Johns Hopkins University Press, 1897.

Steffens, Lincoln. *The Shame of the Cities.* New York: Hill and Wang, 1960.

Still, Bayrd. *Mirror for Gotham.* New York: New York University Press, 1956.

Stoddard, Theodore L. *Master of Manhattan: The Life of Richard Croker.* New York: Longmans, Green and Company, 1931.

Walker, James B. *Fifty Years of Rapid Transit.* New York: The Law Printing Company, 1918.

Warner, Sam B. *The Private City: Philadelphia in Three Periods of Its Growth.* Philadelphia: University of Pennsylvania Press, 1968.

────── *Streetcar Suburbs: The Process of Growth in Boston, 1870-1900.* Cambridge, Massachusetts: Harvard University Press, 1962.

────── *The Urban Wilderness: A History of the American City.* New York: Harper and Row, 1972.

Weber, Adna F. *The Growth of Cities in the Nineteenth Century.* Ithaca, New York: Cornell University Press, 1963.

Wheeler, Everett P. *Sixty Years of American Life.* New York: E. P. Dutton and Company, 1917.

Whitehill, Walter M. *Boston: A Topographical History.* Cambridge, Massachusetts: Belknap Press, 1963.

Willson, Henry B. *The Story of Rapid Transit.* New York: D. Appleton and Company, 1903.

Wilson, George L., James M. Herring, and Roland B. Eutsler. *Public Utility Regulation.* New York: McGraw-Hill Book Company, 1936.

Young, John R., ed. *Memorial History of the City of Philadelphia.* 2 vols. New York: New York History Company, 1895.

C. Unpublished Materials

Brooks, Robert Clarkson. "History of the Street and Rapid Transit Railways of New York City." Ph.D. dissertation, Cornell University, 1903.

Cerillo, August. "Reform in New York City: A Study in Urban Progressivism." Ph.D. dissertation, Northwestern University, 1969.

Dederick, Robert G. "The Economics of Greater Boston's MTA." Ph.D. dissertation, Harvard University, 1957.

Gabel, Jack. "Edward Morse Shepard: Militant Reformer." Ph.D. dissertation, New York University, 1967.

Gillette, Howard F. "Corrupt and Contented: Philadelphia's Political Machine, 1865-1887." Ph.D. dissertation, Yale University, 1970.

Glasgell, William. "West End Street Railway—Factors in Its Early Development." Senior paper, Harvard University, 1970.

Kantor, Harvey A. "Modern Urban Planning in New York City: Origins and Evolution, 1890-1933." Ph.D. dissertation, New York University, 1971.

Latta, Cynthia. "The Return on the Investment in the Interborough Rapid Transit Company." Ph.D. dissertation, Columbia University, 1975.

McCarthy, James W. "An Analysis and Description of the Planning, Construction and Method of Operation of Boston's First Subways." Term paper, Indiana State University, 1971.

McGovern, William T. "The Street Railway Controversy during the Administrations of Mayor Franklin Edson (1883-1885) and William Russell Grace (1885-1887)." Undergraduate thesis, Brooklyn Historical Studies Institute, 1967.

Merino, James A. "A Great City and Its Suburbs: Attempts to Integrate Metropolitan Boston, 1865-1920." Ph.D. dissertation, University of Texas at Austin, 1968.

Miller, Harry A. "History of the Transit System in Philadelphia." MBA thesis, University of Pennsylvania, 1951.

Roth, Louis. "History of Rapid Transit Development in the City of New York." Typescript of 1917 paper in New York City Municipal Reference Library.

Shaw, John M. "Mitten." 2 vols. Typescript of 1930 biography in Philadelphia Free Library.

Skolnick, Richard. "The Crystallization of Reform in New York City, 1890-1917." Ph.D. dissertation, New York University, 1964.

Waterman, Arthur J. "Integration of Rapid Transit Facilities of the City of New York." Ph.D. dissertation, New York University, 1940.

Weber, Robert D. "Rationalizers and Reformers: Chicago Local Transportation in the Nineteenth Century." Ph.D. dissertation, University of Wisconsin, 1971.

Wilder, Nicholas. "A Study of Boston's Public Transit System." Senior honors thesis, Harvard University, 1970.

Index

HARVARD STUDIES IN BUSINESS HISTORY

*Out of print